THE TAKING OF THE BASTILLE, JULY 14, 1789

SO YOU'RE GOING TO PARIS!

AND IF I WERE GOING WITH YOU THESE ARE THE THINGS I'D INVITE YOU TO DO

BY

CLARA E. LAUGHLIN

Author of 'So You're Going to England!' 'So You're Going to France!' 'So You're Going to Italy!' 'So You're Going to Rome!' etc., and Director of the Clara Laughlin Travel Services

FOURTH EDITION

BOSTON AND NEW YORK
HOUGHTON MIFFLIN COMPANY
The Riverside Press Cambridge
1929

914.43

437

The Riverside Press
CAMBRIDGE · MASSACHUSETTS
PRINTED IN THE U.S.A.

TO

MARCELLA BURNS HAHNER

WHO EMBOLDENED ME TO UNDERTAKE THIS BOOK

PREFACE TO THE FOURTH EDITION

FIVE years ago (in the spring of 1924) this little book made its timid bow to a public it hoped to find and serve.

That public — whose extent and whose friendliness no one could have been sufficiently optimistic to expect — has been so gracious in writing me, expressing its pleasure in the little book, and offering suggestions for additions to it which would make it still more serviceable, that I can hardly realize it was a public all undiscovered by me five short years ago.

It is with the warmest appreciation of the welcome accorded my book that I offer this new edition, with many new features.

The main body of the text I have not altered, except here and there a word or line to make a correction necessitated by changes in Paris.

The three Prefaces — two of them embodying matter added to the book in its second and third editions — have been eliminated, and the information contained in them transferred to classified sections in the new Appendix.

I have most gratefully accepted suggestions that I outline a possible program in Paris for the hurried traveller who has but four or five days there. I have offered some hints as to what may be done to make the most of rainy days in Paris. I have outlined what Paris has to offer for children of varying ages.

I have written, briefly, on such theatres in Paris as are most likely to concern the English-speaking visitor; and on the music-halls and cabarets and dancing-places.

I have included a little about sports, as the visitor may be interested in them. I have told where to look for the principal concerts, and listed the leading churches where services are held in English. There is a list of the principal holidays which may affect the program of visitors to Paris. There are addresses of a number of Travel Bureaus that I know and can commend.

Not many new shop addresses appear; for there is now available for readers of So You're Going to Paris that pocket-size list for which so many of my readers have begged, and which is called *Clara Laughlin's Paris Address Book*. In this are a great many shop addresses, classified, with directions for finding the place and some hints as to what you may expect when you get there.

This address book has been compiled by me on the same principle which has directed the selection of addresses included in the text of my books; that is, if I believed an address would be valuable to my readers, I put it in; and if I did not believe it would be valuable to them, nothing could get it in. But in the *Address Book* I have included a very considerable number of addresses; so many that if I were to put them in here, many persons might mistake the character and purpose of this volume. And, furthermore, many, many readers have said they wanted addresses of restaurants and shops in a little booklet which they could carry always with them, in purse or pocket.

The restaurant list, classified by districts, you have often asked for. Here it is! And the same list appears in the *Address Book*; also the list of fascinating places out of town, to which you may go on a short jaunt from Paris.

The Address Book, selling for the trifling sum of fifty cents or two shillings, may be had of any bookseller who carries the 'So You're Going' books, or from my offices; also from a number of other travel offices.

Since the appearance of this book, in the spring of 1924, I have been in communication with so many hundreds of persons, all over the United States, Canada, Mexico, and abroad, who wanted information on foreign travel, that there was only one way for a hard-working author with the long-familiar wolf ever panting on her heels, to keep it up. And that was to do it on a travel-business basis. It costs a great many thousands of dollars a year to maintain an office and adequate staff; to gather and weigh and sift the mass of information, and catalogue it, and keep it up to date, and select from it for the special service of each inquirer.

Such a service, seeking to help that greatly increasing number of persons who distinguish between *travel* and *transportation* from place to place, could be maintained in any one of three ways:

1. By an individual of very considerable private fortune and sufficient zeal for Travel as a Fine Art, and as an Education, to do for it, as a benefaction, one tithe of what is commonly done for the other arts and other forms of education. This has not yet occurred to any person of wealth as a beautiful thing to do. But I believe it will come, some day. And I can only hope that, if it does, the persons in charge will not become perfunctory, because their income is assured.

2. By subsidy from foreign governments, through their bureaus of tourism; or from foreign railways, hotel associations, or the like. This would take care of the costs, but would — inevitably — provide propaganda and 'interested' information; some of which is excellent, indeed, but the intending traveller wants a *completer* viewpoint, and counsel from persons 'without fear or favor'; also, the sort of eagerness to serve which does not often mark the person who has nothing to gain by serving.

3. By selling transportation and hotel arrangements and motor hire *from the whole field of choice*, without restrictions

(except against the unworthy) and without favorites. For this, the transportation companies and hotels pay an accredited agent a small commission, *without augmenting the cost to the traveller*.

Whether it were possible to make the aggregate of these small commissions cover the costs of such a service as many persons seemed ready for, was something that one could not hope to discover without a great deal of effort maintained over a considerable period of time — at least five years.

After a little more than four years of such effort, during which I have had immeasurably the most instructive and satisfying experience of my life, I can say that there must be hundreds of ways of making more money with less effort; but I doubt if there can be a more fascinating and continually educating occupation for any one who has a genuine zeal for the success of other people's travels, and an enormous capacity for work, and patience to wait, not only months, but years, for other 'pay' than satisfaction in doing a worth-while thing and giving a real service.

Literally hundreds of persons, men and women, who enjoy foreign travel and have done more or less of it, have written to me (and still do, at the rate of several per day) to ask me about coming into my business or starting one of their own. I have interviewed a very great many who came to see me on the same errand.

I care so much for the future of Travel Service as it is developing that I cannot look with other than a hopeful eye at any one who may be able to 'carry on,' and carry to a further perfection, this fine profession.

But no amount of optimism could blind me to the perfectly obvious unfitness of nearly every applicant. For the fundamental requisite is ability to feel the situation from

the point of view of each prospective traveller; to thrill with
the privilege of making the projected trip fuller of the experiences that satisfy than it might have been except for
our aid; to set aside personal preferences for *this* or *that*, if
they have no value in the scheme of things favored by the
person we are serving. If a traveller who doesn't yearn for
cathedrals is 'a barbarian' to us (even in our inmost, un-
spoken thought), we cannot hope for more success in this
profession than if a man who wanted his itinerary made so
he could see 'the best modern adaptations of Gothic'
seemed to us to be 'a nut.'

Everybody's desires must interest the person who would
succeed in the travel business. Learning how to serve them
must seem to her a thing eminently worth doing. And the
staggering mass of detail that must be mastered before one
can give anything like adequate service must challenge an
aspirant the way the Matterhorn does a mountaineer. On
top of all this, one must have the ability to *sell;* for, if one
doesn't sell, one can't stay in business.

And the average prospective traveller presents problems
for salesmanship of a very high order.

This is principally because he inclines (in direct proportion to his inexperience and his need of seasoned counsel)
to listen to the contradictory advice of his friends — and
their friends.

I don't know what the sensations of doctors, lawyers, and
others must be, who have devoted many years to the study
of a specialty, have access to the whole accumulation of
knowledge on their subject, and a wide experience of their
own by which to interpret it — and find that almost anybody's haphazard opinions are regarded at least as respectfully as theirs.

But I have learned something of the sensations of travel-
experts trying to deal with prospective voyagers whose

friends have insisted on their taking one of the North
German Lloyd ships to Naples (whither German ships
have not gone since 1914!), or have advised them that two
girls who have never been abroad and speak not a syllable
except English, will have not the slightest difficulty driving
their 'flivver' from Naples to Vienna, Budapest, and elsewhere; and so on.

I have no acquaintance with the proverbial 'fish stories.'
But I have learned a great deal about the sort of swagger
which it is the delight of a certain kind of individual to set
before his friends who have not yet adventured overseas.
Frequently it has to do with vast overcharges; even more
frequently it is a tale of his prowess in 'beating' steamship
companies, hotels, shops, chauffeurs, etc., and achieving
astonishing 'bargains.' One extreme is as likely as the
other to have a shred of truth in it; but the shred is *little*
likely to be of any service to the adventurer who depends
on it.

And even in the case of friends who do not swagger, but
sincerely and in the most willing-to-be-helpful way essay
to counsel, it must be remembered that the hotel or pension
(for instance), to which they tell you to 'be sure and go,' is
probably the only one they know in that place; and there
may be twenty others that would suit you better. It is the
business of your travel-counsellor to know them *all* before
making a selection for you.

Another thing that makes a high degree of salesmanship
necessary in the travel business (if it is to pay rent, salaries,
and other mundane necessities) is the lack of understanding, on the part of the public, as to what a Travel Service is
for, and who supports it.

There are times when I wish that it were possible to serve
everybody, without regard to their willingness to compensate in any way for service asked and rendered. But

when I have tried to do that, I have found it a thankless as well as an unprofitable endeavor.

This I have had to explain, to myself, by supposing that the words 'Travel Service' imply to many persons something existing for their use, and maintained by subsidy — like the Information Offices of foreign railways; and the Personal Service Bureaus of newspapers, public utility corporations, and the like. This would be a natural supposition.

There must, I think, be many persons who vaguely imagine that an 'authorized agent of all steamship lines' is somehow supported by those lines, to furnish information, without regard to what he sells.

It could (surely!) only be some such misapprehension as this which makes some people go to an agent to get a general survey of all the steamship possibilities, together with the agent's recommendations and suggestions, and then — having taken the agent's time and added a few dollars to his cost of doing business — go directly to the office of the company whose ship or cruise he selected as most likely to please them, and do their buying over the counter; thereby cheating the agent of his right, saving themselves not a penny, and adding nothing to the revenue of the salaried clerk who makes out the ticket.

Surely no one would do this unless he did not in the least comprehend the relation of a travel agent to the travelling public and to the travel companies. They are unfair without meaning to be.

As they are, also, when they ask for many hours of an expert's time to work out their plans, recommend hotels, tell rates, and render other services — then use the information in some way that deprives the one who gave it of any recompense for his toil. Every profession has its similar struggle until it has become generally recognized *as* a profession. People no longer ask a half-dozen architects to submit plans for a house, nor a number of interior decorators to submit sketches for refurnishing the living-room; nor try to get legal counsel when they meet a lawyer at dinner. Counsel on foreign travel — counsel which helps people to get out of foreign travel the utmost of whatever they want, and to do it more economically than they could, unaided — is a brand-new profession. Its recognition as a profession has scarcely begun, but it will surely come. And I hold it a most interesting opportunity to have been among the pioneers who are raising the business of selling foreign transportation to the dignity of a fine profession whose scope has scarcely been realized, as yet.

All this might seem to be, properly, no business of an author; or, if of an author (since many authors have had, and many others do have, businesses), no part of a Preface. The tradition dies hard, that authors should be remote from commerce — impractical — unconcerned with stuffs more substantial than those that dreams are made of.

I never entertained such notions. But until five years ago I always looked upon business as something beyond my abilities. I'm not yet sure that I wasn't right! But I know that the effort to *stretch* my abilities has been rich in many kinds of rewards to me, and (I believe) to the books I write.

No author of travel books could conceivably gather, and keep up-to-date and ever-growing, such an accumulation of valuable travel data as a well-known and well-equipped travel office acquires. No author's study could ever be 'open house' for the representatives of scores of foreign-travel factors, each bringing his quota of fresh information and the point of view of his experience; and at the same time for hundreds of the travelling public, each with his own delightful problems to work out — so that the author might know what a wide variety of persons demand in foreign travel and also what a wide variety of foreign factors can supply. Certainly no author could afford to maintain anything like this, even if it were possible to develop it.

To those readers in every State of the Union, in Canada, and Mexico, the Hawaiian Islands and the Philippines, who by becoming clients of The Clara Laughlin Travel Services have kept them going and growing, I make my grateful acknowledgment as collaborators with me in 'trying-out' the feasibility of a kind of service I believed in and was willing to give all the best I had or could attain to prove valuable — or otherwise.

If all this were concerned merely with the intelligent buying of tickets, conserving of funds, selection of routes, etc., it would seem to me to be abundantly worth while — since it is so easy for travellers to get unintelligent direction in all those matters; and the joy of a trip abroad can depend very greatly on

> 'The little more, and how much it is!
> The little less, and what worlds away.'

But the inestimable thing in journeying abroad is spiritual, and it cannot be deduced from a time-table and a hotel rate-book by some one to whom even those compendia are less than keys to Where It All Comes True.

I hold fast to the belief that travel abroad should be, first of all things, a joyous adventure — unto every one according to his concept of Joy. And to the belief that it should be — no matter how oft-repeated — a Voyage of Discovery on which we seek new friends, new knowledge of things long-loved, and new understanding of *ourselves*.

We must all get tired, many times, of ourselves in our familiar routine. We sail away — and from the moment the gangplank's lowered, we may 'set up' any kind of new self we may fancy, for a change from the old one. If, instead of some 'setting up,' we merely 'let down' (as many do), we are sagging — as Age does: whereas travel properly done is the greatest rejuvenation in the world.

People who travel properly are happy, and are continually finding out new things about themselves and those they meet that add immeasurably to their enjoyment and appreciation of this very wonderful old world.

It is these travellers who 'can be the best ambassadors' and who are doing more to strengthen the foundations of international 'peace and good will' than all the other contributing factors combined. To serve them seems to me an opportunity far finer than I should ever have dared aspire to. I am glad, indeed, that it rose in my path and could scarcely be evaded.

These travellers who forge, one by one, the links of friendship and mutual understanding in the chain that binds people together, have had — *still* have! — much to 'live down' in the rancor-breeding behavior of other travellers — savages, who understand few things and instinctively seek to *hurt* what they cannot understand.

But the spirit in travel which is not only admirable, but best serves all the purposes for which one goes abroad, is gaining ascendancy; and with every gain makes travel easier and pleasanter and more profitable for us all.

Let us all conspire together to be among those 'best ambassadors'! And any of you who would like to use the new luggage labels, 'Traveling the Clara Laughlin Way,' which will identify you with this spirit and mark you as an heir of the good will created by your predecessors with the labels, may have some of them from either of my offices. Only —— ! Remember that those who follow you and are likewise labelled will in their turn fall heir to the impressions *you* create. So, if you are a 'grouch,' a 'savage,' I hope you'll continue to fly your own colors. Flying *these* might easily deprive you of the joy of *battling* your way through Europe!

With this new edition of my book go my *very* best wishes to every one whom it helps, in any degree, to get that out of Paris which most richly rewards him for having gone thither.

410 SOUTH MICHIGAN AVENUE, CHICAGO

CONTENTS

ILLUSTRATIONS

SO YOU'RE GOING TO PARIS!

SO YOU'RE GOING TO PARIS!

I

YOUR FIRST PARIS DAY

I HAVE spent a great deal of time, on one occasion and another, planning what seems to me the most delightful, most alluring way to begin acquaintance with Paris. Even with the most fascinating, most satisfying person or place in the world, it is always possible to make a wrong beginning; to happen first on those phases, those characteristics which least sustain his, her, or its reputation for charm and beauty.

I cannot help wanting people I like to be enraptured with Paris. And I've often debated with myself the comparative loveliness of this spot and that, and which of them I'd choose, and what time of day, if I could lead my friend into Paris blindfolded, and at my will tear off the bandage and cry, "Look!"

It doubtless is well that I can do no such thing; for I'd probably never be able to choose the exact spot or moment.

We arrive at railway stations, so bewilderingly "strange" that they do not grow interesting until we are well accustomed to them. And our first glimpses of Paris streets, en route to the hotel, are seldom splendid, or picturesque.

Travellers who come over from England, or down from the Netherlands, are most likely to arrive in the very late afternoon — toward dinner-time. Those who come up from Italy or the Riviera are as likely to arrive in the morning. Transatlantic voyagers arrive at all sorts of hours, but seldom in the middle of the day.

Whatever time one gets there, however, I find that his
first day in Paris seldom (unless he is a rushing tourist) begins very early. He is tired; he is getting settled; and so on.
If he's abroad and on sight-seeing bent by a little before
noon, he's doing well.

So I'm going to assume that it's well past eleven on your
first morning in Paris, and that I'm taking you to a point
which is, all things considered, the best in Paris (in many
persons' opinion) for a beginning: the Place de la Concorde.

Let us stand, with our backs toward the Arc de Triomphe,
near the entrance of the Champs-Élysées, and look about
us — eastward, through the Tuileries Gardens toward the
Louvre; southward, across the Seine, to the Chambre des
Députés; and northward, up rue Royale, toward the Madeleine.

No other part of Paris is so nearly as it was a hundred
years ago, and more. These incomparable vistas are sub-
stantially the same as when the guillotine stood here in
1793-94.

This was far from the heart of mediæval Paris — far,
even, from the frequented parts of Paris of the Renaissance.
The Tuileries were so called because they were built on a
site which had been a vast clay-hole where tiles to roof
Paris were made. Catherine de Médicis began the Tuileries
Palace about 1570; but the clay-hole west of the palace continued for some time; Bernard Palissey, the great potter,
had his kilns there in Catherine's time.

The gardens of the Tuileries were laid out by Lenôtre,
for Louis XIV; but here at this west end they were bounded
by a moat and a great waste space given over to market-
produce.

When Louis XV was still young and "well-beloved," he
lay very near to death at Metz; and in gratitude to God for

his recovery he vowed to build a fine new church to Sainte Geneviève, the patron saint of Paris — which he did; it is now the Panthéon. And when some of his subjects wished to erect an equestrian statue of him to commemorate their joy, he ordered the statue placed "between the moat which terminates our garden of the Tuileries, and the quai which borders the river."

Bouchardon, the greatest sculptor of his time, died soon after this statue (proclaimed the finest equestrian work ever produced in France) was finished. Pigalle designed the pedestal. Then Louis XV commanded his great architect, Gabriel, to construct pavilions and balustrades for the west end of the gardens, and the two splendid buildings on the north side of the square. The eastern one of this pair, now the Ministry of Marine, was the Crown Storehouse, where jewels, plate, pictures, tapestries, and all sorts of valuable belongings were kept when not in use. The one on the other side of rue Royale, was occupied by three great families: the Coislin, the Daumont, and the Crillon; it now houses the Automobile Club, the Union Club, and Hôtel Crillon.

The magnificent wingéd steeds by Coysevox, one bearing Mercury and the other Fame, were made for the royal domain at Marly, near Saint-Germain, but were brought here in 1729 and replaced, at Marly, by those by Coustou which now adorn the entrance to the Champs-Élysées, where they were set up after the Revolution.

The King's statue stood about where the Luxor obelisk now stands. (The fountains and other statues are of a later day.)

In May, 1770, work on the embellishments of the square was still going on, and rue Royale was cumbered with materials for it and for the Madeleine, then building, when a great exhibition of fireworks was given here to celebrate the marriage of the old King's grandson, the Dauphin, with the fifteen-year-old Archduchess Marie Antoinette of Austria, daughter of the Empress Maria Theresa.

There was an accident; some of the fireworks went off prematurely; a panic ensued, the vast crowd sought safety. There was no bridge across the river at this point then — only a ferry — and many fell into the water and were drowned; more were trampled to death in their mad efforts to escape in other directions. One hundred and thirty-three were killed outright, and more than three hundred died of their injuries.

After that, the square was unpopular and little frequented; so much so that the Fair of Sainte Ovide, which had flourished for more than a century in the Place Vendôme until it was burned, in 1771, never had any success after it was transferred to this more commodious, more attractive square. It suffered another fire here in 1777, when all its barracks of canvas and wood, with their inflammable contents, were quickly destroyed; and the distress of the poor proprietors was so great that Nicolet and Audinot, who had successful theatres on the boulevard du Temple, gave a performance for the benefit of the fire sufferers — the first theatrical benefit for the unfortunate ever given in France.

In August, 1792, a mob pulled down the statue of Louis XV and destroyed it. (There is, fortunately for Bouchardon's beautiful work, a fine model of it in bronze in the Salle Houdon of the Modern Sculpture collection in the Louvre.) And the pedestal whereon it had stood was empty on the January day of the year following, when the guillotine was erected here for the first time, and Louis XVI mounted it to his calm, courageous death.

The site of the scaffold, on which more than twenty-eight hundred persons perished in this place alone, was not always exactly the same, but it varied only a few feet.

Some time after the King's execution a plaster statue of Liberty was set up where Louis XV's had been — it was she whom Madame Roland apostrophized with her last breath: "Oh, Liberty! Liberty! How they have mocked thee!" — and the guillotine stood now west of the statue, and now between it and the moat beneath the balustrade of the Tuileries Gardens.

Napoleon many times reviewed here his triumphal armies singing their songs of victory. And in 1814, when the Allies entered Paris, a Te Deum in gratitude for Napoleon's downfall and abdication was here celebrated by them.

Perhaps you will like to " see" (in that way which we shall so greatly employ in all our Paris gazing) Charles X crossing this square on horseback, in July, 1830, fleeing to Rambouillet to abdicate, and thence into exile. And Louis-Philippe, the last of the French kings, stealing out of the Tuileries Gardens in February, 1848, and escaping in a fiacre.

In 1870 the mob surged from here into the Tuileries Gardens, to burn the palace.

Rue de Rivoli, the tourist centre of Paris, is a very modern street in these western parts of it. Napoleon conceived the idea of cutting it, in 1802; but nothing was done, except to name the projected thoroughfare, till 1811; and the first part of the work on it was not finished till 1835. There was so little coming and going hereabouts then that the lots were not deemed worth building on, and the city had to grant the use of them for ninety-nine years without pay, stipulating only that at the end of that period the land and all improvements were to revert to the city.

As we go down rue de Rivoli on this first walk, I think you'll like to re-create it in your mind, as it was in the days preceding and during the Revolution.

On our right is the Terrasse des Feuillants, named for the
Cistercian convent which used to stand near by. All the
space between the Place de la Concorde and on, quite a bit,
past where the Continental Hotel now is, was occupied by
the gardens and some of the buildings of three monasteries
(or convents) and by the manège (or riding-school) built
for Louis XV when he was a little boy.

The first (westernmost) of the convents was that of the
Dames of the Assumption; all that is left of it is the seventeenth-century chapel, at the corner of rue Saint-Honoré
and rue Cambon. (Lafayette was buried from this church.)

Next came the Capucines. And then the Feuillants, in
whose secularized convent Lafayette presided over the
Moderate Club which tried to hold the Revolution within
bounds — and failed.

As we pass the Continental Hotel, on the other side of
the street, we must look for the tablet on one of the garden
pillars recalling that here stood the riding-school where the
National Assembly met, where the first French Republic
was proclaimed, and where Louis XVI was tried and condemned to death.

On August 10, 1792, when the Revolutionary mob
stormed the Tuileries, and the royal family fled to the Assembly for protection, they crossed the gardens and made
their way through a back door into the riding-school where
they sat crowded into a small room during three days; being taken at night, for lodging, into the denuded convent of
the Feuillants, adjoining, where the barest necessities, of a
camping-out sort, were hastily scrambled together for them.

The riding-school covered a space now traversed by rue
de Rivoli. The Tribunal of the President of the Assembly
was where this commemorative tablet is placed. Across
the street, where a pillar of the arcade bears the number
230, was the bar at which the speakers stood.

THE CAPTURE OF THE TUILERIES, AUGUST 10, 1792

Painted by J. Bertaux

Now let us cross to Rumpelmayer's for lunch. It is number 226 and covers part of the site of the Feuillants' garden.

We shall see more Americans here than French; and the food will remind us of the smart confectionery tea-shops at home. But it is a place everybody goes to at least once — the young and the feminine, very often. Going to the counter and selecting pastries is one of the delights of the place.

When we come out, let us walk up rue de Castiglione, which was opened as a street only in 1811, and was named not for that charming gentleman — poet, ambassador, lover of chivalry, friend of popes, emperors, and princes — whose marvellous portrait by his admirer, Raphael, is in the Louvre; but for an Italian town where the French won a victory under Napoleon. It was, before 1811, just a narrow passage between the Feuillants and Capucines convents; though the most frequented entrance to the Tuileries Gardens. While the Assembly was sitting in the riding-school there were great comings and goings through this passage.

The refectory of the Capucines was where the great court of the Continental Hotel is now; the back of their chapel was where we now find numbers 7 and 9 rue Castiglione. And the front of the Feuillants' chapel was across the street where we now find number 14.

Now we are at rue Saint-Honoré, and crossing it, toward the Place Vendôme, which got its name from the mansion of César, Duc de Vendôme (son of Henry IV and Gabrielle d'Estrées), whose wife received this property as a marriage portion from her mother. Louis XIV bought the Vendôme mansion, had it demolished, moved the Capucines Convent over from this side of rue Saint-Honoré (where its properties reached to the city walls on the north) to the south side, and commenced the building of a magnificent square which was to house the royal library, the academies, and the ambassadors-extraordinary to the Court of France.

All this was under the superintendence of Louvois, his minister of war and of building; but Louvois died before the work was well advanced. It was Hardouin Mansart, the architect of Versailles, who designed the square as we see it, and constructed these façades of uniform style; the ground *behind* them being sold to individuals, who were privileged to build thereon as they could and would, so long as they did not disturb the symmetry of the square.

The centre of the square has been occupied by an equestrian statue of Louis XIV (model now in the Louvre), by a statue of Liberty, and by the Column, which has been surmounted by three different statues of Napoleon. The vicissitudes of the column are recounted in your guidebook; so I won't repeat them here.

What you may care more about knowing is a little of some of the celebrated persons who have lived behind these stately façades. John Law was one of them; his house was number 23. He was, you will remember, that Scotchman of frenzied finance (was there ever another?) who blew "The Mississippi Bubble" till it burst. This was under the Regency, in the childhood of Louis XV.

Another celebrated financier who lived here was Antoine Crozat, Law's predecessor in the Mississippi scheme, and a great collector of art treasures. He lived at number 17, and his daughter at number 19. Number 15, the present Hotel Ritz, was once the home of the Duc de Lauzun who there wrote his "Memories of the Eighteenth Century."

Numbers 11 and 13, the Ministry of Justice, was the home of Danton when he was minister of that department, briefly, in 1792.

Hardouin Mansart lived at number 9; this façade and that of number 7 are classed as historic monuments.

Chopin died at number 12, in 1849.

There are some very choice shops here now. I especially suggest visiting Lalique's, on the north side of the square, to see his most exquisite crystals — although the only discourteous shop-assistant I ever encountered in Paris was there, once. Perhaps he's gone now. Coty's perfume shop, also on the north side of the square, seems to me to be one of the most perfect things I have ever seen devoted to trade, even in Paris, where one perfumer's shop is more beautiful than another.

Now we are at the beginning of rue de la Paix, the street of luxury. It was cut through (in 1806) what had once been the Capucines' property, and was called rue Napoléon till 1814. To make it, there was cut away the east part of rue des Capucines, including the church in which many noted persons were buried.

I'm sure you'll delight in a very lingering progress up this street. Flower-boxes in many of the upper windows make it very gay. All the kings and emperors left in the world couldn't (I suppose) buy the jewels that are in the street-level windows. It is a breath-taking bazaar, this street — stocked for the billionaires of all the world. There is much artistry, too, in the fabulous luxury of it; much to admire, even if one cannot (and would not care to) spend.

At the end of it, we enter the Place de l'Opéra, made in 1858, and dominated by the magnificent opera house, about which I won't say anything, because our guidebook says so much.

If it were not so soon after lunch, we'd sit down at a table on the sidewalk, at the Café de la Paix, for a cup of chocolate and a brioche — and a study of the passing throngs and of our neighbors at near-by tables. But we'll do that on another occasion; and on more than one, I doubt not.

Just now, we'll walk past the Café de la Paix and on, along the boulevards, till we reach the Madeleine.

Not all English-speaking persons, I find, remember that *boulevard* is the word from which we get *bulwark*, and means a fortification. When old city walls were taken down, the space they had occupied, together with that of the moat in front of them, was a broad band which the city authorities seldom failed to plant with several rows of trees and to convert into a promenade.

Paris has had several sets of walls, taking down one after another of them as she overflowed their capacity. Of the earliest, we find only here and there a trace. Even the great wall of Philippe-Auguste (1200) has almost completely disappeared, though we shall find fragments of it here and there as we wander about Paris. This section of boulevard we are now on was created by Louis XIV's orders, in the last years of the seventeenth century, clearing away the ramparts erected here under Henry II, more than a hundred years before.

Paris boulevards bear many different names in the course of what is now a continuous thoroughfare, each name commemorating something in the old associations of that section. This part of what are called "the grand boulevards" (stretching from the Bastille to the Madeleine) is the boulevard des Capucines because it marks the north boundary of what was once the enormous property of the Capucines Convent.

The shops along here are interesting. And if this were Saturday, and we had been here a little earlier, around noon, we should have seen, on this elegant avenue, an extraordinary "curb fair" momentarily set up to catch a bit of business as the multitudes of employés hereabouts poured out on their half-holiday.

I once watched here, with the greatest delight, an example of that domesticity with which the French flavor all their petty business life so charmingly: a couple engaged in curb merchandising had set up their little stand of cheap toys or trinkets which, two hours hence, would be doing business in some other and perhaps far distant place; it was time for déjeuner, and Madame, making herself at home where she happened to be, was preparing a good, hearty, appetizing ragout (what we'd call an Irish stew) on the sidewalk's edge — paring potatoes, peeling onions, to add to the meat already cooking on a small portable charcoal stove. The matter-of-fact housewifeliness with which she went about this kept me rooted to a near-by spot for a long time. But nobody else seemed to notice her.

And now we've come to the Madeleine. If we were to cross in front of it and walk up boulevard Malesherbes (named for the heroic lawyer who sacrificed his life by speaking in defence of Louis XVI when the latter was on trial) for two blocks, we'd come to rue de la Ville l'Évêque, or the street of the bishop's town, at the corner of which and rue de la Madeleine (which has disappeared, but which ran about parallel with rue Royale and a little west of it) was the *old* church of the Madeleine. When it was first constructed I don't know; but Charles VIII had it reconstructed and laid the cornerstone of the new structure in 1487. Four years later a sisterhood of Magdalenes were established there. But they let their chapel fall into ruins, and it had to be rebuilt again in 1659, in the early years of Louis XIV's reign. Then, quarrels broke out between the curé of this parish and the curé of Saint-Roch's (more than half a mile away) as to which of them had proper jurisdiction over certain sheep who preferred one fold or the other; and an act of Parlement was necessary to establish the ruling that persons living inside the city limits belonged to Saint-Roch, and the parish of the Madeleine was for those outside. This seems to have been an adverse decision for the Madeleine, for it again fell into ruin. And it was Madame Pompadour who (not long before she died) persuaded Louis XV that the Madeleine deserved something better of him (who had added so many to her sisterhood) than a dilapidated chapel. So Louis ordered a new church, but it was decided to build it on a different site; and that at the head of rue Royale was chosen. Louis himself laid this cornerstone, on April 3, 1764. The first plan was for a building much like Saint Peter's at Rome. Then that architect died, and the next one planned something like the Panthéon. Then he died, and a third architect essayed a grand Greek temple. The columns were erected when the Revolution brought the construction to a stop. And during those stressful years the half-completed structure presented a curious appearance as of rows of Gargantuan candles with extinguishers atop each one. It was Napoleon's intention to make this a monument to the heroes of his armies, bearing the inscription: "The Emperor Napoleon to the soldiers of the Grand Army." His downfall put an end to this. And before Louis XVIII could carry through his intent to make it a memorial to Louis XVI and Marie Antoinette, *he* was gone. The church was finished in 1842.

Go into the church now, if you want to, and if it is open. Or loiter on the east side of it if the flower market is in operation — morning, however, is likely to be a better time for that. Or walk around to the back of the church and look at the statue of Lavoisier, the great chemist and physicist who cleared those sciences from much of their ancient error and laid the foundations for them as we know them to-day. He was the teacher of many distinguished men, and had a high sense of social service. When the foolish zealots of the Revolution condemned him to death, he begged for a few days that he might complete some important work he had in hand. They refused, saying, "The Republic has no need of savants." "They needed," said Lagrange, the famous mathematician, "only a moment to cut his head off, and a hundred years may not suffice to produce such another." Lavoisier lived at number 17 boulevard de la Madeleine.

By this time you may be tired, although you have not walked very far — certainly not two miles. So I recommend a drive to the Bois de Boulogne. We will hail a little fiacre (near the Madeleine is an excellent place to get them) and say, "Bois de Boulogne?" with a rising inflection, which means to the cocher, "Will you go?" It not infrequently happens that he won't. This isn't necessarily because he's disobliging. He makes more in tips on many short hauls than on one long one — and he needs the money! If we say "bon pourboire," we may persuade him. And what he thinks "a good tip" for a couple of hours will not amount to more than what an American driver takes for a few minutes' dash and never even mumbles "Thank you" for. We can jog out the Champs-Élysées and avenue du Bois-de-Boulogne, and through the Bois for an hour or more, and back to our hotel again, for what amounts in American currency to a dollar and a half, or thereabouts. And I know few things so worth the money.

Never mind when rue Royale ceased to become the western wall and became a broad street; just revel in its beautiful shops and gay wares; never mind who made the Champs-Élysées a great pleasure ground. You've had enough of that sort of thing for one day. We'll come here fresh some morning, and eager to know. Just now it's glory enough to *be* — to be alive and in Paris! Up the "Elysian Fields" we go, through such bowers of trees (maybe it's late April or early May, and the thousands of horsechestnuts are in bloom!) as few cities know; on either hand, set in their nests of green, are restaurants de luxe which serve sublimated food in surroundings that make a poetry of dining or lunching. Delightful children, picturesque as if just tumbled out of the pages of a story-book, are playing beneath the trees, attended by nurses in provincial costumes such as we've never before seen off the stage. Here are little goat carriages, and small donkeys, and a carrousel, and other ecstasies for the wee ones. Here are booths full of simple toys to tempt them to further play. Here are little puppet-shows, petits guignols, before which some of the children sit and shout in glee, just as their great-great-great-grandparents did while the Terror was reigning.

On our left are the Petit Palais, housing the municipal art collection, and — across the superb avenue Alexandre III — the Grand Palais where the Salons are held — art, automobile, and others. Look, at your left, across the river, toward the gilded dome of the Invalides, beneath which Napoleon's ashes lie. I hope you will come often to this spot — for the vistas no less than for the palaces. But we'll go on now, with just a glance, right, up avenue Marigny, past the Théâtre Marigny, toward the gardens of the Élysée Palace.

Now we are at the Rond Point, with its brilliant flower-beds, its flashing fountains, its radiating avenues. We shall prowl all about here on foot, some day, re-living a hundred stories. To-day it's enough just to feast our eyes, and to feel ourselves drawn up the slope atop which, silhouetted against the western sky, stands the Arc de Triomphe. Let us descend there, and make our reverence at the grave of the Unknown Soldier; then on, out avenue du Bois-de-Boulogne, to the Porte Dauphine, named in honor of little Marie Antoinette who, as a girl-bride, spent some time at La Muette, half a mile or so southeast of here on the edge of the Bois, and who had this gate opened at the end of what was then the Beautiful Pheasantry.

If you feel like having "tea," you may like to dismiss our fiacre outside the porte (if we dismiss it even a hundred feet *inside*, we must pay our cocher a franc extra; that is a city ordinance — please don't think it has anything special to do with tourists — the Parisian must pay it, too) and walk inside to the Pavillon Dauphine. There we may sit on the lawn, or go back to the very edge of the "wood" where we can smell the sweet, moist forest earth as we listen to the orchestra and sip our refreshment.

It may be necessary to go back outside the porte to get another fiacre for our drive in the park; or we may chance to pick up one returning empty from some farther pavilion.

If we engage the driver without explicit instructions, he will almost certainly take us, at a restful crawl, down the Route de Suresnes to the Carrefour du Bout des Lacs, around the lower lake to the cascade and back again to the Porte Dauphine. If we want a *real* ride, we'll say, "Aux bords de la Seine, s'il vous plaît" [O bore de la Senn, see vou play], and he will go on past the Auteuil race-course and the upper lake, and between the Rothschild estate and the Longchamps course, to the beautiful avenue along the river where the yachts and houseboats are anchored, and past the old mill, to the Allée des Longchamps.

If we want to go back down the Champs-Élysées, we'll find ourselves being taken there without a word. If you'd like another route back, we'll say "Porte Maillot" [port my-ō] and go on thence down the broad avenue de la Grande Armée to the Arc de Triomphe. If we say, "Avenue Friedland et boulevard Haussmann" [Freedlan day boul'var Houseman], that will give us a completely different return. Left to himself, a cocher will *always* take the Champs-Élysées.

Perhaps you're thinking, now, of dinner. It may be that you want to go back to your hotel and rest and dress, or at least "freshen up." We are such gypsies when we're in Paris — evading rather than seeking social entanglements, living as the spirit moves us — that I'm sure I can be no fit guide for those who go to Paris to take it as their schedule of life allows. We bow to schedules at home, because we must, and because we think they're a good thing, at times and in their place; but in Paris we do just what we feel like doing. And I must admit that we only semi-occasionally feel like going home to dress for dinner. We'd much rather drive till seven or after, and then go straight to a restaurant; that is, if we're not going to the opera or theatre.

The first dinner in Paris, each time, is a matter for much consideration. Among so many favorite places, to which shall we go to-night to celebrate our return to the city of enchantment? The weather has much to do with it. If it be warm enough to eat outdoors, I say Ledoyen on the Champs-Élysées just behind the Petit Palais. We'll sit out in front, under the sky, near the fountain, looking east. This is not an inexpensive place; but we need not eat a very expensive dinner (for about forty francs each we can get a good one, which, while exchange continues what it has been these few years past, is very much less than we should pay for a poorer dinner, without wine, in a stuffy hotel at home), and the surroundings are worth a very great deal, besides the delicious food.

After an eight- or nine-hour day like this, *we'd* go home, and to bed at ten or thereabouts. We'd walk home if we were living within any reasonable sort of walking distance. And we'd see that part, at least, of our way lay along the quais beside the glorious Seine.

If the weather does not permit outdoor dining, we shall

hesitate a good while. Shall it be Prunier and lobster Thermidor? Or Marguery, on the boulevards, for the famous sole? Or Foyot, "the king of them all," over the river beside the Luxembourg? Or the Bœuf à la Mode, in rue Valois? It is most likely to be the last, to-night, for many reasons.

If you are foot-loose and fancy-free and feel disposed to trust our choice, say "Buff a la Mode — rue Valwah," and soon find yourselves in a restaurant where Bonaparte loved to go, and Desmoulins and Danton. It is housed in an old mansion which Cardinal Richelieu built and which he loaned to his favorite, Boisrobert, who was responsible for Richelieu's founding the French Academy. Across the street is the Palais Royal where Richelieu lived in more than royal state, and Louis XIV spent his none-too-peaceful boyhood, bossed by Mazarin, who may or may not have been secretly married to Louis's mother, Anne of Austria, widow of Louis XIII.

All this part of Paris teems with stories. We love every stone hereabouts. And we love the Bœuf à la Mode. Better food is hard to find; friendlier service. When we come out, we tingle with excitement, choosing which way to turn. Shall we go over and walk a bit in the Palais-Royal Gardens? Shall we pass the Théâtre-Français and thrill with delight anticipating the evenings we're to spend there? Or shall we cross the Place du Palais-Royal and go under the Pavillon Richelieu into the great court where stand the statues to Lafayette and Gambetta, and look westward, mile on mile, through Tuileries Gardens and Champs-Élysées to the Arc de Triomphe, the whole incomparable vista framed by the Arc du Carrousel through which we are looking? I can't resist this! And then I must cross the Place du Carrousel and stand on the quai looking west to the pont Royal and far beyond its five heavenly arches and their reflection in the river, toward the Trocadéro towers and the Eiffel that carries all eyes heavenward from wheresoe'er they be, these many miles around.

"And so," as old Sam Pepys said, "home and to bed."

II

YOUR FIRST SUNDAY IN PARIS

IT seems to happen that many persons find their second day in Paris to be a Sunday. I am writing most of these chapters with reference to certain days of the week when certain things are best done or can only be done. Also, I am keeping in mind how much more it is possible to enjoy seeing if we vary it properly — now strolling, now riding; now indoors, now out; now the old and historic, now the new and promising; now the museum and now the park or quai; now the shop or café, and now the church.

Sunday in Paris is as different from the same day in London as if the two cities were not only poles apart, but centuries. The proportion of church-going is probably as high in one place as in another; but very different ideas prevail as to what should be done with the rest of the day. I find that there are American tourists whose fears of Paris levity in general are exceeded only by their fears of Paris Sunday levity in particular. And to them I can only say that they will easily find (through their hotel concierge) an English-speaking church of almost every conceivable variety; and that if they go to the parks, they will find a good deal more decorum, of the instinctive sort, not the enforced, than prevails in the parks of many a big American city on Sunday afternoons. Also that they will find most of the restaurants quiet and wholly dignified.

Sundays are especially happy days to me in Paris where all my days are glad and my heart sings a continual "Merci" to the Providence that permits my being there. On Sundays one has more opportunities than on other days for glimpses of that family life which is so beautiful in France and which the stranger to her ways seems, somehow, to have heard so little about.

If you were my friend and I had reason to believe that you would enjoy what I enjoy, and this was your first Paris Sunday and I were taking you about, to help you realize how many kinds of a glad day it is, *this* is what I'd probably do:

If we were living on the right bank of the Seine (the north bank, the side the Louvre is on, and all the places you went yesterday), I couldn't resist taking you, if it were a sunshiny, warm day, to the Parc Monceau, about ten-thirty in the morning. As I can't guess what point of the right bank you'd be living in, I can't tell you how we'd go to the park; but it's north of the Champs-Élysées, perhaps half a mile, in the heart of a beautiful residence district. You can go in the Métro [Subway] and get off at the Monceau Station; or take a bus marked "S bis"; or a tram numbered 5, 30, 35, or 36.

In the years just before the Revolution, that profligate Duke of Orléans who hoped (vainly) to save his head by getting himself called Philippe-Égalité (Equality), and whose son went on the throne as Louis-Philippe, had a place out here — it was quite suburban then — with magnificent gardens where most sumptuous fêtes were given. The property was confiscated at the Revolution, and some of the victims of the guillotine were buried there.

Louis XVIII restored the place to his cousin of Orléans, and it belonged to the Orléans family till 1852. It is now a city park. Nearly every vestige of the private pleasure-ground has vanished; but there is the Naumachie, an oval sheet of water flanked by a lovely Corinthian colonnade brought from a church at Saint-Denis built for the sepulchre of the Valois family and demolished more than two

centuries ago. The Renaissance arcade, near by, was part
of the Hôtel de Ville or City Hall of Paris burnt by the
Communards in 1871.

Many monuments to musicians are in the park, and one
to Guy de Maupassant. But it isn't these, nor the wish to
remember the Orléans, that takes me to this lovely place on
so many Sunday mornings. It is the children — the exquisite children so charming in their play, so picturesquely
dressed, so quaintly attended; and the papas! Of all the
men in all the countries where I have watched children,
there seem to be more in France than anywhere else who
have that grace of fellowship with small children. The relation between father and older children may be more
ideal in other countries; but France is full of heart-warming
glimpses of Frenchmen and wee persons "rising six years"
or thereabouts.

If we loaf about the Parc Monceau for an hour, keeping
our eyes and our hearts open even if we cannot understand
much that we hear, we shall come away full of friendliness
for the people whose guests we are. And that is the feeling
I care most about helping my friends to get. Once they
have it, they are astonished to find how different from the
ordinary "touring" is the thing they are embarked upon.

It may be that you will want to go, while we're so close,
to the Russian church, at which we can now see the congregation as well as the edifice.

If I knew that your time in Paris was to extend over
several months, and you could be as leisurely as you liked,
there is much in this vicinity that I'd love to point out to
you. Many famous persons have lived hereabouts. But
if you're a traveller, not a sojourner, you must "take the
high spots"; so I'd probably lead you straight to the
Chapelle Expiatoire, which is not far from here.

This ground was once the kitchen-garden of the Benedic-

tine monks to whom the Madeleine belonged; and the victims of the disaster in the Place de la Concorde, when the
marriage of Louis and Marie Antoinette was being celebrated, were buried here, in 1770. Twenty-two years later,
about one thousand of the Swiss Guard, killed while defending Louis XVI and Marie Antoinette at the Tuileries, were
here interred — many of them shockingly mutilated after
they were thrown out into the courts of the palace, as Napoleon tells us, who was more sickened by the sights he saw
that day than ever thereafter by any of his battle-fields.

Louis XVI was brought here from the Place de la Concorde to be buried from the church of the Madeleine. Nine
months later, the body of Marie Antoinette was brought
here and dumped in a corner and left unburied for two
weeks, awaiting orders that some one forgot to give. Then
the gravedigger, Joly, took it upon himself to dig a grave
and inter the remains without ceremony. This was on the
first of November, sixteen days after her execution. The
bill he submitted, and which was paid, is as follows:

> The widow Capet, for a bier............6 livres
> For the grave and the gravediggers...... 15–35

It cost something like ten dollars to inter the daughter of
the Cæsars!

The twenty-one Girondists were buried there that same
day, and Manon Roland came to share this place of sepulchre on November 8th, a week later. Charlotte Corday had
been lying there since July. Du Barry came in December.
The next year, Camille and Lucile Desmoulins, Danton,
and many more — 2830 in all, 'tis said, without counting
the Swiss.

For about three months in '94, the victims of the guillotine were buried in ground adjoining what is now the Parc
Monceau. Madame Elizabeth, Louis XVI's sister, was in-

terred there; and no trace of her remains has ever been discovered. Both the brothers Robespierre and Simon, the jailer of the little Dauphin, were among those whose graves were in that other cemetery of which no trace now remains, but the site of which is covered by modern buildings about where boulevard Malesherbes crosses rue Miromesnil.

When the Terror had ceased to reign, a lawyer named Desclozeaux, who lived near by and who had witnessed most of the interments in the cemetery of the Madeleine, bought the ground, restored the walls around it, planted trees, erected crosses, and tended the place with reverent care until 1815, when he put it at the disposal of Louis XVIII, who caused the erection of the chapel and tombs we see there, and had what could be found of the royal remains transferred to Saint-Denis, where the kings and queens of France are buried. This transfer took place on the twenty-second anniversary of Louis's death, just a little while before Napoleon's return from Elbe and the beginning of the Hundred Days before Waterloo.

Be sure to buy, of the concierge at the entrance, some of the souvenir postcard pictures, which include photographs of old prints of the royal family in prison, of the executions, and of such inestimably interesting documents as Marie Antoinette's last letter stained with her tears, and the report filed on Louis's death.

That last letter, by the way, never reached Madame Elizabeth. It was found between the mattresses of Robespierre's bed when that Incorruptible's effects were searched after his execution.

There is much that we'd like to recall, here; but we must be on our way, so as to reach Sainte-Chapelle about noon.

We'll take a cab, and drive — past the Opéra, and along the Grands Boulevards to the Porte Saint-Denis (which is not only the way Louis and Marie Antoinette must have come on their last journey, but the porte through which they made their flight to Varennes, in June, 1791), the great triumphal arch erected by the city to commemorate Louis XIV's conquests in Germany and Holland.

The boulevard Sébastopol, down which we're turning, has nothing to commend it except convenience — it is modern, and its story is all to make — but that is just as well, now, else we might be tempted to loiter. A very little to the east of it is the rue Saint-Martin which was the old Roman road to the north. But we shall prowl all along that on foot, some day, and explore many of these streets we're crossing —twelfth- and thirteenth-century streets, some of them.

This beautiful Gothic tower on our left is the Tour Saint-Jacques — all that's left of the old church of Saint Jacques-de-la-Boucherie which was taken down about the time of the Revolution. There had been a church or chapel on this spot for a full thousand years! Pascal used this tower when making some of his experiments in atmospheric pressure.

And now here we've come to the Place du Châtelet where there used, for centuries, to be a great gate with massive towers and deep dungeons, guarding the north end of the Big Bridge (grand pont). Away back under Louis VI, eight hundred years ago, this formidable gateway was made one of the principal fortresses of Paris, and was the special one where offenders against the city were incarcerated — as the Bastille (likewise a city gate and fortification) was used as a state prison. The first publicly maintained light in Paris, now called "the City of Light," was a candle which by a law of 1318 was kept burning near the door of the Châtelet. Molière was in prison here, for debt to *his* candle-maker! And Cartouche, that maker of melodrama, that terror of Paris, was here in chains before he was taken to the near-by Place de Grève to be "broken alive" on the wheel. We shall meet Cartouche (quite safely!) on another day.

LA TOUR DE NESLE
From an old etching

The prison stood about where the fountain now is. It was not taken down till 1802. The Théâtre Sarah Bernhardt is on our left; the Théâtre du Châtelet, built by the same architect a year later, on our right.

Now here we go, over the pont au Change. The old bridge of the money-changers and goldsmiths, whose shops and dwellings cumbered it on both sides, was a wooden structure a little above this. The first stone bridge was built when Louis XIV was a little boy; and it was over this that Marie Antoinette, Madame Elizabeth, and many others rode from the Conciergerie to the guillotine. The present bridge dates only from 1858, and was built slightly to the west of the old one, to be in more direct line with the important thoroughfares of which it is a part. As we cross it, we have a superb view of the Palais de Justice, with its square clock tower at the corner, the roof and flèche (spire) of Sainte-Chapelle, and the round, "pepper-pot" towers flanking the entrance to the Conciergerie.

We are coming to this vicinity again, on Thursday morning when the Conciergerie can be visited, and when the courts are in session in the Palais de Justice. We shall devote ourselves to the palais then. The idea in coming today to see the Sainte-Chapelle is that it should be seen near noon on a brilliant day, and when the fewest people are in it. Experience has taught me that Sunday noon is likely to be a quiet time there. And, moreover, I want you to see the bird market over here, in what is — other days — a flower market.

When we leave the bridge we are on the Île de la Cité (eel de lah ceetay), that boat-shaped island (the prow pointing west, downstream, seaward) where Paris began to be — before the Christian era. The Roman legions, when they first halted at the Seine's edge, found this island inhabited by a feeble tribe of Gauls whose resistance to Roman authority was brief and not very bitter. They were used to dependence, and they seemed to have the same appreciation of the advantage of Roman protection and Roman civilization that many other Gauls had. Soon, the Roman governors were living here on this island, where the palais now stands, and their rather proud new subjects were building a fine temple to Jove, where we shall now find Notre-Dame.

The first race of Frankish kings, beginning with Clovis, succeeded to the Roman governors; but Clovis, after he ceased to live at Soissons, preferred the palace of the emperors over on the south bank. Some of his descendants lived here; but the next dynasty, of Charlemagne, had little to do with Paris, and it was not until Hugh Capet, Duke of France and strongest vassal of Charlemagne's feeble descendants, became King of France, in 987, that there was much royalty hereabouts. Hugh began the old palace of the kings where the Roman governors had lived, and where the Palais de Justice is now. And twelve kings of his great race ruled France from here.

It was the ninth of them, Louis IX (Saint Louis), who built the exquisite chapel that we are going to see. He had brought back with him from the Eighth Crusade what is believed to be the Crown of Thorns, a fragment of the True Cross and a nail therefrom; and he caused this chapel to be erected, so that the relics might be worthily housed, and so that the royal household might worship near them. (Giving them to Notre-Dame, where they now are, does not seem to have occurred to Louis; and we must be glad it didn't — because no architect could, one thinks, have conceived anything so awesomely beautiful as Sainte-Chapelle unless transfigured with the glory of a task like making a shrine for such relics.)

I know few thrills comparable with that I feel each time I

climb the winding, worn stone staircase in the corner turret and emerge into that jewelled chamber which is the upper chapel. It should never be done in company with any but reverent souls capable of being struck dumb before transcendent loveliness. It is like being in "the house not made with hands."

You may want to study the architecture in detail, on this visit; or you may feel that you want nothing, until later, but the overwhelming general impression.

When you have drunk your fill, we will descend our little winding stair, take another look at the lower chapel (which was for the domestics of the royal household), and leave the palais precincts — crossing the boulevard du Palais and going through rue de Lutèce to the bird market, where we shall meet our hosts, the Parisians, in another rôle: that of bird-lovers. We shall see many little "bits" of endearing human comedy, here.

If I were sure of you as a walker, I'd take you along the Quai aux Fleurs, past the site (number 9) of Canon Fulbert's house where Abélard, the great scholar and teacher, loved the Canon's young niece, Héloise, too well; past the bridge connecting this island with its sister isle to the east, Île Saint-Louis, and round the poop or stern of our "ship" with the Morgue at its rudder-point. Thus we'd approach Notre-Dame from the east, as we should. The west approach tends to be a bit disappointing because the towers never got their spires put on; the thirteen steps, however, up which people of earlier centuries were wont to climb to the cathedral, were not at the front but at the south side.

Nothing mars the splendor of the majestic edifice as we come upon it from the east. Indeed, to the *real* pilgrim I would say: See Notre-Dame first from a small boat coming under the pont de la Tournelle; or, in default of that supreme sensation of seeing it from the water level, see it from the above-mentioned pont itself, early on a golden morning when there is direct light on the flying buttresses, or late on a dying day when the whole pile is silhouetted against a flaming sunset.

Fearful, however, of your "giving out" before our day is done, I'll take you straight across rue de la Cité.

The great building on our left is the Hôtel Dieu — God's mansion — the oldest hospital in Paris and, so far as I know, in the world. This building, however, is new.

Now we are come to the Place du Parvis-Notre-Dame (a *parvis* is an open space in front of a church or temple), where the Roman Forum of Paris was. And if we stand here with Notre-Dame on our left, looking south, we shall look over the Petit Pont, successor to the first bridge the Romans built from the mainland to the isle, and on down rue Saint-Jacques which was the old Roman road "back home," to the Eternal City. Then, if we turn about and face due north, we shall look straight up, over pont Notre-Dame, along rue Saint-Martin which was the road the legions followed going north — to Britain and elsewhere.

This great space, dominated by the equestrian statue of Charlemagne, has only rather recently been cleared of the clutter of churches, chapels, asylums, houses, and ancient streets which huddled about Notre-Dame like a huge brood of very small chicks about an ample, motherly hen.

I shall not ask you — let alone urge you — to enter Notre-Dame to-day. It is enough to glimpse it, and come again for further acquaintance.

You're probably thinking of luncheon, now. So we'll cross the Petit Pont; and instead of going along the Quai Saint-Michel, we'll go south of the bridge a few feet and take you into the twelfth-century rue de la Huchette. At number 10 of this narrow old street there used to be a café with lodgings above, where Bonaparte nearly died of hun-

ger in those bitter days just before he stepped overnight
into fame, in 1795.

And on our way, we'll glance up the rue du Chat-qui-
pêche (the cat who fishes), because it will give you an idea
of what hundreds of streets were like which have been
cleared away during the last century.

Now here we are in the Place Saint-Michel, the beginning
of the famous "Boul' Mich'," which takes its name from
the bridge leading over to the palais; and the bridge was
named for a chapel dedicated to Saint Michel, which used to
stand at the entrance of the palais. Philippe-Auguste was
baptized in that chapel, in 1165. This bridge is new; but
you have doubtless been many times on one of its predecessors, with Dumas and Catherine de Médicis, to visit (at
dead o' night!) the shop of René, the Florentine sorcerer
from whom Catherine bought the poison for her deadly purposes — as Dumas relates in his "Marguerite of Valois."

This Place Saint-Michel is the gateway to the famous
Latin Quarter. If you want to lunch inexpensively, we'll go
up the boul' Mich' to Café Harcourt. It's a third of a mile or
so up the boulevard, and if you're tired we'll take a tram.
Café Harcourt is not so famously frequented as it used to
be; but is still very popular, and the food is good, though
the service is plain. We shall see some Latin Quarter
"types," although rather less interesting ones than we'll
find on the boul' Montparnasse.

If you're inclined for a more distinguished luncheon at a
correspondingly distinguished price (but *worth* it! oh, dear,
yes!), we'll stick to the river, and go to Lapérouse on the
Quai des Grands-Augustins. Many gourmets who were
facile and elegant with the pen have sung the praise of
Lapérouse. No word of mine can add aught to his fame.

But if what you're craving to eat is — as was the case
with some American friends I once took there — broiled

lamb chops, don't go to Lapérouse. Not that his lamb chops (cutlets, in France) are less than perfection; but thousands of chefs can grill a cutlet, and scarce one of them can do the things for which Lapérouse is famous. The head waiter all but wept on my shoulder when my friends (for whom I was translating) chose chops. "Why," he moaned, "do they come here to eat what they can get anywhere?" It seemed such a waste of opportunity!

After lunching chez Lapérouse, your interest in Paris will be intensified, many fold. And you will be glad to know (before lunch you might not have cared) that this quai we're on is the first one built in Paris.

Lapérouse is number 51. The church of the Grands-Augustins was next door, at 53; it was begun by Charles V (along about 1370) and not demolished until after the Revolution. Number 55 covers part of the site of the convent (or monastery — the words are interchangeable in French) in which much of interest in French history took place. It was there that Henry III founded the Order of the Holy Spirit, in 1570; there that Marie de Médicis was saluted regent of the realm after Henry IV's murder. Philippe de Commines, the fascinating chronicler of Charles the Bold and Louis XI, was buried in the Grands-Augustins' church.

Standing here at the west end of this picturesque quai, we look north across the pont Neuf which crosses both arms of the river and the "prow" of the island as well. We shall give more attention to it on Thursday when we come to the Palais and Conciergerie. To-day, let us recall that just beyond this end of it, on the river edge, stood the château Gaillard (not to be confounded with Richard Cœur de Lion's of the same name, in Normandy), where Benvenuto Cellini lived while in Paris working for Francis I, and from which he sallied, doubtless, on many a gay adventure. And near it was the Tour de Nesle which can never disappear from the vision of men's inner eye while Dumas holds them spell-bound.

Just beyond us on the quai are the Monnaie (Mint) and the Institut de France. But we're bent, now, upon the Luxembourg Gardens, which are half a mile away. Every possible way of getting there is a stroll through a hundred story-books; but there is a bit of walking to do in the gardens (if we're to see them!) and a bit more I'd like to do in their vicinity. So, perhaps we'd better take a cab (or a bus marked "Q," which we can get at Place Saint-Michel); and as we shall want to be at the northern end of the gardens, later on, we'll go to the rue d'Assas and enter by the south-west gate and the least-frequented corner.

I have lived over here, close to this entrance, and could take you wandering up and down the streets hereabouts, telling stories, indicating "backgrounds"; but such loitering is, I dare say, not for the first visit to Paris, unless it is to be a long one.

Of these gardens there are such worlds to say! There was once a Roman camp on this site; and then there were convent gardens — the Carthusians were here for more than five hundred years, until the suppression of religious houses in 1790.

The street we have just come down (rue Guynemer, named in honor of the splendid young aviator) used to be called rue du Luxembourg. It was near there that the Dukes of Luxembourg had a mansion which Marie de Médicis bought, the year after Henry IV's death; and soon after, she gave orders that it be razed and a magnificent new palace built in the manner of the Pitti, at Florence, where she had passed her youth.

What I specially want you to see, this afternoon, is the family groups with which these gardens swarm. I shall not mind a bit if, after a glance about you, you elect to sit down and spend an hour or more watching the people. We shall see fewer nurses here than at the Parc Monceau or in the Tuileries or the Champs-Élysées or the Bois; and more mamas. On a week day, when we come here again, the vignettes of the "comédie humaine" we see about us, will be quite different; we shall be more aware of "the quarter" then, although it will always seem to belong most of all to the children.

I have occasionally found myself, in Paris, briefly in company with an earnest compatriot who, on entering a place like the Luxembourg Gardens, felt under an awful urge to inspect each statue, learn the name of each terrace and fountain, and then hurry on.

Now, I love to loiter in front of the statues of Paris — they recall so many stories, and they are so likely to be set up in places where the individual commemorated was a familiar object when he was clothed in flesh and going about his business. But Paris would not be so wonderful a Hall of Fame, to me, if it were not also so very full of people who are being moved by their traditions to make beautiful to-days and glorious to-morrows. *Nothing* is dead, here! Everything is going on and on, passed from hand to eager hand like a torch making plain the way of truth and beauty.

The students who are here from all the world, to carry to the uttermost parts what Paris has taught them, are a perpetual thrill to me. Of the children playing around me, some will have their statues here one day, no doubt; some will leave a memory here that will add to the sweet sacredness the place already has. *All* will keep through life a hallowed recollection of these days.

I shall be glad, if from your first visit to the Luxembourg Gardens you carry away nothing much except an impression of their loveliness, and of the generations of youth which have come up in them and gone on into the world to work and fight and love and pray.

Now that you have your mental picture of the broad sunken gardens, the terraces and fountains, the vistas down the long, tree-lined avenues, and the throngs of people so obviously enjoying life in their quiet, decorous way, we'll quit the palace precincts by way of the lovely Fontaine de Médicis, at the northeast corner. You've had a view of the palace, now the French Senate, and of the little Luxembourg, where the President of the Senate lives. Soon we shall pass the former orangery, where the Museum now is. This would be a most unsatisfactory time to take even a glance through the Museum, which is crowded to suffocation on Sunday afternoons.

We'll go up this short rue de Médicis, and walk a few feet along rue de Vaugirard till we come to rue de Condé. The country house which used to stand here (its principal entrance opposite number 20 — and number 20 was recently the home of Boutet de Monvel, painter par excellence of French children, and best known to Americans by his superb Jeanne d'Arc pictures) had Catherine de Médicis for a tenant, once. And, later, Marie de Médicis was so grateful to Henri de Bourbon, Prince of Condé, for having married a lady who came near getting Henry IV away from her, that she gave them this handsome property. Here the great princes of Condé lived until 1773, when the place was sold for a vast sum and cut up.

The rue de l'Odèon was cut through the Condé grounds in 1779; it was the first street in Paris to have sidewalks — in 1782. We can imagine the Parisians of that day flocking here to look at the novelty.

The Odéon Théâtre was built when the street was cut through, and the sidewalks were laid at the time of the dedication. It was the Théâtre-Français then, and was not named Odéon (a corruption of the words meaning "the place where they sing" until it became a music hall, in 1797. Two years later it was burned, and not rebuilt until the Empire. In 1818, it was burned again; and this is the third theatre built on the site in forty years. It is now a state-subsidized theatre, like the Théâtre-Français across the river; and I hope you will come to it more than once. Also, I hope you'll like (on a day when fewer persons are about) to loiter at the book-stalls of Flammarion, beneath the arcades of the theatre. Loitering and "sampling" is genially encouraged there. Georges Cain tells us of one "patron" who read Darwin's "Origin of Species," 450 pages, while standing first on one foot and then on the other in front of the stall where it was exposed for sale. And nobody disturbed him! M. Flammarion told M. Cain that other "clients," less scrupulous, carried away the books they were reading, and forgot to bring them back. But he smiled indulgently and said that "their thirst for instruction had evidently won the day against their delicacy" — meanwhile setting down the petty larceny to "profit and loss."

Everywhere, one finds Paris indulgent, to the point of tenderness, of those who hunger and thirst for the things of the spirit.

At number 22 of that rue de Condé we've just left, there lived, in the seventeen-eighties, the family of a rich bourgeois named Duplessis, who had a charming wife and two lovely daughters. In an attic from whose window he could look down into the elegant and happy home, there lived a young briefless barrister of twenty-five, who used to follow Madame Duplessis and her daughters when they went to walk in the Luxembourg Gardens. He was homely and poor and already bitter because his education was not helping him to find bread, let alone fame or affluence. He fell easily in with those who believed that if their world could be overturned, they might seize a better fortune from the ruins than they were able to build under the old order. His name was Camille Desmoulins; he became acquainted with the Duplessis family, was often entertained by them, and fell in love with the younger daughter, beautiful Lucile, whose dot would be 100,000 francs. It seemed to her father a presumption most preposterous. But Camille was "coming on" in a political way. He had tried to be elected a delegate to the Assembly at Versailles, where the people were to be allowed a voice in national affairs for the first time since Louis XIV said, "I am the state!" Failing that (although his college classmate, Robespierre of Arras, had succeeded), Camille went to Versailles anyway, and attached himself to Mirabeau. He orated; he published pamphlets; he started the attack on the Bastille.

Prudent M. Duplessis may well have looked askance at the young firebrand! But Lucile wanted him — and she got him! They furnished a home for themselves — *here*, above the Café Voltaire; not where the inscription is (that was put up by a committee improperly informed), but at number 22 rue de l'Odéon, on the third floor, their windows looking out on rue Crébillon. They were married in December, 1790, at Saint-Sulpice, and came here to their own home, for their wedding feast — ten at table, among them the bridegroom's schoolmate, Robespierre, who sought the hand of Lucile's sister Adèle, but did not get it. Camille was very, very happy. He didn't want the world overturned. He wanted it to stay just as it was! Their little Horace was born on July 6, 1792; and when his mother was able to go out, the radiant parents took him over to the Luxembourg Gardens to sleep under their tall trees.

But Camille's old friends were rallying him on his desertion of them and of their cause. "You sleep, Camille," they cried, "and Paris is enslaved!" They said that because he was now fortunate, he should not forget the unfortunate. He allowed himself to be drawn back into their ranks.

For some reason that I have not been able to discover, the Desmoulins seem to have left their home here for a short while, and gone to live in an apartment under the Dantons, in Cour du Commerce, in a house now destroyed, but which stood where Danton's statue is, on the boulevard Saint-Germain.

When Horace was a month old, "the reds of the Midi," the Marseillaise, came marching into Paris, bent on "action." Some of them dined with Camille and Lucile on August 9th; and after dinner they all went up to the Dantons! Everybody was greatly excited. The tocsin rang; the people in the streets cried, "Vive la Nation!" Danton, Desmoulins, and the men from the South went to the Hôtel de Ville (the City Hall). Gabrielle Danton came downstairs to be with Lucile. All night long they wept and shuddered. Near dawn, they heard cannon. Gabrielle fainted.

Finally, Camille came back. The Tuileries had been attacked, and taken; the royal family had fled, taking refuge with the National Assembly.

On the 12th, Danton was elected Minister of Justice of the newly proclaimed Republic of France. On the 14th, he moved into the sumptuous palace of the Chancellerie, in the Place Vendôme. A few months later, Gabrielle was dead. She had been through too much.

Danton made Camille his secretary-general; and he and Lucile, too, took up their residence in the palace of the Minister of Justice. Their stay was not long. On September 8th, Danton and Desmoulins were elected to the National Convention, where they voted laws for the Ministry of Justice to execute. Both men tried to moderate the destructive fury of the Revolution, and for that they went together to their death in the Place de la Concorde on April 4, 1794.

On March 20th, Camille, again living here in his honeymoon flat, received from his old home in Guise a black-bordered letter. His mother was dead.

Camille was sitting by a table; he bowed his head, buried his face in his arms, and sobbed. Hour after hour he sat there. Lucile, exhausted with fatigue and anxiety and sorrow, lay down on her bed, beside the cradle of little Horace.

"All at once," writes Lenotre, "the measured step of a patrol disturbs the silence of the street. Camille shudders, raises himself, opens the window, leans out; the soldiers have stopped at his door. He hastens to his wife: 'They have come to arrest me!' he cries. Lucile, rudely awakened, hardly understands: she clasps him in her arms, strains him to her breast to protect him; he disengages himself from this supreme embrace, leans over the cradle of Horace for a last kiss, and himself goes down to open the door. In an instant he is surrounded, bound like a malefactor, and led to the prison of the Luxembourg."

From his cell there, looking out upon the shady paths he and she had so often paced, he wrote to Lucile: "I believe that there is a God. My blood will wash away my faults, my human frailties, and all that was good in me, my virtues, my love of liberty, God will recompense. I shall see you again, some day."

Eight days later she followed him to the guillotine, to expiate the crime of having been his wife. "I go to sleep," she said, "in the calm of innocence."

We may as well go on to the end of this street to where Danton's statue marks the site of that other dwelling.

Close to the Danton statue on this north side of the boulevard Saint-Germain, is the rue de l'Ancienne-Comédie, a very short one, but one that has several things you will like to see. The street owes its name to the Comédie-Française, which was once installed at number 14. Molière's troupe had had several homes since his death. In 1688 they bought an old handball court here, and had it transformed into a theatre which they opened on April 18, 1689, with a performance of Molière's *Médecin Malgré Lui,* and Racine's *Phèdre.* They played here until 1770, when they moved to the Tuileries, waiting the completion of their theatre where the Odéon now stands. Many painters have had studios in this building — notably David. Marat lodged next door, at number 16, in 1790, and it was there that the officers from the Châtelet came to arrest him — but he had escaped, thanks to the complicity of Mademoiselle Fleury, an actress at the Théâtre-Français.

Number 13 is the old Café Procopé, the haunt of Voltaire, Rousseau, Danton, Marat, Robespierre, Talleyrand, Bonaparte, de Musset, George Sand, Gambetta, Verlaine, and many others. It was the first café in Paris; to-day there are more than twelve thousand. When Benjamin Franklin died, the café was hung with mourning.

Number 21 was the residence of Dr. Guillotin, deputy to the National Assembly of 1789. He invented his machine to provide a humane and expeditious way of slaughtering sheep, and the first trials of it were made in the Cour du Commerce, adjoining. The wall of Philippe-Auguste ran here (you may see a fragment of his old ramparts in the Cour de Rouen, opening out of the Cour du Commerce — and may like to remember that here Henry II built a house for Diane de Poitiers) and there was a gate in the wall, here at the top of the Cour du Commerce. This gate, flanked by two towers, was called the porte de Bussy, or Buci; it was betrayed to the Burgundians in 1418, and by it they and their allies, the English, entered Paris. After the English were gone, this gate was walled up.

Now, let us follow rue de Buci till it leads us back, very shortly, to boulevard Saint-Germain — cross the boulevard and take rue du Four to the new rue de Rennes and so down to rue d'Assas again. You may want to ride this little stretch of a half-mile; and if you're at all tired I advise it, as there's nothing much here to reward sauntering.

We are going, now, for the last visit of our day, to a place that all the lovers of old Paris unite in describing as one of the most interesting, most touching spots they know; yet, of all the tourists who go to the Luxembourg Museum and Gardens, probably not one in a thousand goes a few steps beyond, on rue Vaugirard, to the old Carmelite Convent behind its high, gray walls at the corner of rue d'Assas.

Of the Paris priests who in August, 1792, refused to take the oath of loyalty to the new republic, more than one hundred were imprisoned here; and on Sunday, the 2d of September, 1792, they were slaughtered horribly. All the recently filled prisons of Paris were slaughter-houses that day and the next. Scarcely a trace remains of any of those prisons except this; and it has changed hardly at all.

The massacre started here between three and four o'clock on Sunday afternoon; it had been going on for about an hour at the Abbaye prison (up at boulevard Saint-Germain, just beyond where we left it to take the rue du Four) directed by that extraordinary young man, Stanislas Maillard, who had been in the mob that attacked the Bastille, in the mob that brought the royal family in from Versailles, and had now — just *how*, nobody seems to know! — constituted himself, or been appointed, president of a popular tribunal which was taking its own way with those who opposed the new government.

He set up some semblance of judgment. For the most part it consisted of a single question: Have you taken the oath?

Of course they hadn't taken it — those trembling creatures who were dragged or pushed before him; if they had taken it, they wouldn't have been there — and most of them were dead, or dying, a moment after making the admission.

You may still (if you ask permission; the old convent is now part of the Catholic Institute of Paris, but its chapel is a parish church) see the sombre corridor where this travesty of judgment took place — the bloody spots that the sabres of the assassins left on the walls — the door into the garden which opened a hundred and twenty times in three hours, to deliver to the butchers waiting without their hundred and twenty victims.

"From the top of this flight of six steps (into the hitherto peaceful garden of the Carmelites) what a sight met their eyes! — the horde of slayers, their sleeves rolled up, their arms bloody, mopping their sweating brows with hands dripping red. . . . The victim was hurled to the bottom of these six stone steps, was seized, stripped, while they fought for the first chance at him."

Many of the victims made no resistance. Others tried to flee, and were slaughtered in the garden.

Before darkness fell, all was over, here. The next day, toward night, some men of the quarter came, with two wagons; they entered by this gate on rue Vaugirard, closed it behind them, and — laughing and chattering — divided among them the spoils of the dead. Two or three times before dawn, the wagons went, full, to the near-by cemetery of Vaugirard, and returned, empty.

Then the convent was closed, and a sign was put up: National Property, For Sale.

Seventy-five years later, when the city decided to prolong that rue de Rennes down which we have just come, a part of the old garden (dating back, then, more than two hundred and fifty years) had to be cut away. A tradition persisted in the neighborhood that some of the dead had been thrown into an old well in this part of the garden. The well was opened, searched, and bones were found; but they proved to be beef, mutton, and chicken bones.

Then appeared a very old man (all these details are from M. Lenôtre's "Paris Révolutionnaire," a book crowned by the French Academy and by the suffrages of many thousands of readers) who refused to tell his name, but who took one of the diggers by the arm, led him to the middle of the garden, and said, "They are there."

And there, indeed, they were! Some thirty bodies had been carried away for interment, and ninety to ninety-five — at least two of them women and three of them children under ten — were dumped into this well, covered over, and forgotten. But one old, old man remembered. Doubtless he had been among the butchers; and before the grave should yawn for him, he made what reparation he could by pointing out those bones to such as would give them, at last, Christian burial. They repose, now, in a crypt of Saint Joseph's chapel. The tomb of Madame de Soyecourt is there, too. I would like to tell her thrilling story here, but am afraid of making this chapter too long. Those who read French may make acquaintance with it in the second volume of G. Lenôtre's "Vieilles Maisons, Vieux Papiers," in the chapter called "Le Roman d'une Carmélite."

What I do want to remind you of, while we are here, is that this convent became a Revolutionary prison where many well-known persons were incarcerated — notably Joséphine de Beauharnais and Thérézia Cabarrus.

Do you know Thérézia? You must know her, if you want to *be* anybody in Paris of the Directory.

Her father was a Frenchman from Bayonne, who lived much across the border, in Spain, and married a Spanish lady. Thérézia was very beautiful, and when she was still quite young she married a marquis.

One day, before the Revolution, the exquisite marquise was sitting to Madame Lebrun for her portrait, when there came to the studio on some errand or other a workman wearing the white blouse of the print-shops; he saw her, and was ravished; his name was Tallien, and he was the son of a concierge.

Events moved rapidly then. In 1793 the young printer, then a power in the National Convention, was sent to Bordeaux to organize the Reign of Terror there. Among the nobles who were in prison at Bordeaux, and of whom he was expected to make short work with the guillotine, was his lovely lady of the Lebrun studio. He spared her; and for love of her he spared so many others that Robespierre called him back to Paris. Thérézia went with him. In course of time *she* was arrested, and brought here to this Carmelite Convent, and Tallien — himself under suspicion, a pack of spies forever trailing him — wandered, frantic, around these walls. Then, mysteriously, she was taken away in dead of night, transferred to the sinister prison of La Force, out in the Marais quarter where Tallien's mother was still a concierge. Perhaps it was she who discovered where her son's beloved was. She rented from another concierge in the neighborhood a garret from which Tallien could look down upon the court where Thérézia took her exercise. He threw notes to her, assuring her of his devotion.

One day (July 25, 1794) he found on the table in his mother's home a Spanish dagger that he recognized as Thérézia's, and with it a note: "The police administrator has just left here. He came to tell me that to-morrow I go to the Tribunal — that is to say, to the scaffold. This is little in accord with a dream I had last night: Robespierre was no more, and the prisons were open.... But, thanks to your arrant cowardice, there will soon not be anybody left in France who could make this dream come true!"

Then Tallien determined to die saving Thérézia, if he could not do otherwise. He went about among the malcontents of the Convention, seeing which among them he could rally to his cause: not knowing, though, if the support they promised would not give way to terror when they confronted Robespierre. On July 27th — the great day of Thermidor! — Tallien, after hurling his imprecations, his accusations, at the dictator, bounded to the tribune, armed with Thérézia's dagger, seized the tyrant by the throat, and began that terrific combat which ended in Robespierre's arrest; thus saving, as Lenôtre says, "the Republic, France, the world, to snatch from death the woman he loved."

We shall meet Thérézia again and again, in other places. But I'm sure you'll like to think of her here at the old Carmelite Convent because here she made an acquaintance of which much was to come. Here she met Joséphine de Beauharnais.

Joséphine and her husband, the Vicomte de Beauharnais, had not been living together since before the birth of their daughter, Hortense, in 1783; a formal separation had existed for nine years, when the misfortunes of these troubled times brought them together once more under the same roof — that of this convent, where they were both prisoners. Their children were brought here to visit them, and with the children was that dog of Joséphine's, Fortuny, of whom you shall hear more presently. Tucked under Fortuny's collar were notes telling the captives what was being done by their friends to save them.

The children, to insure their safety, had been wrapped in the mantle of democracy, clothed in the garments of toilers; Eugène was supposed to be apprenticed to a carpenter, and Hortense to a dressmaker; thus dressed, the future Viceroy of Italy and Queen of Holland came here to visit their parents.

But not even this display of affiliation with "the people" sufficed to save their father. He went — not from here, but from the Luxembourg to which he seems to have been transferred — to the scaffold on July 23d. If he had been able to dodge the Tribunal for three or four days longer, the life of Napoléon Bonaparte might have been very different.

There is a story to the effect that Joséphine, looking out of the window of her cell at dusk on the evening of Saturday the 29th, saw a woman in the street who conveyed to her joyful intelligence by shaking her dress (robe), picking up a stone (pierre), and drawing her finger significantly across her throat.

Whether this was or was not the way she learned of the tyrant's execution, Joséphine soon knew of it. In ten days she was free, and practically penniless. She was thirty, and had a son twelve years old and a daughter eleven. She may well have been anxious about her future; but she probably wasn't. Joséphine was not of the worrying kind!

We'll walk along rue Vaugirard, now, past the entrance to the Museum, and the palace entrance with its sentries on guard; past Foyot's restaurant where you will often dine, I hope — "Foyot, the king of them all!" — but *we* don't do it on the same day that we have lunched at Lapérouse's.

If you are of like mind with us, we'll dine outdoors, in front of the restaurant Médicis, rue de Médicis. There we can sit on the sidewalk, overlooking the Luxembourg Gardens, near the Médicis fountain and pool, and the statue of Murger who wrote "La Vie de Bôhéme." We shall have a good dinner at a very moderate price; and we shall have hosts of co-diners to watch, and throngs passing our table. Children will come, selling nosegays from their baskets. An ambulant musician or two may sing or play for us, and accept our coppers in a manner not at all mendicant.

Now the dusk is deepening. The gates of the garden are about to close; the last of the lingerers come pouring out.

Barrie says they clear Kensington Gardens at nightfall, and lock them, so the fairies can have the place to themselves.

Do you know why they close the gardens of the Luxembourg? It is that you may realize why, that I have kept you hereabouts till dusk. I want you to *see*.

We'll walk up the boul' Mich' a way, alongside the high iron railings that enclose the gardens. And here, at a point where rue Gay-Lussac ends at the boulevard, we'll stop and look west, through this superb avenue that runs across the gardens. What a vista! Like an illimitable nave; and at the end of it a blazing altar where unseen acolytes are extinguishing the glory. The shadows deepen in the dim aisles where the chapels are. Just the sheer beauty of what our eyes behold is more than enough to fill them with ecstatic tears. And through those tears we shall have *visions*.

Do you see lights, hear music and laughter? Are the parterres about the sunken garden filled with ladies in great hooped skirts? Marie de Médicis gives a fête tonight. There goes the beautiful young queen, Anne of Austria. And there is the namesake of both her parents, Henrietta Maria, Henry IV's last delight, last playfellow. She is going soon to England to be its queen; 'tis said she's very much in love with the handsome Prince Charles who came a-wooing so romantically, passing himself off as Mr.

Brown. You and I can see what's in store for her; but she can't.

They've passed — but others come.

Can you see Madame Duplessis walking there, with Adèle and Lucile — and shabby young Desmoulins watching them, envious of all their bright blessings? Then, unseen by them, though crossing their very path, can you see Lucile with Camille and Horace? Camille envies no one, now. He has no prevision of those days when he is to look out of his cell window on these gardens and see them through the blur of tears that will soon drop on his farewell letter to Lucile.

I see Joséphine, once of the Carmelite prison, now of the Petit-Luxembourg, walking there, among the flowers. And Bonaparte, meditating his move to the Tuileries.

These, and many, many more flit through the dusk, when the gates are closed, for those who know how to see them.

III

A MONDAY IN PARIS

EVERYTHING that can entertain or instruct us is open in France, on Sundays, when most people have their only leisure day; and many places (including all museums) are closed on Monday, for cleaning and to give the employés a rest.

This arrangement used to offend some American visitors who were Sabbatarians in the old sense. But, now that we have so largely (especially in our big cities) taken over the French idea of Sunday, the only objectors are among those who forget about the Monday "day of rest," and fix upon that day for going to galleries, or to Versailles, or Malmaison, or Victor Hugo's house; or what not.

But no one need have a "blue Monday" on that account! There is always so much to do in Paris, so much to see, that it is rather a relief to have the field of possibilities a bit restricted once in a while, so choice is a trifle less difficult.

If I were trying to show Paris to you, I'd know that this Monday morning you'd probably be "all in a fever" to get at the shops. And don't imagine for a moment that I'd be impatient with you therefor! Nobody could possibly love shop-loitering in Paris better than I do, or know better than I how much of an education it may be as well as a delight. Particularly in the little shops, and in those which are not too fashionable, too standardized.

One thing I always beg my friends in Paris *not* to do: Don't begin buying before you have seen a good deal. If you do, you're sure to be regretful.

I haven't the slightest sympathy with those who believe

in "American prices," and live in the conviction that they are constantly being fleeced. But I know that in every city I have ever bought in there is always the probability of finding the same article in different shops at different prices. Everybody knows that the shopkeeper adds to what he has paid for an article its proportionate share of his "overhead" expense and of his idea of profit. If you like to buy in a palatial shop, or in a little bijou of a place, you must expect to contribute your share toward the fitting-up and to the elegant maintenance, as well as to the proprietor's idea of how his business should support him and provide for his old age. You do it everywhere — Paris included. And remember, too, that when you buy a gown or wrap or hat in one of the great "houses" that set the fashions for all the world, what you are paying for is not merely the cost of the materials plus your share of the enormous "overhead" and such profits as a proprietor expects who has made himself a world-master in his line, but also for something designed not merely to be worn (indeed, not primarily to be worn), but to be *copied*. "Buyers" from all over the world can afford to pay a high price for that model you so admire; because each of them will have it reproduced, in whole or in part, many, many times.

If you are stopping at a first-class hotel, your mail-box was probably full, this morning, of attractive invitations to this and that famous establishment, where you are urged to ask for Mademoiselle Germaine, or Madame Yvonne. It is eminently worth while to accept a few of these invitations and see the sumptuous settings, the parade of mannequins, observe the customers, and revel in the gorgeous clothes and accessories. You may feel able to indulge in the "experience" of having something made at one of these places. It is always interesting, and I some-

times think that it is a wise thing to do, at least once, even
for the woman of modest means — who is likely to be
more, and not less, satisfied thereafter with the copies of
these models that she can get for much less money at
many another place.

Paris, we must remember, is the market-place for all the
world. She caters to all tastes. We are not to suppose that
everything we see for sale there represents that genius for
chic, for elegance, which has distinguished France for
centuries. Some of it is made in a spirit of frank concession
to the more barbaric tastes of other peoples.

And it isn't at all true that all Parisiennes are instinctively "smart," or even tasteful. Only a very small
proportion of French women are concerned with fashions
— as you will soon find out. A great majority of them
dress in black, because it is inconspicuous and economical
— can be "matched" and made over and over, and need
not be discarded if somebody of near or remote kinship dies
and every one in the clan must go into mourning. Economy
is a much more ruling passion with most French women
than display; money in the bank makes them happier than
finery on parade.

The great body of Paris women is committed to the
search for bargains. No wonder that the recklessness
with which we spend gives them the idea that there is no
bottom to our "pile"! They take for granted that no one
could indulge in the purchases we make, whose home was
not bought and paid for, whose old age was not insured
against all want, whose children were not educated,
dowered, and set up in business. And, after all those
really important things are done, what can a woman want
of these fol-de-rols? This is the attitude of the generation
before the war. Their children are more like ours; at least,
many of them are. They buy luxuries beyond their means,

beyond their station, just as we do. They work too little, and play too much. Their elders can't think what France is coming to. We've had our big share in producing this change, just as we had our big share in encouraging their Revolution. Our presence in Paris, spending our money like sailors on shore leave, is vitally important to French trade. But the effect of it on the morale of French youth has been a bit disturbing.

We shall get a great deal more satisfaction out of our shopping tours if we keep this in mind.

And let us remember that in the small shops of Paris, particularly in those that are off the highways frequented by the world's greatest spenders (among whom South Americans are prominent for prodigality), there is a wealth of quiet friendliness awaiting us if only we go in the spirit that calls it forth.

I should hate to be in Paris with anybody who likes to turn night into day, and to come forth, stretching and still heavy-eyed, not earlier than 1 P.M. For Paris mornings are like no other mornings that I know anywhere; although mornings are nearly always lovely to me.

It is delicious to be abroad in Paris streets while they are still fresh from their nightly washing, and while the light still has some of that tender, glorifying quality which makes it easy to believe that if, perchance, there were mistakes yesterday, and disappointments, to-day is *all new*, and very lovely, and Paris "is so full of a number of things that I'm sure we should all be as happy as kings."

I don't mean 6 A.M., of course (though the light is lovely, then!), nor even eight. But it's really a pity not to be abroad by ten. That's nine by the sun, in the daylight-saving months, and a delicious hour. *Please* don't take that time to write letters, or to scan the "recent arrivals" in the Paris edition of the American papers!

And if you've been out since ten, wandering about, looking, you'll be glad (I hope!) to meet me at noon in the Palais-Royal Gardens, close by the statue of Camille Desmoulins. We can sit here in the sun or in the shade, as we prefer; and watch the fountain flash as it leaps high in air; see the tiny navigators at the basin's rim launch their wee craft on those broad, trackless waters; look at Rodin's statue of Victor Hugo, gleaming white on the velvety green sward amid the brilliant flowers and beneath the serried rows of trees; notice the little cannon which, for more than a century and a quarter, fired automatically at noon when the sun's rays at zenith struck its burning-glass (this veteran has now gone out of service and become a "monument"), and fraternize, at least mentally, with our neighbors on the benches and the children playing about our feet.

You think I'm an inveterate "park loafer" in Paris. Well, I *am!* But those who loaf with me nearly all get the habit, and delight in it.

Now we can talk about the Palais-Royal, which is in many respects "the heart of Paris."

On part of the ground now covered by the palace — the part where the Court of Honor is — there used to be, centuries ago, the old Hôtel Rambouillet; not the famous one of the salons, but its predecessor, built in the fifteenth century. In 1624, Cardinal Richelieu bought the old mansion; and for a number of years thereafter he kept on buying more and more property hereabouts until he had a great domain in the very heart of Paris, across from the Louvre. And on the south border of this domain, next to the palace of the King (Louis XIII), who was less the monarch of France than his great Cardinal-Minister, he built for himself a sumptuous dwelling of which not many vestiges are left. There Richelieu received, in 1635, the first members of the French Academy he had just founded. There he ruled, in state, despotically. There he died, in 1642, leaving his palace and gardens to Louis XIII, who survived him only five months.

Then Louis's widow, Anne of Austria, came here to live with her two little boys, born to her after so many years of barren wedlock. And here Anne lived in what may or may not have been secret wedlock with her Cardinal-Primate, Mazarin, between whose apartments and her own she had a communicating corridor arranged.

This was the principal background of Louis XIV's childhood, so troubled by those uprisings against Mazarin which are known as the wars of the Fronde. Twice the royal family had to flee hence, to safety outside Paris.

In 1652, when Louis was fourteen, he abandoned this as a residence, and turned it over to his aunt, Henrietta Maria, widow of Charles I of England. She lived here for nine years, and it was here that her youngest child — that Princess Henrietta who was born on the eve of her mother's flight from England, and had to be abandoned there — was married to her cousin, the younger brother of Louis XIV, Philip, Duke of Orléans.

Louis himself, just a few months married to his first cousin, Marie-Thérèse of Spain (her mother was his father's sister and their marriages had occurred at the same time), conceived an ardent fancy for his new sister-in-law, who was also his first cousin, daughter of another of his father's sisters. And when his manifestations of this fancy had begun to cause scandalous talk, his mother, and Henrietta's mother, and Henrietta's husband, all put their heads together to get Louis interested in some other gallantry. Then it was that they fixed upon seventeen-year-old Louise de la Vallière as one who might be thrown in the King's way and made to divert him from flirting with his sister-in-law.

A CAFÉ OF THE PALAIS–ROYAL UNDER THE DIRECTORY

Louise had succeeded in getting herself appointed one of the maids-of-honor of the young Duchess of Orléans; so she was close at hand for the purpose the plotters agreed upon. She was tall and slim and a little lame — but not so much so as to spoil her dancing. Her complexion was very fair, and she had blue eyes full of expression. Her hair was "of a silvery fairness," and her voice was extraordinarily sweet. Above all, she was richly dowered with the sort of charm that makes a person intensely lovable.

Duchess Henrietta lent herself to this plot because she believed that, behind Louise as a screen, she could keep up her ascendancy over the King. And in that same spirit, Louis began dallying with Louise. The Court was at Fontainebleau then, and there was an endless round of gaieties. Within two weeks Louise had become the young King's mistress, and they were so deeply in love that they could conceal it from nobody at Court — except the Queen.

For more than two years, as this affair went on, Louise continued in the service of Madame (of Orléans) living in a small garret room wherever the Duchess happened to be, enjoying no power nor luxury as the King's favorite.

Then he had to take her away. On the rue de Richelieu side of the Palais-Royal Gardens, not far from the palace, there was a little "pleasure house," one story high, and about twenty-four feet by seventy-two. Louis bought it, furnished it, and gave it to Louise. And there, on December 18, 1663, she brought into the world a son who was taken away from her three hours later. There she led, for a time, a retired life, seeing scarcely anybody but the King, her lover.

Her second son was born there little more than a year later. (Her third child was born at Vincennes, and her fourth at Saint-Germain.)

We shall meet Louise again, here and there; but for me

she is, somehow, one of the outstanding women of the Palais-Royal Gardens. And you may like, as I do, to "see" Louis coming from the Louvre to the little house in these gardens, where he was asked for nothing, "used" for nothing — and *given* everything! — by this girl who loved him utterly.

After the death of Louis XIV's brother, the Palais-Royal was occupied by his son who became Regent for little Louis XV on the death of his great-grandfather, Louis XIV, in 1715. It was during the Regency that most of the buildings of Richelieu were demolished to give place to some of those we now see. Peter the Great was received here by the Regent in 1717. And there were scandalous "goings-on" in the palace and in the gardens, until the Regent died, in 1723.

Duke followed duke here, and kept almost the only royal state that Paris knew for more than a hundred years, for the kings preferred Versailles and Fontainebleau and their other country places, and abandoned, for the most part, the Louvre and the Tuileries.

In 1778, Benjamin Franklin was received here, at the time Paris was so wildly enthusiastic about him; and here Paul Jones, also, was royally entertained. Another American associated with the Palais-Royal was John Howard Payne, who was living in an apartment in the Galerie de Valois when he wrote "Home, Sweet Home." These were the "pleasures and palaces" 'mid which he roamed.

It was in 1781 that the duke of Orléans, known to history as Philippe Égalité, wishing to augment his income (and increase his vices), ordered the construction of the buildings now surrounding the gardens, with their shops below and their apartments above; which caused Louis XVI to say to him: "Now that you are going to keep shop, Cousin, we shall see you only on Sundays, I suppose?"

The shops soon filled with purveyors of luxuries, and with cafés; the rooms above, with gambling-houses and houses of prostitution. The gardens continued to be, as they had long been, the Forum of Paris, its great open-air meeting-place; and it was there that the secret agents of Égalité found their most fertile soil for sowing rebellion against the King and Queen.

One day in 1784, a Corsican who was in Paris on business of some sort wrote home that he had been to the Palais-Royal and there had seen Napoléon Bonaparte — a "green" stripling of fifteen, just come to Paris to the military school — gawking about him, as all the "jays" did. Napoléon loved the Palais-Royal, and frequented it a great deal. I "see" him there, often, under the arcades.

But he was not there that Sunday noon, July 12, 1789, when word quickly spread among the crowded cafés that Necker had been dismissed and was on his way to his home in Geneva. (Necker, the Swiss banker, was Louis XVI's minister of finance, and was believed by some people — probably because they knew Marie Antoinette didn't like him — to be the King's wisest counsellor, and one who could save the country from ruin if only he were given the power.)

Camille Desmoulins was sipping his coffee — and talking, doubtless! — in front of the Café Foy which was over there on our left, at numbers 57 to 60 of the Galerie Montpensier. He leaped to his table, as we see him here in this stirring bronze by Boverie, and made the speech which so inflamed his hearers that hundreds of hands were eagerly stretched out to him to receive those green leaves he snatched from the nearest tree and distributed as badges of revolt.

The crowd broke into number 17 of this same gallery, where the Swiss, Curtius, and his niece, whom we know as

Madame Tussaud, kept an exhibition of wax figures they had made of notables; seized the busts of Necker and of the Duke of Orléans (that Égalité in whose pretended democracy they still believed), and with these draped in mourning as a sign that their friendship for the people was frustrated, the crowd started marching, and swelling as it marched.

Once under way, there was no stopping it. And on Tuesday morning, very early, it attacked and took the Bastille. The French Revolution was on. We might follow almost the whole course of it if we stayed here (metaphorically) from that July day to another in '94, when Robespierre went to the guillotine; and to an October day in '95 when our shabby, starving little Corsican leaped from despair to triumph in a few crowded hours.

But we must be on our way soon.

The north end of the Palais-Royal is the Galerie Beaujolais. You will find there a shop dealing in casts from the antique, where you may buy excellent reproductions in plaster of Gothic carvings in stone and wood. Number 98 in that gallery used to be the restaurant of the Three Provençal Brothers, where Bonaparte frequently dined with Barras, who lived at 15 rue Beaujolais, just behind. Number 103 was known during the Revolution as the Café of the Blind, which was frequented by the Sans-Culottes.

The east side of the long rectangle is covered by the Galerie de Valois. At number 177 Galerie de Valois was the shop of a cutler named Badin, from whom Charlotte Corday bought, at seven o'clock on the morning of July 13, 1793, the huge kitchen knife with which, that evening, she was to kill Marat. It was only 6 A.M. when Charlotte reached the shop, and she had to wander about the gardens for an hour before Badin took down his shutters as an in-

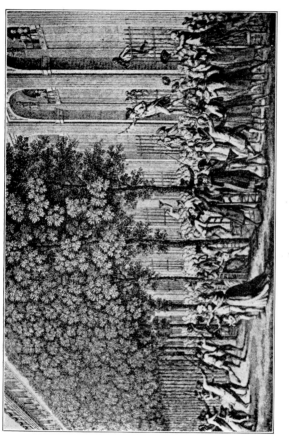

CAMILLE DESMOULINS AT CAFÉ FOY IN THE PALAIS-ROYAL, MAKING THE
SPEECH THAT STARTED THE ATTACK ON THE BASTILLE

dication that he was ready for the day's business. In those days there were stone benches at the foot of each pillar of the arcades. You may see Charlotte sitting on one of them, near here, in the sweet freshness of that summer morning, thinking — we may be sure — on many serious things. That she was about to give her life for her country, whether her attempt on Marat succeeded or failed, she cannot have doubted. Of what, in your guess, was she thinking as she sat there waiting for Badin to take his shutters down? Of what she was to do? Or of what she was to see no more?

Charlotte was twenty-five years old; of medium height and build; grey-eyed; chestnut-haired. "She was not beautiful," said an old woman who had known her in Caen, "but she had an air so sweet, so sweet, that one loved her even before she spoke. She was an angel of the Good God."

Now, let us get up from our bench — if you're rested — and go out into rue de Montpensier and, rounding its lower corner, into rue de Richelieu. We have skirted the side portals of the Théâtre-Français, and of course we're thrilled. But we're not going to stop now to talk about it. We'll do that later.

We're on our way to lunch now; and we'll look, and talk, as we go.

This rue de Richelieu was cut through by the Cardinal's orders, in 1638, and so many things have happened on it that I've often threatened to write a whole book about this street. But I'll let you hurry through it, this first time, with only a few glances to right and left.

In number 23 b, Pierre Mignard died, at the ripe age of eighty-five. He had painted all the beauties and celebrities of his long day, and was about to begin painting the cupola of the Invalides (as, thirty years before, he had painted that of Val de Grace) when death took him. Turenne

sat to him, and Molière, and Bossuet, and Madame de
Maintenon, and Ninon de Lenclos and Madame de Sévigné, Louise de la Vallière and Madame de Montespan,
and countless others. Molière, in speaking of Raphael and
Michelangelo, called them "those Mignards of their age."

At number 26, in the days before the Revolution, was
the shop of Mademoiselle Bertin, Marie Antoinette's milliner, who here made a "Paul Jones" hat for Her Majesty, and a "lightning conductor" dress designed to honor
Franklin.

At the angle of rue de Richelieu and rue Molière is the
Fountain Molière by Visconti, erected by popular sub-
scription in 1844; the statue of Molière is by Seurre; the
figures at his feet are by Pradier who did the "Strasbourg"
of the Place de la Concorde.

Diderot died at number 39. Nearly all his life the great
encyclopædist had lived not only in poverty, but in positive squalor. It has been calculated that the average an-
nual salary received by Diderot for twenty years (from
the contracting booksellers who financed the work) was
about fifty dollars a month. "And then to think," said
Voltaire, "that an army contractor makes four thousand
dollars (eight hundred pounds) in a day!" All the money
he could get went for his beloved books. Diderot, who was
Samuel Johnson's contemporary, had many points of
resemblance with him, one of which was that he also was
a most prodigious and eloquent talker. "When he grew
animated in talk, then he became truly ravishing." What
affection he must have had for his daughter when, to get
her a dower, he sold his library! The Empress Catherine
of Russia bought it, and asked Diderot to keep the books
for her, in Paris, until she needed them. For this service (!)
she paid him a yearly salary. He went to St. Petersburg to
thank her, and spent some months there, in 1773, he and

Catherine engaging in spirited debates on a great variety of subjects.

He had lived in this house only twelve days when death came to him suddenly, in the midst of his loved books. He sleeps, now, in Saint-Roch, close to Corneille.

Number 40, on our right, is the site of Molière's last home. He had lived there but a few months, and when he went there he knew himself to be a dying man. His theatre then was in the Palais-Royal at the corner of rue de Valois, and he could reach it by going through the Palais-Royal Gardens, to which he had access from his own back gate.

Knowing himself too ill to act in any of his old rôles, he wrote "The Imaginary Invalid," which permitted him to sit in an armchair, the back of which let down in the fashion of our later Morris chair. The first performance of this play was on February 10, 1673 — Molière having just recently passed his fifty-first birthday. February 17th, there was to be a fourth performance of the new play, and that day Molière said: "I see plainly that I must give up the struggle. . . . How much a man suffers before he dies!"

Implored not to act that day, he replied: "What can I do? There are fifty poor workpeople who depend on me for a living."

As it drew on toward four o'clock, the hour of the play, he had himself carried across the gardens and into his theatre. All was in readiness, and he went on, and with increasing difficulty played to the end — "with super-human effort held life in his body until the curtain fell." An hour or so later, he was dead. (The armchair in which he played that day is treasured at the Théâtre-Français; an exact copy of it is used by the players of the House of Molière, whenever "The Imaginary Invalid" is presented.)

Two priests who had been sent for refused to come to

give him extreme unction; and it was only with greatest difficulty, and by appealing to the King, that Christian burial was secured for him. The archbishop, in granting permission for Molière's funeral, ordered that it must be accompanied by "no pomp, with only two officiating priests, and must be performed after dark, without day service either in the parish of Saint-Eustache or elsewhere."

So, in silence, and in darkness relieved only by the flaming torches his friends held, he was lowered into the grave, in the cemetery of Saint Joseph, a poor part of Saint-Eustache burial-ground which was situated far from the church, on the right of the old road to Montmartre; the site of Molière's grave is now covered by houses bearing the numbers 142 and 144 rue Montmartre, and numbers 24 and 26 rue Saint-Joseph. In 1792, fearing the desecration of his tomb by the mobs, Molière's remains were removed to the Museum of French Monuments (where the Beaux-Arts now is); and in the early part of the nineteenth century, they were interred at Père-Lachaise.

Number 50 rue de Richelieu is the house where Jeanne-Antoinette Poisson, known to history as Madame de Pompadour, had lived for several years before she went to Saint-Eustache to be married (in March, 1741), when she was fifteen, to the nephew of her mother's "protector." When Jeanne-Antoinette was nine, a fortune-teller named Lebon had predicted that she would one day be the mistress of Louis XV; and ever since then, Jeanne had been preparing herself for it. Her marriage with the rich young seigneur d'Étiolles she regarded but as a stepping-stone to her larger destiny; and so, with her indefatigable efforts, it proved to be.

Now we are nearing rue des Petits-Champs, and here, on our right, is the Bibliothèque Nationale (National Library) about which I shall say nothing now. Your guidebook has the essential particulars. This being Monday, we might go in (the most interesting treasures may be inspected Mondays and Thursdays), but we're moving on to lunch. You may come back here after lunch, if so minded.

On our left is the pretty Place de Louvois with its Visconti fountain of the Four Rivers. Louvois, Louis XIV's minister of war and of buildings, lived here; in 1793 a theatre was built here, which later became the home of the Opéra, in front of which (in 1820) the Duc de Berri, Charles X's son, was assassinated.

In rue de Louvois, number 8, the north side of the square, Antoinette Germaine sells artificial flowers — the loveliest in the world, I think. We must go there, but not now when we are hungry; for it is a hard place to tear one's self away from.

That ancient-looking building behind the Bibliothèque is part of the old Hôtel de Nevers.

Now look, please, at number 62.

César-Marie, Marquis de Talaru, was what we might call the general director of the households of Marie Antoinette — a position of much dignity, many favors to bestow, and, presumably if not certainly, of rich perquisites. In 1785, when he was sixty, he bought for more than a quarter of a million livres a parcel of ground here, on which he had a mansion built and a handsome garden laid out.

When the Revolution took away his job, he had to retrench. And in 1793 he rented the mansion for seven thousand livres a year to a restaurant-keeper who purposed making a hotel of it; Talaru himself taking up his residence in a smaller house, a sort of annex, next door.

But travellers to Paris were few in those days of the busy guillotine, and the hotel lacked patrons. So the proprietor, Gence by name, knowing that all the prisons

were full to overflowing, had the profitable thought to
make his place into a sort of boarding-house where
suspected persons awaiting trial might stay, if they were
able to pay handsomely for the privilege. What they paid
for, and got, was not merely a considerable degree of
comfort or even luxury, but "to be a boarder of the Talaru
house was a sort of guarantee of being forgot; for by a sort
of occult providence, the emissaries of the tragic Tribunal
seemed to steer clear of this jail."

But one fine morning an armed squad came and arrested
Talaru, in his modest annex, charging that he had been
faithful as long as he could — to August 10, 1792 — to
Marie Antoinette.

Pleading his age and his infirmities (he was nearly
seventy) Talaru begged to be allowed to board in his old
mansion until called for trial. Gence rented him a miserable garret, and charged him for it exactly as much as he
paid Talaru for the whole establishment.

But Talaru was not "overlooked." On the 20th of July,
1794, he was summoned to appear before the Tribunal,
and taken to the Conciergerie. The next day he was
"tried," condemned, and executed. And five days later
those who were still in detention at his old mansion heard
the news-venders in the street crying, "All about the
arrest of 'Catiline' Robespierre and his accomplices." If
Talaru could have waited trial a week longer, all would
have been well with him!

Number 102 was bought by Voltaire shortly before his
death and was being made ready for occupancy by him
when he died. He left it to his niece, Madame Denis, who
had so long been his housekeeper. At 109, Dumas worked
on "The Three Musketeers" and "The Count of Monte
Cristo"; and at 112, Balzac had for years a refuge to which
he could retire when he had need of it — which was often!

At number 96 is the restaurant Gauclair, a thoroughly French sort of place, popular with French journalists and little frequented by tourists. If we see any of our countrymen here, they are likely to be such as Will Irwin or Robert Haven Schauffler or others of the Coffee-House crowd in New York — men supremely "at home" in Paris; even more so, perhaps, than in New York; and men good to meet anywhere.

We shall have an excellent lunch (as the French conceive it — but not of the American soda-counter variety) and an opportunity to watch interesting types. And then, I hope, we shall be ready for a further stroll. (Perhaps you think we have walked a long way; but we are only half a mile from where I met you, by Desmoulins's statue in the Palais-Royal Gardens.)

Let us retrace our steps for a few feet on rue de Richelieu, to rue Saint-Marc, and go through that street past rue Vivienne to the entrance of the passage des Panoramas, so called because of the two circular buildings which Robert Fulton erected in 1799, one at the boulevard end of this passage, and the other across the boulevard. In these structures were displayed cycloramas of Rome, Naples, Florence, and Jerusalem. And with the money he earned thus, Fulton was able to continue his experiments in steam navigation.

Now, down rue des Panoramas to rue Feydau, at number 21 in which the Feydau Theatre stood, from 1791 to 1830.

On the night of October 4, 1795, a lachrymose drama called "The Good Son" was playing there, and a young man who was in the audience may have chosen it because, while he seemed to be a failure in everything else in life, he *knew* he was a good son. That evening he had said to his friend Barras: "I *must* get a job! If I can't get one here,

I'll go to Constantinople; they need good artillerymen there."

The play over, about ten o'clock, he came out into the streets, walked down this tiny rue des Colonnes to rue des Filles-Saint-Thomas, and turned east, on his way back to his miserable hotel "At the Sign of Liberty" on what is now called rue d'Aboukir.

Here, at the corner of rue Vivienne, he witnessed a sight which made his blood boil.

The Bourse was not there, then; that ground was still covered by the gardens and old buildings of the ex-convent of the Filles-Saint-Thomas, suppressed by the Revolution, but always a secret centre of Royalist sympathies in which this section of the city was notably strong. Paris was full of misery in those days following the collapse of the Terror; scant rations distributed by card to long bread lines; profiteering in all the necessities of life; terrible depreciation of currency, so that a gold louis, instead of being worth twenty-five francs, was worth twelve hundred and fifty-five! "We were better off under our kings," people were muttering in many places. And this quarter of Paris was known to be the heart of the monarchical movement, and to be fomenting an outbreak. So, that night, more than twenty thousand troops of the Paris garrison had invaded the quarter, under command of General Menou; and rue Vivienne, when our jobless young man got to it, was full of foot and horse soldiers and artillery, and officers galloping up and down the street — getting nowhere! A young Royalist named De Lallot was haranguing the Republican troops — and they were listening! "In the name of the Law," cried the insurgent, "I call on you to withdraw." And they did!

Our young man, who was on the eve of becoming a Turk because his own country would not make use of him, was stupefied — then furious. He followed the retiring troops toward the Tuileries where the National Assembly was in session, and witnessed the commotion there when the Congress of the Republic learned that its troops had fallen back from the fire, not of the Royalists' guns, but of their street oratory. Menou was at once removed from command. But, where to find a successor?

"There is," said Barras, "nothing easier. I have the man we need. He is a little Corsican officer."

And there, standing among the staring mob of on-lookers, was his little Corsican, our theatre-goer; thin and pale, with burning eyes and long, stringy hair; his boots broken, his long coat worn threadbare, his hat — evidently a "hand-me-down" — too big for his head.

Barras was empowered to offer him the command. Napoleon asked "time to consider!" "I will give you three minutes," Barras said. At the end of that time Bonaparte said, "I will take it, on one condition. If I unsheathe my sword, I will not return it to its scabbard till the job is done." Granted.

The next day, in front of the Church of Saint-Roch —! But we shall meet him there.

We'll walk on now, down rue Vivienne, along the east side of the Bibliothèque Nationale, till we come to rue des Petits-Champs, turning out of the latter (where it ends) into rue des Petits-Pères, so that we may glance in at the Church of Notre-Dame-des-Victoires where so many white tapers are always flickering in the enshrouding gloom — each symbolizing a prayer for some loved one's safety or for the success of his endeavor in war or peace.

As we come out of the church, glance up rue du Mail, where Bonaparte lodged in 1790, at the Hôtel de Metz, sharing a room with Junot, Marmont, and young Louis Bonaparte, which cost them each about six cents a day.

(There was a restaurant on rue des Petits-Pères where they dined for six sous each.) And up the next street, rue d'Aboukir, where he was lodging when he went to see "The Good Son."

We are now in the Place des Victoires, with its equestrian statue of Louis XIV. This square, designed by Mansart, was once very elegant; its architecture all of one plan, and its residents rich and splendid. But it has not succeeded in keeping its uniformity nor its dignity. At this corner of the square where we are turning down rue Croix-des-Petits-Champs, Bossuet, the great preacher, once lived (3 Place des Victoires).

If we take a few steps east, on rue Coquillière (the northern section of Philippe-Auguste's city wall ran along here; and at number 7 there is a fragment of it, about twenty-five feet high and nearly twenty feet thick), we shall come to rue Hérold, at number 14 in which was the Hôtel Providence where Charlotte Corday lodged, and whence she went to slay Marat. (The hotel was closed as a public hostelry the day following the murder and the building was torn down in 1893.) In a few minutes we shall see where her stage from Caen set her down. It was about noon on July 11th that she came here, following a "runner" for this hotel, who carried her bag on his shoulder. She was shown to room 7, and — fatigued by her two nights en route — went at once to bed, sleeping till night. Then she went downstairs and asked an old woman employed in the hotel if Marat went to the Convention every day. (Which was about like asking a chambermaid in a New York hotel what are the daily habits of the Police Commissioner.) There was nothing in the old woman's reply to indicate that she had ever heard of Marat. So Charlotte went back to her room. The next day she spent trying to reach Marat at the Tuileries where she supposed him to be. She resolved to go to his home. The next morning, very early (as we have seen), she bought her knife. Then she came up rue Croix-des-Petits-Champs, to which we are now returning, and followed it to the Place des Victoires where there was a cabstand for fiacres. Approaching a cab, she directed the cocher to drive her to Marat's house. When he said he didn't know where it was, she replied, "Find out."

About nine o'clock she was at Marat's house, over near the Odéon, but could not gain entrance. So she returned to the Hôtel Providence, and spent the day writing her "Appeal to Posterity."

Toward 6 P.M. she changed her gown, came out, hailed a cab, and gave the address: "20, rue des Cordeliers."

Before we leave rue Hérold you will, I am sure, like to recall that here, at number 12 (now gone), Alexandre Dumas had his first Paris lodging.

The house numbered 10 (where Hérold, the pianist and composer of many operas, was born in 1791) is as Charlotte saw it.

Now, back to rue Croix-des-Petits-Champs, number 23 in which was the mansion of that rich tax-collector who was the "protector" of Pompadour's mother and the uncle of Pompadour's husband. Madame Poisson (the mother) died here on Christmas Eve, 1745, full of regret at leaving the world just when her daughter had become the King's mistress. Some writers say that the first rendezvous between Louis XV and Pompadour occurred here.

Next door, at number 21, there are still, at the back of the court, some remains of a mansion where Henrietta Maria of England lived for a time before taking up her residence in the Palais-Royal.

Now we come to rue du Bouloi, named in the thirteen-hundreds because of a bowling game there. At number 2

is an arched entrance-way above which we read Galerie
Véro-Dodat. If we step within, we shall find ourselves in
one of those long, glass-roofed arcades with many shops
and chambers above, of which Paris has a number —
though none on the magnificent scale of those recently
built in some Italian cities. This passage was built in 1826.
I like to bring my friends here for a special reason which
has nothing to do with anything to be *seen*.

Among the most impassioned lovers and chroniclers of
Paris in recent times was M. Georges Cain, late conservator
of the Carnavalet Museum and of the historic collections
of the City of Paris. He spent his life in an atmosphere
of Old Paris — among such memorials of it as the Carnavalet conserves; roaming the streets and reënacting
other days; and finding his fellowships with living men in
that elect company of worshippers to whom Paris is, in
a way, almost a religion.

Well, here we are staring at the Galerie Véro-Dodat.

One day, not so many years ago, M. Cain was passing
here when a sudden shower forced him to take refuge under
this glass roof. He was not seeking this place — which he
knew well, of course — but was much interested to find
himself unexpectedly sheltered there; because, only the
evening before, he had been re-reading a delightful chapter
of Alfred de Musset in which the poet described a memorable supper enjoyed with Rachel in her lodgings at 38
Galerie Véro-Dodat in May, 1839.

De Musset had been to the Comédie-Française to see
Rachel in "Tancrède," and after he left the theatre had
met her, under the galleries of the Palais-Royal, followed
by a squadron of youthful admirers. (She, herself, was
only eighteen, then!)

"I am taking you home to supper," she said to Alfred.

They had been home but a few minutes when Rachel

found that she had left her rings and bracelets at the theatre; so she sent her one-and-only servant for them, and she herself cooked the supper — including beefsteaks. Her mother was present, nodding and snoring in her chair. After food, *talk!* And *punch!*

Rachel wanted to play Racine's "Phèdre" (destined to be her greatest part) and the powers that were told her she was too young, too thin, "and a hundred other foolish things."

She brought the book, carrying it — Musset said — with the religious air of an officiant bringing the sacred vessels to the altar; and began to read. Musset could never forget the scene: the table in disorder; the candle with flickering flame by whose light she read; the mother sleeping in her chair, but no less capable sleeping than waking of comprehending the young goddess who had — by what mystery! — sprung from her loins. As a picture, Musset said, it was worthy of Rembrandt; as a pen-picture, of Goethe's "Wilhelm Meister."

All this was vividly in M. Cain's mind that day as he stepped forth into the streets of Paris on some errand or other. Rain! And no umbrella. He went into a passage for shelter — looked about — and it was the very "setting" Musset had described! He went upstairs to what had been Rachel's apartment — and lived it all over again.

That is Paris! To-day we read and are enchanted; to-morrow, on our rounds, we may walk straight into the frame of that which thrills us with the romance of other days.

Nothing is *dead*, in Paris! All the charms of all the pasts are there — not hidden away in dusty libraries, but beckoning us on every hand, no matter where we go. There is no wall between romance and reality; we step from one into the other, freely, continually.

We go to the Opéra-Comique to hear Manon, and we come out into the night and stroll through an ancient street or two into rue Vivienne, where Manon and des Grieux had their lodging; or we drive homeward (if we live near the Luxembourg) past the old Seminary of Saint-Sulpice where the third Act with that great final scene takes place — and the moon is shining between the tall towers of Saint-Sulpice Church, and into the garden, near by, where Massenet lived when he was writing "Manon." Or, we go to see "Les Misérables," at the Odéon; and next day we find ourselves, on some other quest, in that garden of the Little Picpus Convent into which we saw Jean Valjean and Cosette drop from Javert's sight and clutch, in the final scene of the drama.

Ever and ever it is like that, in Paris. The story-books, the histories, the picture galleries, are *all alive;* and *we* are "in" them, *not* on the outside.

Well, well!

I said, awhile back, that we would come, presently, to where the stage set down Charlotte Corday, and many another, with work to do in Paris. It was close to this gallery; but no trace of it remains.

Perhaps you're tired of walking (although we haven't walked a mile since luncheon) or of old streets and houses.

We'll drive out to the Hôtel de Ville, which is new and magnificent. It is about a mile away. And we'll instruct our cocher or chauffeur to go down rue du Louvre, past the colonnaded east front of the palace, and Saint-Germain l'Auxerrois across the way, along the shaded quais. I won't mention anything that happened anywhere; one "takes in" just so much of that in any one day — and no more. We'll look as beauty-lovers, now, over toward the Conciergerie, and the flèche of Sainte-Chapelle, and the squat towers of Notre-Dame, and the dome of the Panthéon crowning Sainte-Geneviève's hill.

The Hôtel de Ville is shown to visitors from two to four every day. And aside from its beauty, its gorgeous state apartments, its wealth of mural paintings and sculpture, it is for its *majesty* a sight which no American should miss who has ever staggered through the foul corridors, over the breastwork of cuspidors, in his city hall at home, cursing the necessity which brought him there.

Some day we shall take a cue from Paris and have a mayor and a seat of government for each one of our big-city wards; and our centre of city government will be a place reflecting our civic pride, fit for our civic hospitality; not a market for peddlers' licenses, a loafing-place for the dreadful henchmen of our almost equally dreadful politicians. When we do our business as citizens in a neighborhood hall where we know our office-holders, we shall elect them more intelligently and have a better idea of how they're serving us.

After we have visited the Hôtel de Ville (particulars of which our indispensable guidebooks will give us), we'll go into the Mairie (or Hall) of the fourth arrondissement (or ward) close by.

You may want to go home and rest now. Or you may feel like a drive along the quais on this side of the Seine, past the Trocadéro.

I thought that, if it pleases you, we'd dine to-night at Marguery's on the boulevard de Bonne-Nouvelle (eating the world-famous sole Marguery, of course!) and after dinner stroll along the boulevards, past the theatres, newspaper offices, cafés, to the Musée Grévin, at number 19 boulevard Montmartre, close to the top of rue de Richelieu, where we ate our lunch.

I like my friends to visit Musée Grévin early in their

Paris stay; because I find it helps to vivify many things for them. It is a wax-works show, in the manner of Madame Tussaud's, though not so large.

In the main hall we shall see startlingly lifelike figures of many leading actors in the late war — some of them seeming so real that we shall find ourselves hesitant to discuss them out loud.

But it is the historic groups of earlier days that I specially want you to see: an evening at Malmaison, arranged under the supervision of Fréderic Masson, the eminent Napoleonic authority; the death-bed scene of Napoleon at St. Helena, faithfully reproduced in every tiniest detail; the murder of Marat, showing his room exactly as it looked at the moment, and Marat sitting in the identical bathtub in which he expired; the royal family in their prison at the Temple when the mob thrust up into Marie Antoinette's view the head of her dearest friend, the Princesse de Lamballe, hacked to pieces at La Force Prison during those September massacres we recalled yesterday at the Carmelites'. And so on.

An hour or so here suffices; and the cost is slight.

After we come out, you may like to sit at a sidewalk table in some of these many cafés, and have a coffee, an ice, a liqueur, or what you will, and watch the crowds go by. Or you may want to go exploring the night life up Montmartre-way. I'm no guide for that. It is one of the few aspects of Paris about which I cannot get up any enthusiasm. I've been there, a few times, and seen the same sorts of things I could see any night in New York or even in Chicago, if I could find them worth the feeling I have next day after spending night hours in a close room thick with smoke and fumes and crashing with jazz. I've no objection to smoke or to drink or to jazz — *except* that, on the day after associating with a lot of them in a close room, I feel no better than if I had been imprisoned in the Black Hole of Calcutta. And I hate to feel that way in Paris, of all places!

And there's really more of Paris, and less of Cedar-Rapids-let-loose, here in a popular café, under the sky.

IV
A TUESDAY PROGRAMME

THE Louvre is open every day but Mondays; it is in the very heart of Paris, and accessible from the street most frequented by tourists; it is always there! Availing one's self of what it offers ought to be as easy a thing as anybody ever did. Yet I find that many of my compatriots have a strange attitude toward the Louvre and the Luxembourg — the only art museums that concern them much. They regard them almost resentfully (or at best only resignedly) as something that has "*got* to be ' done,'" because it would be awful to go home and say we hadn't; but, "Oh, dear! there are so many other things I'd rather do."

Now, the truth is that few of us have the museum habit at home, even those of us who live in cities that own very good art collections. Perhaps we went in droves herded by Teacher, when we were in school. Perhaps our club has a "gallery tour" led by an artist (and *followed* by a luncheon!) one morning in every year. Perhaps we semi-occasionally take our country cousins to the museum — if they'll go. But we don't frequent museums — we frequent movies! — and we don't feel at home in them.

In Europe, though, we seem to feel that we *must*.

Now, I'm a heretic: I say we *mustn't* — unless there's nothing we'd rather do. I say that the museum habit can't be learned all at once, even if one wishes to; and that trailing through galleries so as to be able to say one has "done" them is an unpardonable waste of time which might be better spent doing something we can delight in and comprehend.

I *never* go into the Louvre because I feel that I ought to! The way I do is this:

I am reading over certain parts of Cellini's "Autobiography," and I note what he says about "The Nymph of Fontainebleau" which he executed for the palace, but which, a note by the editor reminds me, is in the Louvre. The next time I am in the vicinity of the Louvre, I go in and look at it; and then I note that my guidebook suggests that one compare the Nymph and Goujon's Diana in the next room. So I do it — just to see why it was suggested. And I look at the cast of it employed in the Salle des Cariatides. Then I start on my out-bound way. Perhaps I pursue it hastily — perhaps I don't. It all depends!

Or, I have been reading about the outdoor salons that were held, two centuries ago, in the Place Dauphine; and that among the pictures there exhibited (because rejected by the regular Salon) in 1728 were some of the Chardins now in the gallery of French painting of the eighteenth century at the Louvre (and fabulous prices they cost, too!). So, first time I can, I go to look at the Chardins.

Or, I find myself suddenly smitten with a new interest in Clouet's portraits; and in I go to enjoy them in a way I never did before.

And so on.

There are miles of galleries in the Louvre, and there must be several miles of them that I haven't seen, haven't even walked through. No one in a single lifetime could know them all. I'm quite content if my desire of them grows deeper and a little broader, every year.

So, you see, I could never be the sort of guide who'd say: "Punctually at ten to-morrow morning, friends, we shall assemble at the Pavillon Denon entrance of the Louvre. And let no one be late, please; because we shall have to be both punctual and brisk to see it all in two hours."

But if, for instance, Sunday morning had been chill and wet, instead of bright and warm for the babies and the flowers at Parc Monceau, I might have said, "Let's go to the Louvre for an hour or so." And it might have been that we'd have gone no further than the Venus de Milo; that we might have spent our hour there, looking at her from every angle, and watching people approach her. Many an hour have I spent doing just that! (Knowing her charms, this adorable woman considerately provides us with benches on which to sit, enraptured, before her — or behind her — or on either side.)

And so it might be that in laying before you my suggestions for this Tuesday, and telling you why I choose it for Saint-Germain and "points en route," I'd say that if, before our early lunch, you felt like spending an hour in the Louvre, I'd be glad to go with you. But I'd be sure to add that if you'd rather shop, or loaf along the quais, I'd never "hold it against you." If you go to the Louvre because you think you ought to, I'm going to let you go alone. I've gone there, sometimes, with people in that spirit; and — well! I think I've done it times *enough*.

If, however, you're really eager to begin your acquaintance with that greatest of all treasure-houses; and if you have no special thing in mind that you want to see first, I'd say:

Let's do this: let's go over and have a look. Mornings are the ideal time for galleries; we're fresher then, and so are they — that is, their air is fresher; and fewer people are in them. The regulations about when certain parts of the Louvre are and when they are not open have changed frequently of late; but our hotel concierge will tell us if we may see the Greek and Roman sculpture this morning. If not, we'll stay outside.

Abhorring as I do those books which devote pages and

pages to telling us what to look at in museums and what to feel when looking and what to say after having looked, I may be *too* hesitant about making suggestions to be of any service as a guide. I'd so much rather, always, that a friend should let himself be drawn wherever anything beckons to him than that he should look at anything because *I* find it interesting or admirable.

But the Louvre is vast; it is possible to spend a great deal of time there without finding any of the things you'd like best to see. So, if you are like many of those with whom I've come on their first visit there, I'd say we'll see the Venus de Milo and the Winged Victory, and the Salle des Cariatides, and anything else that engages your interest on our way to and from those objectives.

The Pavillon Denon, by which we'll enter, is in the wing nearest the river. We'll go through the glorious Place du Carrousel (not without many a look about us, in every direction) and easily find our doorway, between the Gambetta and the Lafayette statues.

This section of the palace (which grew, much like a sectional bookcase, in a way; only the sections are — happily — not uniform) was built by (or for) Napoleon III.

We'll turn to our left, on entering, and go straight on, as far as we can go; and there we shall find Venus, in a room by herself, against a background of dark curtains the color of which I cannot (many times though I have seen them) tell you; all I know about them is that they throw her into admirable relief, and perform this their function so perfectly that we can be unaware of them. I hope we have brought Rodin's little brochure on Venus, so we can sit here and read it. It is like having him with us.

We are in the oldest existing part of the Louvre — the part built by Francis I about 1546; and on top of the foundations of the oldest Louvre, built by Philippe-

Auguste about 1200. These are the rooms (these and those above) in which the kings and queens lived in the days of Francis I, and his son Henry II, and the three sons of Henry II, and Henry IV. This is Pierre Lescot's work. And it is here that we must "set" many of the most familiar dramas of the Renaissance — beginning with the sumptuous festivities prepared by Francis I for the Emperor Charles V. It was during this week's round of splendid gaieties that Charles (whose prisoner of war Francis had once been, at Madrid) said: "Other cities are merely cities; Paris is a world."

We'll take a look, now, at the Salle des Cariatides which, if walls could talk, might tell us breath-taking tales for days on end: of Catherine de Médicis and Saint Bartholomew's Eve; of Henry IV and Marie de Médicis; of Louis XIII and Richelieu and Anne of Austria; and of Louis XIV. The contents of the room may not specially interest us; but the room itself certainly does.

If, as we retrace our steps toward the door by which we entered, we turn to our left in the Rotunde (or round room), we shall find ourselves in the apartments of the first wing that Catherine de Médicis built; over our heads is the superb Galerie d'Apollon which, however, was not added till later. The ceiling paintings in these rooms, done for Marie de Médicis by Romanelli, suggest those of her Pitti Palace in Florence.

The top landing of the Escalier (stairway) Daru contains the Niké of Samothrace, which we call the Winged Victory. And after having paid tribute to her, you may feel that you are satisfied with your first glimpse of the Louvre.

I would infinitely rather that a friend of mine should leave the Louvre, thinking eagerly of getting back to it soon and often, than that he should be the victim of a too intense zeal and not leave until he was footsore and eye-weary and headachy.

If the sunshine is of a friendly warmth as we come out into the Place du Carrousel, I suggest that we sit down near Paul Bartlett's statue of Lafayette, which our school-children paid for with their pennies and presented to France.

There is so much to talk about, right here!

Get out your Guide to Paris and turn to the page where-on the description of the palace and galleries of the Louvre begins. Opposite, you will find a diagram in colors.

Near the top of the page, inside the completely enclosed Cour du Louvre, you will see the faint tracings of Philippe-Auguste's old castle, with its great round donjon and its battlemented walls. It was a suburban retreat, in those days; outside Philippe's great wall. The bristling remind-ers of the old fortress did not disappear until Louis XIV cleared them away, castles having become obsolete and palaces the mode.

The western wall of Paris in Philippe's day (1200) was just about where the eastern end of the Louvre now is — the colonnade of Louis XIV.

A century and a half later, Charles V refortified the larger Paris, and *his* west wall was about on a line with where we're sitting now. So, then the Louvre was "in town." But by that time the kings, who had really lived there very little (preferring the palais on the Ile), were be-ginning to tire of the discomforts of castles and to feel sufficiently secure behind their city walls; so they lived, for the most part, in the Saint-Paul palaces until Cather-ine de Médicis ordered the last of them (the Tournelles) razed, because her husband had died there, and moved her numerous family to the Louvre, which she almost immedi-ately began to expand.

The only really habitable part, when she went there, was the small section (colored orange on your Blue Guide plan) which her father-in-law had built just before his death. To this, she added the green sections on your right; and also she built the Tuileries Palace which lay between the two pavilions now marking the western ends of the Louvre. When we are on our way to the pont Royal we are crossing ground that was immediately behind the Tuileries, or across their west façade.

You will see, on your diagram, that Henry IV started to connect the two palaces with a gallery along the quai des Tuileries, intended to meet his unlamented mother-in-law's gallery along the quai du Louvre. He also put a second story on her first construction, adjoining the Francis I wing.

Then his son, Louis XIII, employed Lemercier, the architect of the Palais-Royal, to add a wing adjoining that of Francis I. And Louis XIV demolished the last of the old castle, completing the palace of the old Louvre.

After that, nothing was added until Napoleon's time. The first Napoleon built a wing which was to connect the Tuileries with the Louvre on the north, as Henry IV's wing and Catherine's did on the south; but it was only half finished when he was deposed. The most extensive of all the builders was Napoleon III whose contributions to the vast pile are colored pale yellow on your diagram.

There was, you see, nothing between the Louvre and the Tuileries (quarter of a mile away) for more than two centuries, except the galleries along the river-bank.

These beautiful great spaces were close-packed with old streets and buildings.

The western wall of Charles V, coming from the river up here across the Place du Carrousel, was taken down only in Louis XIII's time, when the western fortifications were moved in a line with the grand basin of the Tuileries Gardens and the rue Cambon. At the river edge, near where the pont du Carrousel now is (but a little west of it), there was a city gate in Charles's wall; the Porte-Neuve it was called, and by it Henry IV entered Paris as its king. (He had fled from it, barely escaping with his life, more than eighteen years before.) I think you may like to look down there now, and see him riding in, very early on a March morning in 1594. Gabrielle d'Estrées was there to see him do it; he had brought her with him. She needed some "impressing" — that Gabrielle who had seen him so shabby and poor.

The Place du Carrousel, laid out on the site of the old moat and ramparts, got its present name from a magnificent entertainment which Louis XIV gave there on the 2d of June, 1662. Some say it was given for Louise de la Vallière; but that is improbable, because he was then trying to be a little discreet about Louise, who was still in his sister-in-law's service. She was *there*, however.

At the north of this square there was the great enclosure of that hospital for the blind, the Quinze-Vingt, which Saint Louis had founded to care for three hundred Crusader knights whose eyes the Saracens had put out; and which grew and grew until, under Louis XVI, it had five thousand inmates. It was moved away, in 1779, and several streets cut through its grounds.

Between the place where Gambetta's statue now stands and the west front of the Louvre, there was a labyrinth of old streets and historic houses. It might be confusing to enumerate too many of them; but I'm sure you'll like to know that the famous Hôtel de Rambouillet, where the first and greatest of all the French salons were held, was just opposite the door by which we entered the Louvre — where the Pavillon Richelieu is now.

The Place du Carrousel was the theatre of many dreadful scenes during the Revolution — populace rioting, bodies burning, gutters running red with blood. The guillotine stood here before Louis's execution, and was again in operation here after his death.

Shall we visit the Tuileries now? Not a vestige of the palace is left except that southwest pavilion, Pavillon du Flore. And, incredible as it may seem, there is not in existence even a plan of that edifice where so much history was made, and which housed an imperial court within the memory of men still living. But that indefatigable delver in the dustiest, least-disturbed bundles of yellowing papers in the Archives, M. Lenôtre, has not only reconstituted the Tuileries for us by patiently piecing together this and that bit of topography scattered through state documents, but he has done it as he has done all his work: evoking the most stirring drama from those documents in which another searcher would have found only dead, dry bones. The most apparently insignificant details have a way of fairly leaping from their burial-places at the approach of this chronicler (that is the effect; the truth is that he toils mightily to find them and to relate them one to another, and to corroborate them), who knows how to handle them so that his citations from the Archives have more glamour of romance about them, more glow of life, than most novels or dramas.

In his "Paris Révolutionnaire," M. Lenôtre rebuilds the Tuileries for us; and *more:* he re-peoples it. (I am sure that the Minister of Education, under whose direction are all public monuments in France, is one of M. Lenôtre's profound admirers. And I wish he would let M. Lenôtre persuade him that the interest of more sight-seers would be served if the official guides who conduct persons through palaces were to make their remarks less like a furniture

catalogue and more of a reference to history. It cannot be
that the majority of tourists are interior decorators or
buyers of antique French furniture. Why, then, the in-
variable chant about Beauvais chairs, Aubusson carpets,
Gobelin tapestries, clocks by So-and-So and tables made
of this-and-that? Why not: "Here Napoléon took last
leave of the little King of Rome"; "Here Louis XIV and
Louise de la Vallière had their first, secret trysts"; etc.?
M. Lenôtre makes the Tuileries much more vividly
realizable to us than are many of the palaces which exist
intact.)

I shall not ask you to go through it, room by room, re-
living one scene after another of its so varied and so
tumultuous history. But I am sure you will like to know
that its more attractive rooms were toward the gardens,
looking west; though its main entrance was from the Cour
du Carrousel, here, on the east. The grand stairway
mounted from the doorway of the central pavilion —
which was in a direct line with the Arc du Carrousel that
Napoleon set up here. At the first landing was the Chapel.
Then the stairs divided into two flights approaching the
grand state apartments which all overlooked this court.
The living-rooms of the royal family looked out on to the
gardens.

Louis XV lived at the Tuileries, on occasions, during his
youth. But after that, it was not a royal residence again
till October, 1789, when the Parisian mob went out to
Versailles and brought back with it the rulers and their
family and an enormous retinue of their retainers. A
courier, galloping in advance of the slow-moving mob and
their captives, announced to the superintendent of the
Tuileries that the palace must at once be made ready for
the King and court.

Now, this didn't mean airing the rooms and ordering

clean linen put out, and seeing that there were flowers in the vases.

For eighty years, or thereabouts, the palace had been "granted" out, bit by bit, to an extraordinary assortment of needy persons who had, or thought they had, some claim on royal bounty. Actors, artists, seedy lords and shabby ladies, old servitors suffering from all sorts of disabilities — a miscellaneous horde of these crowded to the roof rooms which had been designed for far other purposes. Great state apartments were divided up, not only vertically, but horizontally, to make honeycombs of little cells; doors were cut; ladder-like staircases were introduced; small shops catering to the wants of the tenants were opened in vestibules, under stairways, and in the courts; three theatres were established there; the Chapel served as parish church to this motley flock.

Within an hour, on the afternoon of October 6, 1789, the palace was emptied! Everybody and his lares and penates was sitting outside or scurrying to seek another shelter. And inside, an army of workers was trying to make the rooms habitable for royalty.

There Louis XVI and Marie Antoinette lived, a hollow semblance of power masking their actual captivity, for nearly three years. From here they made their melodramatic escape in June, 1791; thither they were brought back from Varennes, a few days later; there, on August 10, 1792, Louis wrote his last order as king — that command to the Swiss Guard to cease firing in his defence; the pathetic scrap of paper is in the Carnavalet, whither we are going to-morrow — and, taking the Dauphin by the hand, led his family across the gardens to the back door of the riding-school. "How early," was his only comment on that flight from immediate destruction to waiting death, "how early the leaves are falling this year!"

We shall come here again and again. I won't weary you with further details now. I just want you to see it with your mind's eye, when we're passing hereabouts — that palace which played such a part in Paris history.

Perhaps you want to go back to your hotel before we start on our long jaunt to Saint-Germain. We shall not come back till evening. We can lunch at or near the hotel — anywhere, so we're not too long about it, and start it early.

If you're feeling affluent, you may want to hire an automobile for this trip. It will cost two hundred francs, I think — though the concierge at the hotel can tell us more exactly. If we are saving our motor money for other trips, we can make this one by steam tram from the Arc de Triomphe; going out the broad avenue de la Grande Armée, through the Porte-Maillot and across Neuilly — where the Fair may be in progress, if it's late June or early July; if it is, we'll stop off here coming back.

Our first objective this afternoon is Reuil, about six miles from Paris, where Richelieu once had a magnificent château of which there are no traces now. What we've come to see are the tombs of Joséphine and Hortense, in the church.

Then on, by the tram again, to La Malmaison, three quarters of a mile away, where Joséphine died.

It is intensely interesting — Malmaison! — but one goes through it in a group (usually very large) at a pace which seems a gallop; and hears that standard chant about the origin of the clocks and carpets.

Perhaps it is unreasonable to ask more. When I recall the comments I have heard on such occasions, and try to compute how many thousands more of the same sort the attendants must have heard, it is not in my heart to blame them for their disbelief in our intelligence.

There were, for instance, those two American women near whom I stood once, in the garden, here. Very elegantly dressed, they were; and a few minutes later I saw them enter a superb motor, at the gate. But their lives had, evidently, been very little troubled by any "Who's who" outside their social register.

"*Just* who," one of them, lowering her voice discreetly, asked the other, "was this Josephine?"

"Why-ee," the second woman began, hesitatingly; "she — er — lived here, with Napoleon."

"Were they — er — married?"

"I believe so."

It may be argued against the guides that they cannot understand what "we" say; and pleaded in their extenuation that if they told really interesting things, we English-speaking persons, who make up so large a proportion of their crowds, would not understand them. And I am glad to say that no other country of my acquaintance does half so well in this particular as France. But no other country that I know has anything like her ardor for sharing her treasures with all the world. So I respectfully submit my suggestion that a really informing little talk on each of her great show-places would be a work of education genuinely worthy of her; and that one English-speaking guide in each such place ought not to be difficult to provide. (In the Catacombs of Saint Calixtus, at Rome, for example, one goes through with a group of English-speaking, or French-speaking, or German-speaking persons, as one chooses; and for each, there is a Trappist monk who discourses in the language of that group. It is not an impracticable idea, for a place visited by many thousands of persons yearly.)

From Malmaison to Saint-Germain-en-Laye is five miles, by that same steam tramway which brought us from

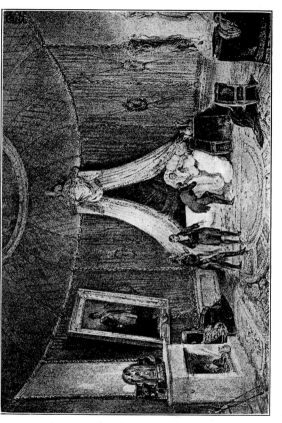

DEATH OF THE EMPRESS JOSEPHINE AT MALMAISON, JUNE 29, 1814

Lithograph by Tirpenne and Monthelier

Paris. The museum at Saint-Germain closes at five; and, in order to see it, we ought to leave Malmaison by three-thirty at latest. (Sundays, Tuesdays, and Thursdays are the only days the château is open to persons without a special permission; Sundays are too crowded; Thursdays we are saving for certain things accessible only on that day; so we must see Saint-Germain to-day.)

There has been a castle here for eight hundred years and more. But the present one was built by Francis I while he was still M. d'Angoulême. He was married here to Claude, daughter of Louis XII and of Anne of Brittany. Anne had opposed this match for her daughter, in spite of Francis being heir to the crown; and that delicious old Court gossip, the Abbé Brantôme, says it was partly because Anne had not relinquished hope of bringing her husband an heir who would put a different aspect upon the eligibility of Francis. Anne was only thirty-seven when she died; and it was not unreasonable for her to entertain hope of a son. But when she was gone, Louis consented to the union. He was, however, so afflicted with grief for Anne that he refused to put off mourning, or to let the Court put it off, for the wedding. And, in consequence, "the bridegroom and bride were vestured and clothed in black cloth, honestly cut in mourning shape," and all the Court was garbed likewise.

Perhaps that gloomy wedding had something to do with starting the new château off wrong. Because, for that reason or some other, it seems to have, in spite of its magnificent situation, an undue share of sombre associations, of tear-drenched atmosphere.

The son of Francis and Claude, Henry II, must have felt that his father's château left something to be desired; for he started another, practically alongside, and his son-in-law, Henry IV, completed it. But of this latter, not much is left.

The old château has recently been restored and now contains a museum of antiquities which will interest us if we have read a good bit about the Gauls and their conquest by the Romans, and not a great deal if we haven't. But everybody ought to see something of the interior of the château; to visit the thirteenth-century chapel, and to go to the church, across the way, where James II of England wished to be temporarily buried — but was not. He died at the château where he had lived for more than twelve years, handsomely supplied by his cousin Louis XIV with everything that he could wish for himself, his family, and his followers. And as he lay dying, he was assured by Louis that "Whenever it shall please God to call Your Majesty out of this world, I will take your family under my protection, and will recognize your son, the Prince of Wales, as the heir of your three realms."

Which should have restrained *some*body in the household of James from adding to those three crowns another, and within an hour of James II's death proclaiming his son, at the gate of the château, "by the title of James III, King of England, Scotland, Ireland, and *France*."

But Louis XIV seems to have borne no ill-will on this account. He continued his bounty to Mary Beatrice of Modena (James II's widow) as long as he lived.

It was hoped that when "James III" was invested with his numerous crowns he would remove his father's remains to Westminster. Meanwhile, instead of interring them at Saint-Germain, they were taken into Paris, to the church of the English Benedictines at 269 rue Faubourg Saint-Jacques, where the lead coffin containing them was opened, in 1793, by a mob opposed to kings of any creed or dynasty, and the bones thrown into a ditch with many others likewise disturbed.

If it is five o'clock, now, let us engage a carriage for a

drive of an hour in the forest. Then, when we come back, we shall have time for an hour on the terrace, before we order dinner at the Pavillon Henri-Quatre.

This pavilion is all that is left of the château Henry II started and Henry IV continued. But little as it is, it is interesting for many reasons. Louis XIV was born here, and we shall see the room where he came into the world. And all the rest of the reasons are, that we shall dine superlatively, here, while enjoying a view unrivalled in the world.

In the birthplace of Louis XIV you may like to refresh your memory a bit and gather together some of the odds and ends about his birth which are scattered through it, here and there.

To-morrow we are going to the Bastille, where the Man with the Iron Mask died; and to the Cemetery of Saint-Paul, where he is buried. Recollections of Dumas are pressing to the fore. You are beginning to remember something about an older brother of Louis XIV being smuggled away; to recall that breath-taking episode wherein Dumas brings him back, years later, for a brief period, and puts Louis XIV in the Bastille.

We know, now, that the Man with the Iron Mask was not Louis XIV's brother. But in Dumas's history of "Louis XIV and His Century," there are some details about the coming-into-the-world of that prince which you may like to have in mind here, in his place of advent.

Louis XIII had been married, at fourteen, to the Spanish princess known to history as Anne of Austria; and, after twenty-three years of married life, was still childless. The relations between his queen and himself varied from indifference to hate. Much of the time they kept out of each other's way. Louis had women friends; but some writers (Dumas among them) have believed that his relations with them were irreproachable. The best-known among them, Mademoiselle de la Fayette, had, in consequence of some plotting against Richelieu into which she had been led, sought refuge in a convent the site of which we shall visit to-morrow, on rue Saint-Antoine. On December 5, 1637, Louis went there to visit her. He arrived at four in the afternoon. He left at eight in the evening. He was domiciled, then, at Grosbois, about fifteen miles southeast of Paris. It was raining hard, and very dark. The King's coachman asked if the King wished to return to Grosbois.

"Louis XIII," Dumas says, "seemed to struggle with himself, and after a moment's silence he said: 'No, we go to the Louvre.'"

"Arrived at the Louvre," Dumas goes on, "the King went up to the Queen's apartments, greatly astonishing her by his appearance; because, for a long time, Louis XIII and Anne of Austria had rarely met. She rose and saluted him respectfully. Louis XIII went to her, kissed her hand with the same timidity he would have felt toward a woman whom he saw for the first time, and in an embarrassed tone said to her: 'Madame, the weather is so very bad that I cannot return to Grosbois; so I have come to ask you for some supper and a lodging for to-night.'

"'I shall be greatly honored and delighted to offer them to Your Majesty,' the Queen replied, 'and I now thank God for this storm which terrified me awhile ago.'"

The next morning, Louis returned to Grosbois. Dumas thought the tempest a mere pretext. He believed that Mademoiselle de la Fayette had urged him to effect a reconciliation with the Queen.

In May, Her Majesty's physician told the King (who seems to have thought very little more about the reconciliation) that Her Majesty was about to make him a father.

The news spread quickly through France and throughout Europe, and so eager were the people of Paris to hear without delay the happy announcement they hoped for that they had messengers so thickly stationed all along the route to Saint-Germain that they could signal to one another. If the child were a girl, the news was to be conveyed by silence and folded arms; if a dauphin were born, it was to be made known by hats thrown in air and joyful cries.

At half-past eleven on Sunday morning, September 5, 1638, Louis XIII received from the hands of the attendant midwife the child just born, and going with it to the window held it up and cried:

"A son, gentlemen, a son!"

Along the living "telegraph" the announcement flew; and in a very few minutes, Paris was wild with joy.

Then, here in this chamber of his birth, the Dauphin was privately baptized by the Bishop of Meaux, in the presence of as many princes, princesses, lords, ladies, and Court functionaries as could be crowded into the Queen's room. After which, the King and Court went to the chapel of the old château, where a Te Deum was sung with great pomp.

The bells of Paris rang, the cannon at the Bastille and the Arsenal boomed in salute. That night all the mansions were illuminated; candles of white wax burned in thousands of windows; paper lanterns hung in the streets where tables were set that every one might eat and drink and be merry. A mighty bonfire seemed trying to tell the glad news to the stars.

As we stand on the terrace of the Pavillon Henri-Quatre, looking away toward Paris, perhaps we can see those messengers stationed along the route, throwing their hats in air on that September noon, nearly three centuries ago.

Louis XIV is said to have disliked Saint-Germain as a residence because he could see from here the Church of Saint-Denis which was to be his sepulchre. That, they say, is why he built Versailles. But there were, doubtless, many other reasons.

Perhaps you are tired thinking of Louis, now, and want to give yourself up to the enjoyment of your dinner (which includes Saint-Germain soup, of course!) and of the view.

If the night is fine, you will get for the picture-gallery of your memory a landscape that will delight you as long as you live. Seen from this height, the windings of the silver Seine are of an incomparable loveliness. That bower of green on the horizon is Paris. Above it soars the ethereal Eiffel Tower. Occasionally one catches a glimpse of gleaming Sacré-Cœur.

The air is full of the perfume of flowers and of fruit ripening on southern walls. The Seine begins to reflect the afterglow. Down a river rosy-red comes a black barge, bound for Rouen or for Havre. We walk along the garden terrace, and the world seems full of lovers. It must be very wonderful to be in love, at Saint-Germain! But then! it's very wonderful to be there at all.

V

YOUR FIFTH PARIS DAY

I'LL ask you (if to-day is *not* rainy) to meet me at the Carnavalet Museum at ten-thirty. Take the Métro to the Saint-Paul Station, or a cab to the museum door.

The quarter of Paris with which you are to begin your acquaintance this morning is one of the most fascinating in the world, and has been more passionately beloved by great romancers, more frequented by them, than any similar area on earth; for, the deeper we get into the heart of this district (still known as "the Marais" because it was once a marsh), the more it seems to us as if every man, woman, and child who ever lived here had felt in duty bound to make himself or herself into a story that could be told and re-told forevermore. The books that have been written about the Marais and its inhabitants (many of them *by* its inhabitants!) would fill a very, very large library. If we lived here for years, and went story-hunting every day, we should by no means overtake them all. So you may know that we shall not do much in two or three brief strolls through this labyrinth of old streets. But I'll do my best to give you an inkling of what's to be found there.

Your driver, if you came by cab, has probably brought you out rue de Rivoli, past the Hôtel de Ville, to where it joins old rue Saint-Antoine that was the Roman road to the east. Those masters of all that pertained to roads kept this one diked, to prevent its partaking of the soggy, boggy nature of the river-bank or of the low land to the north — the marsh, the Marais. And then, bit by bit, the bog on

both sides of the road was filled in, planted, cultivated,
built upon. Philippe-Auguste took a good deal of it within
his city when he built his great wall. Charles V took in the
rest of it, a century and a half later. Charles, when he
succeeded to the throne, in 1364, announced that henceforth the new palace in the Marais was to be the chief
royal residence, although he would continue to hold court
at the palais on the island and to entertain guests at the
Louvre.

The Marais district had, up to that time, been largely
occupied by convents and their gardens and dependencies.
Now it began to be fashionable; and for more than three
hundred years it was the elegant section of Paris.

At the Jesuit Church of Saint-Paul-Saint-Louis, which
we shall visit, later, your way turns north into rue de
Sévigné, which received its present name only in 1867, but
was an important thoroughfare more than six centuries before that. Number 11 contains an east wall of the old
prison of La Force, which played such a sinister part in
Revolutionary history; it lay between here and the street
west. Another wall of the prison is in the caserne, at
numbers 7 and 9. (This is the prison where the Princesse
de Lamballe was butchered on Sunday, September 2, 1792
— her head was thrust up, soon afterwards, at Marie
Antoinette's window; where du Barry was held until her
removal to the Conciergerie; whence Thérézia Cabarrus
sent the note and dagger to Tallien.)

At the corner of rue de Sévigné and rue des Francs-
Bourgeois is the Carnavalet. The president of the
parlement of Paris bought this ground in 1544, and
commissioned Pierre Lescot to build him a mansion and
Jean Goujon to embellish it with his peerless sculptures.
When Francis I saw what they were accomplishing, he
ordered them to build for him that wing of the Louvre

which we visited yesterday, and this work was continued
by Jean Bullant, who, young though he was, had just
shown his mastery in the magnificent château he was building at Écouen, ten miles north of Paris, for the Constable
Anne de Montmorency. (Bullant was, later, one of the
architects of the Tuileries.) Du Cerceau the youngest
worked on it, too — nearly a century later — and the elder
Mansart in the generation after that. So it is in itself, as a
building, no inconsiderable history of Paris architecture.
And aside from its many beauties of design and workmanship, and all the treasures it contains, it is worth a pilgrimage if for no other reason than that Madame de Sévigné
was tenant of part of it during the last nineteen years of
her life, and from here wrote many of those letters which
are among the supreme things alike in epistolary literature
and in pictures of high life in Louis XIV's reign.

I have, about seeming to select what may interest you in
the Carnavalet collection, the same hesitancy that I have in
making suggestions about the Louvre and other museums.
You may be fascinated by the Gallic and Roman articles
which tombs or the muddy bed of the Seine have yielded
up; and you need not be an archæologist to find them
interesting. You may care for the architectural fragments,
survivals of buildings in which history has been made for
fifteen hundred years. You may decide to come often and
spend hours on the pictures and plans of old Paris. You
may care, most of all, for Madame de Sévigné's rooms and
the objects they contain belonging to her time and her
brilliant world.

But whatever else may or may not interest you, I am
sure you will be deeply, absorbingly interested in the
rooms devoted to the Revolutionary period. We are on
our way to the site of the Bastille; you will be able to re-
construct it in your mind's eye, after you have seen these

models of it. One of the abuses that made the Bastille so
hated were the lettres de cachet by which a person could
be arrested, immured in this fortress, kept from all communication with the world outside, and so held, in-
definitely, without charge or trial; often these letters or
warrants were made out *in blank* and given to persons
in royal favor, who could use them to effect the seizure of
any one they wanted out of the way. And it frequently
happened that no one belonging to the captives knew what
had become of them. Here, in a glass case, are some lettres
de cachet. There was a man named Latude who escaped
from the Bastille by means of a rope ladder and who spent
thirty-six years in imprisonment. Here is his portrait, and
here is the very ladder.

Here is that pathetic scrap of paper on which Louis XVI
signed his last order as King of France. Here is a case of
documents relating to his execution. Here are the furnishings of Marie Antoinette's room in the Temple prison; and
the widow's weeds she wore; and the playthings of her
little son. And so on.

It is a place to lure one back and back again, this beautiful old mansion with its great memories and its collection
of treasures which mean more and more to us on each visit,
as we have learned to know more and more about Paris.

At number 29 rue de Sévigné (just north of the
Carnavalet) is the Historical Library of the City of Paris.

This rue des Francs-Bourgeois which runs along the
south side of the Carnavalet is one of the most story-telling
old streets any one ever loitered along. In the thirteenth
century there were almshouses along here, sheltering those
"free burghers" whose civil status was such that they had
the legal right to change their domicile (which serfs of the
country soil and many petty city folk had *not*) so long as
they did not move out of the same district; but whose

financial status was such that they couldn't move, and they even had to be exempted from many of the taxes paid by Paris citizens. Many grand folk dwelt hereabouts, too, and at the same time; but it was the free burghers who gave the street its most enduring name.

If it were not that we shall come back into this street again on Sunday, we'd wander in it a bit now. But for the present, we'll just go to the west end of the Carnavalet (farthest from the entrance), cross the street, and look at the beautiful Hôtel Lamoignon built a little later than the Carnavalet, for Diane de France, Duchess of Angoulême, legitimated daughter of Henry II — not, say the historians, by his great mistress, Diane de Poitiers, but by an Italian who seems to have played no part in his life save that of giving him this daughter of whom he was extremely fond; perhaps she did not even do that, for there are good students of French history, besides Dumas, who believe that she was Diane de Poitiers' daughter. What is certain is, that one of the first acts of Henry as king was to legitimate her. And as Diane de Poitiers ruled him, absolutely, it seems unlikely that she would have permitted such honor to the child of another woman and that one of low estate. Dumas, in "The Two Dianas," makes the Italian girl a fiction to cover the maternity of the great lady. You may think with Dumas or with the cyclopædias. But in any case, Diane de France was a fine woman, of good character and good sense; infinitely the best child that Henry begot, and the most comfort to him. Her half brothers were devoted to her, too, and she had the right of entrée into their royal councils at any time. It was she who effected the reconciliation between Henry III and Henry of Navarre.

Diane left this mansion to her bastard nephew, the son of Charles IX and Marie Touchet. Later, when it had be-

come the Hôtel Lamoignon, it saw much of Molière, of
Racine, of Boileau, and others of that great group. In
1721 a boy was born here who was to die on the guillotine
in '93 for having defended his king; Lamoignon de Malesherbes was his name. To-morrow we shall see his statue
in the great hall of the Palais de Justice. And if we go
back into a small court which is all that is left of the
once extensive garden, we may look up at the windows of
an apartment where Alphonse Daudet lived in 1867, and
wrote "Fromont jeune et Risler aisne," and was visited in
his "sky salon" by many notables of his day.

Rue des Rosiers, which we are now crossing, is a little
ghetto containing many old houses, but none with a history
of special interest for us.

As we continue on our way back to rue Saint-Antoine,
we are again on ground associated with the prison of La
Force. This street, rue du Roi-de-Sicile that we are crossing, was so called because here, in the thirteenth century,
Charles of Anjou, younger brother of Saint Louis (Louis
IX), had a palace; and Charles was King of Naples and
of Sicily. It was a part of this palace, many times restored
and rebuilt, that became the main prison of La Force;
the women's prison, La Petite Force, was a new building,
still unfinished, when it began to receive Revolutionary
prisoners. The court where the massacres took place was
at the corner of rue Malher and rue du Roi-de-Sicile. The
Princesse de Lamballe and one hundred and sixty-seven
other Royalists were butchered there on that Sunday afternoon and evening of September 2, 1792. That unhappy
Cardinal Balue, whom Louis XI kept in a cage for eleven
years (and who survived it!), was once the master of this
princely hôtel; and there were many other interesting
and great folk who lived in this street.

Now we'll cross rue Saint-Antoine and glance down rue

du Prévôt, with its ancient houses. Until 1908 there was still in existence one turreted building of the fourteenth-century mansion from which this street took its name and about which so many memories clung that it is hard to forgive anybody who was responsible for its demolition.

If we go through this narrow passage Charlemagne to rue Charlemagne, we shall find back of the Lycée Charlemagne (a boys' school) the Petit Lycée Charlemagne, a school for girls, which has its gas meter in the remains of an old tower of Philippe-Auguste, called the Tour Montgoméry. Philippe's wall ran north along here from the Seine to rue Saint-Antoine, and at this point in it there was a gate or postern called the Saint-Paul Gate, between two towers.

This rue Saint-Paul to which we're coming was the western boundary of that tract within which were the palaces, gardens, orchards, menagerie, and other appurtenances of the great royal domain of Saint-Paul. The name came from the very ancient Church of Saint-Paul which stood here until 1729, on the site of an earlier oratory destroyed by the Normans. This church was in a cemetery in which interments were already being made in the seventh century, and continued to be made until the eighteenth. Rabelais was buried here, and so was the Man with the Iron Mask, who was Count Mattioli; we shall say more about Mattioli later, at the Bastille.

Look down this picturesque little old rue Eginhard named for the chronicler of Charlemagne's great deeds, and to our right up this passage Saint-Pierre down which people used to go to the cemetery.

Now a turn to our left on rue Saint-Antoine, and we'll enter the present Church of Saint-Paul-Saint-Louis. The latter name is linked with the former because in the late-sixteenth century the Jesuits, who were installed just west of here (where the Lycée Charlemagne now is), built behind the then existing Church of Saint-Paul a little church dedicated to Saint Louis. In 1727, Louis XIII laid the first stone of a costly church dedicated to Saint Louis (the present edifice) and contributed largely to the building expense. Richelieu paid for the main portal, and celebrated the first Mass here, on May 9, 1641, not long before his death. Until the Revolution his coat of arms was above the door. Until then, too, the hearts of Louis XIII and Louis XIV were here, in magnificent cenotaphs; and the remains of the Grand Condé in a superb mausoleum by Sarazin, and those of Bourdaloue, the great pulpit orator who here preached the Grand Condé's funeral sermon. ("He preached divinely," Madame de Sévigné said of Bourdaloue. "It seems as if nobody had ever preached before" — though Bossuet was but just dead and she had greatly admired him — "I do not draw a breath until he is pleased to finish.")

It is said that at the Revolution the architect who was charged with the work of seeing that royalist and aristocratic tombs were duly desecrated and destroyed, gave the heart of Louis XIV to the painter, Saint-Martin, who thereupon bought the heart of Louis XIII, and sought to extract from these and the drugs used in embalming them a rich brown color for his canvases. Subsequently, a painter named Drolling is said to have bought eleven hearts for the same purpose, including those of Marie-Thérèse, the Duchess of Burgundy, the Regent, and Madame Henriette d'Orléans!

The church is constructed on the model of the Church of Jesus in Rome, and at one time was surpassed by no church in Paris in the splendor of its possessions. Not many of them are left. Perhaps you have, as I have, a great distaste for this style of architecture and decoration. But I think you will like to step inside, if only for a moment, because of the eminent persons who have sat here, on one occasion and another; practically all of that fascinating great world of the mid-seventeenth to mid-eighteenth centuries passed in and out here. If I could have come here but once, then, I would choose that it might have been to the funeral of the Grand Condé.

The Lycée Charlemagne, next door west, occupies, in part, ground that once was the site of two mansions between which ran the wall of Philippe-Auguste; a part of it is still standing, along the entrance corridor of the school. The eastern of these two mansions was the first to become Jesuit property (in 1580), and later they bought the other also, and constructed a great new building. Bourdaloue lived here, and so did Père Lachaise, the confessor of Louis XIV, who married the King to Madame de Maintenon. The present library of the school was the apartment of Père Lachaise, who died there.

Many eminent men of art and letters have been scholars at this school; among them, Gustav Doré, Théophile Gautier, and Michelet the historian (whose father was a printer hereabouts).

Now we'll move eastward along rue Saint-Antoine toward the Bastille. (Our saunter from the Carnavalet has covered very little ground, and lasted perhaps twenty minutes.) It is one of the oldest streets in Paris, this rue Saint-Antoine, which was the Roman road to the east, and which got its name from an abbey of Saint Anthony hereabouts. And it has seen many great spectacles. In the olden days, nearly all the pompous processions into Paris entered by the east gate, the porte Saint-Antoine, built by Étienne Marcel, who tried to deliver it to Charles the Bad. (We'll revert to Marcel when we get to where his gate was.) For the present, as we stroll — we are about a quarter of a mile from the Bastille — let us look to right and left for vestiges of those olden days.

Here, at the corner of rue du Petit-Musc (which was a lovers' lane more than five centuries ago), there is what's left of the Hôtel de Mayenne which Diane de Poitiers bought in 1554, when Henry II was still living some of the time at the palace of the Tournelles, a stone's throw away. Charles V, Charles VI, Charles VII, and Louis IX had all lived in it, though probably not in the part we see, which seems to have been built for Diane after Henry died. The Duc de Mayenne, whose name it bears, was one of the brothers of the House of Guise and the only one who escaped the vengeance of Henry III, whose death they plotted in one of the rooms of this mansion.

Next to it is the one-time chapel (by Mansart) of that convent to which Louis XIII came to visit Mademoiselle de la Fayette. It is now a Protestant church called Sainte-Marie.

On the other side of rue Saint-Antoine, a bit back, is the Hôtel de Sully built by a grandson of the architect that designed Diane's house, and bought in 1634 by Sully who had been Henry IV's great finance minister — the one who opposed Henry's plan to marry his mistress, Gabrielle d'Estrées, causing Henry to say to Gabrielle, "I could do without ten mistresses like you, better than without one minister like him." And at that, Henry loved Gabrielle better than he ever loved any other woman. But Gabrielle had been long, long in her grave when Sully came here to live — and Henry in his, too, for almost a quarter-century.

This narrow street on our right as we approach the Place de la Bastille, is rue Lesdiguières. In 1819, Balzac came there to live in a garret, at number 9 — in a house since demolished. Business of the army had kept his father in Paris for six years; now he was taking his family back to Tours. Honoré wouldn't go; he was determined to stay in Paris, and to be — of all crazy, starvation things! — an *author*. His father was horrified. But Honoré declared his willingness to starve. So his father granted him an allowance that would just keep soul and body together, and his mother found him this garret. The garret was so dark that the new tenant had to spend more on oil than on bread; it was suffocating in summer, and freezing cold in winter, and rains and snows came through the leaky roof on to the young author's bed. But he wrote to his mother: "I am not sick of my hardships — I love them." He was free! Master of his own time and movements, in the great world that is Paris. A short walk and he was in the library of the Arsenal with its wealth of documents as well as of books. All about him were people who were potential books!

"A fire," he writes his mother, "broke out in rue Lesdiguières, number 9, in the head of a poor lad, and no engines have been able to put it out. It was kindled by a beautiful woman whom he does not know. They say she lives at the Quatre-Nations [the Institut de France, where the Academies are housed], the other side of the pont des Arts; she is called Fame. Unfortunately, the burned youth reasons; he says to himself: 'Either I have or I have not genius; in either case I am laying up a store of sorrows. Without genius, I am done for. I must then pass my life in feeling desires I cannot satisfy, in miserable envy, cruel pain. With genius, I shall be persecuted, calumniated; and I know very well that Mademoiselle Fame will have to wipe away abundant tears.'"

At number 3 rue Saint-Antoine, here on our right, is a Bouillon Duval, one of a chain of "popular price" restaurants. The original Duval, and the best, is in rue Montesquieu, near the Palais-Royal; the others are — everywhere.

I cannot say much in their praise, for I seldom patronize them; but I do sometimes go to this one when I am in this vicinity. And as the Duvals are a phase of Paris food-purveying, and you want to try many sorts, this is a good occasion to make acquaintance with one. If you feel disinclined for this, try Les Quatres Sergents de Rochelle, 3 boulevard Beaumarchais, for a hearty luncheon.

After lunching, and resting, we'll step out into the great, busy Place de la Bastille from which streets radiate in every direction, like wheel-spokes — all of them new, except this one that we've followed. The east wall of the city in Philippe-Auguste's day was, as we have just seen, a quarter of a mile west of here, where Lycée Charlemagne is.

Kings came, and went — nine of them, in a century and a quarter following Philippe's death; and then one of them, John, went to England a captive of the Black Prince after the battle of Poitiers; his son Charles the Dauphin became regent, and called a meeting of the States-General (or parliament of people, clergy, and nobles), in which there loomed up, bigger than all else besides, the figure of Étienne Marcel, who, as head of the guilds, or labor unions, of Paris exercised great power and the right to speak for "the masses." In their name and their interests he bought a pillared mansion where the Hôtel de Ville has ever since stood, and set up a city hall for Paris. In the States-General, he demanded many reforms.

"That session," says Alfred Rambaud in his "History of French Civilization," "was one of the most important in our history. There were about eight hundred deputies, of whom the greater part were men of the third estate [the Commons]. . . . Since royalty seemed unable to govern and defend the country, the bourgeoisie intended to take the direction." Before any more money was to be voted, there must be reforms in the way the money was spent. A committee of eighty drafted a bill of the reforms demanded. Charles tried to evade this, but found that the country at large was of the same mind; so he yielded. "In these demands," says Rambaud, "there was not only a vast reform, financial, judicial, administrative, and military; there was a complete revolution . . . the Magna Charta of England contained nothing more. If this reform had endured, the French would have been as free as the English."

But Charles, who eventually won the sobriquet of "The Wise," was not wise yet. He resisted these reforms and restrictions; and Marcel roused the Parisians, led them to the palais, where they slew two of Charles's counsellors, and placed on the Dauphin's head his own cap of red and blue — just as, more than four hundred years later, another mob of the Parisian populace, invading another royal palace, forced Louis XVI to unite those colors with the Bourbon white, and wear the Tricolor of the Revolution, of the Republic.

Then it was war to the death between Marcel and Charles the Dauphin. And the death was Marcel's. He tried to "oust" Charles from power and to put in his place Charles, the King of Navarre, who was doubly descended from Saint Louis and was married to a sister of Dauphin Charles; the attempt failed, though for a time Navarre ruled the city and the Dauphin besieged it. But Navarre was too tricky to rally 'round; he was the sort who enters into negotiations with both sides at once, and makes the better bargain, whatever it is. He deserted Paris and Marcel, "for a consideration." Then changed his mind, joined forces with the English, and came back again.

Meantime, Marcel had been "letting out" the fortifications of Paris, and just here where we are, at the end of rue Saint-Antoine, he built a gate called porte Saint-Antoine.

In the night of July 31, 1358, Marcel came here to open
this gate to Navarre's men and let them in to take Paris.

"The same night," Froissart says, "God inspired
certain burgesses of the city ... who, by divine inspiration,
as it ought to be supposed, were informed that Paris should
be that night destroyed." So they armed, and made their
way here — where we are standing — and found Marcel
with the keys in his hands. Their spokesman asked what
Marcel was doing, and, when denied an answer, said: "By
God, you are not here for any good, at this hour, and I'll
prove it to you." So — though he was Marcel's close
friend — he "gave with an axe on Étienne's head, that he
fell down to the earth."

So died, here where we stand, a mighty man of the
people who would have wrought great good to his country
had he not convinced himself that "the end justifies the
means." His naked body lay exposed to view for days,
just where you turned off rue Saint-Antoine into rue
Sévigné to go to the Carnavalet. And after that it was
thrown into the Seine. You saw his imposing statue on
horseback, at the Hôtel de Ville. There is a broad modern
street named for him. He had a great vision, but he died
caught in a dirty bit of treachery. And it was more than
four centuries before another great act in the drama of
Democracy was enacted on the same spot.

Charles the Dauphin became Charles the King; he
transferred his residence to this district, and ordered the
construction of a strong fortress at the east gate of Paris
where the immemorial road ran toward the Valley of the
Marne, the trodden avenue of invasion.

A line of white traced on the pavement marks the exact
site of the Bastille; and you have in mind how it looked,
after having seen the model in the Carnavalet.

It was not used as a prison, at first, but parts of it were

so used during the reign of Charles VI. While the English were in possession of Paris, after Agincourt, that soldier whom Shakespeare has immortalized (if traduced!) as Falstaff was Governor of the Bastille.

The odious lettres de cachet did not begin until the days of Richelieu; but there had been noted state prisoners there long before that: Cardinal Balue, under Louis XI; Bernard de Palissy, the great potter, who, because he was a Huguenot, died at the Bastille, in 1590; and others.

In 1698, a prisoner wearing a mask, not of iron but of black velvet, was brought to the Bastille. Five years later he died there, and was buried in the Cemetery of Saint-Paul, under the name of "Marchioly." The amount of speculation and research and argument this prisoner has caused is paralleled by nothing in the history of any other prison. Voltaire, who was twice imprisoned at the Bastille, once in 1717 and again in 1726, did a great deal to arouse interest in the man of mystery; he said he had heard many things from persons who were "on the ground" when the masked man was there; he asserted that the man of mystery was a bastard son of Anne of Austria and Mazarin; he hinted that there was more he might say. After Voltaire died, another writer declared that the Man with the Iron Mask (they stuck to the *iron* it sounded so much better than *velvet*) was a legitimate twin brother of Louis XIV. Next came a story that this brother of the great King had a son born to him, of some prison alliance, and this son went to Corsica, took the name of De Buona Parte, and became the ancestor of Napoleon! According to others, he was a son of Louise de la Vallière; he was an illegitimate son of Charles II of England; he was Fouquet, Louis XIV's disgraced minister; and so on. Dumas, in "Le Vicomte de Bragelonne," makes him Louis XIV's older brother.

M. Funck-Brentano, the very scholarly librarian of the

Arsenal Library at Paris, where the archives of the Bastille
are, has given years of research to the mystery, and has
satisfied himself and most (but not all) others that the
masked man was one Mattioli, who had agreed, for one
hundred thousand crowns, to betray to Louis XIV a
frontier fortress at Casale, which he (Mattioli) was holding for the Duke of Mantua. Mattioli "renigged," as we
say; and Louis XIV had him kidnapped and imprisoned —
first at the fortress of Pignérol in Piedmont; then, when
that fortress was given up to Savoy, at Sainte-Marguerite
in the Bay of Cannes; and then, after nineteen years of
captivity, transferred to the Bastille. I am entirely satisfied with M. Funck-Brentano's findings. But in case you
don't care to be convinced by them, you have the support of so eminent an authority as Hugh Chisholm, M.A.,
editor-in-chief of the Eleventh Edition of the Encyclopædia Britannica — who is not convinced by them at
all.

Next to the Man with the Iron Mask, the most "popular" prisoner of the Bastille was Latude, a nameless bit of
human driftwood who thought to curry favor with Madame de Pompadour by sending her a box of poison, and
then hastening to warn her of the wicked plot against her
life. He underestimated the lady's shrewdness. She saw
through his scheme and had him put in the Bastille, in
1749. After a short stay there, he was transferred to
Vincennes, whence he escaped; he was retaken, and sent
back to the Bastille; escaped after six years, and was soon
caught and returned to Vincennes; next year he escaped a
third time, and was soon recaptured. After twenty-eight
years of prison life, he was discharged on condition that he
get out of Paris and keep out. He remained, and was returned to prison for another seven years, his definite release not occurring until 1784. During the Revolution he

was made a hero of, and the heirs of Madame de Pompadour were compelled to pay him sixty thousand francs damages. He died in Paris in 1805, at the age of eighty.

He wrote an account of his imprisonment which had much to do with inflaming the populace of Paris against the Bastille.

As a matter of fact (of records) the Bastille was, for tome persons at least, a quite luxurious prison whose "guests" of all degrees sat at table with the Governor, and often furnished their apartments as they were able, and received their friends. Latude is recorded as having complained that his chicken was not *larded*!

When the Bastille was taken by assault on July 14, 1789, it contained just seven prisoners: four counterfeiters, two madmen, and "another prisoner guilty of a monstrous crime." For entertaining these, the Governor, M. de Launay, was massacred, and his body dragged to the Hôtel de Ville. The vengeance of the people fell at the wrong time, or at the wrong place.

Some of the stones of the Bastille were taken to build the pont de la Concorde. But, though this square was decided upon in 1792, nothing was done about it till 1803. Napoleon thought he would erect an Arc de Triomphe there, to his victorious armies; then he decided, rather, on a monumental fountain, and ordered that this fountain should be in the form of an elephant, cast from Spanish guns. Pending the bronze elephant, a model in wood and plaster was set up. It was in the great belly of this beast that Hugo gave Gavroche lodging, along with the thousands of rats — as readers of "Les Misérables" remember.

The July Column now in the square commemorates the victims of that July street fighting in Paris, to overthrow the last of the Bourbons. It was in this fighting that

Gavroche died; so his monument is here close to where he had his home with the rats!

Some of those who were killed fell near the Louvre, and were buried where they died. When the bones of the three hundred and eighty victims were collected, in 1840, to lay beneath the Column, those beside the Louvre were piously disinterred. But it was found that the same ground contained some Egyptian mummies which had started to decompose in the Museum and had to be disposed of. And as there was some doubt as to which of the human remains were French and which were Pharaohs, they were *all* buried beneath our Column.

Running almost due north from the Column is the boulevard Beaumarchais, named for the famous dramatist of whose "Le Mariage de Figaro" Louis XVI said: "If it is played, the Bastille will go." Beaumarchais was a good friend of our American colonies — influenced his government in our behalf, and lent us money, sent us ships. He had a mansion and great garden here, where the boulevard that bears his name begins, and here he died, in 1799. You may like to remember this when next you are hearing "The Barber of Seville" or "The Marriage of Figaro."

We'll go back to where his statue stands, on rue Saint-Antoine at the foot of rue des Tournelles which marks the eastern boundary of the old palace of the Tournelles, where Charles VI, the mad king, lived; where the Duke of Bedford kept royal state as regent on behalf of the little English prince (later Henry VI) whom his puissant father had caused to be crowned King of France. Then Charles VII lived here — and let the English burn Jeanne d'Arc at Rouen. And his son, Louis XI, brought two brides here. It was here that Louis XII died and left the madcap, Mary Tudor, a virgin widow for Charles Brandon to marry almost before poor Louis's bones were buried. It was here

that Henry II died, after receiving in tournament, near by,
a wound from Montgoméry's lance. Then Catherine de
Médicis ordered the Tournelles demolished, and began to
build the Tuileries.

Number 28 rue des Tournelles has another entrance at
23 boulevard Beaumarchais. The house was either built
by Hardouin Mansart, the architect of Versailles, or inherited by him from his more famous uncle, and was the
last abode of that most fascinating lady, Ninon de Lenclos,
who died here in 1705. Of Ninon it is commonly said that
Richelieu (dead in 1643) was her first admirer, and Voltaire
(born in 1694) her last. In truth, almost threescore full
years and ten lay between the day that the great Cardinal
flashed back his appreciation of the girl's charm and the
day when a notary's little boy, brought here to see her, so
impressed her with his cleverness that in her will she left
him two thousand francs to buy books. And in between
those two, who that ever saw Ninon could resist her? And
of her time, when Olympus was so full of gods, which of
them was there that was not her friend? That was her
genius: friendship! She would never marry, for fear of
losing a friend. But it seems as if she might have kept a
husband as a friend — she who kept as such all her lovers,
even when she was through with them as favorites. "It
is not enough," she said, "to be wise; one must know how
to please." And she did know — supremely. So Le Brun
and Mignard painted her ceilings for her, and Molière
brought her his plays to read and his troubles to share; and
Corneille came, too, and Racine; and La Fontaine and
Boileau; and De la Rochefoucauld and the Grand Condé;
and the Scudérys, brother and sister; and Françoise
Scarron — not yet Madame de Maintenon. From five to
nine Ninon was at home to her friends; and with bite and
sup they came, contributing to the material as well as to

the spiritual cheer. Ninon permitted no talk of religion or politics; no malicious gossip; no grossness; no loud laughter; no card-playing. Conversation was an art and a religion. When she thought of heaven, it was as a place where one talks endlessly with one's friends. Weird tales were invented as to why she did not grow old. But there was nothing weird about it! She was perpetually eager, and always tolerant. And, like Diane de Poitiers, she was addicted to cold baths!

Ninon charms me as utterly as if I had been here to one of her supper parties. I can never forget the air of the man, a concierge in the Place des Vosges, who once pointed out her house to me. If he had been there with Molière, he could not have had a more proprietary pride in her. "There," he said — I had not asked him; it was his fear that I might not know — "lived Ninon de Lenclos." She is still making friends and keeping them.

At rue du Pas-de-la-Mule, we turn for a few steps, to our left, and enter the Place des Vosges.

If you had gone to Paris to see the sights three hundred years ago, one of the first places you would have asked direction to was this great centre of fashion and celebrity.

Part of it was once covered by the Tournelles Palace, and part was then a space which sometimes served as a tilting-yard; but the great tournament at which Henry II got his death-wound was staged on a larger area between here and rue Saint-Antoine. It took place on the last three days of June, 1559, and the occasion for it was the wedding of Elizabeth, the fourteen-year-old daughter of Henry and Catherine de Médicis, with the twice-widowed Philip II of Spain; and of Marguerite, Henry's sister, with Philibert Emanuel of Savoy.

Henry's horoscope had warned him that he should die

THE PLACE ROYALE AT THE TIME OF LOUIS XIV

(Now the Place des Vosges)

Painting in the Musée Carnavalet

in a duel. Catherine's star-gazing convinced her that her husband would meet with disaster if he left the Louvre those last days of June. Nevertheless, Henry went; the first two days he was constantly in the lists, and elated by his skill, his success. The third day, June 30th, was Friday, and the plans for that day's "events" were magnificent. In the "field" were the Duc de Guise, Alphonse d'Este, Duke of Ferrara, and Jacques de Savoie, Duc de Nemours; and the honors went now to one of them and now to another, Henry the King winning his share, but no more.

According to Dumas, Henry was not satisfied with these even honors, and insisted on another combat, although night was falling, and nobody wanted to joust any more. Then Henry commanded the young Captain Montgoméry to oppose him; and in some fashion, that no one quite knows, Montgoméry's lance raised the visor of Henry's casque and pierced the King's eye, entering the brain.

"Ah! I am killed!" Henry said as he was lifted from his horse. "But let no one blame M. de Montgoméry. It was unavoidable. I pardon him."

Then he fainted, and was carried into the Tournelles Palace, where he died on the 10th of July, leaving the crown to his eldest son, François II, not quite sixteen years old, though for more than a year past the adoring husband of young Mary, Queen of Scots.

In the museum of armor at Des Invalides, we shall see King Henry's pierced casque.

Montgoméry was executed, in front of the Hôtel de Ville, in 1574, fifteen years after the fatal tournament — ostensibly for having caused Henry's death, but actually for the crime of being a Protestant. Long before that, however, the Tournelles had disappeared, on Catherine's orders, and this space whereon we now stand was a horse-market and a duelling-ground.

Such it remained for some years, until Henry IV ordered it cleared and plans drawn for the building, not of a palace, but of a whole "quarter," to be devoted to luxurious living. Radiating from the square as from a hub were to be broad, handsome streets bearing the names of all the French provinces, and beautified by mansions of the nobility. Henry had need to break up the return to feudalism which the weakness of his predecessors (Catherine de Médicis's three sons) had fostered. He wanted to group his great lords and princes around himself as the symbol of national unity and national authority; to create a strong central government. He had, in envisioning this quarter, much the same idea that his grandson, Louis XIV, realized at Versailles. It would have been better for France, however, could it have been captained by Navarre, the most magnificent compromiser who ever led captive the hearts of men.

He was so interested in the progress of the work, here, that he came every day to speed it on. Then one of the stupidest of all stupid assassins laid Henry low; and the Place Royale (as it was called in the days of its glory) was never quite what he had intended that it should be. It does, however, contain one most interesting souvenir of him, and that is its vaulted arcades which he wanted because he had learned to love such places in his sunny Southland of Navarre.

On the 6th of March, 1612, there was another tournament held here, to celebrate another double wedding: that of little Louis XIII with the Infanta whom we know in history as Anne of Austria, and of Anne's brother, the future King of Spain, with Louis's little sister. But this time no one was killed.

Of all the many eminent residents in the square we must content ourselves here with mention of only a few.

Number 1 was the birthplace of Madame de Sévigné, who always loved this square.

At number 8, Théophile Gautier once lived, and, succeeding him, Alphonse Daudet.

Rachel, the great tragédienne, lived for a short time in number 9, just before she died near Cannes. In the seventeenth century this mansion was regarded as one of the "sights" of Paris.

Richelieu lived at number 21 while his Palais-Cardinal (now Palais-Royal) was building — and while he was, if the gossips speak true, the lover of Marion Delorme.

Number 25 was in the possession of one family, father to son, for two hundred and seventy years — longer than any other house in Paris.

But it is number 6 that interests us more than all the others. It was built in 1605, and the tenant of it in 1610 was the Marshal de Lavardin who was in the carriage with Henry IV when the latter was assassinated. It was, later, the home of Marion Delorme who there received the masculine part, at least, of the great world of her day. In it are supposed to have taken place many meetings of the conspirators against Richelieu, headed by Marion's lover, the Adonis-like young Cinq-Mars, who lost his handsome head therefor. Alfred de Vigny uses this house as a background in his drama of "Cinq-Mars." Dumas gives it to Lady de Winter for a residence, and hither brings D'Artagnan and lets him see the brand on Milady's shoulder.

Hugo had written his drama "Marion Delorme" before he came here to live, in 1832, just after he had finished "Notre-Dame de Paris." Here he held his noted salons, whither Dumas came, and Musset, and Lamartine, and Gautier, and Nodier, and Charles Dickens, and Prosper Mérimée, and Baryé, the great sculptor, and Delacroix, chief of the insurgents in painting then; and many another.

Here, in the hectic days when Hugo was trying to settle his household and to direct rehearsals of a new play, and to sit to Ingres for his portrait, came to bespeak his favor a young actress who had been a sculptor's model (she sat to Pradier for his figure of Strasbourg, in the Place de la Concorde), Juliette Drouet by name.

Juliette had played several minor parts at the Théâtre Porte Saint-Martin and at the Odéon. She wanted a part in Hugo's forthcoming play, "Lucrèce Borgia." He gave it to her. And thus began that friendship which was to endure for more than fifty years, on scarce one day of which did he fail to write her at least one letter — although there were few of those days on which he did not see her.

Hugo had begun "Les Misérables," in this house, when he had to flee it in 1848, on the downfall of Louis-Philippe, who had made Hugo a peer of France. A squad of the National Guard invaded Hugo's house while he was leading a detachment of the royal forces. In his study the officer of the invading squad picked up some manuscript and began to read it aloud; it was the first pages of "Les Misérables," and they were carefully put back in place.

After we have concluded our visit to this house (than which there is, to me, none in Paris more interesting), I shall not ask you to do any more sight-seeing to-day.

Unless we have unduly loitered somewhere, it should not be much, if any, past three o'clock, now.

Perhaps you want to go home and rest. Perhaps you want to shop.

We'll be hungry for a good dinner to-night. And if there's anything "on" that you like at either Opéra, or at the Théâtre-Français, or the Odéon (where many standard and familiar plays are to be seen), this would be a good time to enter upon the enjoyment of those delights.

If it's the Odéon, let's dine at Foyot's. If it's the

THE TOURNAMENT AT THE PLACE ROYALE (NOW PLACE
DES VOSGES) IN HONOR OF LOUIS XIII'S MARRIAGE, 1612

Painting in the Musée Carnavalet

Théâtre-Français, or the Opéra, suppose we say dinner at Henri's on rue Saint-Augustin, just east of the avenue de l'Opéra which leads straight up to the Opéra and straight down to the Théâtre-Français. If it's the Opéra-Comique (where many of the best-loved operas are sung — like "Manon," "Louise," "Carmen," "La Bohême," etc.), I say let's dine at Paillard's, boulevard des Italiens, just a little west of the Opéra-Comique, where many of the best restaurateurs of Paris were trained. Or, if that's too much luxury along with opera seats (for Paillard's prices are steep — there's no denying it!), let's say the Coq-d'Or, 149 rue Montmartre, which is good, and moderate, and liked by Paris journalists.

This is a long chapter, but it does not mean a day of great exertion. I have not asked you to walk so much as a mile, nor to spend more than two hours at the most in looking at museums.

VI

YOUR SIXTH PARIS DAY

As Thursday is the only day on which visitors are permitted in the Conciergerie, I have planned for you to-day a grouping of things to see in that vicinity. I have often taken friends over this ground, and almost without exception they have declared that this was one of the most interesting of all their Paris days.

We must have a card for the Conciergerie. Your hotel concierge will get it for you; but you must give him a little time or else pay for sending a messenger to get it in person. I do not advise your going after it yourself. The Préfecture of Police, where it must be obtained, is a very bewildering place for a novice, and a great deal of time is consumed there in very small transactions. Ask your concierge not later than Tuesday, and he will have your "permission" for you before you leave the hotel for Thursday's saunterings.

I'll meet you at ten-thirty, under the porch of Saint-Germain-l'Auxerrois, opposite the colonnaded east front of the Louvre.

Most visitors to Paris are, I find, interested in this church because its bell sounded the signal for the Saint Bartholomew massacres.

The story is that Catherine de Médicis from a window of the Louvre gave the order for it by waving her handkerchief. If she did, it was probably from a window of the old castle which Louis XIV cleared away a century later, but we must remember that then there were many buildings between the church and the Louvre.

Paris, you will remind yourself, was full of strangers come to see the festivities attendant upon the wedding of the young King's sister, Marguerite, a Catholic princess, with the Huguenot King of Navarre. Never had there been such a union in the royal family of France, and feeling ran high, not only throughout the country, but far beyond her borders.

"The wedding will be blood-red," the people of Paris said, forebodingly, as they watched the followers of the warring factions pouring into the city and seeking places to lodge.

On August 18th the wedding took place, in front of the great portal of Notre-Dame, on a platform hung and draped with cloth of gold. "I," Marguerite wrote, afterwards, "was robed in royal fashion, with a crown and a cape of spotted ermine which covered the front of my bodice; and I shone with the crown jewels and glistened in my wide blue mantle, with its four yards of train which were borne by three princesses."

But though she was led to this altar like a lamb to slaughter, those who coerced her could not make her say "Yes"; her brother (Charles IX) laid his hand none too gently on her head and made it bob — which the Cardinal de Bourbon accepted as her affirmation. Then the bride and her co-religionists went in to hear the Mass; and the bridegroom with Coligny, the Huguenot leader, and some other gentlemen, paced up and down in the court of the bishop's palace, next door.

Thereupon the feasting and pageantry began, and lasted until the evening of August 21st. The Salle des Caryatides that you visited in the Louvre was the centre of it.

On the 22d, Coligny was shot in the arm, as he was leaving the porte de Bourbon (of the old castle).

"I have," he said to his friends while the King's surgeon

was extracting the bullet that the King's ally had lodged, "no enemy but the Guises."

"Let us kill the Guises, then!" they cried. But Coligny gave them stern orders to do harm to no one; he knew that the time was ripe for a terrible conflict, waiting only an occasion to start.

Charles IX was indignant at the attack on Coligny, ordered it thoroughly investigated, and went to call on his wounded councillor to whom he said, "My father, you have the wound, but *I* have the perpetual pain. May I fail of salvation if I do not take so horrible a vengeance for this that the remembrance of it shall never fade."

Catherine went, too! And Coligny, asking to speak privately to the King, whispered to him to distrust his mother and make his own decisions.

On the way to the Louvre, Catherine tormented her son until she made him tell her what was said in those whispers. And when he had yielded, Charles rushed to his room and shut himself in, distraught by grief and fear and "hectoring."

That night and the next day Paris was aflame with rumors that the Huguenots were going to avenge the attempt on their beloved leader.

Catherine then called a council of her trusty agents (most of them Italians) in the gardens of the Tuileries; and thence she went to the King's apartments and began to lash him into that nervous frenzy wherein she could always make him do her will.

At length, his power of resisting her gave way. "For the love of God," he yelled insanely, "since you want the Admiral [Coligny] killed, then do it! But you must kill all the others, too, so that not one shall be left to reproach me."

Foaming, blaspheming, yelling, he banged out of the

room. And the preparations for the massacre went on. As Henry of Navarre, the bridegroom, was marked for slaughter, Marguerite was the only one of the royal family who was not told what was ordered. Her mother, on the fateful night, roughly ordered her to bed. Better that she should be killed with her unbeloved husband than that he and his attendants should be made suspicious by her absence.

The early dawn of an August morning was just breaking when Catherine gave the signal for the tocsin to be rung from Saint-Germain-l'Auxerrois. Charles was with her, and his brother Henry. It is said that at the last moment Charles made a final effort to assert his will against theirs. If he did, it failed. Soon there was the report of a pistol. The thing was upon them! Terrified, then, they sent word to spare Coligny — and the word came back from Guise: "Too late!"

Bells clanged, cannon roared, victims screamed. "Death and bloodshed ran the streets together" — the Seine was thick with corpses. No one knows how many thousands perished; the number has been put as low as two thousand and as high as eight thousand. The King behaved like a maniac, exulting in the fire he had started. When it was over, his mind was a blank. It was never again anything but a prey to horrors and remorse. He was not twenty-two; and he survived for nearly two years — terrible years, haunted by visions of blood and floating corpses. "What evil counsel was given me!" he cried. "O God, forgive me and have mercy upon me!"

We in this country hear "Les Huguenots," where the drama is subordinated to the florid music of Meyerbeer. But we do not see "La Reine Margot" in the theatre. See it in Paris if you can. If not, re-read the story. They call it "Marguerite of Valois" in translation. Dumas could not have made it more vivid had he been an actor in every scene he depicts.

With this refreshing of your memory concerning things read of Saint Bartholomew's Eve, you have a prelude not unfitting for that later tragedy which is soon to engross us at the Conciergerie.

There is not a great deal to see in the ancient Church of Saint-Germain-l'Auxerrois, of which the belfry (eleventh century) is the most venerable part. There has been a church named for Saint Germain here since the sixth century. In his old age, the Abbé Magnin, who at great risk carried consolation to Marie Antoinette in her death-cell, was the curé here — long after the Queen's execution.

One thing you may like to think on is that Molière was married here. And many noted artists are buried here; they died at the Louvre, where apartments were granted them, and were brought here either for interment or at least for their last rites. Among them are: Coysevox and Coustou, the sculptors; Soufflot and Gabriel, the architects of Louis XV; Nattier, Chardin, Boucher, Coypel, etc., painters.

Between the old château of the Louvre and the Church of Saint-Germain-l'Auxerrois there used to be the Petit Bourbon, a mansion of the Bourbon family, built in 1370 and confiscated by the Crown in 1521, which was the cause of the Constable de Bourbon's treason. The great hall of this mansion was used for a theatre for some years; some of Corneille's plays were presented there, and Molière's troupe gave many performances in it.

Of the many other mansions that were once there and were cleared away to give the Louvre more space and easier access, there are few of great interest to the visitor — although you may like to know that the one in which Jeanne d'Albret, mother of Henry of Navarre, died was on the site now known as 15 rue du Louvre. She was first cousin to

Henry II, her mother having been that learned and learning-loving lady, Marguerite, sister of Francis I, who married the King of Navarre, protected Protestants, and wrote very charming tales and verses which have given her a genuine place in French literature. Jeanne, who inherited her father's kingdom and her mother's character, was in Paris for the wedding of her son, when she died so suddenly as to suggest poison, and Catherine de Médicis was blamed. But while Catherine would willingly have poisoned her, or had her poniarded to death in the massacre, it seems that what Jeanne actually died of was consumption, which she did not know she had. (It was not through her, but through her husband that their son Henry stood next in line for the French throne after Catherine's sons, three of whom were living when Jeanne died. Her husband had been Antoine de Bourbon, descended through twelve generations from Saint Louis whose younger son married the Bourbon heiress. They had a terrible tendency to extinction, those royal lines, though most of them were so prolific.)

Well, if Henry's mother did not die of poison, hereabouts, his beloved Gabrielle probably did. Sully or no Sully, Henry was bent upon marrying her, although he was not yet unmarried from Marguerite. Gabrielle had been at Fontainebleau with him, and it was deemed discreet that she should come away in Holy Week; so she came to Paris, Henry accompanying her a good part of the way. She stopped in the Marais, supping with Henry's friend, Zamet, and, it seemed, supping poison which Sully may or may not have known something about. That was Tuesday evening, and after supping she came down here to the vicinity of Saint-Germain-l'Auxerrois, where her aunt lived. On Easter Saturday morning, 1599, at five o'clock, she died here in agonies so terrible that Henry was not permitted to see her even after she was dead. "The root of my love is dead!" Henry cried. "There will be no spring for me, henceforth." There was! But it had nothing to do with the "fat bankeress" from Florence, Marie de Médicis, to whom he was soon married. It was in what is now rue Perrault (named for the architect of the Louvre colonnade) that Gabrielle died, at number 4. It is north of the church, almost as far as rue de Rivoli; I'll not ask you to walk those steps. But if you're interested in Henry (and who can resist him?), I'll be glad to walk them with you.

In this twelfth-century street behind the church, rue de l'Arbre-Sec (or Dry Tree), stands an eyesore of such hideousness that I shudder whenever I see it: a new structure, looking like Coney Island in its last degeneracy, which houses the department store known as " La Samaritaine," whose "succursales" (or branches) one finds in several places throughout the city. The first hydraulic pump of Paris, which used to stand near the north bridgehead of the Pont-Neuf, and pump water for the Louvre and the Tuileries, was called in memory of the woman of Samaria who gave water to Christ, "La Samaritaine"; and the store appropriated the name.

This unpardonable structure stands on the ground once occupied by the house in which Coligny was murdered and Sophie Arnould, the queen of opera, was born; in which, also, that Duchesse de Montbazan lived and mysteriously disappeared, who was the mistress of the Abbé de Rancé, and left him so grief-stricken that he founded the great Trappist order of silence.

On that ground, too, stood a tavern well-beloved of the Three Musketeers.

I'm sure you'll resent as much as I do the iron gingerbread and yellow paint of "the home of bargains."

Along the south side of the old church is the narrow picturesque little rue des Prêtres-Saint-Germain-l'Auxerrois, where the cloisters used to be. At number 17 is the ancient house in which Murger "set" those bohemians of his imagination who do more to keep alive the fame of Café Momus than all the actual artists and authors who frequented it. You will like to have the place in mind, I think, next time you are hearing "La Bohême."

To stand at the corner of this street and rue de l'Arbre-Sec and *look* north, recalling Coligny and the others, is even better than going nearer.

And right here at number 10 quai du Louvre is where the Café de Parnassus used to be, kept by a man of means, named Charpentier, and much frequented by the men of the law courts at the Palais de Justice and the Châtelet. About 1780 there began to appear, each evening, a shabby young law student who ordered a demi-tasse, played dominoes, and gazed wistfully at Gabrielle, the proprietor's sweet and modest daughter acting as her father's cashier. Georges Danton was the young man's name.

They fell in love — the briefless barrister and the daughter with the big "dot" — and on June 14, 1787, they were married in Saint-Germain-l'Auxerrois. A very happy couple they were, and continued to be until that August night, five years later, of the attack upon the Tuileries. Then, felicity for Gabrielle was all a thing of the past, and life itself was nearly over. She had been in her grave for more than a year when Danton saw the Parnassus café for the last time, on his way to the guillotine to die, leaving a young widow of seventeen, and Gabrielle's two little boys.

Now here we are at the Pont-Neuf, whose first stone was laid by Henry III, and which Henry IV was the first person to cross. It was the westernmost bridge between the north and south banks of the river until the Pont-Royal was built, nearly a century later; the sidewalks of this Pont-Neuf were the first laid in Paris.

Let us pause in front of Henry IV's equestrian statue, and look behind it to the little point of land which is the *prow* of the ship that the island resembles. On that land was burned, in 1314, Jacques de Molay, the last Grand Master of the Knights Templar in France. "I am presently to die," he said as the executioners bound him, "but wrongfully, God knows. Wherefore woe will come ere long to those who condemn us. God will avenge our death." And as the flames leaped up into the evening sky, he called on the Pope and on the King to appear with him before the bar of God. Within forty days the Pope went to his accounting; and within a year the King was gone to his, leaving three sons to reign and to die without heirs (like Henry II's three sons, more than two centuries later) and the Hundred Years' War to descend upon France through the quarrel over the succession. The Valois dynasty began when a King's three sons succeeded him, and left no heirs; it ended when a King's three sons succeeded him, and left no heirs!

The first statue of Henry IV to stand here was by Giovanni de Bologna (creator of the famous "Mercury") and was set up by order of Louis XIII. It was melted down in 1792 and replaced by the present one in 1818.

This always very popular bridge is the one of which it was long said that it could not be crossed without meeting a soldier, a grisette (girl of the streets), and a white horse. I don't know about the soldier, now, or the grisette; but the white horses are very, very scarce.

Henry IV looks eastward over the Place Dauphine which was created in his reign and named in honor of his son, the Dauphin, later Louis XIII. The ground on which it stands, and that west of the bridge, where Molay was burned, were two tiny islets until after the bridge was opened to traffic. Then they were united, and the new square built.

In the eighteenth century, young artists, as yet unrecognized and unable to "make" the Salons of the Academies, were permitted to hang their pictures here for public appraisal on the morning of Saturday before Corpus Christi; or, if it rained that day, on the Thursday morning following. The shopkeepers on the north side of the square hung their façades with white canvas, and to this the aspirants attached their pictures. Boucher, Nattier, and Chardin were among those who thus exhibited.

Number 28 Place Dauphine is the house in which Manon Philipon grew up and lived most of her life until she became Madame Roland. She was *not* born there, as some writers say, but in rue de la Cité over beside the Hôtel Dieu, and she was about two when she came to live in this busy, interesting, fashionable quarter where her father (a master engraver) had his shop on the street level and his very comfortable home on the second floor. There Manon learned to read so early that she was a bookworm when she was four. There she associated much with the artists who frequented her father's shop. You may see her going sedately to Lenten services and carrying "Plutarch's Lives," instead of a prayer book, to read in church. You may see her leaning from her window at night, looking out on the Seine and weeping that she had not been born in Athens or Sparta where there were heroic things for women to do.

Here her mother died, when Manon was twenty-one. Here she began her friendship with M. Roland, twenty years her senior, with whom she alternately quarrelled and made up, and whom she married in 1780; but no wedding feast was celebrated here; for Manon had left her drunken and dissolute father and taken refuge in a convent. And the next association of Manon with the quai de l'Horloge (back of the old home in the Place Dauphine) was on November 8, 1793. When she came out from her trial, in that room to which we are on our way, the cart that was to take her to the guillotine was waiting in the Cour du Mai whither, also, we are bound. She was clad carefully in white muslin, trimmed with blonde (the net that we call "footing") and fastened by a girdle of black velvet. "Her face seemed more animated than usual. Its color was exquisite and she had a smile on her lips. With one hand she held up the train of her gown; the other she had abandoned to a crowd of prisoners who pressed near to kiss it."

When the tumbril crossed the Pont-au-Change (the bridge east of the Pont-Neuf) she looked at the quai de l'Horloge, and at the window whence she had leaned, years ago, wistful to be a heroine. Then she smiled, and doubled her efforts to cheer her companion in death, who was afraid to die.

She was smiling to the last. "O Liberty!" she said to the colossal statue set up there where Louis XV had been, "how they have mocked thee!" She had worshipped that goddess — she refused to betray her — she made common lot with those who sought to save Liberty from shame; therefore she died.

Let us walk along the quai de l'Horloge to the Conciergerie, the prison which some historians date back to Roman times and others deny more than a mere thousand years of existence.

Three round towers with conical tops flank the quai. The westernmost of these, and the only one which preserves its crenellations, is sometimes called the Tower Bon-Bec, sometimes the Saint-Louis Tower. In it was the torture chamber where Ravaillac, Damiens, and many others were subjected to horrible agonies, to make them name their accomplices. And underneath were the terrible oubliettes where prisoners were "forgotten" by all but the ferocious river rats who gnawed them even faster than hunger did.

The first of the twin towers is the Tour d'Argent, or Treasury Tower. The other is the Tour de César, or Cæsar's Tower.

Persons whose way, late at night in 1793 and early the year following, took them along this quai, were wont to gaze shudderingly (or exultingly, as their sort was) up at the Tour d'Argent, where a light in one of the narrow windows of the first floor told them that the terrible prosecutor, Fouquier-Tinville, was at work preparing his lists for the morrow. When he had finished, he would go to bed in the Tour de César. In the morning, he would step directly into the adjoining courtroom where the Revolutionary Tribunal sat in those judgments which were *not* trials. And when the session was over, he would be so exhausted that he could scarcely drag himself back to his room and his bed. When he had rested a little, he would go out to dine with friends. Then, back to his office in the Tour d'Argent. Some time every day or night he went into the prison and acquainted himself with what was going on there. From time to time he visited the other prisons in search of "feed" for the guillotine. It was his job to "run them through" in numbers sufficient to satisfy his bosses.

He was a big, powerful man of forty-seven, pockmarked, beetle-browed, with very black hair. And his costume as public accuser included a black coat and a hat with a bunch of black plumes like a hearse ornament.

In those days the entrance to the prison was not here where we are about to present our card. It was around the corner, in the Cour du Mai. The Conciergerie has undergone many changes since the Revolution — changes by which the lot of its prisoners has been so greatly improved that we cannot lament the destruction of historic backgrounds. But, in spite of all the persons who had intimate knowledge of it as it was under the Terror, we have only the most meagre, and often varying, details wherefrom patient research may reconstitute for us a picture, a plan, of what it was like.

Ramshackle constructions which filled and surrounded the beautiful Gothic halls of Saint Louis's palace have been cleared away until there are few traces left of the prison that the Terror knew.

We enter the Conciergerie by a gate east of Cæsar's Tower, which is opened for us by a prison guard. Inside is the court of the prison, and at our right is a Gothic-arched doorway containing a very narrow door with a wicket through which we can state our business. But, this being Thursday, the many-bolted door opens readily to our request.

We go down a few steps into the Salle des Gardes of the old palace, and there we sit awaiting our summons into the cells, and thinking of the men-at-arms who lounged about here, in generations long by-gone, swapping tales of their fights and their wanderings. Saint Louis's companions on the Seventh and Eighth Crusades, some of them must have been; and, a century later, survivors of the battle of Crécy sat here, doubtless; and after them, men who had narrowly escaped being taken prisoner along with their king and many of their comrades, at Poitiers, by the Black Prince.

In a corner of the Salle des Gardes is the little stairway by which Marie Antoinette is said to have ascended to her trial and descended from it; but the best-informed students doubt this.

And as we sit here we see the inner side of the twin towers, and the entrance to their dungeons. Ravaillac, who killed Henry IV, was confined in Cæsar's Tower; and Damiens, who tried (with better reason) to kill Louis XV, occupied a cell in the Treasury Tower. There was once another tower here, whose exact situation I do not know, which was always called the Montgoméry Tower after the unfortunate man who accidentally killed Henry II went thence to his execution. Later, in that same tower, the celebrated poisoner, the Marquise de Brinvilliers, awaited the hour of her death.

When the guide is ready for us he will tell us a few words about the existing towers, point out "the stairway of the Queen," and lead the way into a vaulted corridor known as the rue de Paris, from which we look, through an iron-barred grill, into the beautiful Salle Saint-Louis, one of the most superb Gothic halls left to us.

We are on our way to the last cell of Marie Antoinette.

She was brought here from the Temple (where she had been for a year lacking but a few days) in the night of August 2–3, 1793. Her son she had not seen for a month; but she was permitted to take a brief leave of her daughter and of her sister-in-law, Madame Elizabeth. At the Conciergerie there was hastily cleared for her a room which had been used as a council chamber, and in which was put a bed of straw with two mattresses, a bolster, and light bedclothing; a wash-basin; a common table and two chairs of the prison-furnishings sort.

It was three o'clock in the morning when she arrived here (you will recall from what you saw at the Carnavalet of her furnishings in the Temple that they were comfortable and even made some effort at daintiness), and the jailer's kitchen maid, Rosalie, has left us a pen-picture of the "astonishment with which the Queen's eyes took in the horrible bareness of this room."

She probably knew (even deprived as she was of all communication with the world, all knowledge of what was going on) that prisoners were taken to the Conciergerie when their summons before the Tribunal was imminent. But she rather welcomed the idea of having her "case" called; for

she felt sure that when it was heard she would be set free —
she and her children and Madame Elizabeth; sent out of
the country, doubtless, but free to return to her own people.

As for those who had her in custody, they were by no
means decided as to what they would do with her; but they
had thought that by transferring her to the Conciergerie
they would remind the Powers of Europe of her peril, and
bring on negotiations for her release. Some there were who
had no intention of considering proposals for her mere
banishment; but for the present, they were biding their
time.

A month rolled by, and nothing was done. Then, on the
night of September 2d, the Committee of Public Safety
held an all-night session at the home of the Mayor of Paris.
One of the secretaries of this terrible committee was a spy
in the employ of the British Government, and it is to his
report of that meeting that we owe our knowledge of *when*
and *why* Marie Antoinette's death was decided upon. It
was Hébert, the gutter-snipe editor of that filthy, scurrilous
sheet called "La Père Duchésne," who said to his confrères
that night: "I have promised the head of Antoinette. I will
cut it off myself, if you're too long giving it to me. I have
promised it to the rabble without whose support you will
soon cease to be. It is her head or ours."

Just when this report reached London, I do not know.
The British Government made no overt move to save the
Queen, but it may have been semi-officially behind "the af-
fair of the carnation" which was even then under way.

You may recall Dumas's thrilling story "The Chevalier
de Maison-Rouge"; or have read Lenôtre's no less thrilling
relation of the same events, not as romance, but as documents from the Archives. In case you have not read either
or your recollection of the details is dim, I will recapitulate,
briefly:

MADAME ELISABETH
Elisabeth de Bourbon, Sister of Louis XVI

A young chevalier named Rougeville who had no special reason for risking his life to save Marie Antoinette, but who was adventurous and who seems to have been acting for other persons (probably in England, and very probably headed by Madame Atkins, of the Walpole family, whose efforts in behalf of the royal family of France were untiring and unsparing of expense), had been making cleverly concealed plans for carrying off the Queen. The director of prisons was an ex-lemonade seller, Michonis, who liked to strut and brag that he could blow tobacco smoke in the widow Capet's face whenever he felt a fancy for that display of power. Rougeville could not seek acquaintance with this dignitary; it would be too obvious. So he scouted around and learned of a crony with whom Michonis liked to drink and dally. Rougeville set his mistress, a young woman of humble sort, to make herself attractive to the crony and then to organize a party including Rougeville. It was a protracted party and they got very well acquainted. Then the crony had a party, and Michonis came to it, and bragged as was his wont. And, very dissemblingly, Rougeville declared he would give most anything to see so rare a sight as Michonis described. So Michonis, vinously expansive, offered to take Rougeville with him on a visit to the Conciergerie. Rougeville accepted, not too eagerly. And by adroit questioning he learned that Marie Antoinette was guarded constantly by two gendarmes and a woman attendant— that detail, and others.

Michonis took him. Rougeville watched his chance in the Queen's cell and whispered to her (without seeming to) that he would drop a carnation. He did, and she managed — with much manœuvring — to pick it up when he was gone, and extract the tightly rolled note it concealed, which told her that she was not forgotten nor forsaken; that her friends were preparing to rescue her; that he would come again on Friday; and that if she needed money to "buy" her guards, it was at her service. All this was couched in careful terms, of course.

Marie Antoinette had no pen nor pencil; but she pricked with a pin on a scrap of paper some sort of reply (I cannot take space here for the details of how she contrived to do this) which she then essayed to get her guard to deliver to Rougeville before he left the prison. She had no gift for such business, poor Marie! She went straight to the point with her request, appealing to the man's goodness of heart. Many persons, in those days, had not lost goodness of heart, but everything was in abeyance to their fear. This fellow was terrified. If the prisoner got away, upon how many would vengeance fall! He took the pin-pricked note, gave it to Madame Richard, the jailer's wife, and she — in equal terror — turned it over to Fouquier-Tinville.

As a consequence of this (although they could not decipher the pin-pricks) Richard was removed from office and thrown into a cell in another prison; the jailer from La Force was brought to replace him; the Queen's cell was changed, and the rigors of her captivity were increased many-fold. Rougeville escaped. That infinitely pathetic scrap of pin-pricked paper, still undeciphered, is in the Archives.

She was brought to this cell on September 11th, and left it on the morning of October 15th, to go upstairs to her trial.

Of what we see, nothing is as she saw it save the flooring. Previous to her transfer hither, this space was occupied by the prison pharmacy; next to it was the infirmary, "the most horrible hospital in the world," and the chapel. While she occupied this place, it seems to have been a rather large, square room, with a low screen scarcely four feet high which afforded the captive, briefly, the only respites she had from the gendarmes' scrutiny.

Knitting and sewing needles were denied her. She read a little, but the light was poor, her eyesight had failed terribly, and she had never been fond of books. No lights were permitted her after the daylight faded. You may see her here, pulling some threads from her counterpane and "knitting" them on some wooden toothpicks as children knit worsted on pins stuck in a cork; or standing beside the table whereat her guards almost incessantly played backgammon, watching them for a relief from the torture of her thoughts. She was well fed, and her preferences were considered in the kitchen of the jailer where Rosalie prepared her food. But in no other wise was anything allowed to ameliorate her lot. Even her watch was taken from her; so she could not mark how the hours dragged. When she first came to the Conciergerie, the heat was excessive, stifling. But here, in this cell, in the late September and early October days she suffered sorely from the chill and damp.

On Sunday, the 6th of October, Hébert and some of his associates (including the Mayor) went to the Temple and there made the little Dauphin swear to charges against his mother and his aunt, so hideous that they can scarcely be hinted at even in the necessary frankness of the historian. This accusation the pretty child signed in scrawling characters so unlike his usual neat handwriting (practised under his father's care until they were separated) as to give evidence that he was either drunk or terror-stricken.

With this document in hand, all was ready for Marie Antoinette's "trial." It began at eight o'clock on Tuesday morning, October 15th, and lasted until four on Wednesday morning, with an intermission from four in the afternoon till five. After sentence was pronounced, the Queen was conducted back to her cell to await the hour of her execution and to write that farewell letter to Madame Elizabeth. About seven, Rosalie came in to see if the Queen would take any food. Marie Antoinette said: "My girl, I no longer have need of anything; all is finished for me." But when Rosalie ventured to urge that the Queen needed strength for the coming ordeal, she was permitted to fetch a cup of bouillon, of which Marie Antoinette could swallow but a few spoonfuls.

Then came a priest who offered to hear her confession. But, knowing he must be one who had taken the oath to this government, she refused his offices. (She had already had the consolation of more than one secret visit from the Abbé Mangin, and had received the communion on Saturday night from another priest secretly brought in to her.) At eight o'clock, Marie Antoinette made her last toilet. At ten the executioner came; her hands were tied behind her, her hair was cut off, and she was led, or driven, to the court where the tumbril awaited her. She had given the letter to her sister-in-law to the jailer, Bault, who turned it over to Fouquier-Tinville. It was found between the mattresses of Robespierre's bed after he was executed, nearly nine months later.

The cell next to Marie Antoinette's is said to be the one where Robespierre spent a few hours before his condemnation to death and his journey to the scaffold.

In the chapel, the twenty-one Girondists passed their last night. "The death of Marie Antoinette is to gratify the rabble," Hébert had said; "the Girondists must go to safeguard us."

They were, you will remember, the Moderates — those men who were sometimes called Brissotins because Brissot was one of the leaders, and sometimes Girondists because a number of them came from the Gironde; that is to say, from near Bordeaux — and they were not so much a party as they were kindred souls, men who drew together because they had a common attitude toward what was going on around them. Idealists, all. Patriots above everything. Republicans at any cost but that of tyranny. Better a little headway, rightly won, than too much destruction — and chaos. The Rolands were of their number; he had escaped from Paris, but she had been in prison since June 1st. The twenty-two Girondists who were members of the National Convention were voted out of that body by the Terrorist majority on May 31, 1793, and their trial was ordered. It did not begin, however, until the 23d of October, a week after the Queen's execution; and it lasted seven days, at the end of which time all of the accused were declared "guilty of having conspired against the unity and indivisibility of the republic," and condemned to death. It was eleven o'clock at night, and the excitement in and outside of the courtroom was intense. Valaze, one of the twenty-two, had managed to conceal a dagger in his clothes; and when the verdict was pronounced, he killed himself; the others left the court singing the "Marseillaise" with such fervor that it resounded through the prison as they made their way to this chapel where they were to spend their last night.

Four gendarmes carried the body of Valaze and laid it in a corner. It was to go to the scaffold with the twenty-one, and into the grave with them in the cemetery of the Madeleine where Marie Antoinette was lying still unburied. Those about to die kissed, one by one, the hand of their dead comrade, murmuring as they did so: "Until to-morrow!"

One of their friends, who was in hiding in Paris, had promised to send them a farewell supper ere they left the Conciergerie either for liberty or for death. It was brought — the finest foods, the choicest wines, the fairest flowers. And there they sat, holding high converse on life and death, until the dawn broke. . . . As they entered the tumbrils they again sang the "Marseillaise." And, still singing it, they mounted the scaffold. At last, only one voice was left; it was that of Vergniaud, the golden-tongued orator. Then, silence. There are few pages in history more touching than those which describe the last days of these young men, all of whom were gifted, most of whom were handsome; who had so much to live for, but who were so glad to die for a cause they believed in.

Madame Roland went to the scaffold a week later than her friends. Charlotte Corday had gone in July. Their cells looked down into this Cour des Femmes, or Women's Court, from which Marie Antoinette's was also lighted. That court was the scene of many episodes of the Revolution, varying from the efforts of great ladies to make their toilet at the fountain to the frightful shambles of the September massacres.

The chapel of the Girondists is now the historical museum of the Conciergerie, though many objects which properly belong here are scattered through other collections — notably the Carnavalet, the museum of the Préfecture of Police, the Archives, and so on; not forgetting Madame Tussaud's in London.

Here are three paintings of Marie Antoinette in prison; but the one depicting her communion is fanciful rather than historic in its details. There are also some engravings depicting her last hours; her ivory crucifix; an armchair of which she was fond at the Tuileries, brought here under Louis XVIII; and so on — including old locks and bolts of the prison.

Now we return, through Robespierre's cell, to the Queen's, which would have been an infinitely more impressive memorial to her if Louis XVIII (who never liked her, and made poor work of all his pretences in that direction) had ordered the place of her detention returned as nearly as possible to the state in which she left it, and so kept. One resents the altar, the stained glass, and — most of all — the transformations in the very cell itself.

Leaving the Queen's cell, we are taken into a corridor through which many of the condemned passed on their way to the tumbrils; are shown where their hair was cut — but I am afraid it is not the actual place of that sinister ceremony; and then we retrace our steps — after we have tipped our guide.

As we go back through the rue de Paris, you may try to picture what it must have been like when there were as many as two hundred and fifty prisoners living in it. There were two classes of prisoners during the Revolution: those who could pay four or five francs a day for the luxury of a cell; and those who had to herd with others on the filthy straw laid on the floor of some dark corridor like this.

When we emerge from the Conciergerie on to the quai de l'Horloge again, we continue our way to the great square clock-tower on the corner. Saint Louis's grandson built this tower and ordered placed on it a splendid clock. The clock which now serves is of the time of Henry III, and the exquisite design of it is by Germain Pilon.

Now we follow the boulevard du Palais till we come to the great gilded iron grill and gates of the Cour du Mai, at the back of which is the imposing stairway to the Law Courts of the palais. We'll go up these stairs, enter a gallery or vestibule, turn to the right, and find ourselves in what is called the "Salle des Pas-Perdus." It used to be the audience hall of the palace, and was the scene of so many events in French history that I dare not begin here to remind you of them, for fear of not knowing how to leave off. Probably the picture most vivid in your mind as you stand here, is that from Victor Hugo's "Notre-Dame de Paris," describing the presentation here of Gringoire's play. The great marble table which was used for royal banquets, for councils, and for a stage, was long since broken and destroyed. The hall has been burned and restored many times.

I think you will like the dignified appearance of the French advocates we see hereabouts, in their gowns and rabats; and if you want to visit some of the courts in session, I'll gladly go with you. They are very impressive.

In the Salle des Pas-Perdus is the imposing monument to Malesherbes who went to the scaffold for having defended Louis XVI at his trial.

Standing in front of this, let us look across the hall and then to the corner of that side which is on our left. There is the door to what is called the Première Chambre. It was Saint Louis's bedroom (it is just above the Salle des Gardes where we sat waiting in the Conciergerie) and was so used by Louis XII also.

Francis I held a court of royal justice here. It was here that Parlement proclaimed Louis XIII's coming of age. Here the Fronde was born. It was here that Louis XIV, booted and spurred, strode unexpectedly in while Parlement was discussing some of his edicts, ordered that in future his decrees should become laws without discussion; and, declaring, "I am the State!" went out. He never again appeared at the palais during all the sixty remaining years of his reign. (He was only seventeen when he gave this childish performance.) But he was scarcely dead when his will was broken, here in this very room, in the uncomprehending presence of that frail, pretty child of five who had just begun to be called Louis XV.

On the 10th of March, 1793, this room became the seat of the terrible Revolutionary Tribunal. Here Charlotte Corday was condemned to death, and Marie Antoinette, and the Girondists, and Madame Roland, and hundreds of others.

After sentence was pronounced, they were taken below.

Those who were sentenced early in the day, as Charlotte Corday was and Madame Roland, went at once to the guillotine. Those whose trials were prolonged, or called late, spent the night in the jailer's quarters, near the entrance of the prison. It frequently happened that a new arrival brought (usually in a fiacre) to the Conciergerie to await trial met in the jailer's office some friend who — hair cut, hands tied — was leaving it for the journey to the guillotine.

We'll go back down the staircase now, and reënter the Cour du Mai — so called because here, long ago, the clerks of the law courts used to set up their Maypole. At our left, as we descend, is a small court reached by a few steps going down from the Cour du Mai. The buffet of the law courts is here now, and we shall see advocates and clerks snatching rather hasty luncheons before returning to their labors. Here, where they eat, was the old office of the jailer. This door, through which they come and go, was the entrance to the prison. At the top of these steps is the place where the tumbrils stood. (They were ordered in the morning, before the "trials" began. Fouquier-Tinville could tell in advance how many carts would be needed, at twenty francs apiece, for the journey.)

The usual hour for starting to the guillotine was about four in the afternoon, though many executions took place earlier in the day.

"Toward four o'clock," George Cain says, "one by one the condemned came through the grey door, surrounded by jailers, gendarmes, bailiffs, executioner's assistants; men and women, all had their hair cut short and their hands tied behind their backs; their eyes, red with weeping, were scarcely able to bear the sudden emergence from prison gloom to daylight; they trembled and paled under the insults with which they were assailed by the waiting mob;

filth rained down on them as they crossed this little court and went up the steps at the top of which Sanson (the executioner) awaited them, his carts drawn up against the grill. It was there that the executioner, almost always clad in a long brown redingote and wearing a high, peaked hat, checked off his victims on the death-lists he held, before ordering them tied to the board on which they were to sit, facing the crowd that followed them to the scaffold."

Some there were who scorned to weep — *many*, indeed! Some smiled. Nearly all were brave.

Sardou laid the last act of "Thermidor" here in this court. He was an impassioned student of this place and all its memories.

I would like to linger here with him, and with many another who has written of these scenes with supreme pity and supreme understanding; but I realize that we must be on our way, and that I must not crowd upon you details (however engrossing) too numerous for such a hurried survey as most travellers must make.

We will leave the Cour du Mai now, and follow the course that the tumbrils took on their way to the Place de la Concorde. It is a considerable walk, so we'll hail a fiacre and jog along not much faster than the death carts went, over the pont au Change and on to the quai opposite the Conciergerie. If you speak no French, *write* the directions on a card and hand it to your cocher:

"Pont au Change; quai de la Mégisserie; rue de la Monnaie; rue du Roule; rue Saint-Honoré jusqu'à la rue Cambon."

This rue Saint-Honoré we're traversing is a very ancient street. Keep a lookout on your right, first, for a house numbered 96, on the site of Molière's birthplace. The house in which he was born in 1622 was demolished in 1801.

On your left, as you pass the Louvre colonnade, at num-

ber 145 is the church, or temple, of the Oratoire, a famous
place of Protestant worship now, although in the days of
Louis XIII, XIV, and XV it was the Court chapel. Napoleon gave the Protestants three churches, including Saint-
Louis-du-Louvre which was taken down to enlarge the
Place du Carrousel, and this was substituted for that.
This site is where Philippe Auguste's wall formed the west
boundary of Paris. In a much later day, Gabrielle d'Estrées lived in a fine mansion here.

To number 161 we are coming to-morrow, so you need
not give it any special thought now.

Number 280 is where Jeanne Vaubernier worked as a
milliner's saleswoman, not very long before she became
Madame du Barry and ruled France.

Now we cross rue des Pyramides and come to the Church
of Saint-Roch which has so much of interest in it and about
it that we'll come back here after lunch. Across the street,
before there was a church here, was a humble hostelry
called the Three Pigeons, at which Ravaillac lodged while
he was seeking his chance to kill Henry IV. Later, there
was a café here which was so much frequented by Robespierre that it came to be called, briefly, by his name.

But it was in another café, a few doors farther on, that
Robespierre was sitting while Marie Antoinette was still on
trial. One of those with him had just come from the courtroom, and he told Robespierre about the monstrous charges
Hébert had preferred against the Queen. "That fool!"
Robespierre cried, dashing his plate on the ground. He was
shrewd enough to know the mistake made in charging
Marie Antoinette with a crime of which no one would ever
seriously believe her guilty, instead of piling up against her
accusations of a political nature.

This occurred in the Café Venua, housed in a part of
what had been the Hôtel de Noailles — and is now the

Hôtel Saint-James-and-Albany, at 211 rue Saint-Honoré. This was the home of Lafayette's bride, and here the very young couple (he, sixteen, and she, fourteen and a half) came to live after their marriage.

At number 350 (you have noticed that the numbers are much higher on the "even" side of the street than on the "odd" or south side) Napoleon signed his marriage contract, in the office of Joséphine's attorney to whom the young general, asked what his possessions were, replied, "What I have on." This house is also associated with Savalette de Langes whose story is one of the most melodramatic of all Revolutionary tales, and quite unique among them; but I don't dare embark upon it here, with so much else that should be said first, and a long chapter growing longer.

Madame de Condorcet kept a little shop at 352, and painted miniatures, and slipped away when she could to visit her eminent husband in his hiding-place which you shall visit next week. (After that, you'll look with greater interest at this house.)

Number 374 was called "The Ministry of Society" when Madame Geoffrin held her salon there in the middle of the eighteenth century. Horace Walpole came here in 1766, and made a memorable pen-picture of her. She was of humble origin and scant education, but she gathered the greatest men of her great day about her. Walpole said she had "more common-sense than I almost ever met with." She seems to have used it in judging herself as well as in judging others. For when one of her eminent friends proposed dedicating a grammar to her, she said, "Why, I don't even know how to spell."

Perhaps the dinners (she had married a rich manufacturer) had something to do with attracting Voltaire and Hume and Gibbon and Grimm and other such to her house. But I doubt it. There was no dearth of tables in

Paris at which the spiritual fare was as distinguished as the material, and these men were welcome at them all. You may like to "see" them coming here — the artists on Monday nights, the men of letters on Wednesdays. Or you may care more for the shade of Chateaubriand, who lived here after Madame Geoffrin's long day was done.

Now here we are at rue Cambon. The tumbrils went on to rue Royale, but we'll stop here. At the southeast corner of this street and rue Saint-Honoré is Voisin's, founded in 1813, one of the most famous of all the famous eating-places of Paris; but very, very expensive. Perhaps you are so hungry you don't care about expense. If so, you can have a meal here that you'll never forget, and wine (be sure to choose Burgundy or red Bordeaux) from one of the greatest cellars in Paris. Voisin's is frequented by diplomats, and it is said that "the man who knew Voisin's wine-list would be the greatest authority in the world on claret." But as for *me*, I'll probably go down a short block, past rue Mont-Thabor, to one of the English tea-rooms — the Marlborough or the Columbine — and content myself with a good lunch of a "lighter" and less costly sort.

The church across from Voisin's is the Assumption. It used to be the chapel of the convent belonging to the Dames of the Assumption. Lafayette, as I reminded you in Chapter I, was buried from there.

After you have lunched, you will, perhaps, enjoy the shops of rue Saint-Honoré and hereabouts. The most attractive are this side (west) of Saint-Roch; from there to the Élysée Palace and even beyond. But you may not want to walk so far; and it is impossible to enjoy shops except on foot — sauntering. There are some interesting ones on rue Cambon north of Saint-Honoré — behind the Ritz.

Suppose, however, that we stroll along the south side of Saint-Honoré as far as Saint-Roch, looking in windows and entering where we are tempted; then cross over to the church and come back westward on that other side.

On Monday, in rue Vivienne, we met the discouraged young Corsican who had about decided to become a Turk; we followed him to the Tuileries and saw him given command of the Paris troops. I promised you that you should see him leap into fame, a few hours later. Well, here he is! The Royalists are massed about this church — not only within gunshot of the Tuileries, but within a veritable stone's throw, or almost that. Up from the gardens, across what was then an open space, come the Republican troops who retired last night under a fire of oratory. But they have a new commander now! A youth in shabby boots, a worn coat, and a hat too big for him. A pale, almost cadaverous-looking person, with scraggly locks of hair and a generally unkempt appearance. But he knows artillery! He gives the reactionaries "a whiff of grape-shot." They retire, and disperse. All Paris becomes curious about the young commander. Turkey will not get him. I wonder what would have happened in Europe if he had gone into the Turkish army? Standing here and looking at the pockmarks he made on the church façade, on the bullets still lodged there, for what are you grateful or regretful? If I could know that, you'd be no stranger to me.

I find that our guidebook tells nearly all the main things about this church, including the fact that Corneille, the father of French tragedy, French classic drama, is buried here; and also Diderot, the encyclopædist, who died on rue Richelieu. Mignard, who also died in that street, is likewise buried here. And so is Lenôtre, the eminent landscape gardener who laid out the gardens of the Tuileries and of Versailles. Bossuet preached here.

These steps were always crowded when the Revolutionary tumbrils passed; and it was from them, as our guidebook reminds us, that a woman spat at Marie Antoinette on her way to death.

Now, then, back on this side of the street, which has many alluring shops.

And after we pass rue Cambon, mind you take a good look up rue Duphot, for it's there that Prunier is, and there he serves such sea-food as there may be elsewhere in the world — but I haven't found it!

A few steps farther, and we shall be at rue Royale, where the tumbrils turned down to the place of execution.

But there are two other houses to look at, as we stroll. One is number 271, across the street, which was the cabaret of the Holy Spirit, dating from the seventeenth century, and a famous place of rendezvous for Revolutionists, especially when the tumbrils were going by.

And the other is on this side, number 398, the house of Duplay, the cabinet-maker, with whom and his family Robespierre lived from July 17, 1791, to July 27, 1794.

On the former date there had been, on the Champ-de-Mars or military manœuvre field, a bloody encounter as a result of which, 'twas said, the leaders of the Revolution were to be thrown into prison. Robespierre, returning to his shabby lodgings in the Marais, was recognized by the crowd in the rue Saint-Honoré, and so noisily acclaimed that he seemed to think it best to "make himself scarce," as we might say. At this juncture Duplay came out of a shop, took in the situation, and offered Robespierre shelter in his house. Robespierre accepted.

"I find eminently tragic," Lenôtre says, "this meeting between these two men. Duplay, the good bourgeois, the peaceable and calm man of small affairs, the happy paterfamilias, taking Robespierre by the hand, introducing him in his home, and at the same time taking into it a terrible unhappiness which was to weigh down him and his."

He never left them.

For three years the Duplays thoroughly enjoyed the distinction of being hosts to this man of constantly growing power. One of the daughters married a young satellite of Robespierre's — Labas — who went to the scaffold with him. Another daughter was engaged to Robespierre, and wore widow's weeds for him for nearly forty years. The mother died in prison, after Robespierre's downfall. The father narrowly escaped the guillotine.

All this was in store for Duplay that July day shortly after the royal family was brought back from its flight, when he offered shelter to a "man in the street."

The history of those three years in this house is of the most absorbing interest. Sardou, making studies of this locale for "Thermidor," grew so fascinated by it that he wrote a book on "The House of Robespierre"; not just the house, of course, but the household and the persons habitual and incidental who came and went in those three years as a consequence of Robespierre's being there — those associates of his so many of whom fell beneath the knife when he suspected their subservience to him to be waning; and those who came to beg him for that pity which he did not have. Lamartine has left a vivid picture of it in his book on "The Girondists" for which he had the assistance of Madame Labas who had been one of the Duplay daughters.

The Duplays adored Robespierre — quite literally adored him. Perhaps because he put them and kept them in prominence. Perhaps because they really believed him to be a great apostle to suffering mankind.

His manner of living was simple, almost austere; but he was dandified in dress and had a hairdresser every morning to "do" his hair. This was almost the only time he could be seen by the crowd. It was like the King's dining in public at Versailles, in the old days.

Let us step into the court of number 398 and look about us. The front of the building is of late date, and so are the upper stories of the back part. At our left is a staircase (enclosed). The third window beyond it on the floor above the street level is the window of Robespierre's room. In his day there was a shed beneath it, and the top of the shed was a sort of balcony whereon he sat to have his hair dressed. People crowded into the court to stare up at him; he took little notice of them; generally he read the paper and ate his breakfast of bread and fruit and a little wine.

Thursday evenings the Duplay family was "at home," and the leaders of the realm thronged the bourgeois "settin' room" with its furnishings of red cotton plush.

Sometimes those callers ceased to stop at the door and come in — they went on, to the rue Royale, and turned down it; they were riding, now, and their hands were tied behind their backs; their hair was cut short.

In the late spring of '94, after Danton and Desmoulins had gone riding past without stopping, Robespierre began to act like a man inside whom something that was his source of energy, of power, has failed suddenly. He made desperate efforts to conceal it from those surrounding him, but his success was only partial. Few, if any, knew what had happened; but many knew that *some*thing had gone amiss.

Was he suffering remorse? Not a bit! The bottom had dropped out of his plans — that was all!

He seems to have had little faith in the possibility of continuing for any length of time a republican government. Perhaps he believed in it as an eventuality; but he had seen too much of war-to-death among would-be leaders, not to know that the country was getting ready to cry out for an indisputable head again. It could be rallied round a Bourbon king — temporarily, at least — if that king were a plastic child, stripped of all old-régime counsellors and under the regency of a constitutionalist, of one who had been indefatigable in ridding France of her tyrants. In a word, it was to be Louis XVII and Robespierre — at least until such times as, perhaps, Louis could be dispensed with.

Others were cherishing the same plan — but with a different regent. Robespierre, however, did not know this.

On the 19th of January, the shoemaker, Simon, and his wife had quit their post at the Temple as guardians of "the little Capet." In all human probability they had smuggled the child out with them; from that day forward the records, hitherto so full of references to him, mention him no more. Robespierre may not have noticed this omission. He was very busy! He had not been at the Temple in two years; but on the evening of May 10th, he went out there. He saw Madame Royale; and he probably took away with him, not then but two weeks later, the little boy designated to him as Charles Louis Capet. After an absence of six days the child seems to have been returned. He was *not* the little Capet! Some one had got him before Robespierre tried.

And that is, in all probability, why Robespierre "from the first days of June seemed visibly 'through.' He deserted the Committee of Public Safety; resigned completely his part as dictator, and left the government to his colleagues. In those days he took long, solitary walks in the Champs-Élysées, followed by his dog Brount, a great Danish hound."

The Revolution, in its desire to destroy all the old authority, had abolished God as well as the kings. Then it began to seem to Robespierre that people need something to believe, some faith to sustain, some reverence to restrain, them. So he allowed the Assembly to grant them a Supreme Being, and permission to expect immortality for their souls.

On the 8th of June there was a great fête to celebrate the inauguration of this new cult, and Robespierre was the central figure of it. He delivered, in the Tuileries Gardens, an oration which was one of the supreme efforts of his life. But his evil genius was with him. When he came back here to the Duplay home, he knew that he had failed. He had seen the handwriting on the wall.

"You will not see me much longer," he said to them that night.

On July 26th he appeared in the Convention for the first time in more than a month, and delivered a harangue which lasted for four hours, in which he declared that the Terror ought to be ended. (In the six weeks just passed, more than twelve hundred had perished on the guillotine!) "They call me a tyrant," he cried. "If I were a tyrant they [meaning his denouncers] would be crawling at my feet."

That evening, he re-read the speech to the Jacobins. "This," he told them, "is my last will and testament." They shouted reassurance to him, and he may have believed — as he said — that "the great body of the Assembly will support me."

The next day, "the great body of the Assembly," rallied by the desperate Tallien, denounced him and ordered his arrest. He never came back to the house of Duplay.

He passed, though — two days later, on his way to the guillotine.

We shall consider, in another place, some of the details of those intervening hours. To-day it will, I think, be enough for you as you stand here to visualize the man of thirty-five going hence on a hot July day, the terrible dictator of France; and, a little more than forty-eight hours later, riding past in a cart, followed by a hooting, howling, execrating mob, on his "rendezvous with death."

It should be now not much past three — unless we've lingered in some shop. We've had four hours or so of sight-seeing in places that make thought grave — but oh! how the recollection of what we've seen to-day will vivify much that we read, forever after.

The rest of the day ought to be gay.

What we shall do depends on the weather, the time of year, and your inclinations.

We are in the midst of the most enticing shops in the world.

Perhaps, though, you'd rather go home, rest a bit, freshen up, and go to tea in a smart place: at the Ritz or the Carlton, in town, or out at Pré-Catélan or Armenonville or Madrid in the Bois — if the season for them is in full swing.

If the salons are open, you may feel like spending an hour in one of them. I always look forward with the utmost delight to taking a friend in Paris on her first visit to the salon of the Société Nationale des Beaux-Arts, in the Grand Palais. The picture galleries, upstairs, are not notably different from many great exhibitions we have known. But if there is anything elsewhere on earth like the main floor where the sculpture is shown, I have never seen it. The effect of all those soft white cheesecloth curtains billowing overhead, and of the gleaming statues set in bowers of deep, ilex-like green, is simply breath-taking in its loveliness, but promptly restorative in its restfulness.

Or, across the broad avenue Alexandre III is the Petit-Palais, permanently housing the municipal art collection, and in itself (as a building) a thing of beauty. It is "free" to-day (other days, except Sundays, a franc), and, even if you don't feel like looking at pictures or sculpture, I think you could hardly help loving to sit in the colonnaded open court looking into the lily pool and up to the blue sky.

If that is too crowded for the cloistral quiet which brings out its greatest loveliness, we can cross the Champs-Élysées and patronize one of the puppet shows — petits guignols — or sit beneath the trees and watch the children at play.

There is a military band concert in the gardens of the Tuileries and of the Palais-Royal late this afternoon. Or, if we drive out to the Bois and go to the Jardin d'Acclimatation (a delightful place, and always full of interest) we shall hear a good open-air concert or — if the weather is bad — listen to it in the gorgeous Palmarium or palmhouse.

It's hard to suggest about dinner, unless I know where you'll be before dinner and what you'll be doing afterwards.

It might be the best possible night to go over the river to the Tour d'Argent and eat duck prepared as only the disciples of Frederick (he's gone, now!) can prepare it. This is 15 quai de la Tournelle, quite a bit east of Notre-Dame, and *not* a good place to go to if you're going to opera or theatre. In the latter event, I'd say Prunier (if it's open — closed in summer) or Ciro's in the rue Danou, or — if you like a good table-d'hôte at a moderate price — Romano's at 14 rue Caumartin, north of boulevard des Capucines.

VII

YOUR SEVENTH PARIS DAY

THIS morning will be a good time (if you feel like it) to spend an hour in the Louvre and begin making acquaintance with its picture treasures.

If you have just come up from Italy, you may be sated with Italian masters or you may be all the keener to see more of them. If you have just landed at Cherbourg or Havre, and the Louvre is your first great European gallery, you will probably want to see the pictures you have heard most about.

We will ascend the Escalier Daru, past the Winged Victory, and take the left-hand one of the two flights into which the stairway divides at the landing. This will lead us to the Rotonde d'Apollon from which we can enter the Galerie d'Apollon, one of the most magnificent apartments in the world and in itself a study. Be sure to note the Gobelin tapestry portraits of the builders of the Louvre. And to look out of the windows!

In the Salon Carré (or Square Room) opening into the south end of the Galerie, many of the greatest pictures used to be grouped. They are, most of them, in the Grande Galerie now, and better lighted; but I am not yet reconciled to the change. Some of them seem — to me at least — to demand a smaller room, a smaller company. But very few great pictures have ever been adequately hung — for lighting, for safeguarding, for surroundings, for accessibility. The problem seems too many-fold for solution. The Sistine Madonna is superbly hung. Rembrandt's "Sortie of Banning Cock's Company" (the so-called "Night Watch") is. Raphael's "Transfiguration" is — in the Vatican galleries. And Rembrandt's "School of Anatomy" at The Hague. But there are not many others. The glass over them tends to make them mirrors reflecting us and our fellow-gazers. None of them was painted to hang in a crowded museum. Every one of them suffers from many things which not even the supremest reverence and skill in their conservators can avoid or overcome. It is well for us to remember these difficulties when we come for the first time to look upon canvases pronounced superlative by all the world; to remind ourselves that our first glance at them is little likely to enthrall us as our hundredth glance will. Deep, searching, reverent acquaintance with a few great pictures will do infinitely more for any one than a "survey" of hundreds. There are thousands in the Louvre.

If you have definite ideas as to what you want to see, you need no one's suggestions.

If, however, you happen to be one of those travellers who have never given much thought to art, but — now that you are where it is a part of every one's life, and where many of the world's greatest treasures are assembled — you want to see something of it, so that you may go home from Europe with a new vision of beauty, I'll venture to suggest that you see, here: Correggio's "Betrothal of Saint Catherine of Alexandria"; Veronese's "Christ in the House of Simon the Pharisee" and his "Marriage at Cana"; Titian's "Man with the Glove" and his "Francis I," and compare these with Raphael's "Castiglione"; Leonardo's "Mona Lisa" and "Virgin and Saint Anne"; Murillo's "Immaculate Conception" and his "Beggar Boy"; Velasquez's "Infanta"; Holbein's "Erasmus"; Van Dyck's "Charles I"; Rembrandt's "Supper at Emmaus."

If you see these on a first visit to the pictures, and do

not try to go into the galleries of French painting until another time, I think you will come away less confused than most persons do.

As we return to the stairway up which we came, we shall pass through a room where photographs of the Louvre treasures are sold. Every sou you spend on such is, to my way of thinking, an investment which will yield many hundred per cent. The people of my acquaintance who get most out of their memories of Europe are those who have brought back the most satisfying collections of postcards, photographs, and pamphlets, which serve to keep vividly in mind what has been seen.

But before you begin your buying of this sort at the Louvre, I want to remind you that directly back of the porte by which we enter the galleries, on the quai du Louvre, is the porte Jean Goujon by which we enter the Musée de Chalcographie, where we may buy prints from hundreds of etched and engraved plates belonging to the Louvre. These are sold at astonishingly low prices. See them first; and then buy photographs; and after that, postcards.

I cannot say too much for picture postcards — of the right sort. We have hundreds upon hundreds of them, and they have been worth their weight in gold.

Now, let us leave the Louvre, cross our glorious Place du Carrousel, go through the Pavillon Richelieu (where the Hôtel Rambouillet stood) and come out into the Place du Palais-Royal.

At our right are the Magasins du Louvre, one of the big department stores of Paris, an excellent place to buy silks, velvets, dress-goods, millinery materials, perfumes and other toilet requisites, and — very specially — kid gloves.

On our left is the Grand Hôtel du Louvre; and the little street which runs past the west end of this hotel is the rue de Rohan. At the corner of rue de Rohan and rue Saint-Honoré is where the porte Saint-Honoré was in Charles V's city wall. It stood here till Richelieu's time, when he had it taken down; the western wall of the city thenceforth for some time was at rue Royale. Jeanne d'Arc was attacking this wall (Paris then being in the hands of the English) when she was wounded and carried into a house which stood where now is number 4 Place du Théâtre-Français. Her camp was on a slope, dotted with windmills, about a quarter of a mile to the north.

At this place, now number 161 rue Saint-Honoré, is the Café de la Régence. This is no time of day to make acquaintance with it, but I want you to know it some time in the late afternoon or after the theatre in the evening. It used to be a few doors farther east, at the corner of the Place du Palais-Royal and rue Saint-Honoré; and it owes its name to the Regent who was living in the Palais-Royal when the café came into being along about 1718. In those days it was a very gay place, much frequented by the gallants of the Regent's "set." But it seems to have had a long association with chess (which certainly is not *gay!*), for we know that Diderot liked to watch the games there. The author of "Gil Blas" used to frequent it, too; likewise Rousseau and Voltaire, Grimm and Franklin, Beaumarchais, and many more — Robespierre, for instance, and Bonaparte.

There is a story to the effect that Robespierre was sitting alone at a table in the Régence one night during the Terror, when a young man seated himself opposite and challenged Robespierre to a game of chess. Robespierre asked what the stakes were, and was answered: "A life! The life of a young man condemned to death." Robespierre seems to have been interested in this, as a game of skill with an unusual element of suspense, of thrill; and he agreed. The young man won; and then — hysterical, no doubt — disclosed the fact that "he" was a young woman, playing for her sweetheart's pardon. They say she got it.

Napoleon's fondness for chess is easy to understand. I would give a good deal to have seen him at it; wouldn't you? The Régence has a table on which he played. The café has been in its present location since 1854, and it is still frequented by lovers of chess.

Now we'll cross the Place du Théâtre-Français, and at least stop to read the announcements of forthcoming performances. If you speak no French at all, you would probably find the purchase of tickets at the box-office a bit bewildering, and it will be better for you to "book" them at your hotel. Or, for instance, the chasseur (footman) at the Bœuf-à-la-Mode, who speaks a little English, never forgets a patron, and makes you feel that the place is terribly lonely when you stay away, can always get excellent seats, and hand them to you when you come to dinner. And when you go to the Théâtre-Français, the Bœuf-à-la-Mode is the logical place to dine. The plays given at the Théâtre-Français and the Odéon are nearly all standard plays, and many — if not most — of them are available in English translation, obtainable at Brentano's (on avenue de l'Opéra) or at Galignani's (on rue de Rivoli). There are few play-going Parisians who have not seen every one of these plays, "over and over," as we say.

If we come by here around six o'clock some evening, we shall find the arcade at the north of the theatre, leading into the Palais-Royal Gardens, already filled with people waiting in line for early chances at the best of the cheap seats. Some of them are eating a light supper as they stand and wait. If you could catechize them, you would find, doubtless, that every one of them has seen this play half a dozen times or more. Why do they come? Not to find out what the play's about, certainly. But to *see it done!* The parts are differently cast, to-night — perhaps; "it will be *most* interesting to see M. Blanc play the young lover to-night, whereas he played the old grandfather when I last saw this drama."

When we, in America, have a play-going public like that, we shall have a different kind of theatre. I wish you might hear, and understand, the animated discussions of plays here, between the acts! In America, the bulk of every audience has come to the theatre, child-like, to be amused, diverted, to hear an unfamiliar story told, and to pronounce it "punk" or "peachy" as its development teases or tickles their ideas of life. In France, they come to see craftsmanship which approximates or attains to Art — come to see how a dramatist develops his thesis; how the actors interpret and illumine character.

At the north end of the Palais-Royal Gardens there is another theatre — the Palais-Royal — devoted to French farces of the type which has given most Americans their one idea of the French theatre. Paris loves gaiety, laughter; she loves musical comedy, and likes it spectacular and highly spiced. She loves comedy — loves to laugh at herself, at her foibles and frailties. But she loves other things, too; and you do not really know her until you have known her at the Théâtre-Français — "the House of Molière."

This broad street running straight away to northward, to the Opéra, is the avenue de l'Opéra which was cut through a network of little old streets between 1854 and 1878. It was the first street lighted by electricity.

One old street which had its end lopped off is the rue d'Argenteuil in which Corneille lived, and died; his house is demolished, but it stood where number 6 now is. And you may like to know that Sardou had the keystone of its front door and the rail of its stairway out at Marly-le-Roi, where he lived amid many such treasures.

The first street on our right as we go up the avenue is rue Molière which runs into rue de Richelieu where the Molière fountain is.

There are few interesting shops along the avenue in this lower end, but more as we near the Opéra.

Rue des Petits-Champs which crosses the avenue about halfway up is well worth loitering along, some day when you feel like it. At number 57 Rousseau lived, early in his connection with Thérèse Lavasseur, when he spent a month trying to teach her to tell time on a neighboring clock — and then gave it up as hopeless.

The tiny rue Méhul which runs from rue des Petits-Champs to the Bank of France annex, opposite where Rousseau lived, is where the Rolands lived, in a magnificent mansion, while he was Minister of the Interior, in 1792. A little farther along rue des Petits-Champs, to the east, is rue des Moulins where Jeanne d'Arc was encamped outside the walls of Paris.

Napoleon wrote his recollection of coming through rue des Petits-Champs on the 20th of June, 1792, and meeting the mob pouring from the markets toward the Tuileries to insult the king and queen. On a pike's point they carried a head. They ordered Napoleon to shout, "Vive la Nation!" "And," he assures us, "I lost no time in doing so."

Now let us cross the avenue to the Brasserie Universelle, for lunch.

We'll go upstairs, and turn either to right or to left as beckoned. This is, as you will see, a most popular restaurant. The food is very good and the prices are not high. It has always been celebrated for its hors d'œuvres. In "the good old days" before the war, one paid eighty centimes (then sixteen cents) for hors d'œuvres, and had some

twenty or thirty varieties presented, from which he chose
all that he wanted and called for more if he wished. Such
liberality is no longer possible; but even at the present
prices, one gets extraordinary quality, variety, and quan-
tity for his money. They cook sole most deliciously here.
Indeed, I know of no item on their extensive bill of fare that
is *not* good. And for a finish to your meal I recommend a
coupe Universelle, made with lemon ice and many fruits,
all drowned at the moment of serving in a generous
libation of champagne.

A little way up the avenue, and we come to rue d'Antin.
Number 3, just west of the avenue on the north side of
the street, is now a bank of the Netherlands. It used to be
the Mairie of this (the Second) Arrondissement. On the
9th of March, 1796, the Mayor was asked to be in readiness to perform a civil ceremony of marriage between a
widow no longer young (as Créole women count youth)
and a bachelor so much her junior that, to decrease the
disparity in their ages, she had taken four years off her
total and he had put eighteen months on to his. But as he
swore (in his application for a marriage license) that he
was born on February 5, 1768, he could not say that he
was born in Corsica; because at that date Corsica was not
yet French — he would be reckoned an alien — there would
be complications. So he said he was born in Paris. After
all, what difference could it make? Who'd ever see that
application?

They are not bothering with any religious ceremony —
that will not come for more than eight years, on the eve
of their coronation at Notre-Dame. But the young bridegroom, who is tremendously in love, cannot bear to go off
on his campaign into Italy, two days hence, and leave this
fascinating widow behind save as his wife.

His residence is not far away, on rue des Capucines

(just where rue Volney now cuts in), and at the corner of that street and the boulevard of the same name is his office where he met the lady who is now to become his bride. He had ordered all weapons held by private citizens to be surrendered. That included the sword which was about all that the Vicomte de Beauharnais had left to his children. Eugène was distraught at giving this up, and his mama suggested that he go to General Bonaparte and ask for its return. The lad's request was granted, and his mama called to present her thanks for the courtesy. The young general was enchanted; he began an ardent courtship. The widow —! Well, she seems less to have been won than to have yielded; perhaps she thought it was the easiest way to cure his insistence. She ought to have married money. But Joséphine was hardly the woman to bother about that. She got what she wanted, and left the bills to Providence; they always seemed to get paid, somehow.

Well, here we are, on that March evening, five months after our young soldier was so narrowly saved from becoming a Turk.

If it is two o'clock (which it shouldn't be) one may step to the door of the bank and ask if we might see "la salle de mariage de Napoléon." (Banks are closed between twelve and two.) This gorgeous apartment, little changed since long before that wedding, is now a bank directors' room, but it is shown, when possible, to pilgrims. It is much gilded, and painted with Cupids and garlands and goddesses; has a massive fireplace in red marble — mirrors in heavy frames — and so on.

Whether we enter it actually or not, we can enter it imaginatively on that March night, 1796. Again it is Lenôtre who leads us:

"Barras, dandified and talkative, is there; and Tallien. They are to sign, as witnesses, the marriage record of their protégé. Camelet, Joséphine's confidential adviser, holds himself modestly apart. The bride, with her undefinable Créole nonchalance, her very sweet smile, her amber skin, her chestnut hair knotted, à la Grecque, wears one of her clinging tunics which reveal so perfectly her body's grace and suppleness. Chin in hand she sits before the fire, in a reverie, her little, arched feet stretched toward the warmth.

"At this hour there is no noise in the deserted street, except that of the cochers talking, and the horses of Barras pawing impatiently. The ticking of the clock on the mantel is plainly heard. Joséphine looks at the time: Bonaparte is late. Perhaps he will not come!

"Two long hours they wait, and as the time dragged by we may imagine what was in the glances exchanged between Joséphine and Barras. While as to the official Leclercq, he sleeps shamelessly, in his armchair behind his desk.

"A little after ten o'clock — the sound of voices on the stairway, the clanking of a sabre on the stone steps — the door opens, and the general appears, followed by his aide-de-camp, Lemarois. He is in a hurry, goes straight to the sleeping mayor, shakes him by the shoulder, and in an impatient tone says: 'Come, M. le Maire, marry us quickly.'"

It is done; the witnesses disperse. The bride and the bridegroom enter Joséphine's carriage and are driven to her house. That carriage and those fine black horses used to belong to the King and Queen of France. They were presented to Joséphine — probably by Barras — to recompense her for those she had had long ago. The gods — of some sort — always *did* provide for Joséphine! She was of those who neither toil nor spin, yet Solomon in all his glory —!

She had a house, too. She had rented it six months ago,

without knowing in the least how she was going to pay the rent. It was in what was then called rue Chantereine, and was soon rechristened by Napoleon rue de la Victoire. (The house is gone now, but it was on the site of 58–60; and the street is north of rue de Lafayette.) When they got there, Joséphine's pug-dog, Fortuny, jumped out of her bed and vociferated his resentment of the intruder.

"I wanted her to put him out," Napoleon wrote about the episode, "but she told me I must accept him for a bedfellow, or seek other quarters. It was take him or leave him — and her. I yielded, but the favorite was less accommodating" — he bit the newcomer in the leg!

Early on the 11th of March, a post-chaise drew up in the court of the house on rue Chantereine; it was loaded with valises filled with books, maps, pistols, etc. Junot and Chauvet were already in their places. "Bonaparte tore himself away from the wife he had so ardently desired, mounted the step, waved good-bye, the door closed behind him, and the carriage started in the direction of the Italian frontier. Thus began the 'fabulous journey' which was destined to end at St. Helena twenty years later."

Now let us walk down rue d'Antin, cross rue des Petits-Champs and rue Gomboust, and look at the Marché Saint-Honoré. It is a little late in the day for a market, but that isn't what we have come especially to see.

We have come to see where the club called the Jacobins used to meet. It had such innocent beginnings — that club wherein the Terror was born and nurtured!

When the Assembly was sitting at Versailles, some of the Breton deputies, and a few from other provinces, used to gather, evenings, at the Café Amaury, and "talk things over." It was very exciting, this being "in politics," and they felt terribly responsible.

When the Assembly moved to Paris, in October, 1789,

the provincial deputies were more than ever in need of a place where they could meet to discuss the problems of their new duties. The Assembly met in the riding-school of the Tuileries. The deputies found lodgings as near by as they could, and then they sought a place where they might meet informally in the fashion that the English called a *club*.

Very convenient to the Tuileries was the convent of the Preaching Friars called Jacobins, who were glad to let their refectory for two hundred francs a year. A like sum sufficed to furnish it. And the deputies who got it under way decided to call it the Society of Friends of the Constitution. But that was too long for everyday use. The people of the neighborhood referred to it as the Jacobins — and that name stuck.

You see, all these men had come to the Assembly just bursting with ideas as to the country's needs and how to save it. Only a few of them could get the floor in the National sittings. And they just *had* to talk!

There were only fifteen or twenty of them at the first meeting, and the number grew so slowly that the monks used to drop in and help make up an audience, and nobody found anything incongruous in the white-robed, black-hooded friars sitting listening to how France should be saved.

Then it was decided to admit as members those who were not deputies. And all those who believed that they knew how France should be saved, and wanted to tell it, flocked to the Jacobins. Within three months the refectory was no longer big enough for the gatherings. There was talk of going elsewhere, but the monks were loath to lose these interesting tenants, so they offered the Jacobins their vast library, which was a kind of upper story of their church, a long, vaulted apartment with excellent ventilation and light. And such was the Preaching Friars' respect for their tenants that they neither removed from their shelves nor made any attempt otherwise to protect their thousands of rare and precious volumes. Even their monastic pictures were not taken from the walls, and an altar at the end of the hall was not disturbed.

The Jacobins installed tiers of seats, a platform for their president, tables below it for the secretaries, and a speaker's stand.

The meetings were held every other evening, from eight o'clock to ten-thirty. The minutes of those meetings are published. They are very like the minutes of a high-school debating society.

Thus the Jacobins began. Thus they continued for almost two years. When they moved out of the refectory into the library, a sort of annex or understudy club took possession of the smaller quarters, and there the workingmen of the quarter "orated" in their best possible imitation of the lawyers, journalists, and economists in the larger body.

On the morning of writing these lines, the papers print a White House sanction of a boycott on sugar to bring the profiteering prices down. On the 30th of January, 1791, a member of the Jacobins held the floor with a speech urging that all his fellow-members join him in a boycott on sugar until the price came down within reason and within the reach of "the largest and most precious part of the people." He said he could picture the joy with which "the great Washington and his companions in arms" would welcome the news of this patriotic fervor. And that so moved another member that he proposed that the abstention include coffee, also. This was carried, enthusiastically. But one commentator was moved to wonder how many of the Jacobins who passed this resolution refrained from going to a neighboring café on their way home for their habitual demi-tasse. Human nature may progress a little, but it doesn't change much.

The new American flag shared with the French and English flags the place of honor on the tribune; Franklin's bust was there with Mirabeau's, and Richard Price's (the English political moralist) with Jean-Jacques Rousseau's.

When the ecclesiastical properties were all secularized and taken over by the state, the Jacobins occupied the whole of the Preaching Friars' convent, which was entered from the rue Saint-Honoré, here at what is now the little rue du Marché-Saint-Honoré. There were three arches in the great portal — a centre one for vehicles and two side ones for persons on foot. Inside was a square court, surrounded by the conventual buildings, including the church.

We cannot stop here for a history of the club; but I thought you would like to stand in the Marché-Saint-Honoré and reconstitute for yourself its "setting," so that when next you read of the terrible Jacobins (and terrible they did indeed become) you may picture the place where they met. After the downfall of Robespierre, the club was disbanded, their quarters were "sealed"; and not much more than five years after popular fury had destroyed the Bastille, symbol of royal tyranny, it turned upon this old convent which had become hateful through the tyranny of demagogues, and left of it not one stone upon another.

There is food for thought in the Marché-Saint-Honoré!

We'll take a cab here, now — a fiacre if possible — and say to the driver, "Aux Invalides (Oz Envaleed), s'il vous plaît."

He will take us to the Place de la Concorde, along the Cour la Reine, and over the superb pont Alexandre III.

I have never seen the Taj Mahal, though I am familiar with pictures of the approach to it and am willing to believe that it may exceed in beauty of a certain sort the approach to Napoleon's tomb. But I doubt if anything in the world equals this place that we're going to in majesty and in *thrill*.

If you're a sentient human being, something's going to happen to you, a few minutes hence, that you will never forget.

This broad Esplanade des Invalides was laid out between 1704 and 1720. There used to be a fountain in it, and on this fountain Napoleon placed in 1804 the venerated, the almost-sacred winged Lion of Saint Mark which he had brought from Venice in 1797. In 1815, when Napoleon had fallen before the Allies, the Austrians (then masters of Venice) took down the Lion, and broke it in so doing. It was mended, and restored to its place in the Piazzetta at Venice, in close proximity to the ancient bronze horses of the Quadriga which Napoleon set on top of his Arc de Triomphe du Carrousel, for a while, and which the Austrians returned to the porch above San Marco's portal, where they had been since 1204. (They have seen the world from many vantage-points, those horses! They were probably on a great arch of Nero, once. Constantine sent them to the city to which he gave his name. And Napoleon brought them to Paris.)

We will go first to the Tomb ("o tom-*bo*") and there dismiss our cab.

All the details about who made the building, the statues, and *when*, are in your guidebook. I shan't repeat them. I'm sure you cannot care about any of them on this first visit. It is about all any mortal can do to contain the emotions, the reflections, that surge up within him like a tidal wave, when he stands looking down into that circular crypt, upon the porphyry sarcophagus flooded with that unearthly radiance.

RETURN OF NAPOLEON'S REMAINS AT THE CHURCH OF THE
INVALIDES

When you are able to tear yourself away from that spot, come with me up to these side chapels where Vauban, the great military engineer of Louis XIV, and Turenne, the greatest of his marshals, lie. Not many people come here; and we should not have great difficulty in finding him we seek. He is a sallow, spindling youth of fifteen, recently come up from Brienne to the military school near by; and we may, I think, be sure that one of the first places he would go, when he had any leisure, was here. When he died, in exile, and in his will desired "that my ashes may rest on the banks of the Seine, in the midst of that French people whom I have so greatly loved," he was probably as far from seeing this majesty of sepulture, this procession of pilgrims as to a shrine, as he was when he wandered here an anxious lad, worrying about the education of his younger brothers and the marriage portion of his little sisters.

One event of Napoleon's association with the Church of the Invalides, that you will doubtless like to recall, is the impressive ceremony which took place here on his orders, February 8, 1800, to mourn the death of George Washington, for whom the officers of the French Army wore mourning, and of whom Napoleon said: "His memory will always be cherished by the French people and especially by the French soldiery who, like him and the American soldiers, fought for equality and liberty."

After leaving the Dôme (Napoleon's tomb), be sure to visit the Church of Saint Louis, behind; and especially see the St. Helena souvenirs in the Napoleon Chapel.

Then go into the Court of Honor, and see the trophies and other memorials of the recent war: the Gothas brought down; the restaurant-wagon (dining-car) in which the Armistice terms were signed, etc.

In the museums it is a good plan to go upstairs first. There is so much to see that, if you are likely to get tired, it will be better to leave off before seeing the ancient armor than before seeing the intimate belongings of Napoleon, Guynemer's plane, and so on. In one of the glass cases in the Salle Guynemer, be sure to note the report which that magnificent and legendary eaglet made out for his commanding officer — that laconic and matter-of-fact listing of breath-taking performances. He rides the winds that blow above France forever—that lad! "No man knows his burial-place," nor eye hath seen the flaming chariot that transported him into eternity. But here, hanging from the low ceiling, is the almost toy-like little machine in which he out-sailed the clouds.

Be sure to see, also, in this room, that aviator's button which, cut open, contained a tiny compass and tight-folded map. Many a bird-man, brought down on enemy soil and escaped from the snare of the fowler, made his way back to safety with the aid of such a "button" on his coat.

When you come out of the Court of Honor, do not fail to get the northward view, the vista along the Esplanade, across the river, past the "palaces" of art, and up to the avenue Gabriel where the gardens of the Élysée Palace are.

Then turn to the east. We are now at the western edge of the old Faubourg Saint-Germain, the quarter that attracted the aristocracy after the Marais had seen its best days. Here is where the early nineteenth-century romancers laid so many of their stories. Some of the old noblesse are still in their stately mansions; but not many. The Bois de Boulogne quarter has attracted some. Others keep no large establishment in town — only in the country — and are apartment-dwellers when in Paris. The great houses of other days are foreign embassies now, or offices of Ministries of the French Government, and so forth. The famous quai d'Orsay is immediately to the north. And from that, south to rue de Babylone, we are in the land of Diplomacy. A very interesting land it is, too, to those who have entrée to it; though not much of it can be glimpsed by the wayfarer.

If you feel like a little stroll hereabouts, we'll take rue de Grenelle as far as the Fountain of the Four Seasons.

Rue de Constantine, which runs north from here, facing the Esplanade, contains a number of mansions belonging to important persons — the Duc de la Rochefoucauld, the Duc Décazes, etc., at number 31. In the hôtel of the Duc de la Rochefoucauld, General Pershing established his Staff Headquarters in June, 1917.

At number 115 rue de Grenelle, at the right of the entrance, there is a marble tablet noting that in this ground (then a vacant waste) Adrienne Lecouvreur was buried in 1730. We shall see, in rue Visconti, another day, where she died, in the arms of her lover, the Marshal de Saxe. Being an actress, she could not be buried in consecrated ground nor with church rites; so she was brought here, in dead o' night, and buried with no ceremony but that of love and tears.

The church we see on our left is Sainte-Clotilde, a new edifice (as churches in Paris go) with a fashionable congregation. The spires are those we glimpse from the Place de la Concorde.

The Ministry of Posts and Telegraph, at number 103, has a court in which one of the telegraph instruments of Claude Chappe was set up. On the boulevard Saint-Germain, not far from here, is the monument to Chappe, showing him with his apparatus which was an optical telegraph or signal-system by means of which a message could be transmitted two hundred miles in fifteen minutes. But it took a lot of "manning," of relaying!

The Ministry of Commerce and Industry is next door, in a mansion built in 1700.

At number 97 the Duc de Saint-Simon, the brilliant but caustic chronicler of Court history under Louis XIV, the Regency, and Louis XV's early reign, edited his famous "Mémoires" for publication, and died — in 1755.

The Duc de Cossé-Brissac, last lover of du Barry, lived at number 118, where the Mairie of the Seventh Arrondissement is now.

Number 85 has been the mansion of the Ducs d'Avaray since 1718. Horace Walpole lived there when he was in Paris in 1767.

Number 79, built in 1709 for the Duchesse d'Estrées, was tenanted later by her nephew, the Duc de Biron, and by other famous persons including the Marquise de Tourzel, who had been the governess of the royal children (of Louis XVI and Marie Antoinette) and accompanied them in their flight to Varennes, and shared with them their early imprisonment. It was the Russian Embassy until Russia ceased to have ambassadors; and the Czar Nicholas II and Czarina were lodged there in 1896.

Number 73 is one of the entrances (the other is on rue de Varennes) of the Italian Embassy which used to be called the Hôtel de Galliffet. It has many memories, but the most interesting are those that relate to Talleyrand, the renegade Bishop of Autun, who proposed the confiscation of church properties. He was excommunicated and expatriated, but went back to France under the Directory; and, thanks to the influence of Madame de Staël (whose lover he seems to have been), Barras made him Minister of Foreign Affairs, in 1796, and he came here to this house to live and to direct his Ministry.

It seems to have been some time before this that he wrote to Barras about a beautiful East-Indian, twenty-five years old, who had had as an adventuress an extraordinary career which we must not attempt to detail here.

She was known as Madame Grand, and she had a husband — somewhere. She was arrested on some charge of conspiracy.

"She is," Talleyrand assured Barras, "the person in all Europe most incapable of meddling in any affair. She is an Indienne, very beautiful, very indolent, the most unoccupied woman I have ever seen. I beseech your interest in her behalf. . . . I love her."

Barras got the lovely lady out of jail. And when Talleyrand came here as Minister, he brought her with him. And here she stayed. Here, some years later, having effected "an arrangement" with M. Grand, she achieved a civil marriage with Talleyrand. This was a concession to the ambassadresses, who objected to paying their respects to a lady in her unsanctioned situation. But if some opinions were softened by the marriage, others were not. The old Duchesse de Talleyrand refused to recognize "that person" as her daughter-in-law; the Vatican was scandalized; and Napoleon was none too well pleased. He conceded the beauty of Madame, but he said she was a fool. The day after her marriage she was presented at the Court of the First Consul, who — with his usual directness of speech — told her that he hoped "the good conduct of the Citizeness Talleyrand would cause the 'lightness' of Madame Grand to be forgotten"; to which she replied that she "could not do better than to follow, in this regard, the example of Citizeness Bonaparte."

If she was a fool, she must have had a fool's temerity about speaking truth!

There are many piquant stories about her; but we must not linger. The marriage was unhappy — although the liaison seems to have been quite satisfying — and they separated in 1815. She died in 1835, and is buried in the Cemetery of Montparnasse.

At number 57–59 is the beautiful Fountain of the Four Seasons, reminiscent of one at Rome. Alfred de Musset lived at number 59 for sixteen years. From there he went to Italy with Georges Sand. Thither he returned, disillusioned.

Now let us turn down the boulevard Raspail. Perhaps you'd like to stop sight-seeing and go shopping at the Bon-Marché, two blocks down the boulevard.

If not, let's wander back along rue de Varennes, and look at number 57, a superb mansion built for the Marshal de Montmorency. Talleyrand was once owner of it. The Comte de Paris lived there in 1884. (He was Louis-Philippe's grandson — oldest son of Louis-Philippe's oldest son — and heir to the crown, if there was ever again to be one.) And in 1886, his daughter Amélie was here betrothed, with great ceremony, to the Duke of Braganza who became King of Portugal under the name of Don Carlos, and who was assassinated in 1908. On this betrothal occasion there was such a Royalist demonstration that it led to those laws being enacted which banished from France the older branches of families once regnant there. The Duchesse de Galliéra, widow of another grandson of Louis-Philippe, gave the mansion to the Emperor of Austria, and it became the Austro-Hungarian Embassy.

At number 61, Thérézia Cabarrus lived, when she had "ditched" poor Tallien and likewise Barras and the rich lover who succeeded him, and become the Princesse de Chimay.

At number 69, the Countess Duchâtel, widow of one of Louis-Philippe's ministers, held her very popular salon of the old régime, when the "upstart" Napoleon III was in his heyday.

Number 77 is the Hôtel Biron, where the Rodin Museum is installed. It is, apart from the collection which is the sculptor's superb gift to the nation, a place full of interest, of memories.

The very rich man for whom it was built had come, a young wig-dresser or barber's boy, to Paris when Louis XIV was king. He had a gift for "business," and his small affairs prospered. Then he led into trouble the daughter of a well-to-do man who obliged our young man to marry the girl. When John Law's "Mississippi Bubble" was dazzling France, this Abraham Peyrenc risked all he had, won an enormous fortune, and got out before the crash came. Then he ordered for himself a mansion which should surpass in elegance the most sumptuous abodes of great nobles or great financiers. In 1730 it was finished, and the gardens laid out; but two years later Peyrenc died, at the age of forty-six. His widow sold this property to the Duchesse du Maine, widow of Louis XIV's favorite son by Montespan. The Duchess died here in 1753. The next proprietor was the Marshal de Biron who lived here thirty-five years in the utmost magnificence. The gardens, in his day, were one of the sights of Paris, and he was very generous in admitting the public to them. His tulips alone were said to have cost more than two hundred thousand francs. He died here, aged eighty-eight, just before the Revolution, and left the property to his nephew the Duc de Lauzun, who went to the guillotine, as did his widow after him, and his aged aunt, the former mistress of this domain. In 1820 the property was sold to the Mesdames of the Sacred Heart who used it as a convent until 1907. The project of cutting it up in "lots" for sale aroused great indignation, stirred and kept alive largely through the efforts of M. André Hallays, of the "Journal des Débats," whose continued protests led the Government to buy it.

You may feel like going into the Rodin Museum to-day (if it isn't too near closing time), or you may prefer a glimpse of the garden where those who love Paris past have had so many reveries. It lies in the very shadow of the golden dome above Napoleon's ashes.

Let us take a fiacre, now, and direct the driver "à l'École Militaire — Champ-de-Mars — Tour Eiffel."

It may be the little Corsican that you will care most to think about as you drive past the Military School. I, for my part, seem to find him there with the utmost difficulty, or not at all. The dominant figure thereabouts, to me, is Foch the Teacher. He had been here as a student, too — called, in 1885, when he had been seven years a captain, to the Superior School of War for two years of intensive training and study. Ten years later he was made associate professor of military history, strategy, and applied tactics at this school for officers; and a year later advanced to head professorship and made a lieutenant-colonel. He was forty-five years old, and had been for a quarter of a century a student of the art of war. Now he was teaching it, and with it teaching great principles. What we owe to the skill and to the spirit he taught in this school is beyond all computation. It was here, as much as on the field of battle, that the war was won.

Between the Eiffel Tower and the river, let us stop a few moments for the view over toward the Trocadéro.

Perhaps you want to go home, now. If not, let us say to our driver, "Boulevard Montparnasse." This is a continuation of the boulevard des Invalides; and after we have followed it a very short distance, we shall come to the Gare Montparnasse, across from which is the big restaurant Lavenue where we like to dine. If the evening is warm, we may sit in the garden. The music here is always good, and the food likewise. After dinner, we like to stroll along the boulevard as far as boulevard Raspail, and then settle down for the evening at one of the popular cafés —

notably the Café du Dôme. It is hereabouts that one sees, nowadays, the outstanding figures of the Quarter — some students, but more men, and some young women, who have begun to *arrive*, who are already being pointed out and talked about.

VIII

YOUR EIGHTH PARIS DAY

IF this happens to be Wednesday or Saturday, and you would like to visit the manufactory of Gobelins tapestries, the expedition I propose should start betimes, as the Gobelins' is open only from one to three. If that visit (interesting as it is) seems of less moment to you than some other things, on your first stay in Paris, you might take the morning for shopping or for a visit to the Musée du Luxembourg, and give the afternoon to sauntering. Or, if you want to go to the races in the afternoon, you could take this stroll in the morning if — you will start about ten.

I shall try to plan so that you can fit it in with any other half-day you choose to link with it.

Since you may elect to combine it with the Luxembourg (which is a rational thing to do, because it is close by, and is indoors, whereas we shall be outdoors for the most part in our further sight-seeing), I'll say to you that you will find this museum infinitely easier to see than the Louvre. It is small. You doubtless know that at the Luxembourg the French Government exhibits its purchases from contemporary artists. Some years after an artist's death, his works in the Luxembourg are transferred, either to the Louvre or to the museums of other French cities. So there is constant change, here, not only in arrangement, but in content. Any picture or piece of sculpture I might especially urge you to seek out is liable to be displayed elsewhere before you read these lines. The thing to keep in mind in the Luxembourg is that these works of art represent what a government committee (invariably made up of the best, the soundest, and also of the most open-minded art authorities in the nation) has adjudged the best and most characteristic work of the most significant artists of the present generation.

After a morning at the Musée, you will easily find your way to Foyot's if you want a very fine lunch, or to Café Médicis, or to Café Harcourt (on the boul' Mich') if you wish to lunch less expensively.

In any case you are close to the Panthéon, where we will start our stroll.

The story of this hill on which the Panthéon stands goes back a long, long way — part of the way in history, and beyond that in legend. I'm not sure how far in retrospect you'll want to go. But I find that many of my American friends are glad to have their memory jogged a bit when they're looking at the superb mural paintings, and before they descend to the tombs.

Sainte Geneviève, in whose honor the church was built, is said to have entered upon the religious life when she was only seven, urged thereto by Saint Germain, Bishop of Auxerre, whose statue you see here. She was born in 422, and was a young woman just past thirty when she rallied the courage of the Parisians as Attila advanced. It was she who persuaded the father of Clovis to erect a tomb over the burial-place of Saint Denis, who had been martyred by the axe two hundred years before. She is very lovely and very *real* as well as very spirituelle, in the exquisite Puvis de Chavannes paintings here. The "Vow" which Clovis is taking in the James Blanc mural is that he made before the battle of Tolbiac wherein he was to meet the Romans for a decisive battle. Clotilde, the wife of Clovis, was a Christian; and her husband vowed that if he was victorious over the Romans, he would adopt her faith. He *was* victorious; he kept his word; and on Christmas

Day, 495, he and three thousand of his warriors, together with their wives and children, were baptized at Reims, by Bishop Remi (or Remigius) whose statue, also, is here. It is in consequence of this baptism of King Clovis, which made Christianity the religion of France, and of the sainte ampoule, believed to have been brought from heaven by a dove for his anointing, that the kings of France were crowned and anointed at Reims. Blanc has a picture of the baptism of Clovis, too. The coronation of Charlemagne, which another artist pictures, was at Saint Peter's, Rome, on Christmas Day, 800. Three hundred years before, Clovis — a Frankish chieftain — had beaten back the Roman legions and set up a sort of royal authority over a small section of what we now call France. Charlemagne's coronation, *in Rome*, was followed by the Pope's kneeling in homage before him who had just been proclaimed "Emperor of all the world." The two pictures suggest a great change in the position of France in Europe.

Next of the Panthéon paintings, in point of time illustrated, are those by Cabanel, of Saint Louis administering justice, founding the Sorbonne, etc. And last come the Jeanne d'Arc pictures, concerning which nobody needs any reminder.

When Mirabeau died, in April, 1791, the feeling was widespread that the man whose vision and counsel were worth most to France in her crisis, had been taken away. Just how much the majority of the people comprehended the wisdom of his policies, the worth of his influence, we cannot gauge. But they knew enough to feel grief-stricken when death threatened him; to hush all sounds about his house (at 42 Chaussée d'Antin) while he lay battling to live; and to declare, when he had lost his fight, that no place but the recently completed Church of Sainte-Geneviève was worthy to be his sepulchre.

FRANCIS I AND CHARLES V VISITING THE TOMB OF
SAINT DENIS
Painting in the Louvre

In consequence of this resolution, the church (already secularized) was constituted a Panthéon, consecrated to the great men of the country. And on April 4th, 400,000 persons followed Mirabeau's body thither, to the sound of martial music, by the light of funeral torches.

In July, Voltaire's body was brought from the abbey of Scellières in Champagne, where it had been hastily and secretly interred in 1778, for reburial in the Panthéon. The night of July 11th it lay in state on the site of the Bastille where Voltaire had twice been a prisoner; and the next morning at eight a great funeral car, drawn by twelve horses, started for the Panthéon. On it was a granite sarcophagus, bearing a recumbent statue of Voltaire, draped in purple and crowned with a diadem of gold stars.

The first stop was on the boulevards near the porte Saint-Martin, where hymns were sung. Then to the house of M. de Villette, where Voltaire had died. There it was awaited by fifty young girls in classic garb, by the actors of the Théâtre-Français wearing the costumes of their most famous rôles, and by children with baskets of blossoms which they were to strew before the chariot. But a drenching rain came down; and it was a dripping, sodden cortège when it got here.

Rousseau's body was brought from Ermenonville in October, 1794, and lay in state for a night in an "Isle of Poplars" constructed for the occasion in the great basin of the Tuileries Gardens. His interment ceremonies were less pompous than Voltaire's, but imposing.

Meanwhile, Mirabeau had been dislodged! When the papers hidden by Louis XVI in his famous iron safe (that he himself had made and secreted in a wall of the Tuileries) were examined, some of Mirabeau's counsels to the King were interpreted — in this violent year of '93 — as proving that Mirabeau had tried to save the King and kingdom;

and his bones were ordered from their honorable sepulture
to be replaced by those of Marat.

Accordingly, Mirabeau's remains were carried away to
the little Cemetery of Clamart where many victims of the
September massacres had been buried; and Marat —
dead more than two months — was hauled through the
crowded streets to the Panthéon where he lay for a few
months only — then was cast out, and thrown into the
"common grave" of the near-by Cemetery of Saint-
Étienne-du-Mont.

Even more interesting than Voltaire and Rousseau to the
average American visitor to the vaults beneath the Panthéon is the last resting-place of Victor Hugo, whose body,
in the poor-man's coffin that he had requested, lay all night
beneath the Arc de Triomphe before its interment here.
Zola's remains are here, also.

The Panthéon is very beautiful, very impressive; but I've
seen scores of burial-places I'd prefer to its vaults.

You may care to look in at the reading-room of the Bibliothèque Sainte-Geneviève, across the square; and to recall
that where this now stands there was once a college,
founded in 1314 by an archbishop of Reims, which counted
among its students men so diverse as Ignatius Loyola,
founder of the Jesuit Order; Erasmus, the great Dutch
thinker; and John Calvin, Protestant theologian — and all
of them within a generation's span!

The School of Law, next door, is part of the Sorbonne, or
University. This is rue Cujas that we're on — behind the
Law School. On the other side of the street is the Lycée
Louis-le-Grand, where Molière was educated, and Condorcet, Desmoulins, Robespierre, and many others who have
written their names variously on the scrolls of remembrance. And it may interest you (as it does *me!*) to know
that when Robespierre was a student here the old convent

of the Jacobins was still here — this street, and many another hereabouts, was cut through its property after the Revolution. The old monastery was founded in 1217. Thomas Aquinas had taught in it; and its church contained the tombs of innumerable royalties. The porte Saint-Jacques of Philippe-Auguste's wall was here, and it was through this gate that Charles VII entered with his troops in 1436.

That is the Sorbonne, across from Lycée Louis-le-Grand; but we are coming to that another day, and are headed in the opposite direction, now.

Straight down this street, behind the Panthéon, is the façade of Saint-Étienne-du-Mont, one of the most picturesque and most interesting churches in Paris. It was begun under Francis I and finished one hundred and seven years later under Louis XIII. Marguerite of Valois laid the first stone of the façade, in 1610. It was a sort of attendant upon the old basilica of Sainte-Geneviève (near where the Panthéon now is) which was then the repository of Sainte Geneviève's remains. They were in a gold reliquary made in the form of a church and covered with precious stones. During the Revolution this casket was sent to the Mint, and the remains (what was left of them after twelve and a half centuries) were burned in front of the Hôtel de Ville where malefactors were executed. Some of the ashes, and a part of the old sarcophagus, are said to be in the modern shrine, here in Saint-Étienne-du-Mont, around which so many white tapers are always flickering. I once saw a young father and mother and their six little children (the tiniest in its mother's arms) in reverence at this shrine. Every one had lighted a little taper before kneeling down — there was even one for the baby — and they made a picture worthy of Van Eyck or Memling. What they hoped — those of them who were old enough to hope anything —

Sainte Geneviève would do for them, I could not guess. But it was a lovely sight to see, and I am grateful for the memory of it.

The carved marble rood-loft, called a jubé, is one of the most beautiful pieces of ecclesiastical decoration anywhere, and more pictured by artists than any other detail of a church interior unless it be the rood-screen at Saint Mark's in Venice. Racine is buried in the crypt of this church, and so are Boileau and Pascal. We must be sure to go back into the chapter-house built in the old cloister, and to see the superb stained glass in some of the small windows there.

This is one of the churches of which I never tire; I welcome every occasion which takes me to it. One day not long ago I was coming out of it after a visit to it with some American friends, when a big sight-seeing car drew up at the curb. It was filled with compatriots of ours, and they had evidently seen several churches — *enough!* Only one of them all would get out of the car and venture in. She was in a hurry, and banged the swinging door behind her as she dashed in. A moment later she was out again, at our heels, shouting at a friend in the car. "Come on in, Em!" she cried encouragingly; "it's real *odd!*" But Em was not to be tempted. I dare say her "feet hurt."

The street that runs behind the Panthéon (to our left as we come out of Saint-Étienne-du-Mont) is rue Clotilde, named for the wife of Clovis. On the other side of it is Lycée Henri IV, and that square tower we see above the walls is part of the old Church of Sainte-Geneviève. It is of the twelfth century, but its foundations are older; and it was the first observatory at Paris.

In this old church (built by order of Clovis about 510, destroyed by the Norsemen in the ninth century, and rebuilt in the twelfth) Clovis and Clotilde were buried.

The Lycée Henri IV was opened, in part of the old con-

ventual buildings of Sainte-Geneviève, in 1800. Alfred de
Musset came here to school; so did Scribe, the dramatist;
Mérimée, the author of "Carmen"; Sainte-Beuve, the eminent critic; and Viollet-le-Duc, the very famous architect of
the Second Empire.

The street which runs south from the Panthéon is the rue
d'Ulm, at number 43 in which was Pasteur's first laboratory.

Crossing it, very near the Panthéon, is the rue de l'Estrapade. The house now numbered 3, built in 1681, but much
rebuilt, is the cradle of the French Encyclopædia, since
Diderot was living there when that great work was projected.

If you are a lover of Balzac you will certainly want to
turn down from the rue de l'Estrapade into rue Tournefort,
at number 24 in which is the house described as the Pension
Vauquer, the shabby dwelling of Père Goriot. Henry James
called this "one of the most portentous settings of the scene
in all the literature of fiction . . . there is a profound corre-
spondence between the background and the action." Balzac gave infinite pains to the selection of this place, and a
kind Providence has preserved it practically as he knew it.

At the end of the rue de l'Estrapade we come to the Place
de la Contrescarpe where the celebrated Café of the
Pomme-de-Pin used to be, frequented by Villon and Rabelais, by Ronsard and Jodelle, by Racine and Boileau and
La Fontaine.

If we take rue Rollin, a dozen steps to the north, we shall
see, at number 2, the site of the house wherein Pascal died;
at number 4, the actual house (built in 1623) where Bernar-
din de Saint-Pierre lived when he wrote "Paul and Vir-
ginia" (later, he was superintendent of the Jardin des
Plantes, near by, and lived there); at number 14, a house in
which lived Descartes, the first great philosopher to write in

French. At the end of the "block" (as we say) we shall come to the Arènes-de-Lutèce (Colosseum of Paris), or, rather, to what remains of it. This amphitheatre was probably built under Hadrian, and destroyed first by the barbarians and then by the early Christians — perhaps because of martyrdoms suffered there. There is not much to be seen here; indeed, the presence of these remains was not suspected until 1869. But you may be glad to know where the Roman Arena was.

Rue de Navarre turns the corner and goes south a few feet. Following it, we shall reach, in a minute, rue Lacépède, at number 4 in which was the entrance to the Augustines convent where Manon Roland was educated. A few doors away (number 11 to 15) was the Revolutionary prison of Sainte-Pélagie, where, in a noisy, ribald company, eluding the watchfulness of the keepers, that same Manon, waiting for the knife to fall and end her days, wrote her sparkling "Memoirs." (The manuscript is in the Bibliothèque Nationale — seven hundred pages of neat, firm writing.)

"So full and natural," says Miss Ida Tarbell in her "Madame Roland," "are these memoirs that they are really the most attractive material we have of the life of her class in the eighteenth century."

And so warm with gayety and tenderness, so scintillant with smiles and tears, that they endear her to us more than all her political fervors.

Joséphine de Beauharnais was in Sainte-Pélagie Prison too — before going to the Carmelites.

We'll follow rue Lacépède back to Place Contrescarpe, and then turn south on rue Mouffetard, one of the most picturesque streets in Old Paris, and little known by tourists.

We shall not, though, find ourselves alone in rue Mouffetard! And in this quaint setting of other days, it is impossible to linger long without being a spectator at one or more episodes of the Comédie-Humaine which has been abundant hereabouts for centuries.

It is said that dwellers in rue Mouffetard have no need to leave their street except to go adventuring. All they require for ordinary purposes is here.

If you like (as I do) to look at shops wherein you have no expectation of buying and therefore no responsibility of making a choice, you will enjoy sauntering on rue Mouffetard. It is the other end of the gamut from rue de la Paix; and some people care only to be dazzled. You will not be dazzled here. But if you are the sort of traveller who's interested to know how much poor folks are paying for food, and what kinds they're buying, and how they do their marketing, and what dry-goods cost them, you can learn a great deal in a street like rue Mouffetard without going inside a shop or asking a single question. It's all spread out for easy knowing.

Let us glance, to our left, along rue Saint-Médard, full of ancient houses, and to our right (farther on) down rue du Pot-de-Fer which neither our century nor its predecessor has invaded with an "improving" pick.

Where the Caserne (barracks) now is, occupied by the Garde Républicaine, there used to be a convent of the Misericordia into which Françoise Scarron withdrew for a time in her penniless early widowhood and while she was yet a great way off from being the wife of Louis XIV.

At number 99 is the entrance to the passage des Patriarches, beloved by etchers and all other lovers of the picturesque.

And presently we come to the Church of Saint-Médard, built in the twelfth century and rebuilt in the sixteenth. It was the first church in Paris restored to the old religion

after the Revolution. If you do not care about going in, I
shall not urge it. There used to be a cemetery here, too; and
one of the tombs in it was supposed to be miracle-working,
so that extraordinary scenes took place here, and the place
was closed by order of Louis XV — which caused a wag to
write on the gate: "By order of the King, God is forbidden
to work any more miracles in this place."

But what I care most to see here is an old man, seventy-
five years of age, sitting on the edge of a well and telling his
beads as he makes mute appeal for alms. Yes, he's here
now; he's always here; he will be here forever; Victor Hugo
has seen to that. You remember that when Jean Valjean
had brought Cosette to Paris and was living in the garret in
boulevard de l'Hôpital, he ventured forth only after dark
and then into quiet streets. He spoke to hardly any one;
but to this old beggar at Saint-Médard's he always gave a
trifle, and at times he accompanied it with a word or two.
One night, Jean went up to the crouching figure and placed
his usual charity in the old man's hand. "The beggar suddenly raised his eyes, looked fixedly at Jean Valjean, and
then let his head hang again. This movement was like a
flash, but Jean Valjean gave a start; he fancied that he had
seen, by the flickering light of the lamp, not the placid and
devout face of the old beadle, but a terrifying and familiar
face . . . an instinct urged Valjean not to utter a syllable."
It was Javert! the terrible police inspector. Valjean's presence in Paris was discovered; his lodging was soon located.
We are on the eve of that breath-taking flight of hunted
man and little nameless child through the streets of Paris
by night, in 1824. If you cannot re-read it all while you are
in Paris, try to go over at least a part of "Les Misérables,"
beginning at chapter ninety-five; see what it means to you
now!

As we cross rue Claude Bernard, glance down rue Broca

which is full of old and very curious houses and is one of the
most picturesque streets in Paris.

The avenue des Gobelins starts here. At the very beginning of it, close by Saint-Médard, a very ancient street
called rue Fer-à-Moulin leads us, in a dozen steps, to rue
Scipion, at number 13 in which is the bakery where all the
bread for Paris hospitals is made in what used to be a very
splendid palace in the best Florentine style.

Catherine de Médicis, although she was only fourteen
when she came to France as a bride, was always very loyal
to the Florentines; and among those of her native city who
flocked to Paris, sure of her favor, after Henry II died, was
one, Scipio Sardini, who was amiable, ingratiating, absolutely unscrupulous, and skilful at fishing in troubled waters. Scipio got himself a contract or commission to collect
the taxes on salt. He "discounted" these for the Crown;
and, not on what he held back from the Crown (we may be
sure), but on what he wrung from the wretched, he soon became scandalously rich. "Those," said a contemporary
writer, "who a short while ago were only little *sardines*,
have become enormous whales; and thus it is that France
fattens the little Italian fishes."

Then Scipio began to look about him for a wife who could
help him to some social prestige, and settled upon one of the
frailest of those frail beauties who formed the famous "flying squadron" of Catherine de Médicis and whose business
it was to intrigue the leading men of the Court and country,
learn their secrets and affiliations, and keep Catherine informed. Isabelle de Limeuil, of the house of the Counts of
Auvergne, was the one of these ladies that Scipio got. She
had been the mistress of Ronsard, the poet, of the Abbé
Brantôme, Court chronicler, of the Prince de Condé, and of
many more besides; and had grown more intent upon her
gallantries than upon her "secret service" to the Queen, to

the extent that Catherine not only dispensed with the lady Isabelle's attendance, but had her locked up where her indiscretions could compromise no one. Condé got her out, and Scipio married her. It is not exactly our idea of marrying for social prestige; but it seems to have been a perfectly good one in Scipio's day. His wealth covered the multitude of Isabelle's sins, and her taste, elegance, and "visiting list" gave his money some expression.

They built this beautiful palace, which in those days had splendid Italian gardens; they entertained magnificently; they bought the château of Chaumont on the Loire; Scipio became a State Councillor, a collector of rare editions, a cultivator of roses, and died an old, peaceful, and happy man, after Catherine and her four sons were long years in their graves, and Henry IV was almost in his. There is no "moral" to this story!

Scipio's great possessions passed on to one, Alexandre Sardini, born — the gossips of the day have told us — to Isabelle a week after her gorgeous wedding fêtes, but not related to Scipio in any way at all. And before Scipio had been many years in his grave, this mansion had become a place where beggars were shut up to keep them off the streets! Later additions to its "guests" were pauper women, girl-mothers and their babies, and other persons of the utmost wretchedness.

History is full of stories of the new-rich: of sudden fortunes and their dazzling display. Exceeding few of those fortunes have been enduring, have founded anything substantial. Their general tendency is gourd-like. A study of some of them would make an interesting book; and one that should have value for many generations, since every decade — almost — seems to bring on its own fresh crop of profiteers.

Scipio, the "sardine" who became a whale, is a fair type.

We cannot go into his old mansion without a special permission, and if we had one, we should not see much save a very efficient and extraordinarily clean bakery. But we can stand in the court and stare about us. Perhaps this doesn't interest you. If so, you have only to stay on the avenue des Gobelins, and omit this tiny détour of a stone's-throw distance.

It might be that now, instead of going to the Gobelins and thereabouts, your interest would lead you along the boulevard Arago, here on our right, and off to the catacombs (which you may enter if it is the first or third Saturday of the month, and if you have a permit) and the Lion of Belfort (by Bartholdi) and the Cemetery of Montparnasse where Bartholdi is buried, and Guy de Maupassant, and César Franck, and Sainte-Beuve; or down the avenue de Montsouris to the pretty park of Montsouris where — as I write — the municipality of Paris is planning to erect a new colony for students and struggling artists who find lodging and studios increasingly difficult to get in the old "Quarter." Or, if you are scientifically minded, you may want to visit the Observatory, just off boulevard Arago. The first Saturday of the month is the principal visiting day here (permission must, however, be obtained in advance), but certain parts can be seen at other times than that. The first and third Saturdays (1 to 4 P.M.) are the visiting days for the Pasteur Institute, which is over in this part of town, but about two miles almost due west of where we're now debating what you may do next.

This is the district of hospitals, asylums, clinics, and medical schools; and, in the part immediately south of us, of tanneries, dye-works, and similar industries, mostly situated along the banks of the Bièvre, a river whose pleasant meandering through this section made it a favorite location for suburban villas long ago.

The Gobelins, Jean and Philibert, who left their name to this quarter, came here, probably from Reims, early in the fifteenth century, and made their mark, and much money, not in tapestry-weaving, but in the manufacture of dyes — particularly a scarlet which only they knew how to make. Rabelais says that they made the Bièvre run red with their waste, so that it was called "the river of the Gobelins"; and under that name Ronsard sings of it in his odes and sonnets that Mary Stuart loved.

As makers of scarlet the Gobelins waxed so rich that in a generation or two their descendants were done with "trade," had purchased titles, and were trying to forget dyestuffs. Flemish weavers set up their looms here on these banks, and in time were succeeded by Frenchmen of the same craft. Early in the reign of Louis XIV the State bought the factory and directed Charles Le Brun, the most eminent artist of the day, to reorganize it for the manufacture of magnificent royal furnishings. Le Brun lived here for more than twenty years, and died here, in 1690 — succeeded by his great rival, Mignard.

Your guidebook is very explicit in the matter of the Gobelins; and I will not duplicate. The visit is a decidedly interesting one; but only a small proportion of tourists, I suppose, would feel that it was an essential or even important part of a first brief stay in Paris. If you go, do not neglect to step into the near-by court of an old mansion popularly associated with "la reine Blanche," the mother of Louis IX. Queens in early times wore white as widow's weeds, and in consequence queens-dowager were frequently called "blanche"; but it is probable that Queen Blanche, widow of the first Valois king, had a country house here, and died in it about 1398. It was razed soon after; but her name clung to the castle built on this spot a century later. Only, by that time people had forgotten which Queen Blanche it was who lived hereabouts, and went a hundred and fifty years or so too far back, to find her. This majestic residence was either built for or soon passed into the hands of a family allied with the later and richer Gobelins.

And under Louis XV the administrative offices of the Gobelins' manufactory were here. To-day it is a tannery. We find it in rue des Gobelins, off the avenue, number 17. And this short street terminates in one of the most picturesque corners of Old Paris, the ruelle des Gobelins, with its exquisite little hunting lodge built in 1735 for M. de Julienne, one of the dyers of this district, on whom Louis XV conferred a patent of nobility — which interests us much less than that Watteau was his friend and often came here.

Beside this pavilion is the entrance to the gardens of the Gobelins, wherein each worker cultivates his own "bit." This corner is certainly "one of the curiosities of Paris," as the Marquis de Rochegude says.

You may care, especially if you are a Napoleon enthusiast, to follow the avenue des Gobelins a little farther, to where it ends at the Place d'Italie. The barrière, or gate, by which the city was entered from Fontainebleau, was there; and through it Napoleon reëntered his capital, from Elbe, on the 20th of March, 1815 — the beginning of the Hundred Days before Waterloo.

If this does not attract you, let us walk through rue de Banquier, almost opposite the Gobelins', to the boulevard de l'Hôpital, where we shall find nothing to remind us of that gloomy abode in which Hugo put Valjean, Cosette, Marius, and the Thénardiers; but it is there for us, notwithstanding. It seems that there was once, at 50–52, just such a place as Hugo describes in such graphic detail. And it will always be there, of course! Anything else occupying, or seeming to occupy, that site is an impertinent intrusion.

To the real Hugo-lover I heartily commend starting here,
"Les Misérables" in hand, and, following Valjean and
Cosette as they dodged through the dark streets, pursued
by Javert — up into rue Mouffetard, skirting the passage
des Patriarches, on toward the pont d'Austerlitz, and over
among the timber-yards of the opposite bank, to the
Little Picpus.

To-day, we'll content ourselves with passing 50–52, and
crossing over to number 47 which is one of the entrances
(the main one) to the Hospice de la Salpêtrière, so called
because under Louis XIII there was an arsenal here, and a
gunpowder magazine. Under Louis XIV new buildings
were erected including a church, and the place was converted into an asylum for paupers and insane persons. In
1678 Louis XIV ordered a strong-house constructed here,
for the incarceration of "undisciplined or incorrigible
women or girls." It is thither that the Abbé Prévost brings
Manon Lescaut; and thence that she starts toward Havre,
on her shameful voyage of deportation to Louisiana.

The Lamotte woman who concocted the plot of the
diamond necklace that gave Marie Antoinette so much
trouble, was imprisoned here, and escaped hence to London. Théroigne de Méricourt, that fury of the Revolutionary mobs, died here, a raving maniac after twenty-five
years in a madhouse — which, as a penalty for violence,
makes the guillotine seem light indeed.

In the latter part of her stay here, Dr. Philippe Penel
was director of the institution, and had begun his memorable work as a pioneer in ameliorating the treatment of
the insane and studying the control and cure of nervous
disorders. Another great man long (thirty-three years)
associated with la Salpêtrière, is Charcot, who may be
called the father of suggestive therapy, and the founder
of a school of healing which is growing in extent and in

variety of application much faster than the old school of *materia medica.*

There are more than five thousand patients at la Salpêtrière. It is a city within a city. Visitors who ask at timely hours are usually permitted to see the Court of the Massacres (where, on that September Sunday in 1792, forty-five of the inmates were butchered — after one hundred and eighty-three prostitutes had been set at liberty), the old buildings of Louis XIV's time, the library and study of Dr. Charcot, etc.

Beside la Salpêtrière is the Jardin des Plantes — another world! And one of so many interests that, if you are a naturalist of any sort, in any degree, you may well decide to spend a good deal of your time there.

It has been beloved by Parisians of all classes for nigh on three centuries. They come here, as you see, at all ages, and for many purposes: to play and to study and to work and to make love and to sit and dream.

The garden has so many kinds of appeal that, not knowing you individually, I cannot guess in which of them I would best direct you.

But you are probably tired of walking. The ground you've covered since I met you is about two miles. You may care more to sit under the cedar of Lebanon and rest than to wander any farther.

The great wine-market is just across the way. You might like a glimpse at that, or at the port, on the quai, where the cargoes of wine coming by waterways to Paris are unloaded. Water transport is a great feature of France and one that visitors should be often aware of in their saunterings; so much that is picturesque and interesting is associated with this canal and river commerce which links the vineyards with the sea. Where the wine-market is, there was once the abbey of Saint-Victor, celebrated for its schools where Abélard, Thomas à Becket, Saint Bernard, and other eminent men were students.

You may want to get back to the shops, or to a smart tea place. You may feel like loitering about here until time to eat a rather early dinner at the Tour d'Argent, which is close by. I must warn you that this is a costly place. But it is one you ought not to miss, even if you have to eat several very economical meals elsewhere, to compensate your "budget."

I could loaf about here, deliciously, for hours. But you may feel that your Paris stay is too short to permit such lingering.

If the river steamers are running, the very pleasantest thing we could do, now, is to take one here at the pont d'Austerlitz, in front of the main entrance to the Jardin des Plantes; go by river all the way to Suresnes, and dine at Saint Cloud, at the Pavillon Bleu. There might be time, on a long day in summer, to drive in the lovely park of Saint Cloud before dining; or, there may be a fête going on in the park to which we can go after dinner.

IX

YOUR SECOND SUNDAY IN PARIS

IF you are the kind of Paris visitor who came in at five or six this Sunday morning, from the cabarets or dance halls, and will still be sleepy when you start for the races after a late breakfast, this chapter is not for you. But if you were that kind of "sight-seer," you wouldn't be cumbered with a book like this.

I'm taking for granted that, without being a "fan" for anything in particular, you are here to see *Paris*, and especially those things in it which will forever after make your reading, your play- and opera-going, your enjoyment of art, infinitely richer and more delightful.

On that presumption, I'm going to ask you to meet me, about ten or ten-thirty, at the east front of the Louvre — the rue de Rivoli corner.

We'll walk up the rue du Louvre to rue Adolphe-Jullien (third turning on the right, as they say in England); and a few steps to the east (right) we shall come to a circular building called the Bourse de Commerce, or Produce Exchange, with a cold-storage of great capacity below.

Much has happened here where this quite uninteresting building stands.

Long ago there was a turreted mansion here, close to the western wall of Philippe-Auguste, which belonged to the \seigneurs de Nesle, and they gave it to their King, Louis IX, who, in turn, bestowed it on his mother, Blanche of Castile, to whom he owed much that made him a good man and a great king. She died here, and left the property to her second son, Charles, King of Sicily. A later tenant was John, the blind King of Bohemia, who was killed fighting

for France at the battle of Crécy — where the Black
Prince took his crest and motto and passed them on to the
Princes of Wales ever since: three ostrich feathers, and
Ich dien (I serve).

The blind King of Bohemia was the grandfather of
Charles V of France; and another tenant of this place was
Charles V's second son, Louis, Duke of Orléans, the builder
of Pierrefonds and rebuilder of many other noble resi-
dences. We are going, presently, to see where Louis met
his death; and also to see where the instigator of his assassination hid after the deed was done.

Charles V had three brothers, the youngest of whom
was Duke of Burgundy and founder of that princely line
which soon became so powerful and so rich that there was
no sovereign in Europe able to compete with their magnificence; their pride, their vast possessions, their ambition,
made them outstanding figures in European history for
three generations.

The elder son of Charles V, who sat on the throne for
forty-two years, was a madman most of the time. His wife
was that Isabeau of Bavaria whose name is more execrated
than that of any other woman in French history. She was
the mother of Charles VII, whose kingdom she tried to bestow on the English; and of that pathetic child, Isabelle,
who went to England at the age of eight, as queen to
Richard II, and after his death was married to her cousin
Charles of Orléans, the poet-prince, who wrote an exquisite
lament for Isabelle when she died in childbed at Blois,
aged two-and-twenty; and (not to mention any more) of
Katharine, wife of King Henry V of England and mother
of Henry VI.

Isabeau was an almost complete summing-up of all the
vices except those which are "defects of quality"; and
among them was a guilty passion for her brother-in-law,

Louis, who lived here with his excellent and adoring Milanese wife and their children, including the future poet-prince who was to become the father of Louis XII.

Louis XII lived here before he acceded to the throne (and the wife) of his kinsman, Charles VIII. Then there were Magdalenes here for fourscore years, until Catherine de Médicis turned them out. It is said that one of the astrologers she was always consulting (and who certainly gave her a lot of very bad advice!) warned her to beware of the vicinity of Saint-Germain l'Auxerrois. And in consequence, she bought a great deal of property hereabouts, including a recently rebuilt mansion, and established herself here after the Massacre of Saint Bartholomew. Here she kept her star-gazers and soothsayers. Here, probably, she read the books and pamphlets decrying her, which were sold almost publicly and read as avidly by Catholic as by Protestant, and which caused her to "laugh till she could hardly hold herself," and to say "that if they had only given her notice before, she would have told them many other things of which they knew nothing."

All that is left of Catherine's palace is the fluted Doric column, one hundred feet high and ten feet in diameter, in which a staircase ascends to the roof where the Queen went with her astrologer to consult the stars.

The first street east of the circular rue de Viarmes which surrounds the Bourse de Commerce, is the rue Vauvilliers, a thirteenth-century street which until 1864 was called the rue Four-Saint-Honoré, evidently because there was a public bake-house or oven there. The east side of it was sacrificed, some years ago, to the new constructions for the markets, and recently the west side of the street has suffered, too. At number 33 there was a house which as lately as 1878 was still the Hôtel de Cherbourg, as it had been for a century or more before that.

One day in October, 1787, a shabby little soldier from Corsica came here to find a cheap lodging, and was given room number 9, on the third floor. He had been home on a furlough, and to get that furlough extended was one of his reasons for being here now; the other was to urge a claim of his mother's against the French Government. They were far from being reconciled yet — those very Italian Buonapartes — to the French purchase of Corsica. And this lad of eighteen, although he and his older brother had been educated by the bounty of the French, was bent upon two things: freeing his island from French rule, and in some way or other making money for his family so that the younger boys might be educated without thanks to France, and the girls might be provided with dowries. The prospect of providing much for the numerous Buonapartes seemed slim indeed on a petty officer's pay; and this boy (whose father had been dead two years) took very seriously his responsibilities as a "family man."

He had so little to spend that he stayed in his room much of the time, *writing a novel*, waiting for news of his affairs, and going out only to eat. His face, still stranger to the razor, was furrowed with premature wrinkles, and his clothes seemed to flap on his lean body. He ate, for six sous, in the passage des Petits-Pères, near the Place des Victoires; and sometimes at the Trois-Bornes in the rue de Valois. He seemed — they could remember, afterward — ashamed of his very small expenditure, and used to wrap his money in his "check" or bill, and carry it to the cashier without saying a word to any one.

The hotel-keeper was named Vedrine. "If," says Lenôtre, "Vedrine had, some time later, the curiosity to go and see his old tenant going to Notre-Dame where the Pope had been waiting for two hours to crown him Emperor, he would scarcely have been able to recognize in the Cæsar saluted by cannon, trumpets, and bells, the stripling with scraggly locks, the little grotesque of five-feet-three whom he had once upon a time lodged for four crowns a month."

This is not the time to see the markets. You should be here about six on a week-day morning, for that; but I cannot see that there is anything to compensate a tourist for the effort of getting here then — except the lovely, the ineffably lovely, light that mornings in Paris have. And if I got up to enjoy the light, the markets with their slaughtered animals, their muck of vegetable-strippings and fish-scales, is one of the last places I should choose to do it in.

It is more picturesque hereabouts between midnight and dawn, when the farmers who have driven in from the country are waiting for the markets to open. There are street-dances here, sometimes, which are strange sights to see, if one comes properly attended. And there are underworld cabarets — one, at least, in some deep-down cells tenanted by monks in days long gone — where the avowed enemies of law, order, and property meet and vaunt their ferocity.

The people of the markets (Les Halles, in French, and pronounced Lay Hal, with the "H" very lightly aspirated, almost eliminated) have always numbered a majority of the violent sort. The nature of their occupation seems to give them too much time for swapping opinions; followed by long periods of nerve-tension and exhausting toil which make them highly irritable, readily inflammable. Their bump of reverence is not merely non-existent; it is a positive concavity! I don't know how much it might take, nowadays, to get one's head stuck on a pike by the market crowd; but I am willing to live and die without trying to find out. I am not, you see, a dévotée of the markets.

Your guidebook gives you some facts and figures about the markets, but omits to tell you that they have occupied this space, or part of it, since the beginning of the twelfth century; and that, for instance, the fishmongers have never changed their location since Saint Louis allotted it to them, nearly seven centuries ago: Pavilion nine, the next to the easternmost in the north row.

Across the broad, modern rue de Rambuteau is the church of Saint-Eustache, next to Notre-Dame the largest in Paris. Let us go there for a bit, at least, of the High Mass. Joseph Bonnet is at the organ, and his choir is one of the finest to be heard. We have been walking, since I met you, only about a scant quarter of a mile. We should be in ample time for this service. (If you are a special lover of the organ, keep your eyes open for notices of recitals here by M. Bonnet; you may be fortunate enough to be in Paris when he is giving a series.)

Saint-Eustache, on the site of a twelfth-century chapel, was over a hundred years in building, and they were years of such sharp transitions in architecture that the great church is, more than most great churches, a medley of styles; and of styles that mingle badly. Some people admire the building greatly; others do not. Viollet-le-Duc, the eminent architect of the Second Empire, said it was "a confused mass of débris borrowed from everywhere, without relation and without harmony; a sort of Gothic skeleton clothed in Roman tatters sewed together like the pieces of a harlequin's suit."

It is imposing, in any case — majestic. One of the loveliest sights I ever saw was a procession, in the evening, winding its way through the dim aisles of this church — hundreds of flickering white tapers in hundreds of hands.

Richelieu was christened here, and Colbert was buried here. The body of the great finance minister (of whom Mazarin had said to the young King, Louis XIV, "Sire, I owe you everything; but I believe I am going to pay my debt by giving you Colbert") had to be brought here in the night, for fear of violence from the populace who hailed Louis for the glory of his conquests, but hated Colbert for the expense of them.

Colbert's tomb was preserved from the Revolutionary mobs which destroyed nearly everything else in the church, by removal to the convent on the other side of the river where the Beaux-Arts is now. We shall tell the story of that convent and the preservation of French monuments, in a later chapter.

Mirabeau's grand funeral took place from Saint-Eustache. You may imagine the demonstration of sorrow and regret made here at the time; and then think of the same populace, demanding, three years later, that his bones be taken out of the Panthéon and tossed into a common grave in the cemetery of Clamart over beside the house of Scipio Sardini.

This was the populace which, when the Feast of Reason was substituted for the Christian faith, turned Saint-Eustache (where the new cult was inaugurated) into a hall of drunken debauchery, resounding with the ribald laughter of persons who hailed the maudlin intoxication of little children as an evidence of "liberty, equality, and fraternity."

When we leave Saint-Eustache, let us take a few steps to the west, back to the rue du Louvre that we came up, and walk a short block to northeast on rue Jean-Jacques-Rousseau.

Here, at the corner where rue de Louvre meets rue Coquillière, there used to be the mansion in which Henry IV's mother, the Queen of Navarre, died. Later, it was occupied by the Duc de Bellegarde who had been Henry IV's rival for the affections of Gabrielle d'Estrées. Henry was very jealous of Bellegarde, and everybody knew it. So when, one day, Bellegarde was in Gabrielle's apartment and the King came in unexpectedly, the Duke thought to save a great deal of trouble for all concerned by a quick disappearance. There being no way out but the way the King was coming in, Bellegarde scrambled under the bed. Henry either saw "the last of him" sliding under, or suspected that he was there. So he stayed on and on, enjoying Gabrielle's uneasiness and the elegant Duke's discomfort. The King asked for supper, and ordered it served there. Partridges were brought, and their odor was appetizing. M. le Duc must be hungry, as well as cramped! So the King threw a partridge under the bed, saying, "Everybody has to live!"

It is a trifling episode of gallantry, but the deeper you go into Henry's history and the study of all that made him a great king because he was so much a *man*, the more this partridge tossed to a rival recurs to you as typical of him who fed the Parisians while he was besieging them!

Later, Bellegarde was told to keep away from Court while he was unmarried. So he "very quickly" got him a wife, and settled down here as a model husband.

The mansion was rebuilt in 1615 for the Chancellor Seguier, who welcomed the new French Academy there for its sittings.

A little farther on we come to the Post Office, on the site of a house in which La Fontaine died.

Now, a few feet to eastward, on rue Étienne Marcel, and up rue Montorgueil, for a long time the great oyster market of Paris, and now the place par excellence to eat snails, at l'Escargot, number 38. (Try sole there, if you don't like snails.) If you want a hearty luncheon we can come back here a little later. If you breakfasted late and with American additions, you may not want another "real meal" till dinner.

Do you, by any chance, remember Henry Irving in "The

Lyons Mail"? In it he had one of his great "parts" — or, rather, *two;* for he played both the guilty man, Dubosc, murderer of the courier and robber of the strong-box, and Lesurque, the innocent man condemned to death for a crime of which he knew nothing, but of which even his old father believed him guilty. The play, by Charles Reade, was founded on a French drama of an actual crime committed in 1796. We shall see, on another day, where the coaches of the Lyons Mail had their Paris terminus. Lesurque lived here, at number 38, where the Escargot is.

At numbers 64 to 72 is the most picturesque old inn-yard that is left anywhere in this modern world, to my knowledge. It is called the Compas d'Or, or Golden Compass, and dates from the beginning of the sixteenth century. Mr. E. V. Lucas says that his first pilgrimage, on each arrival in Paris, is to see if this place is still uninvaded by modernity.

The entrance to it is through an archway; and, once inside, we have accomplished a miracle — we have gone back four hundred years. At any moment a dust-covered courier may dash in, fling himself from his foam-flecked horse, and tell us that King Francis had been made prisoner at the battle of Pavia and carried off to Madrid; or a wild-eyed citizen, the first to get here from the tilt at the Tournelles, may shout that King Henry's head had been thrust through by Montgoméry's lance just at the tourney's close.

It is hard to come out; but we must.

And to go hence, where all is as it was, to the Cour des Miracles, where nothing is as it was, would be so hard that I shall not ask you to do it. Although, if your recollection of that old haunt of beggars, thieves, and worse, as Hugo describes it in "Notre-Dame de Paris," makes you want to see where it was located, we can gratify you by a very short walk on to the rue Réaumur. The Cour des Miracles — so called because the professionally halt, lame, and blind became "miraculously" whole when they returned there to enjoy what their simulated sufferings had wrung from the pitiful — was at number 100.

If you are not curious about that, we will leave rue Montorgueil where it ends, at rue Saint-Sauveur, and walk through this ancient and ancient-looking street to rue Dussoubs (one short "block"), turning back south on the latter. At number 21 in this street, Goldoni, "the Italian Molière," whose statue is at the east end of Île de la Cité, back of Notre-Dâme, died in great poverty, in 1793.

Now we cross rue Marie-Stuart, whose early name was a coarse one that shocked the young Scots Queen; and in her honor it was renamed. The celebrated Italian comedian known as Scaramouche lived in this street in 1691. He died, three years later, in rue Tiquetonne to which we are now coming. In this latter street, Dumas gives D'Artagnan lodging at "La Chevrette" — not in "The Three Musketeers," but in "Twenty Years After" — where now is the Hôtel Picardie. A step or two farther, and we are at the Tour de Bourgogne, which is number 20 rue Étienne-Marcel.

This tower, built in 1405, is all that is left of the Paris residence of the Dukes of Burgundy, which covered all the ground between a space south of this street and rue Tiquetonne, and between rue Montorgueil and rue Saint-Denis. (If you will look at your map, you will realize what an extent that was for a vassal of the Crown to occupy with his "town house." But the Dukes of Burgundy had at least a dozen splendid palaces, all the way from Dijon to Bruges. And they owned another in Paris, too! — the old mansion of the Counts of Flanders, where the Post Office now is.)

When this tower was built, the Duke of Burgundy was contending with his cousin, the Duke of Orléans, for the mastery of France. The King (Charles VI) was a madman, shut up in his Saint-Paul palace, neglected to the degree that he was not even kept clean or his surroundings kept decent. The Queen had installed herself in the Hôtel Barbette (to which we shall come, presently) where she was living in debauchery, plundering the royal treasury for her vices and concerning herself about nothing so little as about her unfortunate husband and their seven children.

Burgundy's desire to control the affairs of his unhappy country was not pure patriotism and benevolence, of course; but he really had good reason to believe that other profit than his own would result if he could rid France of the abominable Isabeau and her paramour, Orléans. Burgundy, for instance, wanted to retake Calais from the English, and Orléans refused to sanction it. Burgundy had married his heir to Michelle, one of the mad King's little girls, and his daughter to Louis the Dauphin, and these children of Burgundy were at the Saint-Paul Palace with the children of France. Then, one day, the King's mind cleared, briefly, and he resumed authority. When Isabeau heard this, she and Louis fled toward Milan, leaving orders for the children to be brought there too. Burgundy went after the children (his own were taken, too) and took them back to Paris, and the King made him their guardian — for he knew that his lucidity was a mere interval, and that the shadows would engulf him soon again. They did! And Isabeau and Orléans came back, to resume their old behavior. Things went from bad to worse. The people kneeling in the churches prayed: "Jesus in Heaven, send some one to deliver us from Orléans."

On the night of November 23, 1407, Orléans was at supper with the Queen when a messenger came to him, begging his immediate attendance upon the King, in the Saint-Paul Palace.

Orléans left his sister-in-law, and started for Saint-Paul. He was set upon and murdered by Burgundy's minions — Burgundy, 'tis said, looking on from a dark door-way.

Then the master of this tower came home to it, and climbed to this upper chamber wherein we may stand retelling his story, if you do not mind climbing many a winding stair. (For permission, ask the concierge of the school, at the right.)

At first, he denied connection with the crime; then he confessed it, and fled Paris. But the Court called him back. Nobody but the personal adherents of the Orléans family was sorry about the murder; and almost everybody preferred Burgundy — whatever his designs might be — to Isabeau; so he was reinstated in all his former privileges, and absolved from the crime.

This palace saw much more history, but we can't recapitulate it here. The feud between Burgundy's descendants and the descendants of Orléans reached to the third and fourth generation, and far beyond. Orléans's great-grandson was Francis I; and the vast possessions of Burgundy were united with those of Austria and of Spain in Emperor Charles V, who was the direct heir of this Duke John the Fearless that we've been talking about. Francis and Charles were forever fighting and making terms; and as a result of one of their treaties, Charles relinquished all the Burgundian possessions in France, including — of course — this mansion which had been unoccupied for a long time and was in a sad state of decay. The large parcel of ground was cut up into lots and sold. But, if anybody bought the tower and the buildings about it, the Crown must somehow have got them back again; for Louis XIII traded them to some monks for a part of their land near the Place des Vosges. And the monks set up a soup-kitchen for the poor, in the tower of John the Fearless. It was a Père Vincent who was in charge of this benevolence and so many others that

he was canonized, and is revered throughout the Christian
world as Saint Vincent de Paul.

The plot on the southwest corner of the Burgundy estate
was bought by a band of players, and became the cradle of
the French Theatre and, subsequently, of French Opera.
(For the tablet recalling this, we must cross the rue Étienne-
Marcel to number 29, on the side opposite the tower.)

These players had had earlier quarters near by — at the
northeast corner of rue Saint-Denis and rue Greneta. There
they had been installed for a hundred and forty years, in
the hall of a "hospital" whose *hospitality* was not for the
sick, but for the travellers who arrived at the city gate after
curfew and couldn't be admitted until morning. That north
gate (in Philippe-Auguste's wall) was where number 135
rue Saint-Denis is now. The shelter for the belated was
where number 142 is. So the first plays given by Paris persons who made a business of acting were given just outside
the walls.

There they had their stage constructed in three levels,
the highest representing heaven, with God enthroned; the
middle one, earth; and the lowest, hell — in the form of a
dragon's mouth.

The plays presented were called Mysteries, and the players were called the Brethren of the Passion of our Lord,
Jesus Christ. It was the same sort of performance which
previously had been given, on occasions, by the churches.
The only difference was that these Brethren were not re-
cruited from the congregation to perform now and then;
they made a business of acting, and gave regular performances, for pay.

They prospered; and when the Burgundy property was
put up for sale, they were able to buy a parcel of it for their
exclusive purposes—so that, for the first time in the history
of Paris, there was a group of "professionals" chartered by

the Government and owning their own theatre. There they had a large but low hall, which accommodated a very deep stage and about two thousand spectators. The "Standing Room Only" sign might have been hung out at every performance; for there were no seats, except in the boxes.

Now, here is something for the Little Theatre folk of to-day to take fresh courage from! The development of the modern theatre did not have its birth in the big hall, with the huge stage, among the professional players. It started with the "amateurs," on the outside!

One company of these was made up from law clerks in the Palais de Justice, who gave their plays in the great hall of the palace that is now called the Salle des Pas-Perdus. (Hugo has given us a vivid description of their performances, in "Notre-Dame de Paris.") They called their dramas Moralities, and they left heaven and hell alone and stuck to this plane that we know more about; dealing with life as they saw it; hitting at abuses, vices, and absurdities.

People preferred this to Mysteries. The more it made them laugh, the more they preferred it. In the Mysteries, no one was funny but Satan. In the Moralities, many characters were funny. It was inevitable that some of the "progressives" who played with the law clerks and "got a lot of laughs" (in the parlance of the stage, to-day) should withdraw from Moralities and form a new company to play Follies. And the Follies were most popular of all.

The Brethren of the Passion took note of all this. And of course they tried to profit by the other fellows' success, just like theatrical managers to-day; nearly every one of whom hastens to put on any sort of show similar to one out of which some enterprising (or merely lucky) fellow has made a "hit." But they wouldn't abandon their type of play. What they did was what a Broadway manager in this year of grace would call "jazz it up a bit." They tried to make heaven and hell as funny as the Follies. And people were shocked.

They had been in their new theatre only four years when they were ordered to abandon Mysteries and confine themselves to secular subjects. But they, who had horrified Paris with their unseemly jocularities on sacred subjects, didn't "believe in" secular plays! That is, they wouldn't play them; but they would rent their theatre to the Care-free Children who played the Follies of 1548! Which they did. And then the Brethren, while continuing to draw rent from the Follies, gave up their time and energies to denouncing the stage and arraying the Church against it! In a little while, acting — child of the Church — was a proscribed calling when the Church had lost control of it; and those who professed it were denied Holy Communion or Christian burial.

But the Moralities and the Follies both "wore thin." With all of life to draw from, they seemed not to know how to keep themselves abreast of the times. Perhaps it was asking too much of anybody to make entertainment out of the times of Catherine de Médicis. At any rate, it was in her day that business, for the Care-free Children, was so bad they shut up shop; and the Brethren rented their hall to a travelling company.

After some ten years, differences of opinion developed in this company, and it split — the conservatives staying, and the progressives leaving to form that *Marais* company whose competition with the older house did much to stimulate French drama. Corneille's "Mélite," his first play and the first comedy written about decent, well-bred people, was produced here in 1629. Racine's "Alexander the Great" and "Andromache" in 1665 and 1667.

The Opéra-Comique used the hall of Hôtel Burgundy

(or Bourgogne) until 1783; but not a vestige of it is left, now.

Let us walk east to rue Saint-Denis along which (the story goes) Saint Denis went after his execution, with his severed head in his hand, to the place where he wished to be buried. (You see him thus in sculptures on façades of old churches.) The street was laid out, they say, in his foot-prints on that journey; it isn't very straight, but Haw-thorne thought it was as well done as one could reasonably expect in the circumstances. Saint-Denis's street is one of the oldest in Paris; and in the Middle Ages it was the long-est, richest, and most beautiful street in the city. There were four different gates in it, in the four successive walls; the last of them still standing, on the boulevard Saint-Denis.

Down this street came, always, the monarchs of France making their "joyous entry" into Paris after their corona-tion at Reims. Up this street went such of them as died in Paris, to be buried at Saint-Denis.

Here on our left is the Church of Saint-Lou-Saint-Gilles, an old abbey church of the early fourteenth century. Near it, many centuries ago, there used to be a street shrine to the Virgin whose image therein a soldier struck with his knife. According to the l gend, the image bled profusely. The sacrilegious soldier was tortured and executed; and for more than three hundred years, down almost to the Revo-lution, there was kept, to preserve the memory of this, a three-day fête during which a manikin representing the im-pious soldier was paraded through the streets and finally burned, here, in the midst of an illumination and a display of fireworks. A picture of the crime and its expiation is in the first chapel of the old church, on the south aisle.

In the eighteenth century there used to be seen here "a curious *ex-voto* representing Louis XV, at the age of six,

PROCLAMATION OF THE CONSTITUTION IN THE PLACE DU MARCHÉ DES INNOCENTS,
SEPTEMBER 14, 1791

kneeling before Saint Lou and asking to be cured of fear —
that fear which later became such extreme timidity that
every strange face made the king suffer."

Isn't that an unexpected "angle" on Louis XV?

On we go until we reach the Square des Innocents on
part of the ground where the ancient cemetery of the Innocents used to be. Interments were made there during seven
centuries, to the aggregate of 1,200,000 bodies, till the earth
was so full of decay that a body consigned to it was said to
be consumed in nine days. The poor were buried in caves
containing about 1500 bodies each, into which they were
carried down a ladder. In 1780, the odors arising from the
place were so dreadful that it was cleared away, and the
millions of bones removed to the Catacombs. La Fontaine
was buried here on April 14, 1695. What are believed to be
his remains are now at Père-Lachaise. Some writers say
that Madame Pompadour was buried here; others maintain that she was buried in the Capucines church, rue
Saint-Honoré.

By order of Philippe-Auguste, the cemetery (ancient
then) was walled, surrounded by cloisters, decorated with
frescoes of La Danse Macabre, or Dance of Death; and in
the walls were several of those "living tombs" wherein misguided persons immured themselves to wait for death.

The Church of the Holy Innocents was built in 1150 and
stood till 1790, alongside rue Saint-Denis and over to that
part of the present square where the fountain is. The cemetery stretched away, to the north, over a good part of the
ground now occupied by the markets. The old market,
called the Market of the Innocents, was a string of booths
along the outer side of the north cloister.

The lovely fountain of Pierre Lescot and Jean Goujón
was not designed to stand out in an open space as it does; it
was originally on the south side of the church. If you will

try to imagine it without that disastrous "cupola," and without the steps or base, you will the more readily understand its reputation for great beauty. I have read a story to the effect that it was Henry II's delight in this fountain which caused him to commission Lescot and Goujon for the Louvre. But they had already done their incomparable "wing" there for Henry's father, when this fountain was executed.

I was here, once, with my brother, who had never seen the fountain, when a workingman in his smock joined us to point out the beauties of Lescot's design and Goujon's decorations. The water was not running, and he was distressed. We ought to see it with the water running. If we would wait a minute, he would find the man whose responsibility it is to turn the water off and on. He did; and came back, beaming, to enjoy our increased appreciation.

"Things like that never happen to *me* in Paris!" people often say, when I mention some incident of this sort. To which I can reply only that they "happen to me" by scores; that the byways of Paris are, for me, full of memories of kindlinesses from the people who were my hosts. Perhaps my love of their beautiful things is more evident than some others'. Perhaps I am a less formidable looking person than they — look more obviously "folksy." I don't know. All I know is that in my experience it seems that there are few persons here who, seeing that I love their Paris, show any unwillingness to love *me*.

Over here on the south side of the Square, we'll pass beneath one of those arches into the rue de la Ferronnerie which has kept its name since the days of Saint Louis when it was a street of ironmongers. It was very narrow, and Henry II gave orders for its widening — but nothing was done.

Up and down this street and some neighboring streets,

the Bell-Ringer of the Dead used to go, wearing a black tunic painted in skulls and cross-bones, ringing an enormous bell, and in a sepulchral voice calling out: "Wake, sleeping people! Pray for the dead!"

The great interest attaching to the rue de la Ferronnerie, however, is that here, on Friday, the 14th of May, 1610, Henry IV was assassinated.

He was on the eve of leaving Paris for a campaign against Austria. Dissatisfied with the limited authority she was to have in his absence, Marie de Médicis demanded to be crowned. She had been married ten years, had brought the King six children, and yet had never worn the crown of France. Henry quite frankly detested her; she had neither beauty nor intelligence, she was cold but violent. He had married her because she was the Pope's niece, and because she had the largest *dot* of the epoch. But they quarrelled incessantly. Henry wanted to exile her, but Sully (his great minister of finance) thought it would be politically imprudent. She knew Henry's desire — and she demanded to be crowned. He demurred, saying it had been predicted that he would be killed after a grand ceremony. She insisted; and the ceremony took place at Saint-Denis on May 13th.

In January there had come to Paris one, François Ravaillac, who had been a novice at the Feuillants Convent in Paris, then had gone back to his native place, Angoulême, to teach school. He came up to Paris to try to persuade the King to revoke the Edict of Nantes which granted freedom of religious worship. But his appearance was so forbidding that he was repulsed, everywhere. So he returned home. In April, he was back; and it began to be noised about in Paris that "the murderer of the King" had come.

He had tried to find lodging at an inn, near where the Théâtre-Français is now; but Paris was crowded — the inn was full. As he came out, he saw (in a cutler's shop, I suppose) a huge knife shaped like a bayonet, with a very sharp point, and a stag-horn handle. Of this he possessed himself; and he carried it about with him for nigh on three weeks. Every morning he took up his station outside the Louvre, watching for his chance. Every evening he returned to his lodging in the humble hostelry of the Three Pigeons, across from where the portal of Saint-Roch's now is.

At length, discouraged, he started to go home, and had got as far on the way as Étampes, where he chanced in some way to break off about an inch of his knife-blade; and being, when it happened, in front of the wayside crucifix outside Étampes, he got the idea that there was some mandatory significance between the two — as a result of which he went back to Paris, resolved to stay till the deed was done.

On Friday morning, May 14th, he was outside the Louvre again.

That day, the Duc de Vendôme, Henry's son by Gabrielle, told his father that an astrologer, La Brosse, had predicted this day would be fatal to the King.

"La Brosse," answered the King, "is an old trickster who wants your money, and you are a young fool to believe him. Our days are counted by God."

Nevertheless, he was troubled — restless. It was hot. At four o'clock he decided to go to Sully; he always took his troubles to Sully. The minister was ill, at the Arsenal. So Henry ordered an open carriage, and set out. With him was the Duc d'Épernon (in whose arms Henry III had died, of an assassin's thrust), the Marshal Laverdin, and three other gentlemen. Ravaillac saw them go, and followed.

When the little cortège reached this narrow and much-encumbered street, the footmen took to the cloisters of the cemetery, to leave more room for the carriage, and went on to meet it at the rue Saint-Denis.

In this street were two carts, taking up so much of the

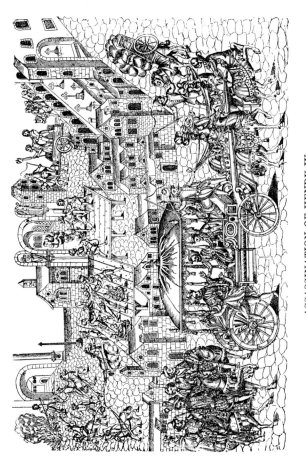

ASSASSINATION OF HENRY IV

Hand-bill sold in the streets of Paris representing the murder of the king and the
punishment of Ravaillac

scant space that the King's carriage had to squeeze close
to the shops to pass them.   This was Ravaillac's opportunity.   The carriage stopped, whilst some one rolled the carts
away.   And in the wait Ravaillac jumped up on the wheel
and drove his long knife into Henry's heart.   Then, without
trying to flee, or even to throw away his knife, the assassin
stood, awaiting the fate he knew would be his.   The by-
standers would have killed him then and there but for the
intervention of the gentlemen-in-attendance.   Henry died
in Épernon's arms; but the curtains of the royal carriage
were closed, the people were told that the King was only
wounded, and the way to the Louvre was retraced.   Con-
sternation — terror! — reigned there when it was known
the King was dead.   They laid him in the Salle des Caryatides, where his wedding to Marguerite had been celebrated,
just before Saint Bartholomew's bloody Eve; and the palace was barricaded.   No one believed that Ravaillac was an
irresponsible fanatic, driven to desperation by a rumor that
the King was going to make war upon the Pope.   Everybody believed him the tool of a party thus preparing to
seize the power.   *Which* party?

We can't go into that, here.   The probability is that Ravaillac was nobody's "tool," but the victim of delusions
that bigotry breeds.

He was tried — not to fix his guilt, for that was indisputable — but to discover his accomplices; and hideously tortured, not so much to avenge his deed as to wring accusations from him.   All to no avail.   Ravaillac was executed on
the Place de Grève, in front of the Hôtel de Ville, and his
body was quartered and burned.

The house numbered 11 of rue de la Ferronnerie was
built under Louis XIV on the site of the one before which
his grandfather was assassinated.

Madame du Barry, when she was Jeanne Vaubernier,

worked in the rue Ferronnerie as errand-girl for a dress-maker whose establishment had furnished Louis XV with another fascinator: Mademoiselle Morphise.

Back to rue Saint-Denis, now; and down it for a very short distance to the rue des Lombards, where the pawn-brokers used to abound and the Italian money-lenders. Boccaccio is said to have been born here.

Now, across boulevard de Sébastopol, and up rue Saint-Martin. But on our way to it, through rue des Lombards, glance up rue Quincampoix, one of the most ancient streets in Paris, where, for more than five centuries, the Mercers, or silk merchants, had their headquarters. During the speculation frenzy of John Law, in 1718, his bank was here, and this quaint old street was called "The Mississippi."

On rue Saint-Martin, at the end of rue des Lombards, is the Church of Saint-Merri, beloved by etchers. The stained glass in the choir is well worth going to see; and the crypt is interesting. But if you feel disinclined to go in, just now, you shall not be urged. There is much to delight even the passer-by.

This street was, as I have elsewhere reminded you, the great Roman highway to the northern provinces. Like rue Saint-Denis, it had four successive gates as the walls moved out; the first one was here where Saint-Merri is.

Let us see rue du Cloître-Saint-Merri, along the north side of the church, and glance up rue Taillepain and rue Brisemisch, two of the quaintest, most picturesque bits of old Paris.

When we have returned to rue Saint-Martin, we must glance to the left, on that street, into the Impasse Saint-Fiacre, where — long, long ago — there was a house be-longing to a man who owned some coaches for hire, and who gave publicity (after the advertising fashion of his day) to his business by hanging out as a sign a picture of "Saint"

Fiacre. There was probably some local humor in this; for Fiacre was no saint at all — he was a liveryman! He had carriages to let, and his place of business was near where the Palais-Royal is now. His name has clung to horse-cabs in France ever since.

A few steps farther on, the street we cross is named Saint-Merri east of us, and Aubrey-le-Boucher to west. Both are picturesque, and sinister; they seem to have been designed as backgrounds for blood-curdling stories of the sort that make us afraid to turn out the light and go to sleep. These are scenes such as Eugène Sue describes in "The Mysteries of Paris." (And when that engrossing "thriller" was running serially in the "Journal des Débats" it was impossible to print enough papers to meet the demand; so copies were *rented* for ten cents the half-hour!) This passage Jarbach marks the spot where, in the early days of Louis XIV, a rich banker named Jarbach had his mansion. He was a great collector of fine pictures, and when he died his pictures were bought by Colbert and became the nucleus of the Louvre Museum.

The rue de Venise, to which we now come, looks more like a fissure in a blackened rock than like a thoroughfare. More perfectly, perhaps, than any street still existing, it helps us to re-create the Paris that Villon the Vagabond knew.

At the corner of rue de Venise and rue Quincampoix is a low drinking-place which used to be the cabaret of the Wooden Sword, frequented by Racine and his literary friends.

My Paris friends incline to be appalled when I report my saunterings in these places. I can only say that I have been here many, many times, and have never met with anything to make me the least afraid. Before the war, this quarter was reputed to be the hiding-place of the most terrible "Apaches." Perhaps it was one of their chiefs who, when first I went to locate the Wooden Sword, helped me most courteously to find it. I did not, before accepting his kindness, demand his history. If you are fearful of squalid streets, you need not venture off rue Saint-Martin, which is still a highway.

Where this broad, modern rue Rambuteau that we're crossing now is, there used to be, in the thirteenth century, the Street of the Jugglers.

In the passage Molière, on our left, was the theatre in which Rachel made her début.

The north wall of Philippe-Auguste's city crossed rue Saint-Martin between Impasse de Clairvaux and rue Grenier-Saint-Lazare; the porte Saint-Martin was here, for a long time. This rue Aux Ours, on our left, dates back to 1300, so it must have hugged the wall of Philippe. You are probably saying to yourself: "What is it that I ought to remember about the rue Aux Ours? Why does it sound familiar to me? Ah! *Porthos!* It was here he came to Madame Coquenard's, and ate her stingy dinner and flattered her until she made her husband's strong-box yield him the money for that equipment wherewith he kept up before his three companions his fiction about the duchess who adored him."

In the rue de Montmorency, on our right, the mansion of the great Montmorencys stood for more than four centuries.

Now we have come to the Church of Saint-Nicholas-des-Champs, which is beautiful, and interesting because part of it is Gothic of the time of Charles VI and part of it is Renaissance of the time of Henry III.

Opposite the church is one of the principal entrances to the Paris sewers, the trip through which may be made on the second and fourth Wednesdays of each month. It is interesting and in no way offensive.

On the other side of rue Réaumur is the Conservatoire

TRIAL OF MARIE ANTOINETTE BEFORE THE REVOLUTIONARY TRIBUNAL

des Arts et Métiers, occupying part of the ground of the old abbey of Saint-Martin-in-the-Fields. The abbey was outside the city, so it had need to be surrounded by high walls, crenellated and flanked with eighteen defence towers. A fragment of this wall and one of the towers, the Tour Vertbois — constructed in 1140 — are to be seen at the corner of rue Saint-Martin and rue Vertbois, just north of the Conservatoire. It was saved from demolition in 1877 by the ringing protests of Victor Hugo and other lovers of old Paris. The refectory of the monks was built by the same inspired architect to whose genius we owe Sainte-Chapelle — Pierre de Montereau — and is a gem too little seen by visitors to Paris. Even if the Museum does not interest you, the refectory, now used as a library, surely must. The old abbey church is an exhibition hall.

We have now walked a good two miles. It is probably past noon. You may be hungry. The boulevards are close at hand. If you are very hungry, let's go to Maire's, 14 boulevard Saint-Denis — which is quarter of a mile east. If you want a lighter lunch, come into Café Prévost, across the way from Marguery, and celebrated for its chocolate and brioche.

After luncheon, we can take a cab, if you're tired, and merely *halt* at the Square du Temple on our way to the Archives Nationales. There is nothing to be seen, where the great stronghold of the Templars stood, but a pretty green square. I'm sure you'll want to see it, though; and for those of you who are interested (as, I find, most people are) in the royal captives of the Temple, I'll try to give you some idea of what it was like in their day. You can read this while you wait for your lunch, and make only a brief halt at the site of the Temple as you drive down the rue du Temple from the Place de la République.

The Knights Templars were installed at Paris about 1148,

after the Second Crusade, and were given a domain of many hundred acres well beyond the city walls. This they fortified so strongly that it was a securer place than any within Philippe-Auguste's bulwarks. The great square donjon was erected about 1300. The domain was so rich and so formidable that the King coveted its treasure and feared its strength; so he suppressed the order, helped himself to its possessions, and gave its property to the Knights of Malta, who usually had, for their Grand Prior, one of the bastards of the royal family. The enclosure was a sanctuary, subject only to the Prior's justice; and he was lenient to other people's debtors and assailants, so that there grew up about him, in his palace, a large colony of persons who durst not venture outside, and also a considerable number who chose the enclosure as a residence because there they paid no Paris taxes and enjoyed protection and many other advantages.

If you will take your guidebook map of this vicinity and draw a line from the top of rue du Temple to rue de Bretagne, and from the latter, up rue de Picardie and inside rue Béranger, you will have (roughly) the extent of the Temple enclosure in the seventeenth and eighteenth centuries; previous to that, it stretched farther to south and to northward. There was a high crenellated wall all about it, flanked with towers. The sole entrance to the vast enclosure was on the rue du Temple side, opposite rue des Fontaines; it was a mediæval-looking gateway, between two big towers.

The palace of the Grand Prior was at the southwest corner, and the present Square covers the site of its garden. The great donjon was where the rue des Archives now runs between the Square and the Mairie of the Third Arrondissement; it was square, very high, and had a small round tower at each corner. In one of these was a winding stair;

THE TOWER OF THE TEMPLE
From a print of the Revolutionary period

the others contained small rooms, one on each floor, opening out of the big apartment of the centre tower.

When the royal family was brought here on the evening of August 13, 1792, nothing was in readiness for them. The King supposed that they were to be lodged in the Prior's palace, which he knew to be elegant in its appointments. But they were permitted to remain in the palace, which was untenanted, only a few hours, and then were taken to a small tower near the great one, and there kept until the donjon could be made ready for them.

This "making ready" consisted in removing all near-by buildings, enclosing the space thus created about the tower with a thick wall some twenty feet high; covering every window in the tower with a chute-shaped thing which permitted light to enter only from an angle of about forty-five degrees, and nothing to be seen from within except a strip of sky; dividing the space on the second and third floors into four small rooms of thirteen by fourteen feet. The second floor was prepared for the King, who was moved into it on September 30th, and remained there till his death; the Dauphin shared his father's room. On the floor above were the Queen, her daughter, and her sister-in-law.

Perhaps these are details enough for you; although, when I go into more and more intimate detail in lectures, I find that people are universally fascinated by it, as I myself am. Two phases of the royal captivity seem especially appealing: Louis XVII and the mystery of his fate; and the personal narratives left by many of the guards and keepers, showing the change in their attitude when brought into close contact with the prisoners.

This chapter is so long that I dare not let myself go on the subject of the Temple, except a little bit about the Dauphin.

To-morrow we shall go to the shabby little cemetery of

Sainte-Marguerite, where Louis XVII is supposed to be buried — and quite certainly is *not*. In all human probability the child was smuggled out of his prison by the Simons, in a hamper of their dirty clothes. What became of him *then* is a mystery. But what is very well established is that the little boy who died in the tower of the Temple in June, 1795, was NOT the son of Louis XVI and Marie Antoinette. Nor was the little fellow so ill-treated as he has been represented. Simon tried to make a "good republican" out of him, and Simon's ideas of "liberty, equality, and fraternity" were about what one might expect of a shoemaker who had never been able to live by his trade, and whose wife was a charwoman. Far more privileged persons than they are obsessed by the idea that democracy is a process of reducing everybody to the lowest level, instead of raising the many to a higher.

The Simons had led, previous to July, 1793, only the most precarious and wretched existence. As guardians of the little King they were paid ten thousand francs a year and provided with an excellent — to them, a luxurious — living. At the end of six months they gave it all up and retired into poverty and obscurity, for no reason discoverable if not for the reason that they were bent upon snatching the child they had come to love from all possibility of harm.

It is not probable that any one would have harmed him — as they understood "harm." He was worth too much as a gage wherewith to negotiate with foreign powers. But the Simons could not comprehend that; so they snatched him away. All the stories of the child in the Temple being "walled up" date from the time in January, 1794, when those successors of the Simons (who had signed a receipt for the person of the "little Capet") found that the child in custody was a deaf-mute. To permit this news to get out would be fatal to many things. Nobody must be allowed near the substituted child. And this led to all the wild talk of his being immured (for eighteen months!) and left to die. As if a delicate child of eight could *live* thus, for a year and a half!

After "slowing up" here, and turning the corner of the Square, let us drive down rue des Archives to the Archives Nationales, which are open to visitors on Sunday afternoons.

There is *every* reason for coming here: beauty for the eye to feast on, memories for the mind to revel in — thousands upon thousands of Yesterdays linked with To-day.

"Whom do you salute?" an old man was asked who, passing the Archives, took off his hat reverently.

"I salute," he answered, "those who are no more and who have made us what we are!"

This thoroughly characteristic French anecdote is told us by Jules Claretie, for many years the eminent director of the Théâtre-Français.

"Do you wish," M. Claretie says, "to know this nation which has fought so much for others, torn herself, exhausted herself, so many times appeared near her end, and always 'come back' more ardent and more proud than ever before? Do you want to know the past of this country of devotion to great causes and beautiful follies? Do you want to know what France is? Look! She is here!"

He quotes Michelet's ardent lines speaking of his visits to the Museum of French monuments (now dispersed, but then where the Beaux-Arts now is) and telling how he began to feel history as a *living* thing. If tombs could make a man feel thus, M. Claretie goes on, what ought we not to feel in the presence of such memorials as are collected in these Archives? "It is not the dead whom we meet here," he says, "but their very souls, their book of life, still burning with their strifes, their tears, their blood." "If," he says, "you feel the need of refortifying yourself with the truth; of asking the past to counsel the present; if you burn with desire to demand of death the secret of life, come here. I know no other place more strengthening to thought. The mind rises and expands, here; the heart takes to itself new courage. One learns to look crime, treason, success, in the face and to depise them. One measures all the glories and all the failures. One comes out more consecrated than ever to sacrifice and justice, more impregnated with love of country."

It is a union, a fusion, an evolution of many historic mansions which is now known as the Hôtel des Archives. This ground belonged to the Templars, and part of it was given to Olivier de Clisson, the famous Constable of Charles VI. (And, by the way, we have curiously corrupted that old French word, *constable*, or count of the stables; it was always a warrior of distinction who was made the count of the king's stables; and in course of time, after having led the army, the constables got to command it.) This magnificently picturesque old doorway at number 58 rue des Archives, with its Gothic arch and its pepper-pot turrets, is as the doughty old Constable de Clisson left it, at the end of the fourteenth century. It had many interesting tenants, even before it was bought, in 1553, by the Guises, along with several other mansions adjoining, and became the cradle of the League, or ultra-Catholic party. When Mary Stuart was a young girl, she must have come here often to visit her uncles the Cardinal of Lorraine and the Duke of Guise — her mother's brothers — whose "court" was hardly second to that of the Valois at the Tournelles or the Louvre.

In 1697 the great mansion which the Guises had constructed here on their collected properties was bought from the widow of the last duke, by Madame de Soubise, then

LOUIS XVII
The Dauphin

very much in favor with Louis XIV who seems to have paid for the palace and also to have furnished the funds wherewith Madame's husband (whom he made a prince) spent years in embellishing it until it became one of the most sumptuous that Paris has ever known.

To attempt even the scantiest summary of documents that may be seen here would be to embark on a task that would weary you. But, to mention a few, there are the volumes of that pathetically "dry" journal which poor Louis XVI kept in the midst of such tremendous events; his last will and testament, and that tear-stained letter of Marie Antoinette's which Robespierre had hidden in his bed. Here is Charlotte Corday's letter begging, "Forgive me, my dear papa, for having disposed of my life without your permission." Here are the papers relating to that affair of the Carnation, at the Conciergerie. Here is a letter of Manon Roland's written from the Abbaye prison, protesting against the illegality of her arrest. Here are the documents of Jeanne d'Arc's trial, and the report of her death. Here is Mary Stuart's marriage certificate, and a letter of Coligny's written on a shirt and so smuggled into Rouen where Montmorency was then besieged. And so on, and on, and on — including many documents in Napoleon's handwriting.

The tables at which persons sit in the public hall, to study documents brought out at their request, are those at which the terrible Revolutionary Tribunal sat. In another room is a study table belonging to Louis XVI at the Tuileries and removed to the rooms of the Committee of Public Safety, whereon Robespierre was laid, bleeding from his broken jaw after he was brought back from the Hôtel de Ville and before he was taken to the Conciergerie.

As we come east along the rue des Francs-Bourgeois,

which is the south front of the Archives, glance in — if you care to — at the Mont-de-Piété, or national pawn-shop, at number 55–57.

At rue Vieille-du-Temple, turn down as far as number 47. It was here (and not in front of 38 rue des Francs-Bourgeois, where an erroneous inscription used to be) that the Duke of Orléans was murdered by Burgundy's minions, on November 23, 1407. In the present house on this site, Beaumarchais wrote the "Mariage de Figaro."

Then, back again, to number 74 on the same street, north of rue des Francs-Bourgeois. This is the Hôtel de Strasbourg or de Rohan — so called because four of the Rohan were Bishops of Strasbourg. They were of the Soubise family, and had their garden in common with that of the mansion behind, now the Archives. If you have this house in mind, and two others that I shall indicate, shortly, they will serve to vivify the story of the diamond necklace when we recall it at Versailles.

Farther up the rue Vieille-du Temple, number 90 is the site of the Marais Theatre, that offshoot of the Hôtel de Bourgogne of which we spoke. It came here, to a tennis court, in 1635; and here the first performances of Corneille's "Le Cid" took place, at the end of 1636.

If you are interested in famous French salons you will want to look, as you return toward rue des Francs-Bourgeois, at number 22 rue des Quatre-Fils, where Madame du Deffand held her intellectual court for many years, and was found still charming by Horace Walpole when she was seventy-three and had been blind for a decade.

At the northeast corner of rues des Francs-Bourgeois and Vieille-du-Temple is the charming little tourelle of the Hôtel Barbette where Isabeau lived and, later, Diane de Poitiers. It is said that Diane was looking out of this window when Francis I had his first glimpse of her. The opera, "Rigoletto," is based on Victor Hugo's drama, "Le Roi s'Amuse," which is a story of Francis and Diane. It loses much, to my thinking, in being recast as an Italian story.

Number 31 rue des Francs-Bourgeois is the Hôtel d'Albret. Françoise Scarron lived there or visited there; and this is the place where Madame de Montespan (so they say) persuaded the widow Scarron to become governess for the semi-royal children.

On, past the Carnavalet (you may like to go in, for a half-hour or so) to the rue de Turenne. Number 66–70 is where the great Marshal Turenne lived, who sleeps at Des Invalides. Number 56 is where Paul Scarron died, and where — in the last six years of his life — he was visited by half the notables of his day. There he sat, year in and year out, chained to his paralytic's chair, nothing nimble about him but his wit and his tongue; and the young girl who was his Platonic wife was learning much that was to serve her when, a quarter of a century later, she became the wife of Louis XIV. From this house that young wife sallied forth into the streets to gaze at the royal cortège when the King brought home his Spanish cousin-bride; and back hither she came, saying how happy Marie-Thérèse should be, with such a husband.

At number 10 rue Saint-Gilles lived the Countess de Lamotte, of the diamond necklace plot.

A little farther along in rue de Turenne we come to the rue Saint-Claude, at number 1 in which was the apartment of Cagliostro, the Sicilian necromancer — also implicated in the Necklace scandal — to which many persons of the greatest wealth, the highest fashion, the utmost beauty, trooped in quest of "magic."

It must now be well on toward four o'clock. If the afternoon is fine, a restful and delightful way to finish it would be at the concert in the Tuileries Gardens; or having tea in the Bois de Boulogne — at Pré-Catélan, or Dauphine, or l'Ermitage, or Pavillon de la Cascade.

If you dine in town, you might like the Franco-Italian restaurant on avenue Matignon, in the house wherein Heine died. This is tremendously popular on Sundays, and there are many "types" to watch. The food is good, and the prices are not high. Avenue Matignon runs north from the Rond Point des Champs-Élysées. Des Gauffres, at the corner of Matignon and the Rond Point, is excellent, too.

X

YOUR TENTH PARIS DAY

MONDAY would be a good day for this programme, unless you are bent upon getting into the Château de Vincennes, for which you have provided yourself with a permit issued by the Military Governor of Paris at the Invalides, and valid for Sunday or Thursday. In that case, you would "do" this section of Paris on one of those days.

I recommend taking the Métro (as near to ten o'clock as you can make it) and riding to the Place Martin-Nadaud, from which it is a short walk to the north entrance of Père-Lachaise, the great city of the dead which holds the remains of more illustrious persons than any other place of sepulture except Westminster Abbey. Louis XIV's Jesuit confessor, Père Lachaise, owned a suburban estate here, the King's gift to him; and his name is the one popularly given to the vast cemetery which was opened here in 1804 under the official appellation of the Eastern Cemetery. It is a most fatiguing spot to visit, unless one is willing to confine himself to a very few of the innumerable tombs.

As you come in through the north gate (and please don't hop off too soon, at the Père-Lachaise station of the Métro, which would give you a long walk through a section of the cemetery you will least care to see), you will find facing you avenue Transversale number 2. Follow it a very short way, to avenue des Thuyas; turn to your right and go to avenue Transversale number 1, after crossing which avenue des Thuyas calls itself Chemin-Casimir-Delavigne, for the poet and dramatist who is buried here. Charles Nodier, lover of Paris, librarian at the Arsenal, cultivator of modern romanticism, friend of Hugo, Dumas, Lamartine, Musset, etc., lies here; and Delacroix, the eminent painter; and Barye, the great sculptor of animals; and Michelet, the historian. But the grave we have come especially to see is Balzac's.

It was on August 21, 1850, that Hugo, Dumas, Sainte-Beuve, and Baroche bore Balzac's body here where he had so often sat as a dreaming boy, gazing down on Paris.

"When we reached the grave, which is on the brow of the hill," Hugo wrote, "the crowd was immense. While I was speaking, the sun went down. All Paris lay before me afar off in the splendid mists of the sinking light, the glow of which appeared to fall into the grave at my feet as the dull noise of the earth upon the coffin interrupted my last words: 'No; it is not the Unknown to him. No, I have said it before, and I shall never weary of saying it — no, it is not darkness to him, it is light. It is not the end, but the beginning; not nothingness, but eternity. . . . Such coffins proclaim immortality.'"

If you follow avenue Transversale number 1 for a considerable distance, you will come to a section (25) where the bones of Molière and La Fontaine may or may not be lying beneath those stones which Balzac said "told all and set the passer-by to dreaming"; and where Daudet is buried; and Parmentier, who persuaded the French to eat potatoes when bread was too dear; and Champollion, who found the Rosetta Stone and the key to Egypt's inscriptions; and Pradier, the sculptor; and Corot and Daubigny, beloved painters.

Take the chemin du Bassin to avenue de la Chapelle; follow that a few feet to avenue Saint-Morys, turn to your left and walk to the Monument to the Dead, by Barthol-omé, facing down avenue Principale toward the main entrance to the cemetery. Be sure to see this beautiful and impressive monument. Then take the chemin Denon, named for the Egyptologist and director of museums under Napoleon I, who also is commemorated in the Pavillon Denon by which we enter the Louvre Museum; he lies here, not far from Chopin. (As you entered this path you passed near the grave of Talma, the great tragedian.) Keep on to avenue Casimir-Perier, cross it, and you will see the Gothic canopy under which the bones of Abélard and Héloïse may or may not be lying, but of which their memory makes a shrine excelled in popularity by few love shrines anywhere. Each generation which stands in sentimental reverie before the monument to these illustrious and tragic lovers would probably treat living lovers of their sort no more gently than the twelfth century treated these. This tomb seems to me to be well worth visiting if for no other reason than to demand of ourselves how tender and "comprehending" we could probably bring ourselves to be if Abélard were a living professor of great eminence at, say, the Institut-Catholique, who broke his monastic vows to wed the loved and loving girl he had made a mother.

In the Jewish Cemetery here is the elegant Rothschild chapel and the tomb of Rachel, the great actress.

Following rue du Repos, which describes a right angle, you will find yourself, in a few moments, at the Porte Principale, or Main Entrance. There are many graves and monuments of interest to which I have not directed you, because I know how very, very tired one can get in Père-Lachaise. It is a great pity not to see at all a place about which one reads so much. But to attempt to see all of it is to make one's self too weary to care for anything else that day.

At the entrance, take a cab (preferably a fiacre) and show the cocher, if you can't *tell* him, these directions:

Rue de la Roquette — arrêtez-vous devant la prison; rue

de Charonne 161; Sainte-Marguerite; rue du Faubourg-Saint-Antoine à la Place de la Nation; Cimetière de Picpus; Bois de Vincennes, au bord du lac de Saint-Mandé.

Rue de la Roquette runs into the main entrance of Père-Lachaise.

In about a minute you will pass, on your right, the prison for young offenders — boys under sixteen — similar in purpose but not in method to what we call a reform school. The boys detained here are not known by name even to the keepers. They never come in contact with one another. Each boy is taught a trade, but taught it privately, in his cell. He leaves his solitude for exercise, for chapel, and to visit in the parlor with his relatives; but has no contact with his fellows, no chance to teach or to be taught "tricks," no need to become known as one who has been "in trouble," nor to know others as such. So much solitude for a growing boy may be deplorable; but is it half as bad as what we subject our young offenders to?

Across the street, on your left, is the site of the old prison of La Grande Roquette in front of which, from 1853 to 1899, the public execution of criminals used to take place, very early in the morning, before crowds which had been gathering since midnight for the gruesome spectacle. The five stones on which the guillotine was set may still be seen in the pavement. (In the crooks' argot of an earlier day this prison was called the Abbey of the Five Stones.)

Number 161 rue de Charonne is about five minutes' "jog" south of La Roquette. This building, and the one adjoining (163), which had belonged to the Marquis de Chabanais, had a strange history during the Terror. Number 161 was what in Paris is known as a Maison de Santé (what we would call a private hospital or sanitarium or nursing home) kept by a Dr. Belhomme, who was a friend of Robespierre.

GÉRÔME'S PORTRAIT OF RACHEL

When the prisons — in spite of the busy guillotine — were crowded to suffocation, Dr. Belhomme opened his sanitarium as a "boarding home" for prisoners who could afford to pay him a very fancy price. It was quite generally understood that, in addition to all the comforts and most of the luxuries, his "boarders" were assured of immunity from the Revolutionary Tribunal and the guillotine; Robespierre saw to that for his friend. So, to increase his asylum, Belhomme rented the mansion and great gardens of the erstwhile Marquis de Chabannais; and his list of "guests" was very distinguished. Once in a while, one of them grumbled at the cost. Two duchesses left — and perished on the scaffold a few days later. Belhomme said they were "victims of a misplaced economy."

One day there came to this refuge the widow of Philippe-Égalité, Duke of Orléans. The former mistress of the Palais-Royal who was the richest heiress in France had led a sorry life with her profligate husband, but she supported with calm and uncomplaining courage the indignities he heaped on her, and probably was the most surprised of women when she found that a Revolutionary prison was, for her, not the gateway to release and eternity, but the nursery of her great Romance.

Shortly after her entrance upon the scene at Dr. Belhomme's, there came, from the Carmelite prison on rue Vaugirard, a man from Toulon, Rouzet, who had been a professor of law there, had been elected a deputy to the National Convention, and had suffered many cruel disillusionments in his brief career as a "minority member." He refused to vote for the King's death, protested against the arrest of the Girondists, and otherwise made himself so unpopular with the powers that he was put behind bars and slated for the scaffold. But somehow or other he managed to get himself transferred to Belhomme's refuge; and there he quite promptly fell deeply in love with the recently widowed Duchess of Orléans, who loved him devotedly in return. The whole of their romance of six-and-twenty years' duration is too much to be detailed here. He went into exile with her, never left her, was her faithful, adored, and adoring friend until he died, in 1820, and was buried by her in the magnificent mausoleum she erected at Dreux for the Orléans family, and of which the provincial lawyer who had come to Paris to support republicanism was the first tenant, followed by many sons and daughters of royalty. In the crypt of that bizarre monument, the Duchess had ordered two exactly similar sarcophagi of white marble. In one of these she had Rouzet laid; and into the other she herself hastened soon afterwards. Her son, Louis-Philippe, removed his mother's remains to the upper part of the church he built around her mausoleum, and left Rouzet in the crypt, alone.

This little-known royal romance is one of the few pages of Revolutionary history which record long years of quiet happiness growing out of the terrors and anguish of that great upheaval; and I thought you'd like to drive past here and recall it.

Now you go in a westerly direction along rue de Charonne, and when you pass number 98 you may like to know that there, in 1655, died Cyrano de Bergerac, whom Rostand made more alive than ever Cyrano made himself. He was converted in the chapel of a Dominican convent, here, of which his aunt was prioress, died and was buried there. Three streets past the boulevard Voltaire, you come to rue Saint-Bernard, at number 36 in which is the little Church of Sainte-Marguerite which was built in 1624 as chapel of a convent, and became a parish church in 1712. Girardon, the eminent sculptor, is buried behind the high altar; and the relics of Saint Ovide which gave rise to the great pirgrimage and fair held in the Place Vendôme, and then in the Place de la Concorde, are now here.

The cemetery, adjoining, was the official burial-place for the quarter of the Temple (a mile and a half away), and that was why the child who died in the Temple in July, 1795, was brought here for interment in the common grave or "lot." It was near ten o'clock at night when the body was brought, and very secretly laid away. Twice it has been disinterred for examination — in 1846 and 1894 — when the skeleton was found to be that of a boy over five feet in height and evidently about sixteen years of age.

When you leave Sainte-Marguerite's, you will go down rue Faidherbe to rue Faubourg-Saint-Antoine; and as you turn east in the latter street, look at number 210, where Santerre, the brewer, lived and carried on his business. It was here that the assailants of the Bastille drank so deep, without charge, that it is not to be wondered at that they made Santerre the commanding general of their section. Two of the prisoners released from the Bastille were brought hither. Three years later, he led his battalion and his unenlisted neighbors in the attack on the Tuileries. And, soon after, he was made Commander-in-Chief of the National Guard and warder of the King and royal family. He conducted Louis to trial, notified him of the death sentence passed on him, and was in charge of his execution. In history he is generally charged with having ordered the drums to beat so that the King's last words should be inaudible.

From Santerre's house (the brewery was behind it) to the Place de la Nation is a very short distance. This big, round open space, an ancient cross-roads, near Paris, on the immemorial route from the east, was for a hundred and thirty years called the Place du Trône, because of a throne which was temporarily erected there in 1660 when Louis XIV and his Spanish bride celebrated the Peace of the Pyrenees.

During the Revolution it was called the Place du Trône-Renversé (throne-overturned), and for a time, June 15th to July 27th, in 1794, the guillotine did its work here, when, in forty-nine days, thirteen hundred and seven persons perished, fifty-four of them in one day — June 17th.

The Gingerbread Fair held here every year for three weeks after Easter, is one of many similar events of which there is nearly always one in progress somewhere in or about Paris. No visitor to Paris should fail to spend at least a couple of hours loitering about one of these fairs. My favorite time for doing it is around six to seven-thirty, when the fascinating folk who "follow fairs" for their living are enjoying a little leisure and attending to the business of supper. Family life as it is lived in the gaudy wagons of snake-charmers, sword-swallowers, deep-sea divers, carrousel-keepers, freak photographers, vendors of varied "chances," etc., is intensely interesting as one gets glimpses of it in the "slack" hours.

From the Place de la Nation it is, again, but a very short distance to the Cemetery of Picpus where General Pershing, at Lafayette's tomb, said, on July 4, 1917: "Lafayette, we are here!" For the sake of that soldier-man of ours who expressed himself and us so perfectly in those words, if not for all the other compelling reasons, I hope that no American tourist to Paris will fail to visit this little cemetery at 35 rue de Picpus.

Victor Hugo has told us a great deal about the Convent of the Perpetual Adoration, in whose garden this hastily created cemetery lies. He learned the details he gives us largely from Juliette Drouet, who was long a boarder-pupil there, as he made Cosette. It was over this garden wall that Valjean and Cosette escaped from Javert and found Fauchelevent, the old man who so handsomely paid Valjean the debt of gratitude he owed him. You will remember how Jean was smuggled out of here in the coffin of the nun, and taken hence to the Cemetery of Vaugirard to be all but buried alive.

At nightfall, on each of those forty-nine days at the end of the Reign of Terror, a wagon filled with severed heads and bodies came from the Place de la Nation to this lonely spot where two men stripped the headless corpses of their bloody clothing and threw the mortal remains of hundreds of France's noblest and best men and women into a great ditch which they never covered — so sure were they that on the next night it must needs yawn again.

André Chenier, the exquisite young poet whose life and death are more poignant even than his poems, was one of those thus interred, on July 20th.

For eight years no one knew where those hundreds of victims had been buried. Then, in 1802, the Marquise de Montagu-Noailles, returned from her place of emigration, sought the grave of her mother, the Duchess d'Ayen, executed on July 22, 1794. No one could tell her where it was, until she learned (by chance) that a poor working-girl named Mademoiselle Paris had followed the tumbril carrying her father to execution, and had waited in the vicinity of the reeking scaffold until she saw where the bodies were taken. Every Sunday she had gone to pray on the spot, which she gladly indicated to other mourners when she realized how many there were who desired to mingle their tears with hers. Madame de Noailles bought the ground occupied by the common trench or grave; and, when it became known that here slept the victims of the Terror's last butcheries, many of the very illustrious noble families of France sought and obtained permission to have sepulture near by their martyred relatives. It is among these latter that Lafayette, married to a daughter of the Noailles, lies, the Stars and Stripes fluttering always above his dust.

Every day, in the convent chapel, the nuns of the Perpetual Adoration say a service in memory of those who lie in the Martyrs' Field at the back of their trim garden. And once a year, in the springtime, when the early flowers and the fruit trees are in bloom, there is a solemn service here attended by the families of the Martyrs, in mourning, who wend their way from the chapel to the little enclosure where poplars wave and cypresses stand perpetual guard over the bones of princes and poets, duchesses and simple folk, like the father of Mademoiselle Paris.

I haven't said anything in the itinerary for the cocher about rue de Charenton. Fearful, always, of overcrowding, I did not include this "background" of Cartouche, the notorious bandit of two hundred years ago. But if you are interested in such histories (many people are, I find; and a boon sort they are, too, for fellow-pilgrims to Canterbury or elsewhere — keen, catholic creatures, as alert for a lively thief-chase as for a Gothic portal), you may want to pull your cocher's coat-tails, as he leaves the Picpus, and show him *this:*

Rue de Charenton, 306 — enfin, Bois de Vincennes.

This will take you hardly at all out of your way; and as Cartouche figures not a little in literature (having, with other bandits, engaged the serious attention of M. Funck-Brentano, historian of the Man With the Iron Mask; and also, if my memory be not confused, of the last Henry Irving, Sir Henry's son, who made a study of famous criminals), this slight détour will give you another touch of intimacy to enhance your delight in reading, when you've gone back to your delicious, fireside evenings at home.

Cartouche was a gamin of the Marais quarter, in the last years of Louis XIV. When he was twelve, he ran away with some gypsies whom he met at a fair, and they taught him the tricks of thievery. When he fell ill at Rouen, the gypsies abandoned him, and presently he was back in Paris, where he soon became the leader of a devoted band. He was a gay little fellow, of the sort usually called "the life and soul of the party," and seems to have had a very good time — while it lasted. Both his braggadocio and his sense of humor were tickled by the state of terror that not only Paris but all of France was in because of him. The agents of the law seemed powerless against this laughing, mocking little dare-devil and his outlaws, male and female. Some rumors had it that the police were their accomplices; others, that they were afraid of the Cartouchians. Everybody, high and low, talked and wrote about the crimes of Cartouche as — for instance — everybody talked and wrote, nearly two hundred years later, about Jack the Ripper.

One of the many girls who were carried away by his reputation and his personality was Justine, lady's-maid to the Duchess de Boufflers. One evening, Justine let Cartouche in, through a window, to the Duchess's room. And when he gallantly introduced himself to that noble lady, she almost died of fright. But Cartouche assured her that all he desired was supper and a night's lodging, and promised that he would leave in the morning without having taken a thing. He had a fancy to be a guest, tête-a-tête, of a duchess — that was all.

He found the Duchess's food excellent, but her champagne mediocre; so, a few days afterwards, he sent her, with his thanks and compliments, several baskets of superlative champagne that he had stolen from a noted cellar, telling her that he had great pleasure in providing her with some wine more worthy of her hospitality.

That — in one of his phases — was merry little Cartouche. This house at 306 rue de Charenton belonged to him; and though the police often came here to find him — followed him here, indeed — the most thorough search failed to discover him. In the courtyard he had a well through which he dropped to a level where a concealed opening gave access to a subterranean passage leading to a far and safe exit.

Georges Cain thought it must have been this well of Cartouche which gave Sardou his idea for Angelotti's hiding-place, in "La Tosca"; and that it was a similar one in which Madame Bouquey hid the seven fugitive Girondists in 1793.

It was even rumored that Cartouche forced all thieves not in his band to pay him a tax on their takings.

All sorts of stories grew up about him; he was invested with the legendary characteristics of Robin Hood and endowed with some that not even the balladists ventured to ascribe to the merry-andrew of Sherwood Forest.

When, at last, Cartouche (aged twenty-eight) was caught and lodged in the Grand Châtelet, he had scarcely been in his cell five days when the Comédie-Française was playing a piece based on his exploits.

The end of the laughing lad was horrible — he was broken, alive, on a wheel in front of the Hôtel de Ville. . . .

Now, go on to the beautiful Bois de Vincennes, and there have luncheon in the delightful little restaurant, Café du Chalet-du-Lac, on the Lake Saint-Mandé. If the day is fine, you may be served in a rustic summer-house, and share your bread with the friendly ducks.

The Lake Saint-Mandé is close to the Château; so that, after luncheon, you have to walk but a few steps to see whatever portions of the fortress may be open for inspection. As I write, an historical museum is being installed there, and admission to certain parts of the enclosure is about to be made more frequent and less difficult. The beautiful chapel, with its very fine sixteenth-century windows, and the monument of the poor young Duc d'En-

ghien, is always open to the public at the three Sunday
morning services.

There are so many stories to recall at Vincennes! Saint
Louis sitting under an oak tree to hear the plaints of
his people, as Cabanel has painted him at the Panthéon;
Henry V of England dying here — and his poor, mad
father-in-law; and Charles IX, haunted in his last hours by
all the horrors of Saint Bartholomew, and raving of his
blood-guiltiness — the poor terrorized lad of three-and-
twenty — and Mazarin.

The donjon of Vincennes has had many famous prisoners
— more, even, than the Bastille. Broadly speaking, it may
be said that if an offender against the sacred, inalienable
rights of the Crown was a mere impertinent — irritant, like
a mosquito, but not much more important; like a writer, for
instance — he was sent to the Bastille; whereas, if he were
a Somebody whose dissatisfactions might foment a conspiracy, he went to Vincennes.

The best-known description of the dungeons, torture-
chamber, chapel, etc., is Dumas's in "Marguerite of Valois"; and, as La Môle and Coconnas were veritable persons
who actually suffered what Dumas ascribes to them, there
is as little fiction about that part as about others of the
famous story.

I don't know how a poor encyclopædist like Denis Diderot got here, instead of going to the Bastille; but he did,
and Rousseau came here to visit him. Mirabeau was put
here when he was twenty-eight mainly through the influence of his own father, who had procured, at one time and
another, no fewer than fifty lettres de cachet against members of his own family. It was a drastic treatment, but it
seems to have been justified in this case. Mirabeau stayed
here five years, and emerged a very different man, schooled
for the great leadership he was about to assume. Here he

wrote his influential treatise on the "Lettres de Cachet" which played its part in bringing down the old absolutism.

Of all the prisoners of Vincennes, though, it is the young Duc d'Enghien whose memory is greenest, although he was there but a few hours. He was the last of the great Condé line, the cadet family of Bourbon, and he was born at the superb Château of Chantilly. His father fought against the Revolution — led the Royalist forces gathered outside France, against the armies of the Republic — but although the young duke (then only twenty-one) fought with his people at that time, there is nothing to show that he was active in his father's movement against Napoleon, twelve years later. Enghien had secretly married the Princess Charlotte de Rohan, niece of the "Necklace" Cardinal, and for some reason that I do not know she continued (at his wish) to live in her house in rue Bonaparte, where he went to visit her. His own residence was at Ettenheim in Germany, near the Rhine. His secret visits to Paris were interpreted by Napoleon's police as connected with a Royalist plot, and he was seized — at his home in Germany! — brought to Paris, and lodged in this donjon about five o'clock in the evening of March 20, 1804. His request to see the First Consul was not granted. That evening he was called from his bed to "trial," and shortly after midnight he was dead — shot, by a firing squad, in the moat where a grave had already been dug for him. Napoleon's apologists have tried to exculpate him; but the stain of Enghien's murder is one of those spots that will *not* "out."

In the last war, also, there were firing squads at Vincennes; and one of them faced a woman, the dancer Matahari, convicted as a spy.

If, at the Esplanade in front of the château, we take the route de la Pryamide, it will lead us past the pyramid marking the site of Saint Louis's oak tree, and across the drill-ground toward the confluence of the Seine and Marne.

Return to Paris may be made by steamer or by Métro or by train. If you have shopping in mind, you could easily be in the midst of it by three o'clock, by omitting the walk to the Marne and taking the Métro at the porte de Vincennes close to the château. And as you have walked little since leaving Père-Lachaise, you should not be tired.

If you are in the mood for a very special dinner to-night and don't mind dining indoors, you might try Larue, on rue Royale, across from the Madeleine. Weber, farther down the same street, is good, but not so expensive; and there is the Restaurant Volney in the Volney-Chatham Hotel; or Ciro's across the street from it.

Or, this may be the night you'll elect to dine at the Ambassadeurs in the Champs-Élysées, watching the elaborate theatre programme as you eat.

Americans all seem to know about the Café de Paris; so I don't mention it. I am much less fond of it tha of other places under the same management: Fouquet's on the avenue de Champs-Élysées, and Pré-Catélan and Armenonville in the Bois de Boulogne. The food is superlative at all, and the wine excellent. But the backgrounds and the patronage are, to me, least interesting at the Café de Paris.

XI

VERSAILLES

THERE is no question in anybody's mind about going to Versailles. The only question is as to how, and when.

I strongly advise against going in a sight-seeing party. I advise against that way of seeing anything, but very specially in the case of Versailles. The ride down in a motor is pleasant — it may even be so in one of the big sight-seeing cars loaded with tourists — but it is not worth hiring a car to make it, unless money is no object to you. Better save it toward a trip where the difference between going by auto and going by train is all the difference in the world.

The tram from Paris to Versailles is interesting, but takes too much time. There are three railway lines, and each of them makes the journey in about half an hour. I prefer the Ligne des Invalides-Versailles, which is electric, and runs from the Gare des Invalides in front of the Esplanade leading to Napoleon's tomb.

Ask your concierge about the train schedule; and choose, I pray you, a train that will get you to Versailles not later than ten-thirty; because, whatever you're to see of the château, you should see before luncheon — leaving the afternoon for the Trianons and the gardens.

So much for the *how*. Now for the *when*. Any day but Monday. If you can go but once, and feel that you must see the great fountains play, ask for the nearest date of such an occasion. It is always on Sunday, and the crowds are enormous; so it is a bad time for coming and going, a bad time for service in the restaurants, and a bad time to see the palace and the Trianons.

My advice is to go on a quiet day; Tuesday is a good one.

The weekly cleaning is just over; the attendants have had their holiday; and a nice freshness and serenity reigns over everything.

I shall not repeat all the details your guidebook gives as to how much Versailles cost, and how long it is, and how many people it can hold, etc.; nor can I embark, here, upon a history of the palace, a summary of its noted occupants, a disquisition on its paintings. It is the fashion to speak slightingly of the latter. Perhaps not many of them are notable works of art as the Louvre counts masterpieces; but most of them are, to my mind, decidedly interesting, and with their aid the Château of Versailles is one of the best places I know to study French history. If I could use fairy-godmother magic for the very young persons I love best of all, I would transport them to Versailles to spend a summer as in a story-book incomparable; to play familiarly in those gardens, and wander almost daily in the palace and the pleasure-houses; to meet fairies in the bosquets where the tiny princes and princesses played; to study the early history of France in the great Galerie des Batailles; to re-live the melancholy scenes of October 6th when the Paris mob went away with its royal captives; to meet Napoleon at the Grand Trianon; to see the German Empire born in the Galerie des Glaces, and to witness the German Republic signing the Versailles Treaty, there in that same place. And so on.

But you are probably going to Versailles, not for a summer, but for a day.

I know how overwhelming is the magnitude of what there is to see in a few hours. I know that most persons come away confused and unutterably weary. If I can help you to see "the high spots" with some economy of time and effort, it will be a great deal to accomplish in a chapter.

In approaching Versailles — making your mental as well

as your physical approach — it is important to keep in mind what, besides a gigantic stage for display, Louis XIV had in view when he built this palace, and why it is, more than any other palace in France (perhaps in the world) a symbol, an epitome, of the political history of the past two hundred and fifty years.

Louis XIV may well have had more vanity than any other man of modern times; but it was not mere self-satisfaction — it was also a policy of state.

Louis XI, when he found the sovereign power in France weak and the great vassals too strong, built up the authority of the crown — made France a nation instead of a group of warring factions — by a policy of terror. Shabby, moth-eaten little man that he was, preferring the company of his lowest subjects to that of his highest, he would have been insolently amused at Louis XIV's idea of attracting the nobles about him and eclipsing them. Louis XI went after them in their strongholds, and "squashed 'em."

Gradually, after he was gone, they began to get arrogant again, and powerful; the Crown got conciliatory — sometimes more, sometimes less; but never absolute. Henry IV had to make constant concessions to his nobles to establish the Bourbons on the throne. Richelieu, acting for Louis XIII, laid the foundations of an autocratic, all-sufficient sovereignty. Louis XIV carried it to its utmost lengths possible in a modern age wherein the Renaissance and the Reformation were both "working" like yeast in a mass. His excesses in glorifying the Crown at the expense of every subject, high and low, brought on much suffering for all, himself included; but to overlook *why* they seemed to him not only pardonable but necessary, and to think of him as a mere voluptuary, an insane egotist, a strutting peacock, is to miss all the truth about him. And the truth about Louis XIV is immensely interesting and important.

He created Versailles out of nothing, not only to show what a great king could do and how he should live, but to provide a setting for magnificence so dazzling that none of his people of consequence could bear, or afford, to stay away from it. He wanted them all there, under his eye, looking to him for their pleasure, their distinctions, their aggrandizements. Not to be "at court" in his day, was almost tantamount to being defiant of the sovereign. Magnificent châteaus, all over France, were closed and left to go to seed while their princely or ducal owners intrigued and fawned for the favor of lodging in some comfortless small closet, here, where they might be on hand for the pomp and pageantry — and for the preferments!

That very noble duke who told his valet to call him at eight o'clock, "unless somebody dies," was wholly typical. If anybody died, the Duke was to be called at once, not to mourn, but to see about getting the deceased's place, or his lodging, or what-not.

It is this policy, this plan, we must bear in mind as we approach Versailles — and as we go hence to the Trianons where the monarchs sought escape from the tyranny of that which they had created.

From the station, go straight to the Place d'Armes in front of the château. If you came by the Ligne des Invalides, the walk is not a long one, up the avenue des Sceaux.

At your left, in a side street, just before you come to the Place d'Armes, see the Jeu-de-Paume, or Tennis Court, to which the National Assembly retired after its demands caused its ejection from the very elegant hall originally arranged for it. It was here that the deputies took that famous oath called "Le Serment du Jeu-de-Paume," swearing not to dissolve their body until they had given a constitution to France. This was in June, 1789. The tennis court is now a museum of the Revolution.

The palace really faces the gardens; so that we are going in by the back way, in a sense — although it is the principal entrance. Louis XIV, on his horse in the Cour d'Honneur, looks east — not exactly, but sufficiently for our purpose in identifying the wings of the château. On the ground floor of the south wing is the former Chamber of Deputies (so-used when Versailles was the seat of government of this Third Republic), where the presidents of France are elected. If you want to see it, go into the Cour des Princes, at your left, and back to the entrance to the south wing, where an attendant will conduct you to the chamber. Give him a franc or two.

Then cross the Cour Royale and enter the north wing. There are many things in this wing that are well worth seeing; but for this first visit, I'd suggest that you try to see none of them except the chapel, at the near end of it, and possibly the Opéra (later used as a Senate Chamber) at the far end, but entered from another approach, in rue des Reservoirs. The Opéra was dedicated at the time of Marie Antoinette's marriage, and its memories as an opera house centre about her. The chapel was finished late in Louis XIV's day, and was the scene of many royal weddings. Previous to the construction of this, the chapel was where the Salon d'Hercule now is, alongside, to the north; it was in this earlier, smaller chapel (of which this room formed the upper part) that Louis XIV was married to Madame de Maintenon, in 1685, when he was forty-seven and she was fifty.

The rooms immediately to the west of this, looking over toward the Basin of Neptune, were the grand apartments of the King. The Salle de Diane was the billiard-room; and the Salon de Mars, next, was used as a ballroom under Louis XIV, and here his coffin lay in state for eight days. The next room, the Salon de Mercure, was a bedchamber.

THE OATH OF THE TENNIS-COURT, JUNE 20, 1789

Painting by Couder

Next came the throne-room, the Salon d'Apollon, where the Doge of Venice, bowing in submission before Louis XIV, told the courtiers that what most surprised him at Versailles was to find himself there. It was here that Louis XIV held his last public audience. The last room of this series is the magnificent Salon de la Guerre, from which we enter the celebrated Galerie des Glaces (or Gallery of Mirrors), with its incomparable views from the windows, and its many memories. The German Empire was proclaimed here in 1871; the Treaty of Versailles was signed here, in 1919. Innumerable spectacles, one more gorgeous than another, have defiled here before potentates and favorites. The temptation to recall some of them in detail is very great — but must not be yielded to. I shall permit myself to remind you of only one story connected with this gallery — and that is the arrest, here, for his complicity in the Affair of the Diamond Necklace, of the Cardinal de Rohan, Grand Almoner of France. It is impossible to read anything at all about Marie Antoinette without reading of the diamond necklace. I find that the details of it are hazy in the minds of most Americans abroad, and that they like to clarify the story in their book of memory when they are here where so many of its scenes were enacted. You may like to sit down on one of the fauteuils here in the gallery, looking out on the gardens, and rest while you recall this affair that had so much to do with increasing the disfavor in which Marie Antoinette was popularly held.

On the Quai des Orfèvres (number 54) there used to be a firm of Court jewellers, Boehmer and Bassenge, who had invested a great fortune in diamonds — and diamonds were gone out of favor, since Marie Antoinette had set the fashion, at the Petit Trianon, of muslin dresses and simplicity. The Queen must be induced to restore popularity to diamonds. They made up their choicest stones into a superb necklace valued at 1,600,000 livres, took it to Versailles and induced one of the gentlemen-in-waiting to show it to the King, who was delighted with it and ordered it shown to Marie Antoinette. She said that she had enough diamonds; that such a jewel could not be worn more than three or four times a year; and that the money it would cost might better be invested in a ship for the navy.

Boehmer was in despair. He secured an interview with the Queen, at which he told her that he would be ruined if she did not buy the necklace, and would drown himself. Her common-sense suggestion that he take the ornament apart and sell the gems separately met with no favor with him. He hawked the costly thing all over Europe, but found no purchaser.

The Grand Almoner of France, then, was the Cardinal Prince de Rohan, who had been Ambassador of France at Vienna, where he was heartily disliked by Maria Theresa, of whom he made cruel fun for which Marie Antoinette never forgave him. When he came to her Court, in his position of vast influence, she would not recognize him. This was a terrible chagrin to Rohan, who was of the high nobility, immensely proud and pompous, and bent upon becoming prime minister with power equal to that of Richelieu or Mazarin.

Rohan was also Bishop of Strasbourg; and there he first met that extraordinary charlatan calling himself the Count of Cagliostro, who claimed to be three hundred years old, to have the secret of perpetual youth, the power of reawakening love, the magic of making gold and precious stones, the art of healing, the gift of divination and prophecy — and a few other things.

That was an age of scepticism and rationalism in religion; so the credulity which was unemployed by the Church went out without stint to fakirs like Cagliostro. Rohan, Prince of the Church, was one of Cagliostro's most ardent dupes; he believed that with his own eyes he had seen the magician make gold and gems "out of nothing"; and he was so convinced that Cagliostro could and would remove from his path every obstacle to the summit of human power and splendor, that there was nothing he would not do at the sorcerer's behest.

But a woman's wits were needed to complete the combination working against Marie Antoinette; and they presented themselves, in due time, in the person of an adventuress, Madame de la Motte, who was descended from an illegitimate son of Henry II. This woman and her husband were living in Paris in the direst poverty, their hope being that she might obtain an audience with the Queen and so work upon her sympathies as to get a handsome pension; even their household goods and their clothes were pawned, when it occurred to Madame de la Motte to appeal to the Cardinal de Rohan. He was captivated by her coquetries, but had to admit that he had no influence with the Queen. This gave her the suggestion she needed.

She said she would try again to see the Queen. Soon, she reported to Rohan that she had been granted an interview in which Marie Antoinette told her that her apparent dislike of the Cardinal was only a pretence and that she was seeking some way to let him know her real feeling for him. He believed this. And when the La Motte woman showed him letters purporting to be from the Queen and asking him to loan her large sums of money, this gullible prelate handed over the cash — although the letters begging for it were signed "Marie Antoinette *de France*" which was, he should have known, a signature the Queen would never have used. The clumsy forgeries were made by a renegade named Villette, whom the husband of Madame de la Motte had met in the army. They got 120,000 livres out of the Cardinal so easily that the swindlers soon set about getting a vaster sum. They heard about the necklace, and Madame told the Cardinal that nothing in the world would please the Queen so much as to have that ornament, but that the King opposed the purchase. If the Cardinal, acting as her agent, would negotiate the purchase, the Queen would pay for the gems in four instalments of 400,000 livres each, the first to fall due at the beginning of August. Rohan expressed himself willing to help her get it, if thereby he could win her favor. Cagliostro, consulted, strongly advised it.

La Motte had noticed in the Palais-Royal gardens a young woman of bad repute who in face and figure strikingly resembled the Queen. He followed her to her lodging, and told her that a countess would call on her next day to seek her help in a matter of great importance. This girl, Mademoiselle d'Oliva, was not let into the plot; she believed that she was being employed by the Queen, for some little joke or prank. So she went with the La Motte woman to Versailles and suffered herself to be dressed like the Queen and introduced into the gardens, after dark. There Rohan presented himself believing that he was to have a secret tryst with Marie Antoinette. But scarcely had he approached her whom he supposed to be the Queen than Madame de la Motte hurried up and whispered that the King's sisters-in-law were approaching. All there was time for was the gift, to Rohan, of a rose and a small box with her portrait on it, and the whispered words: "You know what this means." Then the "Queen" vanished.

On the strength of this, Madame got 150,000 more livres from the enraptured prelate "for the Queen's benevolence"; and she was able to satisfy him as to why Marie Antoinette's demeanor toward him continued so cold, although her letters of gratitude were so warm. Also, she got him to act in the purchase of the necklace, which was delivered to him at the end of January, 1785, in his residence in the rue Vieille-du-Temple, and taken by him next day to Versailles, where Madame had a modest lodging in what is now the Place Hoche. There a man wearing the Queen's livery (he was Villette, the forger) appeared to receive the jewel-case, and immediately withdrew.

The necklace was taken to England, broken up, and the stones in it sold separately. The Cardinal wondered that the Queen remained cold to him, and that she never wore the necklace.

August came — and the jewellers received no payment. When they urged their great necessity, the fraud was disclosed.

On Assumption Day (August 15th) the chapel at the château was all in readiness for the Mass; the Galerie des Glaces was full of courtiers waiting for their Majesties, to attend them to the service. The Cardinal, in his magnificent robes of office, was there; suddenly, he was summoned to the King's room, where an explanation was demanded of him. It was far from satisfactory. When he returned to the Galerie, one of the King's ministers gave the bodyguard the order: "Arrest the Cardinal de Rohan."

Soon, all the conspirators, including Cagliostro and his wife, were in the Bastille, except the La Motte man; he was in England and could not be extradited. The trial was a tremendous sensation — not for nine days, but for nine months. Rohan and the La Motte woman had burned all their papers, and evidence was hard to produce. Many people believed that the Queen had made dupes of the persons on trial, and was trying to shield herself by trumped-up accusations of trickery.

There was a vast throng outside the Palais de Justice on the evening of May 31, 1786, when the verdict was rendered. It was acquittal for all but the La Motte woman and

Villette; and it was greeted with roars of applause. When the judges left the Palais, as many of the crowd as could reach them kissed their hands. Wishful to believe ill of the Queen, they did so.

Now, resume your round of the royal apartments. The Queen's suite began at the Salon de la Paix, in the corner, at the south end of the Galerie des Glaces. The next room was the Queen's bedchamber. Two queens (Marie Thérèse and Marie Leczinska) died here — the only other who ever reigned at Versailles died on the guillotine — and nineteen princes and princesses were born here, including Louis XV and his ten children and the four children of Marie Antoinette. The custom of permitting any one who wished to witness a royal birth survived until after Marie Antoinette was nearly smothered here, by the curious crowding about her bed when Madame Royale came into the world.

The private entrance from this room to the King's apartments was through a dark passage, of a sort very common in all palaces, where unobserved communication was a luxury difficult to attain. And from this bedroom, too, Marie Antoinette had access to that suite of little rooms which she had prepared as a refuge from the wearisome pomp of the palace routine. You may see them by asking for the Petits Appartements de la Reine.

The next room was the Queen's salon where her drawing-rooms were held and presentations to her were made; and beyond that was the room in which the Queen dined in public — any one who was decently dressed might stand and gape whilst Royalty ate a most unenviable meal. Benjamin Franklin, when he was a tourist in Paris, before he went there officially, stood here and stared like the rest — just as we should do to-day, doubtless, if queens were still on exhibition.

The Salle des Gardes de la Reine is next; here, three

guards were killed in the early morning of October 6, 1789, while defending the door leading to the Queen's apartments.

One of the things I like most to do at Versailles is to recapitulate — there, where the scenes were laid — the events of those last two days when Versailles was the home of France's king. But to comprehend them, we must go back a little.

On June 4th, Louis and Marie Antoinette had suffered the great grief of losing their elder son, the Dauphin, seven and a half years old. (Two years before, they had lost a baby girl, not quite a year old.) The Dauphin was buried at Saint Denis on June 13th; and on June 17th the Third Estate (or Commons) with some of the clergy withdrew from the States-General (or General Assembly of Nobles, Clergy, and Elected Deputies) and declared itself the National Assembly; and Mirabeau had ordered the King's message-bearer: "Go tell your master that we are here by the power of the people, and that we can be driven away only by the force of bayonets." On July 14th, the Bastille was taken. Two days later the flight from Versailles of many of the royalties and great nobles began. On July 22d, Lafayette was made commander of the new militia, the National Guard.

The Revolution was on.

The morning of October 5th there was a great gathering of the Parisian rabble, mostly women, before the Hôtel de Ville, complaining that there was no bread in the bakers' shops, and shouting "To Versailles!"

Lafayette had a battalion of the National Guard drawn up on the quai de Grève, and he rode up and down trying to persuade the mob to disperse and abandon its plan. But a young man of the Guard stepped out of the ranks, seized the bridle of Lafayette's horse, and said: "General, hitherto you have commanded us; now we are going to lead you."

And Lafayette gave the command to go; but the first lot of rioters had got away hours before the troops.

That morning Marie Antoinette was sitting in the gardens of the Petit Trianon where she had not made a sojourn for about fourteen months. It was dark and rainy, and the autumn wind blew the fallen leaves across the lawns and along the deserted paths. A page from the palace came, begging her to return at once.

The King was hunting, near Meudon; he, too, was recalled by messenger.

The first lot of marchers from Paris, led by a band, plodded along in wind and wet and reached Versailles about four in the afternoon when the rain was falling in torrents. They went first to the National Assembly, and then to the palace where a deputation of five women was received by the King and so kindly treated that they returned to their bedraggled sisters and urged a quiet, orderly return to Paris. For this advice, they nearly lost their lives. The disorder grew. And the rain continued. Lafayette arrived at about ten o'clock — there was much parleying with him, inside the palace, and much discomfort and cursing, without.

About 2 A.M. the King and Queen retired. The town was quiet then. Those of the mob who had not been able to find shelter had made a big fire in the Place d'Armes and were bivouacked there. Lafayette, with an absurd confidence in the "goodness" of the people (as if democracy must needs be so much better represented by those who wear her colors than religion is by those who wear hers!) for which it has been hard to find justification, left the palace in the early morning hours and went to his father-in-law's mansion in the rue de Noailles. There he lay down to rest, and was soon awakened.

At five-thirty in the morning the mob invaded the palace, killing three of the Queen's guard within a few feet of her room. The marble staircase up which the assailants came is here, beside the room in which the Queen's guards were killed.

Marie Antoinette fled from her room, by a door concealed behind the panel on which her portrait hangs, through the dark passage to the King's apartments in the Œil de Bœuf, where their children soon joined them.

This room, in which Louis XIV had slept until he moved (late in his reign) into the one adjoining, where he died, looks out on the Cour Royale, and the furious crowd, seeing their Majesties at the window above, shouted for them to come out on the balcony of the next room, facing the court.

The King complied. There were shouts for "The Queen!"

Marie Antoinette, accompanied by Lafayette, and holding the Dauphin by one hand, her daughter by the other, stepped out on the balcony.

"The Queen alone!" they shouted, from below.

She pushed the children back into the room, and faced the frenzied crowd, expecting nothing else than that they would kill her.

But before her calm courage, they lowered the guns they had raised. Some one cried, "Vive la reine!" Lafayette came to her side and kissed her hand.

"To Paris!" cried the mob.

Preparations were hastily made, and at one o'clock the cavalcade started. Louis XVI, Marie Antoinette, Madame Elizabeth, the Dauphin (probably) looked for the last time at the palace of Versailles.

Close to the Queen's side, through all these scenes, was Count Fersen, the young Swedish nobleman who had loved her for more than fifteen years with a great and irreproachable love, and who was to make the desperate attempt to get her out of the country, two years later.

It was at Versailles, just before she became Queen, that he first saw her. And when he realized that he loved her, and she loved him, he went away, with Rochambeau, to America, and fought for the freedom of our colonies, for which Washington rewarded him with the Order of Cincinnatus. He was not back in France till the fall of 1783. Both he and Marie Antoinette had learned much of self-discipline by that time. Each knew that the other had high and unyielding ideals of honor and duty; they were able to be much in one another's company without fear of weakening. He felt the chill winds of disfavor blowing toward her and was powerless to change them or to keep them from making her cold with apprehension. But his sword was at her service while he had strength to draw it. . . .

He followed her to Paris, with the gentlemen of the King's household.

From the room beyond that in which the guards were killed, you enter the first of three small rooms which formed the apartments of Madame de Maintenon, concerning whom so many of my compatriots have confused ideas that I believe some, at least, among you will be glad to go over, here, this extraordinary woman's story.

Françoise d'Aubigné was born in a prison, where her father was confined — partly for his debts, partly for his religion, and partly on political charges — and lived there until she was three years old; then her father was released and took his family to Martinique, where he died. She was ten when she returned to France and was given to her father's sister "to be raised." Her father's family were Protestant — her mother's Catholic. Françoise became Protestant with her aunt. Her mother then had her removed from that care, and given to her godmother — where Françoise was with much difficulty persuaded to renounce her Protestantism. The penniless girl, with no

prospects, was introduced, when she was about fifteen, to
Paul Scarron, the wit and dramatist, who offered her the
protection of his name and home, the advantages of his
brilliant associations, in return for such care as a daughter
might have given him. For nine years she was wife-in-
name-only to the caustic cripple. Then death took him; and
there followed nine other years of struggle as a widow. She
was on the point of quitting France to go to Portugal when
she met Madame de Montespan, then high in favor with
Louis XIV and on the eve of becoming his acknowledged
mistress. The first two of Montespan's seven children by
the King were born before their relation was admitted;
they must be secretly brought up; the beautiful young
widow Scarron seemed ideal for the purpose, so she was
sought, secured, and installed with her little charges in a
large, isolated house on what is now the boulevard Montparnasse, but was then a suburban road.

After five years of this life, Françoise and her charges are
removed to Versailles. There is nothing to be kept secret
now; the children of Montespan are not merely acknowledged, they are legitimated. The King is extravagantly
fond of them; he feels that they are being passing well
brought up; he is so grateful to Madame Scarron that he
gives her money to buy the estate of Maintenon, and the
right to style herself the Marquise de Maintenon. She is
an admirable woman! Handsome, intelligent, placid, pious.
Versailles is far from finished; it is not yet the royal residence — only a play-house and place of resort, and a residence for the children of the favorite — but the King is here
often enough to become very fond of Madame de Maintenon's society; and the Court is not slow to feel her growing favor and influence. "She is," Madame de Sévigné
writes, "introducing the King to an entirely new region; I
mean the commerce of friendship and conversation without

chicanery and without restraint; and he appears charmed with it."

It was on the 6th of May, 1682, that Versailles became definitely the official residence of the French Court. Montespan's star had passed its zenith and was well on toward setting; Maintenon's was in ascendancy. The relations of the King with his wife were better (thanks to Maintenon's influence) than they had ever been since the first days of their marriage. Marie Thérèse died, in Maintenon's arms, on July 30, 1683; and when Françoise essayed to withdraw, the Duc de la Rochefoucauld said to her: "This is not the time to leave the King; he needs you."

The King himself seems to have known his need. Almost immediately that he was widowed, he offered her his hand. Their marriage occurred early in the following year.

There seems to be an impression quite general among English-speaking people that Maintenon had been the King's mistress. No French historians or students of history believe this; whether they execrate her or ecstasize over her, they know that she was, by every instinct, every conviction, true to her own adage: "There is nothing cleverer than irreproachable conduct." It was by her virtue that she won and held Louis XIV, who, at forty-seven, was weary of complaisance, of flattery, and ready to love a woman of fifty who never hesitated to tell him what he ought to be and do.

Nobody (that I know of) has ever contended that she loved him; she could not, perhaps, have influenced him so profoundly if she had known loving dread of losing his favor. What she cared for was dominion over his conduct. From his magnificence she lived apart; of his wealth she accepted only a modest allowance; it was his soul that was her prize, and his service to the cause of religion, as she interpreted it, that was her constant concern.

In these small apartments (numbered on the plan of the palace, and in your guidebook, 141–143) she lived for more than thirty years; and hither the Sun-King came, as frequently as he could leave the pomp of Court life for a brief interlude of almost bourgeois simplicity. Her bedroom was the one numbered 142. In her day there was a chimney-place in this room; on one side of it stood the King's armchair, with a table in front of it for his papers; on the other side was her armchair, with a table in front of it for her book or needlework. Her bed was in an alcove, in a part of the room now cut away to continue the marble staircase to the floor above. (The apartments of the Dauphin were at the foot of the marble staircase, on the ground floor, immediately beneath those of the Queen.)

You may pretend, if you like, that when you leave these apartments you are in the wake of Louis XIV, who usually spent here the hours between 5 and 10 P.M., going hence to supper with the royal family in the room numbered 121 on your plan. After the supper, he went into his bedroom (until 1695 the room numbered 123 — after that, the one where his bed is, numbered 124) and there chatted with the favorite members of his immediate family until he retired.

When you are in that room (124) you may whisk yourself back two hundred years and more, and see Louis XIV die.

His last years were most melancholy. Wars, excessive taxation, the Huguenot emigration, had reduced industries to a frightful degree. Many towns were decimated; thousands of homes had fallen into ruins; starvation stalked on every hand; on a single journey from Paris to Orléans, one traveller counted thirty dead by the roadside.

Of Louis XIV's six children by his queen, only one survived to maturity, the Dauphin; and he died in April, 1711. In February of the year following died the Dauphin's eldest son and heir, the Duke of Burgundy; the Duchess of

Burgundy; and a few days later, their eldest son, the Duke of Brittany.

Louis XIV went down to his grave knowing that the crown of his distraught kingdom was to go on a baby's head.

The illness which carried him off was gangrene caused by an irritation of the left leg where his garter chafed it. This his doctors treated by giving him wild asses' milk to drink, and bathing the infected part with hot spiced wine.

It was his aged wife (she was eighty) who told him that his days were numbered.

"I am prepared," he said; "being persuaded that there is a Sovereign infinitely higher than earthly kings, to whose orders we must submit. My confessor has told me that I must have great confidence in the compassion of God; but I never can console myself for having offended Him."

His one regret, he said, was in leaving her; but at their age they could not be long separated. He was sorry that he had not been able to make her happier, and thanked her for all the good she had been to him.

He had the tiny heir to the crown brought in to sit in an armchair at the head of the bed. (I'm sure you can see him there, now, listening, round-eyed.)

"My dear child," the dying king said, "you, who are about to become the greatest king in the world, never forget that you owe everything to God."

There was much more good counsel. And, almost up to the last, the old monarch worked at setting his house in order. His sufferings were intense, and the gangrene became frightfully offensive. Long before the last spark of spirit flickered out, the corruptible flesh had become the prey of decomposition. This part of the palace was sedu-lously avoided by all who were not compelled to be here.

On Saturday afternoon, August 31, 1715, he lost con-sciousness. When he had sunk into coma, Madame de

Maintenon gave away her few possessions, and left the palace forever, going to the school she had founded at Saint-Cyr.

Very early on Sunday morning the courtyard was full of people from Paris, waiting to hear that the King was dead.

His last sigh came at eight-fifteen. (It was, you will remember, on a Sunday morning of early September that he came into the world, at Saint-Germain.) And when his jaw was bound up, his eyes closed, his linen changed, and the candles lighted about his bed, the Grand Chamberlain, wearing a black plume in his hat, stepped on to the balcony and cried: "The King is dead!"

Then he went in, changed his black plume for a white one, returned to the balcony and cried, three times, "Long live King Louis the Fifteenth!"

Inside, all the Court was bowing low before the five-year-old king. Somebody then dried his baby tears and took him out to show to the acclaiming crowd in the grand court.

Nearly threescore years later, Louis XV died, of smallpox very pestilent, in the next room but one (numbered 126 on the palace plan), and Louis XVI and Marie Antoinette fell on their knees, exclaiming: "God help us! We are too young to reign."

Louis XV lived here, boy and man, during most of his sixty-four years; but there is not much about him that I care to recall and I am not sure what there is that you might wish I had reminded you of.

"What," he demanded, "would life be worth without coffee? But then, what is it worth even with coffee?"

There you have him, in a nutshell. Bored to extinction, always, satiated with everything.

Of the women who ruled here in his day, Pompadour and Du Barry are interesting. Superficially considered, both are deplorable wantons and wasters of millions wrung from the starving poor; "under the skin," each is an intensely absorbing study, and one that awakes many sympathies. To those who are interested in these women and their psychology, I commend the books of Edmond and Jules de Goncourt — "La Du Barry," and "Madame de Pompadour" — written from the documents of the National Archives, the Bibliothèque de l'Arsenal, and from private papers. I dare not embark, here, upon any summary of their associations with Versailles, for fear of making this chapter unpardonably long.

If you reached the château at eleven, it is probably past noon, now, and will be one o'clock by the time your luncheon is served.

I have not directed you to the great Galerie des Batailles (almost twice as long as the Galerie des Glaces) in the south wing, where, under Louis XIV, the Duke of Orléans and his children were housed. I am very fond of this Galerie, and my one thought in keeping you clear of it is to save you fatigue. If you are hardy, and do not want to miss it, enter this wing of the château before you go into Madame de Maintenon's apartments. And if you are *very* hardy, see something of the galleries of historic paintings in the north wing. They do a great deal toward re-creating for us the outstanding scenes of French history.

And before leaving the palace you will, I am sure, like to refresh your recollections of its history since that October day when Louis XVI and Marie Antoinette left it as captives of the Paris mob.

A Russian traveller who came to Versailles only a year later (in 1790) found the town so desolate that he could scarcely get a wretched meal.

After the Republic was declared, the furniture of the palace was sold, and the building was left to go to ruin. In

1800, two thousand wounded veterans of Napoleon's armies were installed in the central wing and in the apartments of Louis XV and Louis XVI. Five years later, Napoleon gave orders for the restoration of the palace and the Trianons; and in February of that year he gave a ball in the Salon d'Hercule. When he resided at Versailles, it was at the Grand Trianon.

Louis XVIII and Charles X seldom came here to their birthplace, after the Revolution. Louis-Philippe got from the Chambers (of Deputies and Senators) money for the restoration of the palace (which work had not gone far under Napoleon), but only on condition that it should become an historical museum.

The Museum was inaugurated June 10, 1837, at a grand state dinner in the Galerie des Glaces, and a gala performance in the theatre.

In August, 1855, Queen Victoria and the Prince Consort were entertained here by Napoleon III and the Empress Eugénie. A magnificent ball was given in the Galerie des Glaces; there were elaborate fireworks in the park; and a supper in the theatre.

On September 19, 1870, the victorious Germans — their bands playing the "Marseillaise"! — entered Versailles. On January 8, 1871, "an altar covered with a red cloth was raised in the Galerie des Glaces, opposite the windows looking out upon the park. On this red cloth was the figure of the Iron Cross of Prussia. Around the altar stood officers holding flags. At one in the afternoon, King William, surrounded by representatives of all the reigning families of Germany, by the members of his family, his generals, and his ministers, entered and took his place before the altar. ... The new German Empire was about to be established."

On leaving the château, go for luncheon either to the Hôtel des Reservoirs, in rue des Reservoirs which runs in front of the north wing of the palace; or to the Hôtel Trianon Palace, which you may reach by turning to your left at the boulevard de la Reine (just past Hôtel des Réservoirs) and continuing on it to the avenue Saint-Antoine. The first of these hotels is housed in an old mansion of Madame de Pompadour's. The second is new. Both are good, but expensive. Your guidebook gives the names of several restaurants, but as I have not patronized them I cannot say what their merits are.

The boulevard de la Reine runs into the avenue de Trianon just beyond the Trianon Palace Hôtel, and leads, in about half a mile, to the Grand Trianon. If you feel unequal to this walk, you will find cabs plentiful.

Long before the palace of Versailles was finished, Louis XIV had a little refuge here, a tiny place to which he could come, briefly, for a respite from the fatiguing ceremonies and crowds of his Court. And so happy was he in the simpler atmosphere that in some degree resembled a home that, soon after his marriage to Madame de Maintenon, he replaced the first Trianon (where Madame de Montespan had presided) with this glorified marble "bungalow" where he and his wife could entertain their intimates, and Madame could be recognized as the mistress of the house. (At Court, her position was perfectly understood, and respected; but her status was unprecedented and undefined — she was the King's wife, but she was not the Queen; so she avoided causing problems of conduct, by keeping much to her own simple routine of life.)

Both the Trianons have to be visited in charge of guides who run their herds through to the accompaniment of the usual sing-song about clocks, tables, carpets, and candelabra — most of which is drowned in the noise of shuffling feet and private conversations.

Near by is the Musée des Voitures, with gilded state carriages which seem to belong in a fairy-tale.

And then we come to the Petit Trianon, which Louis XV began for Pompadour and finished for Du Barry, but which is principally associated in most minds with Marie Antoinette.

The visit to the villa is moderately satisfying; but the visit to the garden is, to my mind, one of the most delicious experiences that fall to the human lot in journeying through this world that is so full of beauty. Whether you re-create the past here or merely revel in the present, there is as much as your soul can hold. Get as deep into this garden as you can; let its quiet loveliness "sink in." Exquisite memories of the time you spend here will stay with you as long as you live, and delight you always.

From this garden, go back to the great gardens of the palace, which are superb, but not as "sympathetic." And spend here all the time — and energy — you have left.

If you have no reason for hurrying back to Paris, you will find it very well worth while to dine at Versailles and loiter about the town a bit.

XII

YOUR TWELFTH PARIS DAY

IF you were at Versailles yesterday, you are probably not feeling extraordinarily ambitious this morning; so I have planned for you a day which you may start late, finish early, and still see some very interesting and important parts of Paris, with a very moderate amount of walking.

Suppose you say that you will be at Notre-Dame at eleven o'clock, or thereabouts. If you think you will want to climb the towers (which is a bit fatiguing, but well worth doing, not for the view alone, but for the impression one gets, at close range, of the infinite and beautiful detail of Gothic architecture — "flowering stone"), it would be well to start at least half an hour earlier.

I have gone very often to Notre-Dame with friends who were seeing it for the first time, and I cannot remember that any of them seemed avid for many facts about it or disposed to study it architecturally or archæologically. Most people who read, who have any "background," have thought so much about seeing Notre-Dame, looked forward to it so long and so eagerly, that when they at last find themselves there they are more or less overcome by emotion; and as this seems to me so eminently right, I never want to disturb their ecstasy by a single nudge or suggestion. I like going with people who feel thus about it; and I like going with others who have been there many times and have long since begun to have special enthusiasms. One friend of mine has been fascinated by gargoyles and has given a world of study to those fantastic water-spouts; she tells me delightful things about the famous ones of Notre-

Dame. Another friend is a close student of ancient stained glass, and tells me much that enhances my appreciation of those (and other) glorious windows. Many friends I have who are architects specializing in Gothic, or teachers and lecturers in Gothic art; going to Notre-Dame with them is a liberal education. Other friends are etchers, and I know few things more interesting than going round and round Notre-Dame with one of them, looking for a vantage-point from which to sketch — unless it be going round and round, inside and out, with one of those other friends who can re-create before my inner eye Notre-Dame as it was in days long-gone. I have been there, too, with friends who were students of sacred music, and who have told me what would make a fascinating book about music at Notre-Dame.

I have tried to choose from all that I have read about Notre-Dame, and all that I have been told about it, and all that I have seen there, what might best serve you on your first (and perhaps only) visit to it. And after weeks of consideration, I have come to the conclusion that the thing to do here, in a book, is the thing I should do were I there with you in the flesh. And if I were actually escorting you thither for your first visit, I'd never, *never* halt you outside to remind you when this cathedral was begun and when finished, to urge you to study the sculptures of the façade or the details of the portals. If you wanted to stop, guidebook in hand, and inform yourself about those things, I'd be respectful of your desire; if you were not yet ready for them, we'd go in; and I'd never, never tell you how long the nave is, nor how high (I don't know), nor prod you to notice the double aisles. I'd follow you silently, as you chose your way and revelled in your own reflections. Some, on their first visit, are overcome by the awesome beauty of what their eyes behold; others are thrilled by the thought of

waking with their footsteps the echoes of others who have
trod these stones in ages long gone by: the little Corsican
coming hither to be crowned and to make Joséphine "more
than queen"; Marie Antoinette, at the Te Deum giving
thanks for the birth of the Dauphin; Henry IV hearing that
Mass which he deemed a kingdom to be well worth; Mary
Stuart, walking out in her proud young beauty, wearing the
crown of the queens of France; the mother and brothers of
Jeanne d'Arc, brought here to witness the ceremony at
which the Church expressed its deep contrition for having
found the Maid of France a heretic; and so on. Or perhaps
it is the thought of the millions of feet which have stepped
reverently here, in nigh on eight hundred years, which fills
you with a new sense of kinship with "them that have
believed."

It may be that you will witness a church ceremony of
some sort. An unforgettable one I once saw at Notre-Dame
was the funeral of an old cocher, or cab-driver. An exceedingly humble funeral it was, following the pompous beadle
down one of the shadowy right aisles, his heavy staff-of-
office thumping measuredly on the stone pavement to
announce the coming of His Majesty, Death — the King of
Kings. Saint Louis was buried from here, with more pomp
than my cocher, but with no more reverence. I was very
deeply touched by the way that poor man's obsequies
seemed perfectly *at home* in the glorious old Cathedral;
there was not the slightest incongruity about their being
there. And I tried to think whether this triumph of democracy was due to Christianity or to the French spirit.
I dare say both were responsible; but when I tried to think
of a cab-driver's funeral at Westminster Abbey or Canterbury Cathedral or Saint Thomas's on Fifth Avenue, I had
to grant the French attitude toward death the greater
credit.

You have, I'm sure, been impressed by the universal respect shown the dead as they pass through the streets of France on their last journey: every man's head bared to them as they go by. Death has often been called the great leveller; in France, he seems more to be the great elevator, raising everybody, at last, to a dignity beyond that of kings.

You may want to visit the Treasury, where the reliquaries of the Crown of Thorns and the Nail of the True Cross are kept, and Thomas à Becket's cross, and other relics — some sacred, and some interesting for other reasons, like Napoleon's coronation mantle. Of course you'll pay your respects to Notre-Dame de Paris, the famous statue of the Virgin which has been venerated for more than five centuries. You will walk around the ambulatory, and see the choir-stalls, and perhaps ascend the north tower. If you haven't had a good view of the apse, walk around to the east, and gaze up at those marvellous flying buttresses.

To the north of the Cathedral, where the old cloister used to be, with its fifty-one houses for the canons, is a district with many interesting associations. I would like to take you "prowling" there; but that is, perhaps, for the leisurely sojourner in Paris rather than for the tourist. So, while you take a few moments' rest after your descent from the tower (you may like to sit in the charming gardens at the south of the Cathedral, for this), we'll recall Hugo's "Notre-Dame de Paris," which he wrote in 1831, when he was twenty-nine years old and had just made a sensation in the theatre world with his "Hernani." He had a contract with a publisher, to write a novel; but the social distractions consequent upon his success in the drama were so many that he could not seem to "get down to" the novel. He was living, then, in the rue Jean-Goujon, near where the Grand-Palais is now; and one day he went out, bought himself a big bottle of ink, a supply of quills for pens, and a coarse

gray robe like a monk's habit. When he got home, he locked
up all his good clothes (he was quite a "dandy") and denied
himself to everybody. In five months and a half of prodigious industry, he completed his book, writing the last
words of it with the last drop of ink. He thought, first, of
calling it "What There Is in a Bottle of Ink," but gave that
title to his friend, Alphonse Karr, and chose for his story
"Notre-Dame de Paris." Goethe damned it as "a dull and
tiresome show of marionettes." Perhaps Quasimodo is a
marionette; and Gringoire, and Esmeralda, and Claude
Frollo, and Captain Phœbus. But with their aid, Hugo
made fifteenth-century Paris live again and forevermore, as
no other writer has ever done, though many a one has tried
to paint that vivid, eventful time.

Now, cross the pont-au-Double, close to Notre-Dame,
and reach the quai de Montebello. The street which runs
from the bridge-head is rue Lagrange; and a few feet south
of the bridge, on your right, is a street called rue du Fouarre,
or street of the straw or fodder. In the Middle Ages there
were many colleges here; and by an edict of Pope Urban V
the students were forbidden to sit on benches when listening
to lectures, but were obliged to sit on the ground. When the
ground was muddy, they threw down bundles of straw.
Hence the name of the street, which Dante mentions in his
"Paradiso," and where he probably sat at the feet of Siger
de Brabant and of the Florentine, his fellow-exile, Brunetto
Latini, in 1304. Follow this street (past some half-dozen
houses, only) to the rue Galande, also a very ancient street
with many quaint old houses; and turn, again to your right,
into rue Saint-Julien-le-Pauvre, in which you will find the
little old church of the same name. There was a chapel and
a "religious lodging house" here away back in the sixth
century when Saint Gregory of Tours was sheltered there.
The present church is a little older than the oldest part of

Notre-Dame. It was the chapel of the Hôtel-Dieu (the hospital) for many years; and is now used by Greek Catholics subject to the Pope of Rome. Saint Julien the Poor was a humble man who served his poor fellows by ferrying them across the river. One day a leper whom he had thus served revealed himself as Christ. This story is told in sculptural relief over a door at 42 rue Galande. In the yard north of Saint Julien's church is a considerable fragment of Philippe-Auguste's wall. The view of Notre-Dame from this little garden is splendidly impressive.

Now another step or two in rue Saint-Julien-le-Pauvre and you reach rue Saint-Jacques, and across that street you will see the apse of Saint-Séverin, one of the most exquisite architectural gems of Paris, and by some authorities considered the most interesting of all Paris churches. The rue Saint-Séverin, on the north of the church, is one of the oldest in Paris. In it, beside the church, long ago, there was a sort of prison where erring girls were shut in and left, for their subsistence, to the charity of passers-by. It may have been that thinking of this, as he passed to and fro, gave the Abbé Prévost, who lived in this street, some impulse toward writing the story of "Manon Lescaut." We know "Manon" better through Massenet than in the printed page; but it is well to remember that this perfectly written, poignant tale has had an immense influence on fiction for nigh on two centuries.

The Church of Saint-Séverin (where Saint-Saëns was long the organist — sitting at an organ whose case was built in 1417) has some superb stained-glass windows, a number of which were at one time in Saint-Germain-des-Prés.

The apse of this church, Huysmans says, is "one of the most astounding tabernacles that the artists of other days ever executed to shelter the altar of the Holy Sacrament. They seem to have borrowed the theme of it from the vegetation of the country where Christ was born, because they have created here a lofty forest of palm trees from which the ruby light before the Host drops like blood-red fruit."

You will, I think, be interested in the multitude of supplicative and grateful plaques hanging about the chapel altars — entreaties that a student's examination may be successfully passed, that a marriage may be happy, that a journey may be safely made, a malady may be cured. And when these prayers were answered, those who had made them hung up a "Merci" or "Thanks" plaque, to attest what had been done for them.

The street in front of the church, called rue des Prêtres-Saint-Séverin, crosses (close beside the church) the quaint old rue de la Parcheminerie, so called since 1387 when it had become a centre for copyists, illuminers, and other workers on parchment; and beyond the street of the parchment-workers (which leads, a few feet farther on, to the rue de la Harpe, where Madame Roland lived when she was arrested — it was her last home) the rue des Prêtres-Saint-Séverin becomes the rue Boutebrie, which ends, a stone's throw beyond, at the boulevard Saint-Germain, in front of the Cluny Museum.

You are probably thinking of lunch, now. So, cross the boulevard Saint-Germain and the boul' Mich' (boulevard Saint-Michel — you are in the very hub of the Latin Quarter, now) and follow rue Pierre-Sarrazin to rue Haute-feuille. At number 5 rue Pierre-Sarrazin, corner of the Impasse Hautefeuille, note the turret on a remaining part of the "town house" of the abbots of Fécamp. (In that Impasse lived Christophe Le Blon, inventor of engraving in color.) Giorgione, the Venetian painter, lived in the tur-reted house in 1560 or thereabouts.

A turn to the left, a few steps, and you are in the rue de l'École-de-Médecine, with the huge buildings of the Schools of Medicine on both sides of you. There is much here to interest physicians and surgeons. But to non-medical visitors the chief reason for coming here is the association of this section with those extremists of the Revolution who were called the Cordeliers.

The original Cordeliers were Franciscans, followers of the gentle saint of Assisi, who were girt with a knotted cord; they came to Paris in 1217, and it was Saint Louis who bought this ground for them, from the vast abbey domain of Saint-Germain-des-Prés. The Church of the Cordeliers was one of the largest in Paris, and one of the most popular; it was very long and very narrow, and occupied the ground now covered by the Place de l'École-de-Médecine. There the Chevaliers of the Order of Saint Michael held their glittering Assemblies; and there the members of the French Academy convened to eulogize their deceased confrères.

But from the beginning of the eighteenth century, novices had been few; the rule of the Order was severe, and the taste of the times was not for austerity. So, gradually, parts of the great convent were allotted to secular bodies.

Notwithstanding the spectacular part they played in the Revolution, the Cordeliers as a body have left us very scanty records. If they kept any minutes, they have perished. I do not know who started the society (whose official name was Friends of the Rights of Man and Citizen); but it had a large membership of butchers, and a butcher, Légendre, was at one time its president; he lived in this street, which had twenty-two butcher-stalls in it; and so did Marat, Danton, and Simon the shoemaker who was destined to become the Dauphin's jailer. It is said that Légendre did not know how to read, but he had a violence of speech which won him great favor with certain sorts. It was he who, in the Cordeliers, demanding the death of Louis XVI, had shouted: "Let us cut the pig's throat! Let us make as many pieces of him as there are departments of France, and send a morsel to each one; the head shall remain in Paris, hung to the vaulting of this hall." It was he who proposed to requisition butchers' blocks whereon to cut up the aristocrats and the rich. "As for me," he yelled, "I shall eviscerate, with pleasure a noble, a rich man, a statesman, or a man of letters, and I will eat his heart."

It was an assembly responding delightedly to such sentiments which deified Marat, and whose acclaim Marat courted when his intellectual peers (men of science and philosophy) scorned him for his truculence and then persecuted him for his retaliation. We incline to think of Marat solely as a violent "Red," hiding in sewers and emerging into prominence only when sewer-filth overflowed; we incline to forget that he was more than nationally eminent in medicine, as an oculist, and as an experimenter with electricity; that he was a brilliant linguist, and a man of encyclopædic erudition; that many of his attacks were upon indefensible abuses, and that much of his constructive critical reasoning was very clearly to the point. He became an arch-Terrorist because of his bitterness over the failure of his abilities to convince and lead able men.

His house was number 20 rue des Cordeliers (now rue de l'École de Médecine) and no trace of it nor of the street, as he knew it, remains; nor of the meeting-place of the Cordeliers, who did not use the refactory (now the Musée Dupuytren of the Medical School) as their assembly hall, as most of the guidebooks erroneously state; they met in the Salle Théologique of the chapter-house, on a spot now covered by one of the amphitheatres of anatomy.

But as you are on your direct way to lunch, you may like to imagine the scene in this street on that July evening of 1793, the eve of the Bastille anniversary, when a fiacre with a young woman passenger drove up to the door of number 20, and stood waiting at the curb while the young woman went within.

Marat's apartment was on the first floor above the stores; there was a roomy salon, a good-sized bedroom, and a study, on the street front, and a kitchen, dining-room, and bath-room behind, lighted from the court. Charlotte was ad-mitted by the servant, Jeannette. The household consisted of Simonne Evrard, Marat's "common-law wife," her sister, Catherine, and his sister, Albertine — the latter in Switzer-land at the time of the murder. Simonne was in the small, tile-floored cabinet, back of the bedroom, where Marat sat in the shoe-shaped bathtub you saw at the Musée Grévin, on the top of which he had his papers outspread as on a desk. Catherine, Jeannette, and the concierge of the build-ing, whom Marat employed to fold his printed sheets, were all in the small inner hall between the kitchen and dining-room, when Charlotte was admitted. There arrived, almost at the same moment as Charlotte, two men; one, named Pillet, came to present a bill, and the other was Laurent Bas, a messenger who frequently executed errands for Marat and who now brought a supply of print-paper. How many more persons there might be in the apartment, Charlotte had no means of knowing. Pillet was directed to the bath-room, presented his bill, had it approved, and left. When he came out, he saw Charlotte, and heard the concierge trying to persuade her that it was useless to try to see Marat. Charlotte persisted; and the argument brought Simonne, who, when she knew that Charlotte was the girl who had been there that morning, consented to ask Marat if he would receive her. He consented, and Simonne escorted the stranger through the dining-room and into the bath-cabinet. A minute later she was back again, to see what was happen-ing; she found Charlotte sitting near the bathtub, with her back to the window. Some conversation passed between

Marat and Simonne, relative to a remedial drink she was preparing for him (he had contracted a loathsome and painful skin disease, when hiding in the sewers; and the bath he was sitting in was a sulphurated one, to relieve his tortures), and then she left, taking back to the kitchen with her two plates of sweetbreads and calves' brains which she had bought for supper and left there on a previous visit to the bath-cabinet. Scarcely had she reached the kitchen with these when she heard a raucous cry, and ran back. Marat was bleeding profusely, horribly; a jet of blood as big as his thumb was gushing from the wound in his naked breast; Charlotte, very pale, was standing against the window; the knife was among the blood-stained papers upon which Marat's head had dropped. (M. Anatole France owns those papers now.) Simonne's cries brought the three other women and Charlotte profited by the confusion to slip out and regain the hall; but the messenger, Laurent Bas, was there, and he knocked her down and beat her with his fists. A dentist who was a tenant of the house rushed to the aid of the stricken man; and soon the house was full of the curious, the resentful, and the representatives of the law. The first examination of Charlotte took place in the salon of the apartment. It was with extreme difficulty that she was got through the furious crowd and taken to the Abbaye prison, near by.

Go through rue Antoine-Dubois and rue Casimir-Delavigne, to the Place de l'Odéon, and lunch at Café Voltaire, number 1 in the square — still frequented, as it was two centuries ago, by men of letters.

After lunch, take rue Racine back (one block) to the Cluny. George Sand lived at number 3 rue Racine, on the fourth floor, for a time, and was visited there by the Brownings; and Longfellow twice had lodgings in this street: once at number 49 and once at number 5.

CHARLOTTE CORDAY

You may find that a half-hour's visit to the Cluny Museum will suffice you; or you may feel resentful that you were not directed to go there on one of your first days in Paris, so you could plan to make many visits. If, however, you are one of those to whom the Cluny is an inexhaustible treasure-house, you have almost certainly known before coming to Paris that this would be a main objective, and have lost no time getting here. Students and workers in the applied arts find here thousands of the choicest examples in the world of ceramics and enamels and glass; of carved ivory and wood, and wrought iron, and bronze; of jewelry and reliquaries and altar ornaments; of tapestries and textiles and embroideries and lace; and so on. Collectors find here, in greater abundance perhaps than anywhere else in the world, the rare and precious things they most covet. Designers get more from the Cluny than from any other place. If you belong to any of the above classifications, you will find yourself, at the Cluny, in the midst of objects about which you have heard, read, studied so much that you will feel like a pilgrim come at last to Mecca.

The sight-seer without special art education and without the museum habit is, on the other hand, apt to be less engrossed by the sixteen thousand articles housed here than by the exquisite casket in which they are contained, and by the remains of the Roman baths.

You enter the Cluny from the rue du Sommerard, named for the eminent collector whose treasures form the major part of the museum.

I think that most persons who are capable of any "thrill" at all feel that they are leaving a workaday world behind and stepping into the heart of Romance when they enter, through the arched gateway in those crenellated walls, the courtyard of the Hôtel de Cluny, and find themselves face-to-face with that lovely octagonal turret, beside the old well of Tristan l'Hermite.

Do you find *doors*, or doorways, intensely suggestive? I do. I could name a number of doors the merest glimpse of which brings up out of the depths of my imagination all the poetry, the mystery, the once-upon-a-time-ness that ever went into me from without or generated in me from within. Both the larger and smaller gateways in the Cluny wall are among the number; and the doorway of the octagonal tower is high up near the top of the list. "Special interests" always add greatly to the value of travel; they need not, should not, mean that the heart and mind are closed to the million-and-one other appeals; but a hobby has a way of making us intensive; and they travel best who are on some special quest as well as on many general ones. If you have no hobby of your own, try doorways (if they interest you) for a while; and note how many delightful things will fall under your observation while you're looking for lovely or unusual doors. Make a collection of pictures of doors. I have one, and I cannot tell you, here, all the kinds of pleasure and profit it has been to me and to others.

This exquisite house that you're entering was built by the abbots of Cluny, and finished about 1490. For some reason the monks lived in it very little, and seemed to prefer renting it to distinguished tenants. One of the first of these was Mary Tudor, the madcap young widow of poor old Louis XII, best known to this generation as the heroine of "When Knighthood was in Flower." It was here that her husband's successor, Francis I, surprised her with Charles Brandon and ordered an immediate wedding for them. (Francis could be very "proper" — at times!) It was here that Francis, twenty-one years later, married his daughter Madeleine to James V of Scotland. Rather strangely, the Hôtel de Cluny later became the residence of the House of

Lorraine from which James V took his second wife by whom he became the father of Mary, Queen of Scots.

The mansion had tenants of many sorts in the seventeenth and eighteenth centuries; and in 1833 M. Alphonse du Sommerard rented it to house his immensely valuable collection of antiques of the Middle Ages and the Renaissance. He was a Vendéan and a monarchist, the son of a financier and a member of the Cour des Comtes. The furious destructiveness of the Revolution horrified him. "The Vandals of the fifth century (Attila's hordes) did not destroy so many works of art," he said. And he gave himself, piously, to the gathering together of precious things which had survived the storm of human passions. He was forty years collecting these, and he was fortunate (as well as wise) enough to get as a repository for them one of the most exquisite examples of domestic architecture created in the era which gave birth, also, to the objects of his collection.

On the death of M. du Sommerard, his heirs, wishing the collection to remain intact and benefit the largest possible number of persons, sold it for a very small sum to the directors of Fine Arts; and a few years later, the Government also bought the mansion. About the same time the city of Paris bought the ruins of the old palace and baths of the Roman emperors, adjoining, and presented them to the nation to be, with the Hôtel de Cluny and the du Sommerard collection, a museum. The son of M. Alphonse du Sommerard was curator of the museum until his death.

All of us who love old Paris spend a great deal of time lamenting what has been swept away by the rebuilders. We have much to deplore; but we also have some things wherein we are more fortunate than earlier generations. If we had lived a hundred years ago, we should have found the Hôtel de Cluny "let out" to a variety of tenants; and the baths of the Roman emperors used as a cooper's shop, with a vegetable garden growing in the thick soil that hid priceless fragments. There was a proposition made, under Louis XVI, to buy this property and convert it into a museum; but the storm broke before anything was done about it.

It was Constantius Chlorus, conqueror of England, who built the palace of which these baths were a part, during the five years that Paris was his headquarters — 287 to 292 A.D. Julian the Apostate was here proclaimed emperor, tradition says. And Childebert, at least, of the descendants of Clovis, lived here. But the splendor of the emperors seems to have descended into ruin and neglect more than a thousand years ago.

If you have no special interests among the Cluny exhibits, and want only a general impression of its treasures, you might walk through rooms, I, III, IV, V, VI, and VII, into IX which has a number of specially beautiful things. There are three interesting rooms to your left as you turn into room IX; but if you find yourself not greatly attracted by what you see in room IX, you may omit these (the carriages, in room XV, are rather less interesting than those you saw yesterday at Versailles) and take the staircase in room VIII for the floor above. (That staircase was brought from the old Chambre des Comtes and bears the arms of Henry IV and Marie de Médicis.) On that floor you will, I think, want to see the ceramics, especially those in rooms XVII (note the Bernard Palissay things, because you are going, presently, to see where he lived) and XVIII, and the enamels in room XX; and to see room XXIV with its sixteenth-century furniture; and room XXV, which was Mary Tudor's bedroom. If you must cut short your visit, you might omit further exploration of this floor; but you will miss some exceedingly beautiful things if you do.

The Roman baths are entered from room IX, in which is

the main doorway of the Church of Saint-Benoît whose chaplain was foster-father of Villon; it was in the very precincts of Saint-Benoît that Villon killed a priest, Philippe Sermoise, who was his rival in love. The Church of Saint-Benoît was at the corner of rue Saint-Jacques and rue des Écoles where the Sorbonne is now.

After visiting the baths, spare at least a little time for the garden, between the Cluny and boulevard Saint-Germain; it is charming.

When you come out of the Cluny, you are but a stone's throw from the Sorbonne. Walk a few steps east in rue du Sommerard to rue Saint-Jacques, and down the latter a few steps to rue des Écoles. After you have crossed this street, you will have the Collège de France on your left and the Sorbonne on your right.

Robert de Sorbon, chaplain to Saint Louis, is usually credited with the founding of the Sorbonne; but it was really Robert de Douai, physician to Marguerite of Provence, Saint Louis's wife, who left fifteen hundred livres to found a college and confided the execution of his bequest to Robert de Sorbon. A "college," then, meant a group of men of the same profession — literally, colleagues. It was Abélard who first drew students toward this quarter, away from the doctors of Notre-Dame. And Robert of Sorbon's first college, aided by a gift of lands and houses from the King, opened its doors in 1255 to sixteen poor students. But soon the faculty of theology took up residence in the college, and the students shifted for themselves as best they could. The first books printed in France (examples of which you may see in the Galerie Mazarine of the Bibliothèque Nationale) were done here in 1470; and on the Grand Staircase of the Sorbonne you may see that first French printing-press pictured in a fine mural by Flameng.

Apply at door VII in the rue des Écoles for permission to

visit the Sorbonne, which now houses only two of the many faculties it controls: Sciences and Letters. There are about seventeen thousand students always in attendance at the various faculties of the Sorbonne. The famous old university has had many ups and downs in its centuries of existence. It was suppressed by the Revolution — of course! — and, equally of course, reopened by Napoleon; but after his downfall it had little support. The present building was begun in 1889 and finished in 1901.

I hope you will see the murals of the Sorbonne. You have already seen those of the Hôtel de Ville and of the Panthéon. Think what French appreciation of this great form of art has done to encourage it in the past generation! We in this country have made tremendous strides, during that same time, in architecture; but our art leaders have not yet been able to get American millionaires, corporations, or government committees to give any adequate patronage to mural painters. It is the next important step in our development of the beautiful; and every one of us who comes home with a definite feeling in favor of it will be a help in hastening it.

The Church of the Sorbonne was rebuilt by Lemercier (architect of the Palais-Royal, of part of the Louvre, etc.) for Cardinal Richelieu, who, on being elected head of his Alma Mater, in 1624, rebuilt it, handsomely, at his own expense. Richelieu was buried here, in a superb tomb designed by le Brun and sculptured by Girardon. In 1793 his tomb was violated and his skull was stolen and passed from hand to hand until it reached a little village of Brittany, whence it was returned, in 1866, to its rightful resting-place. The tomb, Girardon's masterpiece, was saved from destruction at the hands of the mob only by the heroism of Alexandre Lenoir who threw himself upon the exquisite thing and in his own body received the hurts intended for it. You shall hear Lenoir's story when you go to the Beaux-

Arts; it is one of the most moving tales that Paris has to tell.

Over the tomb hangs Richelieu's red hat. And there are some interesting murals here, too.

I am not sure that the Collège de France will be of much interest to the average visitor; nor that there will be anything to repay him for walking across the street to take a closer look at the Lycée Louis-le-Grand. This was the Jesuit college of Clermont, and Molière, Voltaire, Robespierre, and Camille Desmoulins were among the students; but nothing remains of the buildings they knew.

There is, however, a fairly short détour easy to make from here, which will be very interesting to some readers.

The rue Saint-Jacques, you will remember, was the old Roman highway. If you loiter on it o' nights, with your ear not to windward, but toward that retreat where the echoes stay — the echoes of yester-years — when no one is summoning them forth, you may distinctly hear the tramping feet of Rome's legions. Those that sound a little weary are coming up from the south — it has been a long march; the springier steps are those of men returning from Rome's outposts to Rome's very self.

A pause; a lapse of ages; then the soft footfalls of another from the south, a lone man, his pace beating the measure of a sad heart, the heart of a man who wrote of life as "the time of my debt" and endured it as one endures a prison sentence. Dante is coming to call on Jean de Meung, author of the second part of "Le Roman de la Rose" which was for two centuries and more the most celebrated work of French literature. Jean lived at 218 rue Saint-Jacques. His house is, of course, long since gone; but you may like to visit the spot.

As you continue down the old highway, look to your left along rue des Fueillantines (it is just beyond the big National Institute for Deaf-Mutes); for here was the delicious old convent garden in which Victor Hugo spent those enchanted years of his imaginative childhood which he has so exquisitely described in "The Last Day of a Condemned Man," and in "What Went on in the Feuillantines around 1813." It was an idyllic place for such a child, and we have reason to be grateful for it.

At number 269, where Vincent d'Indy now has his Schola Cantorum, or school of choral singing, there used to be the convent of the English Benedictines, in whose chapel James II of England and his daughter Louise-Marie were buried.

At number 284, at the back of a mean little "yard," is a portal between two columns. Through it, on an April day in 1674, Louise de la Vallière entered the Convent of the Carmelites to begin that penance so harsh that nobody expected her to survive it for very long, but which she endured for thirty-six years. She was not quite thirty when she came here, and at the height of her beauty; but for seven years past she had been supplanted in the King's affections by Madame de Montespan. Her two children were with her — Louis XIV's children — and friends and relatives followed in another carriage. "Thirteen years earlier — day for day!" says her biographer, Jules Lair, "little La Vallière, Maid-of-Honor, had set out, in innocent young gladness, for Fontainebleau; and now she was going to a living grave."

She at once put on the coarse serge habit of the Order; and that night with her own hands she sheared away her golden hair. In the Galerie Mollien of the Louvre, containing French paintings of the seventeenth century, you may see a picture by Lebrun of Mary Magdalene which used to hang in one of the chapels of the Carmelite church, and which is sometimes said to be a likeness of Louise de la Vallière. This latter is an obvious error; but the picture was

there when she passed her long vigils in prayer, and doubtless helped to sustain her in her arduous penance. If you
are especially interested in La Vallière, you may like to go
through to rue Pierre-Nicole, immediately behind rue Saint-
Jacques, on your right, and see at number 17 *bis* what is
called the Oratory of La Vallière; it was a "station" in the
garden of the Carmelites.

Across the street is the hospital of Val-de-Grâce. This
was once a Benedictine convent, and the present buildings,
including the church, were erected by Anne of Austria in
thanksgiving for the birth of Louis XIV. It is now a military hospital which still houses and nurses a great number
of victims of the late war. The church, whose dome is one
of the dominant features of the Paris sky-line hereabouts, is
in the style of Saint Peter's at Rome, and the high-altar is a
copy of Bernini's in Saint Peter's. Mignard painted the
dome frescoes, which some authorities pronounce "perhaps
the most important mural that France possesses." And
Molière wrote a poem to celebrate the completion of Mignard's work.

The hearts of many royalties were buried here: Anne of
Austria; her sister-in-law, Queen Henrietta-Maria of England; Louis XIV's eldest daugher, dead in infancy; and so
on, down to the first dauphin of Louis XVI and Marie Antoinette, the little boy who died at Meudon in June, 1789.
It is said that his is the only one of all those royal hearts
which was not snatched from its resting-place by the mobs
of '93.

When you leave the Val-de-Grâce you are almost to the
boulevard Port-Royal, across which, on the opposite side
also of rue Saint-Jacques is the Maternity Hospital where
one of the shells from "Big Bertha" wrought such dreadful
havoc among mothers and new-born babies in the spring of
1918. (This was a branch of the Jansenist abbey of Port-

Royal-des-Champs, and had many interesting associations in the late seventeenth century.)

At this corner you may board a bus, route A, which will take you, in five minutes, to Saint-Sulpice — to which those who have not cared to make this détour may proceed from the Sorbonne by way of rue Vaugirard and up rue Fé-rou. Just before reaching this latter street, on Vaugirard, you pass Massenet's house (48 Vaugirard), and number 54, where Voltaire's adopted daughter, "Belle et Bonne," the Marquise de Villette, died in 1822.

You may think that this day has too many churches in it. I cannot blame you — for Saint-Sulpice is the sixth. But there is, I think, not one of them (unless it be the Val-de-Grâce) which you would not be regretful to miss. And as a compensation, I shall not ask you to visit one to-morrow, and very few more in all the course of our Paris days.

You really ought to come to Saint-Sulpice for a service, to hear the magnificent organ, superbly played, and the famous choir. And if you love such things, you ought to come to a service in the Students' Chapel at nine some Sunday morning, and hear the little organ of the Dauphin (Louis XV's son) on which Mozart played at Versailles.

I am fond of Saint-Sulpice for many reasons. I love this "neighborhood," as we'd call it. I can walk these streets and meet so many sorts of people who fascinate me. At almost every turning I encounter one of the Musketeers. Athos lived here in rue Férou, within two steps of the Luxembourg; D'Artagnan's lodging, in the house of Bonacieux, was in what was then rue des Fossoyeurs and is now Servandoni; Porthos had that apartment, to which he invited no one, in rue du Vieux-Colombier, to the north of the square; and Aramis lived in rue Vaugirard, just east of rue de Cassette, his windows overlooking the Luxembourg Gardens.

No wonder that Booth Tarkington described this vicinity to Arthur Bartlett Maurice, as "just around the corner from the places where Aramis and Company used to hang out." (And if, by the way, you belong to the delightful company of those who love "footsteps," I commend to you most heartily Mr. Maurice's book on "The Paris of the Novelists," with the aid of which you may follow many a trail of romance and immeasurably intensify your joy in reading.)

You come up rue Férou toward Saint-Sulpice, along the east side of the old Seminary of Saint-Sulpice, which ceased to be a seminary in 1906, and was under discussion as a more commodious housing for the Luxembourg Museum when the war came and filled it with fleeing refugees from the invaded districts. It is in a parlor of this seminary that the fourth act of "Manon Lescaut" is laid — but that would be in the older buildings which disappeared soon after the Revolution. The superior of the seminary at the time of the Revolution was the Abbé Eméry, who was imprisoned in the Conciergerie; but from there, under the very nose of Fouquier-Tinville, directed the maintenance of the suppressed faith, not only in the Conciergerie (where Mass was celebrated every day), but in all the prisons of Paris. And when the condemned were not able to receive the sacraments before leaving for the scaffold, they were secretly notified where, along the *via dolorosa*, a priest would be standing to give them absolution as they passed. All this was organized and directed by this intrepid man of sixty from the depths of his own cell which was above that of Marie Antoinette whom he comforted at least once, if not oftener, with a midnight ministration.

It was in the new seminary, however, that Ernest Renan was a student, and from which, casting aside his soutane, he walked out, in October, 1845, and went to a modest lodging-house on the other side of Place Saint-Sulpice — to do his own thinking, thenceforth.

I come to Saint-Sulpice for many "occasions": now on a late December day in 1790 to see Lucille Duplessis married to Camille Desmoulins; to follow the bridal party into the sacristy, and to shudder as one of the witnesses signs the marriage register with the name Maximilien Robespierre. He is the bridegroom's schoolmate; he aspires to wed the sister of the bride; yet within little more than three years he will send both these young spouses to the guillotine. Again, I come here on a June day in 1821, when Victor Hugo and his brothers carried their mother's body across the Place, from the house at number 10 rue des Mézières, where she died, to the Church of Saint-Sulpice, and thence to the Cemetery of Montparnasse; and, in October of 1822, I come to see Victor married here in the same chapel of the Virgin from which his mother had been buried.

Rue Servandoni (where D'Artagnan lodged) runs south from the church to rue Vaugirard. On the façade of number 14 you may see a medallion showing Servandoni, the architect, unrolling his plans for Saint-Sulpice. At number 15, the French sculptor François Vernet died in 1784; and to his widow, still living here in 1793, came certain persons who asked her if she would give shelter to a proscribed man. This heroic woman did not hesitate a moment, although she knew that the penalty for hiding one proscribed was death. She did not even ask the name of the man she was to harbor. All she sought to know was if he was honest. "Then, let him come," she said, "and lose not a moment, for while we talk he may be seized."

So he came. He was the Marquis de Condorcet, fifty years old, a member of the Academy of Sciences and of the French Academy, also of the academies of Turin, Saint Petersburg, Bologna, and Philadelphia; the friend of almost all the distinguished men of his time. He had been inspector-general of the Mint, and had lived at the Hôtel des Monnaies, where his young wife (one of the most beautiful women of her time) held a salon that was famed throughout Europe — because she was not merely the beautiful wife of a brilliant man, but was herself an intellectual of remarkable sort. Condorcet was an anti-Royalist, an anti-Clerical, a secretary of the Legislative Assembly, and a member of its committee on public instruction; the plan which he drafted for a system of state education laid the foundations on which the modern educational scheme of France is built. He was one of the first to declare in favor of a republic, and to resign his offices and titles; but he voted against the death of the King, denounced the arrest of the Girondists, and was accused of conspiring against the Republic, condemned, and declared an outlaw, subject to the Revolutionary Tribunal.

This was the man Madame Vernet received into her home. When he realized the risk she ran to shield him, he declared he must leave. "I am outlawed," he said, "and if I am discovered, you will meet the same end as myself." To which Madame Vernet replied: "The Convention, Monsieur, has the right to declare you beyond the protection of the law; it has not the power to declare you beyond the protection of humanity."

And stay he did, though his hostess had to keep constant surveillance over him lest he change his mind and steal away. His wife came often, in greatest stealth, to see him; and it was she who persuaded him to employ his time in writing that which he had long contemplated: his "Historic Outline of the Mind's Progress," in which he presented his arguments for his belief in "the infinite perfectibility of the human species." In the midst of the Terror, hunted by the men who had the power to show what perfectibility there was in free creatures, this calm, dauntless philosopher preserved not only his courage, but his cheerful faith in mankind.

At length he fell a prey to fears, not for himself, but for the heroic woman who was hiding him; and, eluding her vigilance, he stole away from her house and began wandering, forlornly, denied other shelter. Three days and three nights he hid in the quarries of Clamart; then, driven forth by hunger, he entered a humble tavern and called for an omelet. When asked for his papers, he had none to show. He was searched and a volume of Horace was found on him. Sufficient proof that he was a dangerous man! He was thrown into a damp cell in the jail at Bourg-la-Reine, and found dead there on the floor, next morning — whether of exhaustion or of poison, no one knows.

I think that all of us who are idealists and who suffer, at times, abysmal despair over the human race and its conduct when given the rein, must needs regard this house in rue Servandoni with the utmost reverence and with profound renewal of faith. For the bloody Terrorists of '93 passed; and out of all the suffering they caused emerged a new France in which the possible perfectibility of the human species has been demonstrated as it has seldom been elsewhere in the annals of mankind.

There is a great deal more in this vicinity that you might enjoy seeing on another day. But for the present you have, I am sure, had enough.

You may like to sit for an hour or so in the Luxembourg Gardens, and then dine at Michaud's, on the northeast corner of rue Saints-Pères and rue Jacob, where you can get excellent food, plain service, and good company, for a very modest sum. Or you may want to spend an hour or so in the fascinating antique shops which you will find between boulevard Saint-Germain and the Seine on several streets: rue Saints-Pères, rue Mazarine, rue de Beaune, etc.

If by any chance "Manon" is "on" to-night at the Opéra-Comique, think what a time 'twould be to see and hear it!

Should you be going to the Comique, you might like to dine at Noël-Peters, 24–30 passage des Princes, just off rue de Richelieu; or at Lapré's, 24 rue Drouot, north of the boulevard immediately across from rue de Richelieu.

Or, if the night is warm and you are inclined for outdoor dining, and disinclined to spend a great deal, suppose you take at place Saint-Sulpice a bus marked "A E" and ride out past the Lion of Belfort to the Parc de Montsouris, where you may dine very well at the Pavillon du Lac, and hear a band concert.

XIII

YOUR THIRTEENTH DAY IN PARIS

THE saunter I propose for to-day is one which will richly reward lovers of "old Paris," bring admirers of "the little Corsican" very close to him in his first Paris day, and give glimpses of the Mint and of the Institut de France. (Those who wish to see the Mint must have a permit, issued, on written application, by the Directeur des Monnaies, 11 Quai Conti.)

Those who feel that they have had their fill of "old Paris" and of Bonaparte, and are not specially interested in the Mint and the Institute, would do well to take this day (Thursday) for a trip to Chantilly, which I outline in the chapter called "Here and There."

On the supposition that you want this stroll (which to my way of thinking is one of the most fascinating in the world, but which might bore some persons to tears) I'll suggest that you take the "Métro" (about ten-thirty) to the Saint Paul station, at the beginning of rue Saint-Antoine, and walk back, west, from the station, to the rue du Prévôt; down that short street to rue Charlemagne, and (a step to your right, across rue Charlemagne) into rue du Figuier which dates back to 1300, and was named for a fig tree which stood here until 1605, at the corner of what is now the rue de l'Hôtel-de-Ville, but used (for many centuries) to be the rue de la Mortellerie.

At this corner is the Hôtel de Sens, which was begun in 1474 for the archbishops of Sens who were, until 1623, the ecclesiastical lords of Paris; a curiously protracted survival from those very early days when Sens was an important

Roman town and "Lutetia" was an unimportant outpost and dependency.

The great lords of the Church who lived here seem to have been, almost without exception, a rascally lot, and given to the lowest infamies, personal and political. Louis de Guise, Cardinal of Lorraine, uncle of Mary Stuart, was one of the tenants, and it was his influence, perhaps, which made this, after his death, a favored meeting-place of the Ligue or ultra-Catholic party opposed to Henry III and even more to Henry IV. Some historians aver that Henry IV's death was plotted here, in those days when he was fighting for his kingdom. What we know is that the then master of this mansion, the Cardinal de Pellève, died here, suddenly, when he heard that Henry IV had entered Paris.

After Henry's marriage with "the fat bankeress from Florence" (Marie de Médicis) there seemed to Marguerite de Valois, his divorced wife, no reason why she should not come back to Paris and its gaieties. Nor did good-natured Henry see any reason, either. So he provided her with a suitable dwelling on the outskirts of town. But "Margot" had no suburban tastes. She complained to Henry that she was too far from the centre of things; and he, always anxious to please, gave her this Hôtel de Sens. She had not been here very long when her favorite of the moment (Marguerite was fifty-two, but she liked young lovers) was killed, at her side, by her favorite-of-the-moment-before. The murdered youth, a curly-haired youngster of eighteen, was her page; and the murderer was a "man of twenty." Margot was returning from Mass at the Célestins, and the pretty page was helping her from her carriage when the jealous ex-favorite slew his rival. Whereupon Margot swore that she would neither eat nor drink till she had seen the crime avenged. 'Tis said she went in person to Henry to tell him her troubles. It would not have seemed incongruous to either of them. At any rate, swift justice was meted out; and on the morrow of the crime, Margot sat in her window and saw her erstwhile lover ascend a scaffold, draped in black velvet, on the spot where the page was slain, and tried to think she was glad when the headsman's axe flashed and a second lad went into eternity on her account. But she had none of her mother's indifference to violent death; and she never again could bear the Hôtel de Sens. Henry, sympathetic, then gave her a great grant of land on the south bank, and there she spent the last decade of her disorderly but fascinating life. She is often called "the best of the brood" of that unnatural she-wolf Catherine de Médicis; but this is an injustice to that poor young martyr, Elizabeth, who succeeded "Bloody Mary" in the Bluebeard-ly succession of Philip II's wives. I have to confess that nearly all of Catherine's children fill me with an enormous pity — not exepting Charles IX. I suppose that Margot wrung more from life than any of them. She was the only one who scratched any gray hairs, or came within a mile of doing so. And she seems to have learned, at a fairly early age, how to fend for herself in matters of pleasure. She has had her eulogists, like Brantôme; and those who wanted to throw stones at her were never at a loss for stones to throw. But it is Dumas who has kept her, for all time, the living woman of passionate flesh that-she really was, and I am sure that she is ardently grateful to him, and tells him so, whenever they meet in the Otherwhere.

Long after Margot's day, the Hôtel de Sens was the Paris starting-point for the coaches of the Lyons Mail.

At half-past five on the evening of April 27, 1796, the coach for Lyons left here, carrying a large sum in gold and bank notes.

Near Fontainebleau the coach was held up, the driver killed, and the treasure carried off. Joseph Lesurque, a man of blameless life, living at 38 rue Montorgueil, Paris, was "recognized" by several passengers as the murderer and robber, and executed, on October 30th. Two years later the real perpetrator, Dubosc, was captured and guillotined. This is the episode which furnished the Henry Irvings, father and son, with one of their most popular plays, "The Lyons Mail." I am not sure but it is still given sometimes in Paris (at the Odéon, probably), but if I ever see it announced, I'll not miss it. They call it "Le Courrier de Lyon." Keep a lookout for it.

After the rue du Figuier crosses the rue du Fauconnier, it becomes the rue de l'Ave-Maria.

Look up the rue du Fauconnier. It was there in 1265, and I don't know how long before. It used to be inhabited by women of evil repute.

The rue de l'Ave-Maria got its name from a convent that Saint Louis founded. At number 15 is the doorway through which Molière and his companions came and went to their dressing-rooms and stage when "The Illustrious Theatre," as they were pleased to call it, played in the deserted tennis court of the Black Cross. They came here, from another tennis court across the river, in January, 1645, on the eve of Molière's twenty-third birthday, and set up their tragic Muse under the very noses of the rich and fashionable, who inclined no more then than they do now to devote any of their abundant leisure to Hecuba wailing on the walls of Troy — or similar entertainment. Molière's "Little Theatre" was a dismal failure, like most of ours; he was arrested, because he could not pay for the candles he burned to light his echoing playhouse, and haled to prison in the Grand Châtelet. That was in August, '45. And not long thereafter, Molière left Paris, in an ox-cart, for those twelve years of weary wanderings which taught him to make people laugh if he would eat.

He must have come by here, often, in later years; and I like to conjecture what his reflections were. He lodged, when playing here, at either 5 or 7 rue des Jardins hard by — across the street from where Rabelais, the other great, mordant comic genius of France, had died in 1553. Look up that street, which has eight centuries of history, and let your spirit salute those of the great satirists who lived there. (The tablet recalling the Illustrious Theatre is at number 32 quai des Celestins; but the existing remains are at 15 rue de l'Ave-Maria.)

At the end of rue de l'Ave-Maria, rue Saint-Paul runs northward, along what was the western boundary of the royal enclosure known as the Saint-Paul Palace, or group of mansions and their dependencies. The grand old mansion at number 4 rue Saint-Paul dates back to the end of the fifteenth century, and has so much history that M. Lucien Lambeau, secretary of the Old Paris Commission, published a résumé of it, in 1907; but there is no outstanding feature of it which I feel sure you would care to muse upon as you make your way up the ancient street on a little détour of four short blocks which some of you may decide to "skip."

The first street on your right as you go up rue Saint-Paul, is rue des Lions, so named because thereabouts the menagerie of the kings used to be. In a wretched garret here Rachel lived when she was a little urchin singing for coppers in the streets and winning the notice of Victor Hugo.

A few steps farther, and you come to rue Charles V, commemorating the founder of the Saint-Paul domain. And at number 12 in this street is the mansion of the Marquise de Brinvilliers, whose story became a part of literature because Madame de Sévigné and other writers of her day made so many comments on it; and continues so because M. Funck-Brentano has made a so-complete story of it in his "Drama of Poisons."

She was a dainty, appealing little thing, that Marie-Madeleine Dreux d'Aubray, with big blue eyes, extraordinarily white skin and a childishly innocent face. When she was twenty-one, her father, who was Lieutenant of the Châtelet Prison, found her a rich husband in the person of the dissolute Marquis de Brinvilliers, of the famous Gobelins family, who went on with his own gallantries and either encouraged or permitted the girl Marquise to amuse herself with "affairs." One of her lovers was a handsome young cavalry officer of bad reputation, named Godin de Sainte-Croix; and their "carryings-on" soon became such a nasty scandal that her father decided to intervene. One day when the Marquise and Sainte-Croix were riding in her carriage, the carriage was stopped by officers of the Crown furnished with a lettre de cachet, who seized Sainte-Croix and hurried him to the Bastille, where he stayed for a year, sharing a cell with an Italian poisoner who boasted that he had made away with one hundred and fifty persons in Rome alone.

Sainte-Croix's interest in learning of poisons was principally, at first, that he might safely avenge himself on the Marquise's father, and, in getting him out of the way, remove his interference and secure his estate. Brinvilliers had fled town to escape his creditors, and Marie-Madeleine was living at her father's house. Her sister had become a Carmelite nun, and it seemed that Marie-Madeleine was inclining toward a life of service — so much time did she spend in hospitals and in visiting the sick poor in their homes. She was a devoted nurse, but it could not be said that she was successful; an extraordinary number of her patients died. Marie-Madeleine was trying on them the slow poisons that Sainte-Croix had learned to brew. He, freed from the Bastille, had taken rooms in the Impasse Maubert over on the Left Bank, and there he distilled and prepared

the poisons that she administered. Even the servants of
her household became subjects of her experiments; and in
time her father died, of a lingering and unnamed malady.
She nursed him devotedly to the end, and seemed to mourn
him sincerely. Then her two brothers succumbed. When she
purposed poisoning her sister and sister-in-law, her secretary and accomplice, a man named Briancourt, was horrified
and tried to dissuade her. He began to moralize. "Enough,"
he doubtless said, "was enough"; he thought she should go
no farther. Marie-Madeleine told Sainte-Croix and they
decided that Briancourt should "disappear." He knew too
much about their methods to be easily poisoned; so it was
planned that Marie-Madeleine should give a midnight rendezvous to Briancourt, and that Sainte-Croix should appear
and kill him. Briancourt was madly in love with the lily-
fair Marquise, and could not wait for the time to come
when she was to receive him. He hid himself in a corridor
of the same floor on which her chamber was, and through a
half-closed window he could see her as she made her preparations for the night, dismissed her maids, and locked the
door. Then, a torch in her hand, she went to the fireplace;
it was summer, and the aperture was closed. She slid back
the covering, and Sainte-Croix emerged. There were kisses,
caresses, directions; then Sainte-Croix went back to his
hiding-place.

Briancourt was so frightened when he realized the trap
prepared for him that he leaned too heavily against his window and either broke it or in some other wise attracted
Marie-Madeleine's attention to his fear-frozen face. She
taunted him for not coming to keep the rendezvous, and he
went in. Sainte-Croix leaped from the fireplace, but Briancourt did some leaping too, and lived to tell his tale at
Marie-Madeleine's trial.

She had been giving poisons to her husband (Marie-Madeleine was rich, now, and he was back to spend her money), but they seemed powerless.

Then, one day, the glass mask that Sainte-Croix wore when bending over his death-distilling broke, and he died of the fumes. The police came to search his papers for some clue to relatives or properties, and found, instead, Marie-Madeleine's letters to him revealing their crimes.

Somehow, she got wind of his death in time to flee before they came to arrest her; and when they arrived at this portal, she was on her way north, in a coach, bound for England. There she heard that her capture was planned; so she fled to Liège and entered a convent. There, after some time, she met a handsome young priest who made love to her and persuaded her to "fly" with him. The carriage crossed the French frontier, the "priest" tore off his clerical disguise and revealed himself as Desgrais, a clever police officer, and Marie-Madeleine went to the Bastille, thence to the Conciergerie where she was subjected to the water-torture and made to confess. It is said that when she saw the preparations for her torture she summoned a coquettish bit of raillery and said, "Surely, gentlemen, you don't think that a little body like mine can hold those three buckets of water." But soon the show of courage vanished, and the admissions that she made were beyond even what had been suspected.

After sentence of death had been passed upon her, she was denied the consolations of the Church; but on the way to execution, she was taken to Notre-Dame and made to kneel in front of it and confess afresh. Clad in a hooded gown, her feet bare, a rope around her neck, a lighted taper in her hands, she publicly admitted her manifold guilt; then resumed her place in the tumbril and her way to the Place de Grève (in front of the Hôtel de Ville), where she was first beheaded and then burned. Her husband wept beside her the whole way. "Everybody and his wife" were there to see her die. Some say she rallied the women of rank and fashion on the entertainment she was providing for them. But I doubt it. Charles Le Brun made a drawing of her as she passed in her tumbril. (It is in the gallery of Old French Designs, in the Louvre.) And unless he imputed to her a terror she did not feel, she was a creature well-nigh dead of horror as they dragged her through the streets. Her execution took place late on the afternoon of July 16, 1676, and was graphically described in a letter next day by Madame de Sévigné who witnessed it.

If you have come to look at her house, you will find yourself, a few paces beyond it, at rue Beautrellis, at number 16 in which Sardou was born, in 1831. Across the way from him, when he was a little boy, was an old mansion which had subterranean passages leading to the Seine, to the Bastille, and ('tis said) to the house where the Marquise de Brinvilliers lived; and its garden was part of the old Saint-Paul cemetery whe e Rabelais was buried, and the Man with the Iron Mask. Is it any wonder that he became such a weaver of spells, such a passionate lover of this old Paris?

A stone's throw beyond rue Beautrellis, is rue du Petit-Musc. If you are specially interested in Gabrielle d'Estrées, you may care to cross it and follow rue de la Cérisaie (street of the cherry trees) to number 10, where she supped with Zamet, the Italian financier, on Tuesday, April 6, 1599. Her wedding garments were made. Henry had given her the ring with which, at his coronation, he had wedded France. She was queen in all but name. There were many, however, who had other plans for Henry — and Gabrielle died. The house has other memories, too. Peter the Great was a guest there of the Maréchal de Villeroi, in 1717. But nothing that he ate made him violently ill. Perhaps nothing could!

Go down rue du Petit-Musc to the quai des Célestins. At

the northwest corner of the quai and Petit-Musc, you will
see an extraordinary-looking building, now occupied by the
École Massillon. Hardouin Mansart (architect of Versailles) built it for Fieubert, chancellor of Anne of Austria;
but it has suffered many vicissitudes since then — the
worst of them from those who thought they were doing
most to restore or to embellish it. In front of the school are
some remains of one of the Bastille towers, uncovered in
1899 when the Métro was digging on the site of the old fortress, and removed hither. Next door to it (number 4) is
where Antoine Louis Barye died, June 25, 1875, after a long
struggle with poverty. Almost everybody, in every land,
knows Barye's small bronzes and something of his great
groups; knows that he was the greatest artist of animal life
of the French school and perhaps of any school. But not
everybody knows that he was once a goldsmith, like Verroc-
chio and Cellini, and that he did not suspect his real genius
until long after he had left the Beaux-Arts. He delighted in
the Jardin des Plantes, and, from making vigorous drawings of the animals in their menagerie, went on to model-
ling them. You have seen his groups in the Tuileries Gardens. There is a whole room devoted to his works in the
Louvre. You will soon see his monument on the Île Saint-
Louis.

This quai des Célestins got its name from the old convent of the Célestins founded here in 1365, under Charles
V. The Célestins' church was very popular with royalty,
even after royalty deserted its dwellings hereabouts for
the Louvre. The Duke of Orléans, murdered by his cousin
of Burgundy, was buried here, and so was his wife. And
here were the hearts of poor little Francis II and of his
father, Henry II, and of his brother, Charles IX, and of
Catherine de Médicis, and of the Constable du Montmorency. Germain Pilon's "Three Graces," now at the Louvre,

was here, too — though how the severe Célestins tolerated those lovely ladies I am at a loss to know.

This church was not demolished until 1849. It stood about where number 12 boulevard Henri IV is now, and where the conductor of the famous band of the Garde Ré-publicaine lives, at the corner of the rue de Sully. The Ca-serne (barracks) des Célestins houses the Garde Républi-caine.

This is the Arsenal quarter, and to the lovers of old Paris there is magic in the very name — not because of the Arse-nal, which Louis XVI suppressed, but because of the library which once belonged to his brother Charles, and of the as-sociations that collection of books and manuscripts has had in the last ninety years or so.

Let us give the old uses of the Arsenal their due, and then pass on to those which make it a veritable shrine.

Francis I began the casting of cannon here, and Henry II made the place into a vast factory for war; it occupied all the ground between the Seine, which used to be where the boulevard Morland is now, and the Bastille, and contained, among other things, many powder mills. There was a grand explosion, about the time of the Saint Bartholomew massa-cre, and when Henry IV had become King and fought his way into Paris and found a little time to settle down, he or-dered a new arsenal built. Of all that was constructed for him, nothing remains except the residence of the Grand Master, which you are about to visit. Sully lodged here, and it was on his way hither to see his sick minister that Henry IV was assassinated. They will show you (if you ask) some apartments that are said to be Sully's. The most searching writers aver that, while the panelling and other decorations are those of Sully's suite, the rooms he actually occupied were on the other side of the building, facing the river. It was here, in this building, that the Marquise de

Brinvilliers was tried and condemned; and here, also, was Fouquet's celebrated trial which had all France agog.

After the death of Louis XIV and the breaking of his will (by which he left the regency of the Kingdom to the Duc de Maine, his dearly beloved son by Montespan), the Duke and Duchess of Maine, cheated of regnant dwelling at Versailles and Marly and Fontainebleau, came here to live for a while. If you ask to see their apartments you will, doubtless, he permitted to do so. They are very charming; and besides being in themselves well worth seeing, they contain some of the treasures of the library.

This library was founded by M. de Voyer d'Argenson, Marquis de Paulmy, who was the last governor or grand master of the Arsenal. He was so proud of it (as he well might be!) that he was very anxious to guard against its breaking up after his death. So he sold it to the Comte d'Artois, younger of Louis XVI's two brothers. Just what that wild young rake was supposed to do with a library, I cannot imagine; but doubtless it was considered a "genteel" and princely thing for him to own. And two years later he acquired a large part of the superb library of the Duc de la Vallière, grandson of Louis XIV and Louise. Buying libraries was not costly for Artois — he just promised to pay, and then forgot both the books and the promise. His books became national property in 1792, and four years later were open to the public. Louis XVIII returned them to his brother, in 1814; and in 1830, when Artois had been chased from the throne after six inglorious years as Charles X, the library of the Arsenal became a public treasury for all time.

Charles Nodier had been librarian of this collection since 1824, and he continued in his post till 1844, when he died. There have been other eminent librarians here — poets, dramatists, booklovers, members, all, of the Immortal

Forty — and each of them has done notable work as a result of his tenure of this vantage-point. But no name associated with the Arsenal library shines with such refulgence as Nodier's. Indeed, I do not know that anywhere in the annals of libraries there is a story comparable with his as an ideal of all that a librarian can be, though few of them seem to aspire thereto.

Nodier was a native of Besançon, the same border town that gave Hugo to the world, and was a librarian there in his youth. His father was a Jacobin, and Charles seems to have been one, too, when he was only twelve years old. It was the safest thing to be, just then! But, somehow or other, he had got to be a Royalist by the time the Bourbons came back — enough of one, anyway, to get this job from Charles X — and grateful, indeed, ought we all to be that he had. For those were years when extraordinary young persons were "coming up" in Paris: Hugo and Balzac and Dumas and Musset and Vigny and Sainte-Beuve and Lamartine — and others; and Nodier had a great gift for perceiving literary talent and for encouraging it. The circle he gathered about him at the Arsenal, the suggestions he made, the critical discussions he started, had more to do than any one will ever be able to compute, with the extraordinary fruition of the romanticists.

There has never again been so great a galaxy of first-magnitude stars; but each decade or thereabouts has had its luminaries, and nearly all of them have been more or less lighted at the Arsenal.

For the lover of books it is a place of delicious reverie — far from the madding crowds, quiet, redolent of ageing volumes and of unexplored documents which may yield to the indefatigable delver, some day, the solution of dear-knows-what teasing mystery. For, in addition to more than 600,-000 volumes (as compared with 3,600,000 in the Bibliothèque Nationale) and about 120,000 engravings, this library has about 10,000 manuscripts, including the archives of the Bastille, the love-letters of Henry IV (charming they are, too!), the records of Brinvilliers' trial, all the papers in the Affair of the Diamond Necklace, and all the evidence relating to the Man with the Iron Mask. M. Funck-Brentano, the present librarian, has been splendidly true to the traditions of his place and has enriched French literature with many scholarly studies of the manuscript treasures in his charge. It is to him that we are indebted for the solution of the Iron Mask mystery.

Ask to see the psalter of Saint Louis and the fragment of his mantle of blue silk sewn with gold fleurs-de-lis; and Charles V's Bible, in which he wrote: "This is my book, the King of France." He owned about nine hundred books — did Charles — which was a goodly number, a century before printing was thought of — but in the evil days of his poor drivelling son, Charles VI, the collection was dispersed, and a great part of it went over to England with the Duke of Bedford, "regent" for Henry VI of England, who was crowned King of France in Notre-Dame, in 1431.

You are probably thinking of lunch, now. But if there is any good restaurant near here, I do not know it. I hope you can defer lunching, to-day, until about one-thirty; by that time, you shall be where there are many good places to choose from.

When you leave the Arsenal, go back to the quai des Célestins, and look down at the port Saint-Paul, beneath this quai, and let your "mind's eye" do some seeing for you. It is about four-thirty on the afternoon of October 30, 1784, and you, not being very busy, are watching the clumsy big barge which is warping in to unload her cargo of country produce and her three hundred cheap passengers some of whom have been forty-eight hours on the way from points whence the coaches would have brought them in a third or a quarter of that time.

Among the first to debark, by a narrow gangplank, was a Minim friar convoying five lads, all under sixteen, whom he was bringing from Brienne to the École Militaire. They scrambled up to the pont Marie, and crossed it to the Île Saint-Louis. The street which bisects Île Saint-Louis, between pont Marie and pont de la Tournelle, is called rue des Deux-Ponts. On it, in those days you are reliving, there was a restaurant called the Coq Hardi. And thither the friar leads his charges, for a meal on which (I surmise) the restaurateur did not make a sou. When they have eaten as much as they can get, they continue on their way, cross pont de la Tournelle (whence they have the incomparable view of Notre-Dame's flying buttresses and belfried towers, silhouetted against the afterglow) and are on the quais of the Left Bank, of which they have heard so much. One of the boys finds an old, well-worn book on a stall, and covets it — but lacks even the few sous that would make it his. A comrade, in funds, lends the price; and the sale is effected. The book is Le Sage's "Gil Blas." The new owner is a lad just past fifteen, undersized, stoop-shouldered, hollow-chested, sallow, with thin legs and scraggly locks; he speaks French badly, with a strong Italian accent, and is a taciturn chap, taking life very gravely, and having to bite his tongue, often, to hold back the resentment he feels against France; he is being educated by the French King's bounty, and he may not speak his mind; but he is very bitter because France, having purchased his island home, will not permit it to become free. His name — as he now writes it — is Napoleon Buonaparte; he has gallicized Nabuleone, of which his schoolfellows made such fun; but he has a fierce pride in thinking that there is nothing French about him, and never will be.

If this were not your first visit to the Île Saint-Louis, I'd suggest that you follow this lad, with his "Gil Blas," as the friar leads his charges along the quais and up (probably the street now called rue Bonaparte, then called rue des Vieux-Augustines) to prayers; thence to the École Militaire, where he took leave of them. But as you must economize steps, in this great wonderland of Paris, I'll not ask you to go farther now with Napoleon in his first Paris footsteps than across the pont Marie.

What is now called Île Saint-Louis was, before 1614, two uninhabited islands, one called Île Notre-Dame, and belonging (ever since the ninth century) to the bishopric of Paris; and the other called the Île aux Vaches, or island of the cows. In 1614, a man named Marie who was chief of the department of roads and bridges of France, and two associates, got a grant of the two islands in consideration of their willingness to pay therefor by filling up the channel between them and building a bridge linking them to the north bank. In addition to this, they promised that the channel between the Île de la Cité and the new island should never be filled in.

Building on the united isles began in 1630, and by 1664 they were completely built up.

I am not able to guess what you may think of Île Saint-Louis. You may find it "a dull little backwater" on which you care to bestow no more than a glance; or you may find it one of the most interesting spots in Paris in which to dream and re-create. Artists, writers, antiquarians, and such folk, look upon it as a very isle of enchantment, a sort of sleeping beauty of the marvellous seventeenth century, breathing the charm of those stately years, deaf to the panting hurly-burly all about her.

If you are of this fellowship, you will come here more than once, and will linger longer on each successive visit.

To-day, mindful that you have not yet lunched, I shall suggest no more than that you turn to your left, midway of rue des Deux-Ponts, and follow rue Saint-Louis-en-l'Île, past the church and the magnificent Hôtel Lambert (where Voltaire lived, with Madame du Châtelet) to the boulevard Henri IV. The rue Poulletier which runs back of the church marks the site of the old waterway between the two islands. At the east end of the Île, beyond the boulevard, in the little square, is the monument which French and American admirers raised to Barye, in 1894. To this spot, Georges Cain tells us, Barye, "unrecognized, scoffed at, harassed by his creditors, came often in the evening, from his modest studio on the quai des Célestins, to forget his sorrows and to dream before the splendid panorama of Paris crowned by the noble silhouette of the Panthéon."

If the pont de la Tournelle (rebuilding as I write) is finished, walk to it along the quai de Béthune, and cross by it to the south bank, so that you may get the view that Napoleon had, that first evening in Paris, of Notre-Dame, where he was to be crowned Emperor of France in twenty years. If that does not appeal to you, cross by the pont Sully, and take a tram numbered 103, 104, or 105, running west along the quais. (That is, unless you feel able, as to appetite and as to purse, to lunch at the Tour d'Argent, which is close to the pont de la Tournelle.) If you want to go to Lapérouse, these trams will take you past the door (51 quai des Grands-Augustins). For an economical and good luncheon, get off at rue Saints-Pères and walk up to Michaud's, at the corner of rue Jacob. There is excellent food to be had at the Hôtel d'Orsay, farther west on the quai d'Orsay; but the prices are rather high and there is nothing distinctive in the surroundings.

Not knowing which place will be your choice, I cannot do better than to say: "After lunch, go to the Hôtel des Monnaies, or Mint."

I don't urge the Mint; I merely suggest it; and Thursday is one of the days when it may be visited, between 1 and 3 P.M. Next door to it, quai Conti 13, is where the Permon family, erstwhile of Corsica, were living while Bonaparte was a student at the École Militaire, and where, according to Madame Junot (née Permon) and others, he was a frequent visitor. Hither, she says, he came in the splendor of his new uniform as second lieutenant; and was so funny, with his thin little legs in his high, shiny boots, that her sister burst out laughing and called him "Puss-in-Boots." This made him furious. And if you like, you may see him striding forth, raging at the lack of reverence for his new dignity. He was sixteen, and very serious.

Nor am I sure that many visitors to Paris will be eager to see the Palais de l'Institut, or Institut de France. Thursday is not a visiting day; but if a respectful pilgrim applies at the secretary's office, I think he will not be denied permission to see at least the Salle des Séances Solonnelles where the meetings of the French Academy are held.

The quais hereabouts are lined with bookstalls where the most surprising treasures often reward the loiterer — not treasures in the catalogue sense, perhaps, but things one is delighted to find, and blissful to own. One of my favorite places in Paris (which means in the world) is along these left-bank quais in the neighborhood of the pont du Carrousel. And if you really love this sort of thing — lingering and looking and listening — be sure that you come here *alone*, and take your own time about everything. Perhaps you will fall into another habit of mine — which is to cross the river by the pont du Carrousel whenever I can, especially in the late afternoon and early evening; the pont Royal, the next bridge west or downstream, is to my eye one of the loveliest things that stone and water ever composed; the span of those five arches, their reflection in the river, and the vista behind them "when the blazing sun is set" thrill me, in actuality and in recollection, like the sublimest music.

The bridges of Paris are not just structures across a stream. They are nearly all things of beauty, and of extreme *personality*. Not to have your ardent memories of certain among them, your special tendernesses, is to miss one of the deep delights which bind together in close confraternity the lovers of Paris. I shall have something to say, three chapters hence, about "a bridge at midnight." But I must pay tribute here to the bridges of Paris (most of them) at any hour.

A stroll along the left-bank quais as far as the Chambre des Députés will give you a variety of interests.

This quai Malaquais, between the pont des Arts and the pont du Carrousel, commands a fine view of the Louvre. Number 5, before which Voltaire's statue is, has nearly three centuries of history. The Maréchal Maurice de Saxe lived there, and died there in 1750. Some years later, a tenant of the house was a Russian lady, Baroness de Korff, widow of a colonel, who was the mistress of Quintin Crawford and called herself, for some reason, Madame Sullivan. Crawford was a wealthy Englishman ("slightly lunatic like all the English at that time," Lenôtre says) who had collected in Italy art works of great value, and who lived in a magnificent mansion in the rue de Clichy, far away on the other side of the river, north of the gare Saint-Lazare. Crawford and "Madame Sullivan" were friends of Count Fersen, and it was in her name that he procured Marie Antoinette's passport for the flight; in Crawford's name that he ordered the travelling coach built.

Number 9 was once a fashionable gaming-house, and there the abbé Prévost laid the scene of Des Grieux at the card tables.

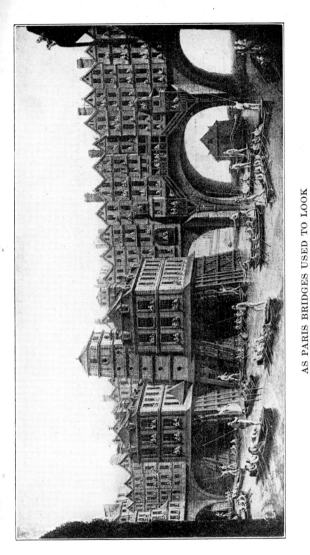

AS PARIS BRIDGES USED TO LOOK

PONT NOTRE-DAME IN THE SEVENTEENTH CENTURY

Painting by Raguenet

At number 11 Fouché lived, and from there he sent, every night, to the Emperor a notebook of twenty pages summarizing all that his spies had learned in twenty-four hours about persons inimical to the Bonaparte régime. This building is now a part of the École des Beaux-Arts, to which I shall direct you on Sunday.

Numbers 15 and 17, likewise part of the Beaux-Arts, were built by the elder Mansart. Henrietta Maria of England lived there at one time during the years that her brother, her sister-in-law, and her nephew had her "on their hands," so to speak, and seem to have kept her considerably on the move. But the most interesting associations with this place are those created by Marie Mancini, Duchess de Bouillon, who there entertained La Fontaine.

West of the pont du Carrousel, the quai is called quai Voltaire. At number 15 lived Georges Cain, late curator of the Carnavalet and author of many charming books about old Paris. Alfred de Musset was once a tenant of number 25. And number 27, corner of the rue de Beaune, is — as a tablet tells you — the house where Voltaire died. André Hallays in his book on Paris devotes a chapter to this house with so many interesting facts not commonly known that I am going to pass some of them on to you. (If you read French, I heartily commend to you the book in its entirety.)

When Voltaire came here, in 1778, for those final triumphs whose excitements hastened him into his grave, he was not — M. Hallays reminds us — a stranger to this house. He had lived here fifty-four years before. "He was thirty, then, and already celebrated for his verses, his freakishness, and his wantonness. . . . He had spent a year in the Bastille and written three tragedies, of which the first 'Œdipus,' had been praised to the skies, the second, 'Artémise,' had been outrageously hissed, and the third, 'Mari-

anne,' had fallen flat. He had finished 'La Henriade.' He
was very ill: stricken with smallpox (that time when Adrienne Lécouvreur, the splendid creature, disregarding the
risk to her beauty and her career, sat and read to him!) he
had finished the ruin of his health at the waters of Forges,
which he said were made of vitriol. He came back to Paris
very ill, and as he did not like lodging in hotels, he engaged
board at the home of President de Bernières for eighteen
hundred francs a year, with his friend Thiériot. . . . Infernal noise prevented him from working by day or sleeping by
night. At the end of a week, this racket had thrown him
into a terrible fever and he was forced to pack up and return to his hotel. But, some days later, he was back again
and again ill. 'You will find me,' he wrote to Madame
de Bernières (who was in the country), 'with a horrible
mange which covers all my body.'"

That is about all we know about his stay here in 1724.

When he returned to this house, in 1778, it had recently
become the property of the Marquis de Villette who was
still in his honeymoon with Voltaire's ward, "Belle et
Bonne," or "Beautiful and Good."

Villette had inherited a great fortune from his father, and
owned eight estates or mansions before he acquired this
one. He was notorious for his evil living; but that did not
make Voltaire hesitate to give him in marriage the sweet
child of eighteen whom Voltaire had rescued from consign-
ment, by her family, to a nunnery.

The wedding, at midnight, in the chapel at Fernay, was
scarcely over when Voltaire determined upon his return
to Paris; and the Villettes hastened thither to give him
hospitality.

The rooms he occupied were on the first floor of the wing
looking on rue de Beaune; they were two in number, a large
chamber with an alcove, and a dressing-room. The rooms

were so ill-lighted that he had to burn candles there at mid-day. For his great receptions of "all the world," however, he used the grand salon overlooking the quai. There Gluck came to see him, and Madame Necker, and Madame· du Deffand, and Madame du Barry! There the old man made his one English speech, holding out his hands over the grandson Franklin brought to see him, and saying "God and Liberty!" with such emotion that twenty spectators were dissolved in tears.

"For each of these visitors, Voltaire had a smile, a caress, a tear or a sally."

But all these efforts proved too much for him, and he died. The midnight, secret burial of his old friend, Adrienne, interred in a vacant lot, like a dog or cat, because she was an actress and without benefit of clergy, had haunted Voltaire. "I don't want to be thrown into the roadway," were almost his last words. So, hardly had the breath left his wasted body when it was placed, dressed for journeying, in a travelling carriage and driven with all haste to Scellières in Champagne where his nephew, the abbé Mignot, got it into the crypt of the church just before orders came from the Bishop of Troyes warning against Christian burial for Voltaire.

Thirteen years later, the body was brought back in great triumph and given a funeral the like of which Paris had never seen before. We recalled it Saturday, at the Panthéon.

The street leading to pont Royal is rue du Bac, so called because about 1560 when the Tuileries was begun a ferry (bac) was installed here to transport materials brought from this side of the river (principally stone from the quarries south of Paris); and the road to the ferry was called rue du Bac. There are not many other streets in Paris which have managed to keep one name during nearly four centuries. It is an interesting old thoroughfare to saunter in, but I don't know that there is anything in it to tempt the somewhat-hurried visitor on his first trip to Paris.

You are now at the east end of the famous quai d'Orsay, the heart of French democracy and diplomacy.

At number 1 quai d'Orsay the abbé Edgeworth lived. If you have ever wondered why it was an Irish priest who attended Louis XVI on the scaffold, you may be interested to know that Henry Essex Edgeworth had lived in France since he was three years old (or forty-five years, at the time of Louis's death), his father having emigrated from Ireland when he resigned his rectorship in the ancestral "living" and joined the Church of Rome. The son was educated by the Jesuits, and was the confessor of Madame Elizabeth, who commended him to her brother when the King's trial was impending. In spite of the danger he ran, the abbé Edgeworth refused to leave France until there was no longer any possibility of his being of service to Madame Elizabeth — who was not executed until May, 1794.

The gare d'Orléans is a handsome (and most convenient) railway station; but its erection at this spot on the quai d'Orsay was violently opposed by lovers of the picturesque who lamented the demolition, not of an ancient building, but of the ruins of a quite modern one. The Palais d'Orsay, begun in 1804, was still unfinished in 1820, and work on it was halted, not to be resumed till 1833. Nine years later the Cour des Comtes (or accounting office of all departments of the French Government) was moved there from the vicinity of Sainte-Chapelle, and the State Department from the rue Saint-Dominique. And in May, 1871, the Communards burned the building, which stood in splendid ruins for a quarter of a century. The architect, said Édouard Drumont, from whose book "My Old Paris" I quote, "was without genius; but Providence, one fine day, laid his own upon it, majestically," and it was a lovely thing, indeed, with its luxuriant growths of vegetation. Drumont and many another mourned its passing and bitterly bewailed the crass cupidity of those who replaced it with a railway station. It is a thousand pities that anything so exquisite should have had to go. But I dare say that the march of progress, if it must not be ruthless, must make its respectful concessions, should also take its toll. There was nothing consecrate about the Palais d'Orsay; it was picturesque but inutile, and it was in the way; it had to go. Paris is still the most beautiful city in the world, incomparably the most interesting to live in, and embalms her past more perfectly than any other, unless it be Venice which has — so to speak — no present to contend with the past.

Across from the west end of the gare d'Orléans is the palais de la Légion d'Honneur. The Légion was instituted by Bonaparte in 1802 as a general military and civil order of merit. The President of France is grand master of the Order, and the administration is in the hands of a grand chancellor and chancellery named by the President and housed in this palace which was built in 1786 for a Prince de Salm-Kyrburg who had married a Hohenzollern. It was said of this prince that nobody could deny that he had an intellect, but nobody could believe that he had common sense. Although he had not the money to pay for this mansion, he gave a prodigally lavish fête to celebrate his "house-warming," and this was attended by so vast a throng that the Prince said to one of his friends: "Many of those who are here must think I am also a guest." The next year, his architect distrained the Prince from ownership in the unpaid-for palace, but permitted him to live there as a rent-paying tenant.

The Prince pretended to be a republican (when that way, if any, safety lay) and Lafayette gave him a command in the National Guard and set up a Reform Club in this lovely palace. But Fouquier-Tinville, working night and day to keep the guillotine busy, ordered "the citizen Salm, ex-Prince of Germany," to the Carmelite prison, brought him to trial before the Revolutionary Tribunal, and sent him to the guillotine. The palace, confiscated, was put up for a lottery and won by an extraordinary person named Lieuthraud who had been a wigmaker's apprentice and had suddenly and inexplicably grown so rich that he had bought Bagatelle (in the Bois) and was known to be maintaining a mistress whose price was "ten thousand francs a day, payable in advance." He gave, here, a fête which cost 1,200,-000 francs (or livres) and had so many jonquils that most of the guests were made ill by the heavy perfume. A few weeks later he was arrested, condemned as a counterfeiter, sentenced to be branded, and to serve four years in irons. But he disappeared, without leaving a trace.

During the Directory, Madame de Staël and Benjamin Constant gathered about them, here, the members of the Constitutional Club. And in 1804 Napoleon installed here the Chancellery of the Legion of Honor.

Beyond rue de Solferino is the German Embassy, built in the early years of the eighteenth century. Prince Eugène de Beauharnais (Joséphine's son) spent a million and a half francs on decorations here when he was the tenant, and greatly disgusted Napoleon with this extravagance. In 1815 it was sold to the King of Prussia. The entrance of the mansion is in the rue de Lille, and opposite to it (at number 79) lived that Madame Atkins, née Charlotte Walpole, former actress at Drury Lane, who played so mysterious a rôle in the drama of the Temple, spent more than three millions to save the Dauphin, and visited Marie Antoinette in prison, offering to change places with her. (Was this, perhaps, what gave Dickens his idea for "A Tale of Two Cities"? And why has no ingenious romancer founded a story on the supposition that Marie Antoinette acquiesced? It could be done with less stretch of probabilities than Dumas used in exchanging Louis XIV for the Iron Mask thirty-odd years before the masked man was brought to the Bastille.)

Concerning the pont de la Concorde, with its stones from the Bastille, and the Palais Bourbon (Chambre des Députés) your guidebook, whether it be a Baedeker or Muirhead, is sufficiently informative. If there is a session on and you cannot enter the Chambre now, I hope you will come again, if only to see the paintings, especially those by Delacroix.

You may want to walk back a few steps along the boulevard Saint-Germain, to the Ministry of War, which was the residence of Madame Mère, or Lætitia Bonaparte, whose boudoir is still conserved there.

Next west of the Palais Bourbon is the Petit Bourbon, residence of the president of the Chamber of Deputies — corresponding somewhat to our Speaker of the House. And beyond that is the Ministry of Foreign Affairs, which has many times been used to lodge royalties on state visits.

Now you are at the Esplanade des Invalides, and you may not care to walk farther. The reasons why you should are not compelling. You might be mildly interested to see rue Jean-Nicot (which runs north from rue Saint-Dominique, a little west of the esplanade), named in memory of the French ambassador to Lisbon who introduced "My Lady Nicotine" into France in 1560, a quarter-century before Raleigh terrified his servant by smoking the first "Bull Durham" at Durham House in London. And you might care to know that at this point in the river, so close to this south bank as to be separated from it only by a tiny streamlet, there used to be an island (now one with the mainland)

called the Isle of Swans after Colbert stocked it with them
in 1676, and before that, Mackerel Isle. Many persons who
died of pestilence were buried here; and so were great numbers of Huguenots massacred on the eve of Saint Bartholomew.

I do not think there is anything in Magic City to attract
an American (except the crowd, and that is seen to better
advantage at fairs), but it was truly magic, or the scene of
magic, once in my experience when, on the night of King
George's coronation, I saw the street pageantry of the coronation in moving pictures, exhibited here, two hundred and
eighty miles away, some eight or nine hours after the scenes
were enacted.

Beyond the pont d'Alma, around the bend in the quai, is
the storehouse (garde-meuble), descendant of that which
used to be on the Place de la Concorde where the Ministry of
Marine now is, and filled with magnificent tapestries, paintings, marbles, furniture belonging to the nation and destined to be distributed, some day, among the palaces of the
Republic. Next are the stables of the French presidents.

But all these things are as well heard about as looked at.
And if I were you I would (supposing that you are not
otherwise engaged) take a steamer at the pont de la Concorde, opposite side, for Sèvres; see the porcelain factory
(open till five) then drive to Ville-d'Avray, see Villa des Jar-
dies where Balzac lived and where Gambetta died, then
back to Meudon. You may be in time to get into Rodin's
house. You certainly can see his tomb, with his "Penseur,"
in unending reverie above it. Or, you could omit either
Sèvres or Ville-d'Avray, or both, and go direct to Meudon,
spending the late afternoon walking or driving in the
beautiful Bois de Meudon.

XIV

YOUR FOURTEENTH DAY IN PARIS

FOR to-day I suggest that you start at the Trocadéro, at eleven, when the doors open. Only one bus line goes there; it is numbered B; you can transfer to it, of course, from any of the others. The Métro goes, and there is a Trocadéro station. And a pleasant way to go is by the river steamers to the pont d'Iena landing. Trams 1 and 2 also go along the quai, which is the ideal way to approach the Trocadéro, rather than from behind, as by Métro and bus.

Ever since you came to Paris, the twin towers of the Trocadéro have been a familiar feature of the western skyscape. If you visited the Champ-de-Mars, a week ago to-day, after leaving Napoleon's tomb, you had a fine view of the Trocadéro from that side of the river.

Perhaps, if you are very adept in bridging time, you saw beside you on the "Field of Mars" (then a very desert sort of place) a short man, grown stoutish, who used to stand there frequently — in the morning, usually — gazing over at these heights of Chaillot and with his eye of vision seeing them covered with palaces more extensive, more magnificent than those wherewith the Cæsars had capped the Palatine. I want to tell you about that vision of his. But, first, let us go back a bit in the story of those slopes that we're ascending. You may be interested to know that the seignory of this hilly hamlet fell to the crown domain in 1450; and when Louis XI was seeking to make Philippe de Commines believe him a more worth-while master than the splendid Charles the Bold, this property was one of the many gifts he gave him. The "father of modern history" owned this seignory for thirty-five years; then it either reverted to or was purchased by the Crown, and half-a-century or so later, Catherine de Médicis built a château here.

It was here that Henrietta Maria established her convent of the Visitandines; its chapel (where many of the hearts of the Stuarts were interred) stood where the water basin of the Trocadéro Gardens is now. It was in this chapel that Bossuet preached his very celebrated funeral sermon for the daughter of Henry IV and widow of Charles I. When Henrietta's younger son, James II of England, died in exile at Saint-Germain, it was hither that his grief-stricken widow came in her fresh sorrow, before his burial. It was here that Louise de la Vallière twice took refuge, before she became a Carmelite; the first time the King himself came and entreated her return; the second time, Colbert, sent by the King, fetched her back to Versailles to act as a screen for his affair with Montespan!

The aqueduct of Chaillot was built by Bernard de Palissy, on Catherine de Médicis' orders, to bring water from Saint-Cloud to the gardens of the Tuileries.

It was along this stretch of river-front, below where the Trocadéro now stands, that Robert Fulton made his first experiments with a power-driven boat. (You will remember that he was earning the money for those experiments by keeping "Panoramas" on the boulevard.)

The convent of Henrietta was suppressed at the Revolution. And about 1811 Napoleon had the buildings removed to clear the ground for the imperial magnificence which was to surround the tiny King of Rome and to make the traditions of Versailles and the Sun-King shabby and second-rate by comparison.

The Champ-de-Mars was, in Napoleon's plan, to contain a great group of edifices housing thousands of persons serving as satellites to the little Corsican's heir; here a barracks for ten thousand foot soldiers, there another for ten thousand horsemen; here, a palace of the Arts, sheltering the university, the archives; there, another palace for all the artists and savants whose presence at Court could contribute to its glory or its fame. Around these, the Ministries, and other state buildings, making a continuous line with the École Militaire, the Invalides, the Palais Législative and Cour des Comtes, along the south bank of the Seine to the Pont Royal.

From this south bank, the approach to the palace of the King of Rome was to be over the pont d'Iena and from that, by gentle rises, beneath colonnades like Bernini's before Saint Peter's, permitting carriages to come under cover to the foot of the grand stairway of the palace. Back of one of these curving colonnades there was to be the Court of the Ministers, and back of the other, the Court of the Princes; between them was to lie the great Court of Honor. The palace was to contain an immense gallery for fêtes, all across the south façade, flanked on one side by a chapel and on the other by an opera house; the imperial apartments were to be on the north side, with a majestic outlook reaching to the Bois de Boulogne which was destined to serve as a sort of "backyard" and hunting-ground for the domain.

All this was not merely projected; it was actually under way when the Empire dissolved like a phantom in the mist. A few years later, Louis XVIII planned the erection, here, of a huge war memorial, with arch of triumph, monumental column, fountains, etc. But that, too, failed to materialize.

In August, 1826, a sham battle was held here on the third anniversary of the taking of Trocadéro from the Spaniards by the Duc d'Angoulême. It was then that the hill was named, and the cornerstone was laid of an immense barracks that was to crown the height. But the second stone was never added. And a later project, to build a "garden city," died a-borning, like the rest. Then the present palace was erected, for the international exposition of 1878; and after the exposition was over, sold to the city.

Your guidebook gives you all the details about the building, the gardens, the two museums, and the aquarium. If you love monumental and architectural sculpture, you will revel in this superb collection founded by Viollet-le-Duc, the great Mediævalist of the Second Empire, restorer of many of France's monuments of the Middle Ages, and author of a dictionary of architecture which is one of the most fascinating books I know.

It is scarcely probable that you will leave the Trocadéro before twelve or twelve-thirty; and for your next steps I have most carefully weighed, not once but many times, the attractions of everything in this quarter, against the pressing claims of things to be seen elsewhere, and have decided to give you a choice of three courses.

What used to be the avenue du Trocadéro, running east from the Place du Trocadéro, is now named avenue du Président Wilson. I think that most Americans will want to walk along this avenue at least as far as the Place d'Iena, where stands the equestrian statue of George Washington, by Daniel Chester French and Edward Potter, presented to Paris by the women of the United States "in memory of the friendship and assistance given their fathers by France during the war for independence."

If you are tired, or otherwise indisposed to walk much, take bus B here, and ride to the rue Faubourg Saint-Honoré; then walk east along that to rue Royale and lunch at Ixe, for a light lunch, or at Weber's, or at Lucas's (9 Place de la Madeleine). You will find rue Faubourg Saint-Honoré described a little farther on in these pages.

Another course is for those who love art collections. Let them go a step or two up rue Pierre-Premier-de-Serbie, and see the Musée Galliéra, the mansion of the Duchess de Galliéra. The house is in itself a gem, "a work of pure art in architecture." And although the Duchess left the bulk of her superb art collection to Genoa (where you may have seen it in the Palazzo Rosso and Palazzo Bianco), she left to Paris her house and her tapestries, which are magnificent. There is also, on the other (west) side of avenue d'Iena, the Musée Guimet, devoted to the religions, history, and art of the Far East and of classical antiquity. This is for special students of those things rather than for the average individual.

You may like to follow avenue d'Iena a little way toward the Arc de Triomphe, and see the Place des États-Unis (or United States) of which we used to hear so much during the Peace Conference. If you do that, you might go past the Washington and Lafayette monument and on to rue la Pérouse, following the latter toward the Arc till you come to the Hotel Majestic, which was British headquarters during the Conference. It is a most attractive and luxurious hotel, delightful for the not-too-hurried sojourner in Paris who does not mind paying a good price for superlative comfort. A luncheon there will be a restful experience, and the food is excellent. Or, you may prefer to turn the other way at the Place des États-Unis, and follow rue Bassano to the Champs-Élysées, lunching at Fouquet's at the corner of avenue George V. This also is expensive, but well worth the money — if you can afford it. Then take tram 16, at Place des États-Unis, and get off at rue de Courcelles, to visit the Musée Jacquemart-André, at 158 boulevard Haussmann.

I hope that you will be moved to come here. If you find that your enthusiasm for art collections is waning, I would urge you to sacrifice something in the way of "galleries" rather than miss a collection like this which exemplifies not only what is possible to two individuals of taste and means, in the way of gathering together objects of great worth and rare beauty, but how those objects may be used with most perfect taste in a home. We see a great deal of art in galleries (for which little, if any, of it was designed) and a great deal in churches where it is well "set," but execrably lighted. Of art in a home, most of us see little unless we happen to have access to some of the houses of very rich collectors. To my mind, this home of M. Édouard André and his wife, Madame Nélie Jacquemart-André (a well-known painter of portraits), is one of the things in Paris which should not be missed. It was bequeathed to the Institut de France, and M. Pierre de Nolhac, former curator of Versailles, is in charge of it.

If you go to it, come down rue de Courcelles (at number 38 in which Charles Dickens lived when he was gathering data for "A Tale of Two Cities") to the Church of Saint-Philippe-du-Roule (from which Balzac was buried), and as you pass rue de la Baume you may like to know that number 15 in that street is the home of Frédéric Masson, of the French Academy, the eminent authority on Napoleon. (Jules Claretie, director of the Comédie-Française, lived at 155 boulevard Haussmann, and Henri Bernstein, dramatist, and André Messager, director of the Opéra, were his next-door neighbors at 157 — both of these across from the Musée Jacquemart-André). And from the church start your walk along rue Faubourg Saint-Honoré.

The third route from the Trocadéro that I propose is that from the Place d'Iena you follow avenue du Président Wilson to the Place de l'Alma, and turn up avenue Montaigne.

Close to the river-edge here, at the end of avenue Montaigne, there was, at the time of the Terror, a thatched cottage known as La Chaumière, to which on the evening of December 26, 1794, Tallien brought his bride, that beautiful marquise whom he had twice snatched from the guillotine.

The rond-point of the Champs-Élysées (toward which you are now making your way) then resembled a carrefours in a royal forest, except that toward the river it was given over to vegetable gardens and glass-covered forcing-beds. What is now called avenue Montaigne was then known as l'allée des Veuves, or Widows' Walk. The road, beneath great twisted elms, was grass-grown; and the narrow foot-paths were trodden principally by gardeners, washer-women, and cultivators from the vineyards of Chaillot.

Even before the delayed formality of her marriage, Thé-rézia was the idol of Paris. "Our Lady of Thermidor" they called her, and did homage to her as to Tallien for saving them from Robespierre.

She had a strong sense for the theatric (as, perhaps, most beautiful women, especially adventurous ones, must have to be effective), and it may have been that which brought her here to the thatched cottage, which she had had painted "like a comic-opera farm" with "antiqued" tim-bers and weather-mottled bricks.

In this setting she shone startlingly. She was more ex-otic than Marie Antoinette at the farm of Petit Trianon.

(Those who would know a great deal of Thérézia's part in the Revolution and the Directory should read the three absorbing novels of the Baroness Léonie Aminoff: "Revo-lution," "Love," and "Ambition.")

Among those who moved about her, here, were Barras and Bonaparte; Vernet and Joseph Chénier; Cherubini and Auber; and Joséphine de Beauharnais. It was Auber who said that "when she entered her salon she made night and day — day for herself and night for the others."

Tallien adored her so that he was completely satisfied in knowing she was his. His associates had enriched themselves out of the spoils of revolution. He asked nothing more than Thérézia. Short-sighted man! He did not even scheme for more power. His reach had equalled his grasp; there was nothing more he wanted.

As soon as Thérézia realized this, she was through with him. She wanted more worlds to conquer, and she found them. Barras seems to have had her favors as well as Joséphine's; then it was a millionaire banker, named Ouvrard, who installed her in an exquisite love-nest in the rue de Babylone, where she bore him four children in four years, at the end of which time she married another man, and became a princess — the Princess Caraman-Chimay.

Tallien, meantime, had left France, seeking to forget her. Futile quest! Bonaparte took him to Egypt, but he was soon back. Then he was given the consulship at Alicante, where he had yellow fever, lost an eye, and was sadly disfigured in face by fever-blotches. Tallien had reached his zenith before he was thirty. The rest of the way — for twenty-five years — was steadily downhill into the ever-deepening shadows. During the last years he lived here on avenue Montaigne, in a little cottage belonging to one of the truck-farmers. "He lived there," says Lenôtre, from whose "Old Age of Tallien" I quote, "alone with a servant, no longer writing nor even reading, but just remembering. He was often to be met under the elms of the avenue, walking with short, gouty steps, leaning on his cane. He hobbled on, to the Seine, and halted there, gazing at the former Chaumière, transformed into a roadhouse where an old tree surviving from Thérézia's garden bore the sign 'The Acacia.' The place was frequented only by teamsters and washerwomen, and no one knew who this sad stroller was, nor what he was seeing.

"He was dreaming: in front of this perron, crowded with drinkers, had pawed the horses of that ox-blood carriage which all Paris knew. He saw Thérézia again at his side, 'clothed like a cloud,' white-skinned, smiling, besieged with silent homage. . . . His thoughts go farther back . . . he sees himself, eyes on fire, body hot with agony and with fever, among the stupefied tremblers entering the jelly-fish Assembly, seizing Robespierre by the gorge, pushing him out of the tribune, and saving — without caring that he was doing so, without realizing it, perhaps — the Republic, France, the world, to snatch from death the woman that he loved. . . .

"She is a princess, now; she has forgotten these things; she has forgotten him."

Poverty strips him, slowly, of all but his recollections. Lot by lot his great collection of Revolutionary documents go. Then his books. When his old servant asks money to buy fire or food, he makes up a packet and goes down the Champs-Élysées, across the Place de la Concorde, where *they* died — they whom he had hunted, they who hunted with him, and they who had hunted him! — and along the terrace beside the Tuileries where he had reigned as master, to the river, and across to the quai Voltaire, where he stops before the stalls of the dealers in second-hand books. Then he comes sadly back to the Widows' Walk, and gives his servant two crowns.

Early one November morning in 1820, attended by no one but the faithful old woman servant, Tallien died — broken and forgotten — an old, old man of fifty-three, who had lived only in his memories for more than twenty years.

Perhaps you don't feel that this story makes the avenue Montaigne any more interesting to you. If not, you may prefer to pass along the quai, along the Cours-la-Reine, the western part of which has been renamed in honor of Albert I, King of the Belgians. It was Marie de Médicis who ordered this beautiful drive along the river made, in 1618, and it was the fashionable promenade for long afterwards. The quai below is called the quai de la Conférence because there the Spanish ambassadors debarked when they came to Paris in 1660 to confer with Mazarin on the proposed marriage between Louis XIV and his cousin, Marie-Thérèse.

The exquisite house at number 16 Cours Albert Ier is said to have been built by François I either for his sister, Marguerite, or for Diane de Poitiers. It was originally at Moret, near Fontainebleau, and was brought to Paris in 1826. The sculptures are by Jean Goujon. The Latin inscription on the façade means: "He who knows how to hold his tongue and conquer his senses is mightier than he who takes cities by force."

If you have come this far, go up avenue Victor Emmanuel III to the Rond-Point des Champs-Élysées, cross, and lunch at Des Gauffres, on the corner of the Rond-Point and avenue Matignon, or at the Franco-Italien, 5 avenue Matignon.

Those who have come up avenue Montaigne may stop for luncheon in the Hôtel Plaza-Athénée, which is, to my way of thinking, quite the nicest hotel in the world. This part of Paris is absolutely ideal for the sojourner — quiet, elegant, very accessible and convenient. The Plaza-Athénée is a beautiful new hotel, under the same incomparable management which made the old de l'Athénée, up near the Opéra, hold its distinguished patronage so successfully. The Plaza-Athénée is what in Paris they call a "serious" hotel. The shoddy and noisy are absolutely "discouraged." It is restful in the extreme, and lovely. The food is perfection. Our American Consul-General makes his home there — and so do I, when I am most fortunate!

If you do not feel like lunching in a hotel, go on, up to the Champs-Élysées and lunch at Des Gauffres or the Franco-Italien.

In either case, walk up rue Matignon (continuation of the avenue) to rue Faubourg-Saint-Honoré, so you may pass, at number 17 rue Matignon, the mansion in which Count Axel Fersen lived at the time he planned and executed the flight to Varennes. It was here that he kept the travelling carriage he had ordered for the journey, and which he stocked with necessaries for the comfort of the royal family.

Now turn east, toward rue Royale. Avenue de Marigny, to which you come, presently, was cut through and created by the Marquis de Marigny, brother of Madame de Pompadour, who lived in the mansion that is now the palace of the Presidents of France. This house was built in 1718 and bought by la Pompadour in 1753, for 500,000 francs, and greatly beautified and enlarged. Her last wishes, when she lay a-dying eleven years later, at Versailles, were that her body be brought hither before being taken for interment to the Church of the Capucines. She had left this property to Louis XV, whose only comment on her death was made when he saw her body being driven away from Versailles in a pouring rain. "She has a bad day for her journey," he remarked, without feeling.

Caroline Bonaparte and her husband, Murat, lived here. And at the time of the divorce, Napoleon gave it to Joséphine, who preferred Malmaison and sold this back to the Emperor. It was here that he signed his second abdication, and hence that he set out for Malmaison to say his farewells to his family. The next tenants of it were the Duke of Wellington and the Emperor of Russia. Louis-Napoleon was living here when he prepared the coup d'état by which he made himself emperor. From here he moved to the Tuileries.

Rue de l'Élysée, to the east of the palace, was cut through by order of Louis-Napoleon, to isolate the presidential dwelling. A little later, the Empress Eugénie

bought the property at the northeast corner of this street
and avenue Gabriel, and had a handsome residence built
there for her mother, the Countess de Montijo. This was
bought in 1873 by Baron de Hirsch who used the home of
an empress's mother as a mere wing of the magnificent palace he there constructed. Do you know anything about him?
Perhaps not, unless your memory goes back nearly thirty
years, when the world's press used to be full of his enormous
gifts to charity. He was a German Jewish banker, who lived
principally in Paris and London; and his gifts, chiefly
to Jewish agencies, totalled nearly a hundred million dollars. Yet I dare say that of the strangers who pass by number 2 rue de l'Élysée to-day, an overwhelming majority
have no idea who Baron de Hirsch was or what he did.
So hard it seems for money, no matter how wisely and
generously bestowed, to get its donor remembered.

Number 41 rue Faubourg-Saint-Honoré is the mansion of
Baron Edmond de Rothschild. (Another Baron de Rothschild lives at number 23 avenue de Marigny, across from
the west side of the Élysée Palace.) And number 39 is
where Pauline Bonaparte lived during the Empire, after the
fall of which it became the British Embassy, the Duke of
Wellington negotiating the sale. Queen Victoria was entertained there in 1867, and Edward VII stopped there many
times.

Guizot lived at number 52 for ten years.

The shops along here are fascinating, but — of course —
expensive. It costs nothing to look, however. And presently you are at rue Royale. More shops, delightful and
expensive.

This afternoon, if it is fine, might be a good time for you
to see something of Montmartre.

The basilica of Sacre-Cœur is best from "a great way off."
I would never advise any one to ascend the mountain for

the purpose of making closer acquaintance with it. The
more unreal and distant it can seem to you, the more you
will enjoy it as a feature of the Paris skyscape. There is no
"fitness" about it; it has nothing in the wide world to do
with the Martyrs' Hill, with France, with the Christian religion! Nevertheless, it is incomparably lovely on "the
back drop" of Paris. Seen from the boulevards, at rue Lafitte; from boulevard Saint-Germain at rue de Solferino;
from the terrace at Saint-Cloud; from the avenue Montaigne, especially when the chestnut trees are in flower, it 's
thrillingly beautiful because so strange, so white, so much
more like a fantastic thing slipped down out of the clouds
(the sort of unrelated thing one sees in dreams) than like a
structure built of earth's substances.

If you are very poetic, very sensitive, I say "Keep
away" — even though, to do so, you must miss Saint-
Pierre-de-Montmartre.

If you want to go, you can go quickly by taking the Nord-
Sud (North and South underground) at the Madeleine, and
getting off at the station called Abbesses. But you'll see
more, en route, if you take the bus marked "A Q," which
you can get by walking up boulevard Malesherbes (running
northwest from the Madeleine) to its intersection with the
boulevard Haussmann.

The ideal way to go is afoot; but there are not many who
can stand the walking and have any energy left for exploring when they get there.

The fact of the matter is that Montmartre is really not
for tourists, except those night-revellers who like to go and
look at other tourists in crowded dance halls which are no
different from resorts of like character anywhere in the western world. Montmartre is for the leisurely sojourner who
can wander up there on many days when in the mood to
care greatly for seeing where Berlioz died, where Henri

Murger was born, or where Turgueniev had his Paris home, or beautiful Delphine Gay held her salons.

I have spent an incredible amount of time trying to figure out a "course" for a single visit to Montmartre which might include a fair number of its points of interest and not exhaust the visitor. Few travellers, except the night revellers, get up that way more than once. And in one survey, it is very hard to get much of an impression.

However, suppose you try this:

At rue Royale, take either a fiacre — they are always plentiful thereabouts — or a bus marked "A C," and ride to the corner of the boulevard des Capucines and rue Chaussée-d'Antin — just beyond the Place de l'Opéra. Then either walk, or drive very slowly, up rue Chaussée-d'Antin. Many interesting people have been closely identified with that street. Number 2 was the residence of Rossini. When rue Meyerbeer was cut through, in 1860, some memory-laden houses were sacrificed. One of them, numbered 5 Chaussée-d'Antin, was the home of Madame d'Épinay, the brilliant woman who was the mistress and benefactress of Jean-Jacques Rousseau and Baron von Grimm, the friend of Diderot, D'Alembert, and other eminent men. Mozart visited her here and stopped as her guest five months. Next door to her, at number 7, lived the Neckers, including the future Madame de Staël; Gibbon was their guest here in 1777; and under the Directory, this was the home of Madame Récamier. Years after (1831) it was Chopin's home. Number 11 (also cut away) was built for the mistress of the Prince du Soubise, and was decorated by Fragonard. In a house back of the building now numbered 23, Napoleon installed the Countess Walewska, the lovely Polish girl whom he had made a mother. Mirabeau died at number 40. And Joséphine de Beauharnais lived at number 62; some writers say that it was there Napoleon "proposed" to her. Napoleon's uncle, the Cardinal Fesch, lived at number 68. And it was on rue de la Victoire (then rue Chantereine) that Napoleon went to live when he married Joséphine. She had rented, six months before, the house of Madame Talma. Napoleon bought it two years later. It was where number 60 rue de la Victoire now is, but nothing of the historic house remains. Louis Bonaparte and his wife (Hortense de Beauharnais) lived for a time at number 44, where the synogogue now is; here their eldest son, Napoleon-Charles, was born.

Now go up rue Lafitte, and return toward Chaussée-d'Antin on rue Châteaudun. To your right as you turn out of rue de la Victoire is the site of the cemetery where Molière had his torchlighted burial. Rue Châteaudun is not especially interesting except for some of its "antique" shops; but it is the way to get back to the Place de la Trinité, from which you may take your choice of three streets leading up to Montmartre.

The westernmost of these is rue de Clichy, which follows the course of an old Roman road between Paris and Rouen; it leads to the Place de Clichy, and there is no reason why you should choose it. The easternmost is rue Pigalle, leading to the Place Pigalle, the centre of Montmartre's gaudy night-life. Henner and Puvis de Chavannes used to have their studios at number 11 Place Pigalle; Eugène Scribe (said to have made the largest fortune ever acquired by a French author) was living at number 12 rue Pigalle when he entered his carriage, February 20, 1861, to pay a visit to a friend; he died en route. Scribe wrote and collaborated on the enormous total of more than four hundred plays. But as his stage activities covered fifty-one years, and everything from one-act vaudeville sketches to five-act dramas, perhaps the total is not so surprising. We know his plays very little, in this country, but are more familiar with some of his opera libretti: "La Juive," "La Muette de Portici," "Les Huguenots." Many people went to Scribe with "plots"; with many of them he "collaborated." When the play was finished, there was, usually, exceedingly little in it that the "collaborator" had supplied, but he received half the royalty, nevertheless. Scribe grew rich in spite of being just and generous, or *because* of so being — as you like! If you want to see where he lived, go up rue Pigalle as far as number 12, then return to the junction of rue Pigalle with rue Blanche (at the northeast corner of the church), and — if you are afoot and may grow weary — take bus A Q to avenue Rachel and the main entrance of Montmartre Cemetery. Another easy détour from Place de la Trinité is south of the beginning of rue Pigalle, into the rue de la Tour-des-Dames — so called because the windmill of the Dames (or abbesses) de Montmartre used to be here. At number 1, Mademoiselle Mars, of the Théâtre-Français, lived and held a salon which was the rendezvous of the élite in the artistic world. She had been a great favorite of Napoleon, and when the Bourbons came back she would not make any pretence of welcoming them.

Horace Vernet, the military painter, who lived at number 5, was also an ardent Bonapartist, but he could be a Royalist too, and he enjoyed many favors from the Bourbons and the House of Orléans including appointment as head of the French Academy at Rome. His beautiful daughter was the wife of Paul Delaroche, who lived next door, at number 7. Delaroche was by no means so great a painter as his friend Delacroix, but there are few artists so many of whose canvases are familiar to thousands, through reproductions, as some of those by Delaroche: "The Death of Queen Elizabeth," "The Execution of Lady Jane Grey," "The Princes in the Tower," "Stafford led to Execution," "The Execution of the Duc de Guise at Blois," "Richelieu Going to the Execution of Cinq-Mars," "Napoleon at Fontainebleau," "Marie Antoinette leaving the Convention" — these are among the best-known pictures of modern times. Delaroche died here, in 1856. Talma died at number 9 thirty years before. Everything about Talma is interesting; he is one of the best sources of piquant anecdote in all the realm of biography. I came across an old biography of him recently, published soon after his death, which was even "meatier" (if such were possible) than Talma's own mémoires, edited by Dumas. The temptation to tell tale upon tale about him is all-but irresistible, but must be repressed here. I find that many persons accustomed to think of him, rather vaguely, as the friend of Napoleon, as the great tragedian, the founder of historic realism on the stage in costume and scenery, in which he was inestimably aided by David, feel a keener interest in him when reminded that he was a successful dentist who was encouraged by his successes in amateur theatricals to go upon the professional stage. The story of how he prepared himself for the theatre as a career is one that I wish might be very widely read to-day, not only by stage aspirants, but by drama-lovers generally.

You may want to make a little pilgrimage to rue de Calais, to see where Berlioz died, and to rue de Douai, to see where Ivan Turgueniév lived, and Gustave Doré and Ludovic Halévy, and Jules Claretie and Francisque Sarcey. Rue de Calais is on your left as you approach Place Blanche. Berlioz lived at number 4 rue de Calais for twelve years and died there on March 8, 1869. It was here that he wrote the later parts of those fascinating "Mémoires" which make us feel that we know him as we know few of the still-embodied souls about us. "Victor Hugo," it has been said, "was a romantic, Musset was a romantic, but Berlioz was romanticism itself." "Had he been an architect," said Liszt, "he would have built pyramids, gardens of Semiramis, Roman amphitheatres." But the gorgeous structures he built of tones were slow in bringing him recognition or reward. His musical criticisms for "Le Journal des Débats" continued for seven years after he came here to live. He called it an "infernal chain of article-writing," and said, "I am so ill that the pen falls from my hand every moment, and yet I have to force myself to write to gain my paltry hundred francs. All this time I have my head full of projects and work, which I cannot carry out by reason of my bondage." When he threw off these fetters he was too tired to create. You may like to see him coming out of here and going to walk up and down in front of the lyric theatres, luxuriating in the feeling that he need not go in unless he wants to, and need not hurry away after the performance to write his impressions of it.

Rue de Douai crosses rue Blanche just north of rue de Calais. (The Grand Guignol is a little south of rue de Douai and a little east of rue Blanche; you may want to go there this evening.) Jules Claretie, director of the Comédie-Française, lived at number 10 rue de Douai for a long time. Gustave Doré and Ludovic Halévy lived at number 22. (Halévy also lived at number 69.) And number 50 was the home after 1870 of Turgueniev — that is to say, it was the home of Madame Viardot, the singer, sister of Malibran, and her painter-husband, with whom Turgueniev lived. It was at this house (I think) that Dickens met George Sand, in 1856.

Those who revere Zola will want to make a détour of a few steps from rue de Douai, to number 21 rue de Bruxelles, where he died. At one end of rue de Bruxelles is the Square Berlioz, with the statue of Berlioz by Alfred Lenoir, grandson of Alexandre Lenoir, whose story you shall hear on Sunday at the Beaux-Arts. A nude statue of Napoleon used to stand here, shaded by a willow from St. Helena. At the other end of rue de Bruxelles is Place Blanche, where the celebrated Moulin Rouge used to be.

Avenue Rachel, leading to the main entrance of the cemetery, runs north from boulevard de Clichy, just west of the site of the Moulin Rouge. (Those who do not care to visit the cemetery may take rue Lépic and rue Tholozé north from Place Blanche to the site of the Moulin de la Galette.)

If you will scan the cemetery plan in your guidebook, and follow it as I direct, you can see many of the most famous graves with a minimum of wandering.

Turn to your left on entering, and see, in section 15, the tomb of Alphonsine Plessis, the original of "La Dame aux Camelias" whom we Americans persistently call "Camille," although her name in the play is Marguerite Gauthier. Near her, a little farther on, lies Alfred de Vigny. Turn north into avenue Charles, and follow it a few feet to avenue de Montmorency. Edmond and Jules de Goncourt lie close to the latter avenue as you go north on it. Perhaps you do not read their novels from which, Arthur Symons said, Zola learned everything; perhaps you are not of those who delight in their eighteenth-century studies, so intimate that we who read them are almost ashamed, at times, to enter in; but you hear of them often through the Goncourt prize — the prix de Goncourt — of five thousand francs awarded annually to the author of some work of fiction. This was a provision of Edmond's will. He outlived Jules by more than a quarter-century, dying in 1896, and left his estate for the endowment of an academy to consist of ten members, each of whom receives an annuity of six thousand francs; and these ten members yearly vote a prize of five thousand francs to the author of some work of fiction which seems to them especially meritorious.

Those who are interested in Émile de Girardin and

Delphine Gay may find their tombs on avenue Travot which you will cross, presently; but there are not many of this generation who know much about them. If you continue up avenue de Montmorency past avenue Samson, you will come to a section, on your left, in which are buried the Duchesse d'Abrantès who was Madame Junot of the famous "Memoirs"; she was a Permon, of Corsican birth, and it was her family that Napoleon visited on the quai Conti, and elsewhere, in his struggling days; her husband, Junot, who was his comrade in adversity and his favored friend in prosperity. Ary Scheffer lies in that section, too; and his nephew, Ernest Rénan. On the other side of avenue de Montmorency lies Dumas fils. Murger (author of "La Vie de Bohême"); Delaroche; his father-in-law, Horace Vernet; and Henner lie in a section on the other side of avenue Cordier. To reach Berlioz's resting-place you must cross avenue de Tunnel and continue along avenue des Carrières. Then return on avenue Cordier and on your left is Théophile Gautier; Halévy is a little farther in, in the same section. Round the angle of avenue Cordier and avenue de la Cloche, pass the monument of Viollet-le-Duc and of Meilhac, the dramatist, and face back toward the direction whence you have come. You will have Greuze on your left, and Heinrich Heine a little farther on. Troyon lies in that section, too, nearer the entrance of the cemetery. Beyond Heine's grave there is a path leading to avenue de la Croix, and not far from the end of that path in the avenue de la Croix is the grave of Madame Récamier. If, from there, you turn back to the Carrefour de la Croix (north of which is Zola's tomb, from which his remains were removed to the Panthéon), you can easily regain the cemetery entrance. You will not have seen all the tombs which are shrines for lovers of art, letters, music, science (Foucault is here, for instance, and Ampère, and Dr. Charcot,

Delibes and Offenbach and Ambroise Thomas), but you will have seen a representative number, without traversing more than a tithe of the space.

From avenue Rachel, if you are tired, take the A Q bus to the end of its route; or walk back to Place Blanche and take rue Lépic to the Moulin de la Galette. (Do not follow the winding of rue Lépic, but save many steps by leaving it at the end of its first section, for rue Tholozé).

Montmartre used to be full of windmills whose great creaking arms were the cadence of Paris's bread a-grinding. The Moulin de la Galette, dating from 1275, was one of the last survivors of that horizon-full which was for many generations not only the assurance of the hungry, but the joy of artists, poets, of beauty-lovers both mute and expressive.

This height above Paris where the giant arms of the windmills ground Paris's bread has played a part in much of the military history of the city. On March 30, 1814, the day Paris capitulated to the Allies, a battery of nine guns was installed here, and King Joseph Bonaparte, from his headquarters, sent word to the gunners to hold on, for the Emperor was marching to their aid. But it was the Prussians who were coming; and all was lost. There were four brothers Debray of the family to which this Moulin de la Galette had belonged since 1640. Three of them were killed at once, and the eldest — bent on avenging his brothers' death — refused to obey when the order to cease firing came. A Russian column advanced. Debray pointed his gun and let it bark. The Russians threw themselves on him, but, instead of surrendering, he used his pistol to lay low the commanding officer. Immediately, he was massacred, his body hacked into four pieces, and each of them attached to one of the wings of his mill. He lies, now, up in the little old cemetery of Saint-Pierre, beneath a bronze windmill. You shall see his grave, presently.

His son "carried on" in the ancestral mill and sold milk and rye rolls to the energetic walkers who came there for the view. He was a hard-working man who amused his neighbors by his passion for dancing. He delighted in teaching others to dance. "He did it first for the love of the art," says Sellier in his "Curiosities of Old Montmartre," "then later the idea occurred to him to make a pay course of it. And thus originated the public balls of the Moulin de la Galette." The mill no longer grinds; Paris gets her flour from elsewhere; but dancing continues one of the main "industries" of the Martyr's Mount. That, and the view, is why I wanted you to see the site of the Moulin de la Galette and know something of its story. The name, as Paris knows it now, has no more to do with the old uses of mills than the Moulin Rouge had. It is a public dance hall, belonging to the municipality, and (as I write) about to be moved farther east, to the end of rue Lépic.

The energetic who will walk up rue Girardon to rue Saint-Vincent and along this latter to rue du Mont Cenis, will be rewarded in several ways. The rue Saint-Vincent, one of the most picturesque streets in Paris, contains a thatched cottage which, tradition says, sheltered Henry IV while he was besieging Paris.

On the other hand, those who turn, at the east end of rue Lépic, down rue Ravignan to rue Gabrielle will find at number 39 of the latter street a belvedere from which the view of Paris is the most magnificent to be had anywhere. Both rue Saint-Vincent and rue Gabrielle lead to rue du Mont Cenis, on which is Saint-Pierre de Montmartre, "the dean of the sacred edifices of Paris," consecrated in 1147 by Pope Eugène III and Saint Bernard, and visited by Thomas à Becket in 1169.

You know where Paris was then! Far away to the south, within walls earlier and less extensive even than those of Philippe-Auguste. This "butte," or ridge, is three hundred and thirty-five feet above the Seine; its southern slopes were vineyard-clad in very early days, but soon the vines were torn away and burrowing began; for the quarries here are rich in that gypsum which makes "plaster of Paris."

The Druids once had sacred groves here; then the Romans raised temples to Mercury and Mars; and presently came missionaries preaching a new faith. Three of these were martyred on this hill; and one of them, Saint Denis, took his severed head in his hands — so the story goes — and wandered with it, northward, till he met a pious woman who gave him burial. You shall visit, on your way down the hill, the spot reputed to be that whereon he suffered death. And when you go to see the burial-place of France's kings, you shall realize how far the poor man had to walk to find a sepulchre.

In 1096, some monks established themselves on the ridge; but in 1133 they ceded their territory to the King (Louis VI) who, with his Queen, Adelaide of Savoy, founded a Benedictine Abbey here in 1134. The Church of Saint-Pierre de Montmartre — begun the next year — was used partly for the abbey, and partly as a parish church for the people of the hillside village.

Be sure to spend a few moments in the very ancient cemetery north of the church. Then do as you like about the Basilica next door.

Come down from the Basilica by the funicular into the Square Saint-Pierre and, near the foot of the funicular, take rue Tardieu to rue Antoinette. At number 9 rue Antoinette is a convent in which is a modern chapel (1887) erected on the site of a very early one which Sainte Geneviève caused to be raised over the spot where Saint Denis was martyred. In that old chapel Ignatius Loyola and his companions founded the Jesuit Order, on August 15, 1534. And there, forty years later, La Môle and Coconnas were interred, after their execution on the Place de Grève, through the intercession of their mistresses, Margot of Valois and the Duchesse de Nevers. (Is there anything in all the realm of fiction more gruesome than the scene in "Marguerite of Valois" wherein Dumas describes the two great ladies going to the headsman's house by night and weeping wildly over the mangled bodies of those young men?)

It must be nearing dinner-time, now, and you are not far from the avenue Trudaine, where you may dine luxuriously at L'Écrivisse (number 32), a little less expensively at L'Âne Rouge (number 28), and least expensively at La Poule au Pot (number 10). I have been told that one may dine at some of the notorious night resorts without paying the fantastic prices charged there after 11 P.M., but I cannot testify, not having tried them.

This evening might be a good time to see a performance at the Grand Guignol. And if you are curious about the all-night dance halls, you will find the most noted ones on Place Pigalle, near the theatre.

Should the night be warm, or your inclination be for something different from a theatre, you might like to drive out through the industrial quarters of eastern Paris to the park called Les Buttes Chaumont. But the strongest probability is that you are tired and ready for bed.

You have seen a good deal to-day, over a vastly larger area than on any other day. Those who feel that the day as outlined is too strenuous, might combine the morning part of it with some further explorations in the western quarters, as outlined in the chapter following this. Then come up to Montmartre earlier in another day.

XV

ANY DAY IN PARIS

THE BOULEVARDS AND THEIR NEIGHBORS

THIS chapter is one that you may substitute for any of the others, if you are hurried or if they do not appeal to you, or with which you may supplement them as seems best to you. Everybody goes along the boulevards in Paris, not once, but many times. Some are satisfied with just what they can see as they pass wonderingly along. Others would like to know a little more about what they're seeing. This chapter is for those "others." There is no need to take a day for following it. Read it and have it in mind as you go on your explorations of Paris.

But to give it sequence, order, let us start it at the Madeleine, which marks the western boundary of the "grands boulevards."

The boulevards are not what they used to be; but in this post-war world nothing is as it used to be, and I do not know that the Paris boulevards seem as "different," by half, as many other places do. Everywhere in the western world, now, the persons most in evidence seem to be those whom a sudden and unprepared-for affluence has driven out of their accustomed courses and into ways that they wot not of. The handful of humanity that has savoir-faire, that can give grace, elegance, distinction to what it does, has become hard to find in the hubbub of loud assertiveness, gaudy display, and reckless expenditure which characterizes most persons when they get more money than they have been educated to spend. Paris has not only her own share of these "unexpected" persons; but she has always within her gates a very large share of every other nation's new-rich who have flocked to the world's capital of luxury.

The boulevards are easy to find; they and certain places in their vicinity are the first points of attack by the multitude of pleasure-seekers who are new to Paris and whose idea of what to do in Paris is bounded by the rue de la Paix and the races on the west, by the all-night dance halls of Montmartre on the north, by the glove and feather counters of the Magasin du Louvre on the east, and by dear-knows-what on the south — perhaps the hope of finding a shocking ball in the Latin Quarter, where (by the way) shocking balls seldom, if ever, occur. So you must expect to find along the boulevards a large percentage of "persons from everywhere" who are as strange as fish out of water and who are essaying what they think is "the thing to do in Paris" and are doing it blatantly — as if noise could do other than advertise awkwardness.

Be careful how you judge "Parisians" along the boulevards. Be careful — because they may be Portuguese barbers or Patagonian pork-butchers "seeing the sights" as you are. The boulevards are cosmopolitan in a very high degree; and many elements of the Paris population have withdrawn from them except to use them, when necessary, as thoroughfares. They are interesting as the Main Street of the world rather than as the Main Street of France.

With this in mind, suppose you start at the Madeleine some day, with one sharp-focused and one reminiscent, distance-seeing eye, and saunter along toward the Bastille. You must have your hearing-apparatus adjusted for different wave-lengths, too — for the sounds all about you, and for the distant murmurs of far yesterdays. Your heart will beat responsively to both — but you need not tell to which it answers most happily.

Nor need you say whether you are best able to understand the persons who sit almost cheek-by-jowl with you on the sidewalk-extension of some popular café, or those with whom you have lived and loved and suffered and rejoiced in pages so vivid that they are like the leaves of your own past. All about you in rue Royale, rue Faubourg-Saint-Honoré, in Place Vendôme, and rue de la Paix, are the exquisite shops of the famous perfumers. But what do you know of M. Coty? Or of the present head of the old house of Houbigant? The Paris perfumer you know is the late César Birotteau, whose shop was on the north side of rue Saint-Honoré just west of the rue Castiglione and Place Vendôme. "Boy and man," that was his background. And César, you remember, lost in real estate speculation the fortune he had made in perfumes. The property he believed in and gambled on was around the Madeleine. César had seen values rise in this vicinity. He had known land, that sold (as late as 1805) for eight and a half francs a square metre, to fetch forty-seven francs in 1811. It was 1820 when he bought his three thousand square metres for 300,000 francs — and lost all. Eight years later, they were worth double what he paid for them, and to-day they are worth many millions. César's foresight was good, but *too* good! He saw too far ahead of his contemporaries.

Many of you are thinking of him, I know, as you stand in the Place de la Madeleine and look about you. It was not without reason that Balzac, when he was putting César into his gallery of immortals, broke into a conversation about current affairs, by saying: "Come, let us discuss real people! I must tell you about César Birotteau and the new perfume that he has just invented."

It is difficult — it is almost impossible! — to realize that César was "real" only because Balzac made him so; you probably find yourself wishing, as you stand in the Place de la Madeleine, that he could come back and see it now, and know himself justified.

If there is any special reason why this square was selected as the site for Sardou's monument, I do not know it; but the monument (by Denys Puech) of Jules Simon, across the way, stands in front of the house — number 7 Place de la Madeleine — where Simon lived for fifty years and where he died, in 1896. I am not sure that many Americans of this generation have definite impressions of Simon, who was teacher, statesman, journalist, author; nor that they know as much as their grandparents would have known about Henri Meilhac, the dramatist, who also lived in this house (with Ludovic Halévy he was co-author of many plays once immensely popular, of which "Frou-Frou" is perhaps the only one you know). Saint-Saëns lived at number 4. Lucas, at 9 Place de la Madeleine, is an excellent place to dine; and so is Viel, at 8 boulevard de la Madeleine. If you turn north, up rue de Caumartin, to rue Boudreau, you will find at no. 3 rue Boudreau the establishment of Blanche Lebouvier, Marie-Louise, directrice, whose clothes I like among the best in Paris, and for knowledge of whom many friends have thanked me. It is not a terribly expensive place, and caters to refined, conservative tastes. Ask for Madame Marguerite.

Boulevard de la Madeleine ends at the apex of rue Cambon and rue des Capucines. It was here that the first shots were fired in the revolution of 1848 which unseated Louis-Philippe from the throne. Here stood the mansion, called Hôtel de la Colonnade, where Bonaparte had his office after that memorable October day when he dispersed the Royalists before Saint-Roch. Here Eugène Beauharnais came to ask for the return of his father's sword; and hither came Joséphine to thank the General for his courtesy. He was living, then, a few doors down rue des Capucines, where rue Volney now cuts through.

Boulevard des Capucines is a sort of main artery of such club life as is left in the vicinity of the boulevards, and is more elegant than any other stretch of the old bulwarks, more Parisian still — in spite of its throngs of foreigners from the Grand Hotel, the Hotel Edward VII, from Cook's, and from the American Express. (If you turn off, to your right, into rue Danou, you will find some very attractive, but expensive, shops. The milliner I like best in Paris is Réjane, 15 rue Danou, near rue de la Paix.)

Offenbach "who set all Europe humming," died at number 8 boulevard des Capucines; and Guizot lived at number 16. "The private circle of this great man," said a writer in "Fraser's Magazine" for 1843, "is always one of the most delightful in Paris. Small are his apartments, far too small to admit the crowds of European as well as of French, American, and English literati who seek to claim the honor of his acquaintance. On his reception nights the streets about his house are crowded with carriages. Madame Guizot presides at a tea-table where the simplest fare is distributed." Guizot owned thirty thousand volumes, besides a mass of notes and manuscripts.

Soon after you pass the Place de l'Opéra, going east, the boulevard changes its name to boulevard des Italiens. The very attractive specialty shops continue for a little way on boulevard des Italiens, but for the most part they are behind you now. Liberty's Paris shop is, however, east of the Opéra, and the windows are always fascinating. It is a favorite place with Americans, and deservedly so. Liberty fabrics need no commendation from me, but I am glad to urge them upon the attention of any one who may not know them. Their satins are especially lovely. Their plush robes for auto, or any travelling or home use, are the height of luxury. Their scarves and handbags leave nothing to be desired. I do not, however, recommend having anything made there except children's smocked crêpe frocks, and possibly an evening wrap.

Boulevard des Capucines ends where rue Louis-le-Grand runs into it on your right, and rue Chaussée-d'Antin runs out of it, on your left. Details of the latter street are in Chapter XIV; of the former there is, I think, little that you may care to know, unless it interests you that Madame de Montespan sometimes lived at number 3 in this street, now named for her royal lover (Louis XIV) after she had been supplanted in his favor. Also, the painter, Rigaud, died at number 1, in 1743.

The next street on your right is rue de la Michodière, cut (in 1778) through the grounds of the Hôtel Conti, which belonged to the Princesse de Bourbon-Conti, daughter of Louis XIV and Louise de la Vallière. At number 19 in this street, on the third floor, Bonaparte was a lodger in those days of bitter poverty and chagrin when he came so near going off to be a Turk.

The rue de la Michodière ends at rue Saint-Augustin, in the Carrefour Gaillon, where there is a fountain that was erected in 1707 to honor Louis XIV. The justly famous restaurant of Henry is here, close to this fountain. And Maillabuau, 13 rue Saint-Augustin, is noted for good food and for Burgundy wine. Drouant, at 18 rue Gaillon, corner of rue Saint-Augustin, is also a famous place to dine. And Marguerite, on the south side of rue Saint-Augustin, opposite Maillabuau's, is a favored luncheon place for Americans who are hungry for baked beans, corned-beef hash, and other homely fare.

There are, you see, a lot of "present" reasons why you should mark well that rue de la Michodière. And you may be interested in a "past" reason, too. In 1792 there was erected, at the corner of rue de la Michodière and boulevard des Italiens, a curious-looking structure known as "Les

Bains Chinois," or Chinese Baths. (Just why a Chinese bath should be supposed alluring, I do not know. But neither would I suppose that a Turkish or a Russian bath would promise a superlative cleanness — neither Turks nor Russians, in general, seeming to have developed bathing to a high art.) They were, however, very popular; and the café and restaurant connected with them became the rallying-place for those who mourned the death of their "illustrious Robespierre" and plotted to overthrow the Directory and restore the Terror. A "model" of this structure (which was taken down in 1856) is at the Carnavalet Musée. Curiously enough, the opposite side of the boulevard was then popularly known as "Le Petit Coblentz," because so many Royalists had taken refuge in Coblentz, and this section of the boulevard swarmed with their sympathizers.

Paillard's restaurant (which might be called the Superior School of Restaurant-Keeping, whose graduates are among the most eminent food-artists in the world) is across the boulevard, at the corner of rue Chaussée-d'Antin. The next street running north is rue du Helder, at number 6 in which is the Grill-Room du Helder which may interest you some time when you are hungry. Then you have rue de Choiseul, between which and rue de Grammont, is the great bank building of the Crédit Lyonnais.

North from the boulevard, at this point, diverge rue Taitbout and rue Lafitte. At the corner of rue Taitbout and the boulevard stood, for ninety years, the famous restaurant Tortoni, whose "ices" drew the most elegant of all the great world of Paris under the Second Empire.

The bank of Ouvrard, the millionaire for whom Thérézia Tallien deserted her husband, was at number 11 rue Taitbout; and Thérézia lived, for a time, at number 1 rue Lafitte.

Talleyrand lived, during the Directory, at number 24 rue Taitbout, and with him was his then mistress, Madame Grand. In his "Memoirs" he says:

"A few days before Brumaire 18 [November 9, 1799], General Bonaparte, who was then living in the rue Chantereine [now de la Victoire], called on me one evening to talk about the preliminaries of his intended coup d'état. I was then living in a house in the rue Taitbout, which has, I believe, since been known as number 24. It was situated at the back of a yard, and the first floor of it communicated with rooms overlooking the street.

"We were engrossed in conversation in the drawing-room, which was lighted by a few candles, when, at about one o'clock in the morning, we heard a great noise in the street. It sounded like the riding of carriages and the tramping of horses, such as might be produced by an escort of cavalry. Suddenly the carriages stopped in front of my house. General Bonaparte turned pale, and I quite believe I did the same. We at once thought that people had come to arrest us by order of the Directory. I blew out the candles, and went on tiptoe to one of the front rooms, whence I could see what was going on in the street. Some time elapsed before I could ascertain the cause of all this uproar, which, however, turned out to be simply grotesque. As in those days the streets of Paris were hardly safe at night, all the money of the gambling-houses was collected at closing time and removed in cabs, for which, as in this case, the proprietor obtained from the police an escort of gendarmes to accompany the cabs as far as his residence. On the night in question, one of these cabs had met with an accident exactly opposite my door, thus causing the whole party to stop on their way for nearly a quarter of an hour. We laughed a good deal, the General and I, at our panic, which, however, was but natural on the part of people acquainted as we were with the disposition of the Directory."

Thomas Jefferson lived on rue Taitbout when he was United States Minister to France, 1785–89.

Rue Lafitte has many interesting shops where prints are sold. From 1792 to 1814 it was known as rue Cerutti, and it was on this street, where rue Pillet-Will now cuts into it, that Hortense Beauharnais lived much of her wretched married life with Louis Bonaparte.

Number 2 belonged, under the Restoration, to the Marquis of Hertford whose superb art collection, inherited by his illegitimate son, Richard Wallace, is now, as the Wallace Collection, at Hertford House, London, one of the "sights" of the British Capital.

Number 49 was once the home of the celebrated journalist, Émile de Girardin, and of his beautiful, brilliant wife, Delphine Gay. Thither came Hugo, Balzac, Eugène Sue, Musset, Gautier, and others, to pay homage to Delphine.

On your right, as you follow the boulevard, you have the Opéra-Comique. In 1781 the Duc and Duchesse de Choiseul caused to be built, on part of the grounds belonging to their splendid mansion, a theatre for certain Italian comedians — hence the name of the boulevard. It was burned in 1838, and its successor suffered a like fate in 1887. The present edifice was not finished until 1899.

Rue Favart, on the east of the theatre, was named for the founder of the Opéra-Comique, Charles Favart, and his wife. It has had many player-folk as tenants.

Place Boiëldieu, south of the theatre, is where Alexandre Dumas fils was born — in 1824, of a dressmaker, Marie-Catherine Lebay, living in the house (number 1) where Alexandre Dumas père was lodging, going thence to his work as what we would call a mail-clerk in the offices of the Duc d'Orléans, rue des Bons-Enfants. He was twenty-one — the temerarious young father! — and his income was twenty-five dollars a month, out of which he contributed to his mother's support. He might have been forgiven if he had evaded responsibility for Mademoiselle Lebay's nameless son. But he didn't!

A little farther on is the passage des Princes, in which is the restaurant Noël-Peters, very popular and very good. Opposite, debouches the rue Drouot, where you will find restaurant Lapré, at number 24; good food, not too high-priced.

Boulevard Montmartre — the Paris Rialto — begins here. The passage des Panoramas, with its memories of Robert Fulton, is at number 11 (at number 10 in the passage is the restaurant Beaugé, moderate in prices, and good); and across the way, at number 10, is the Musée Grévin, which you have visited — I hope. Before you come to passage des Panoramas, you pass rue Vivienne, at number 25 in which is the shop of Max, a furrier in high esteem with many of my friends.

Boulevard Montmartre ends where rue Montmartre runs to southward, and rue du Faubourg-Montmartre to northward. To those of you who will follow this latter with me for a considerable walk, I will promise rewards of several sorts.

Rue du Faubourg-Montmartre is a very ancient thoroughfare, and always a very animated one. As you go north on it, the first street on your right is Cité Bergère, where Heine lived in 1834, at number 3. Beyond it you come to rue Bergère, which need not concern you; and, past that, to rue Montyon and rue Geoffroy-Marie; take the latter, and come out on rue Richer, opposite the Folies-Bergère; if you turn to your left here, you will be in rue de Provence, where Liszt and Berlioz and Meissonier and Halévy lived, and Fanny Elssler had a theatre, and where there are many curiosity shops to-day; if you keep to your right on rue Richer, a few steps will take you to Cité Trévise, at number 2, in which, on the second floor, you will find the establishment of Mademoiselle Féhner, who makes the most exquisite lingerie in the world (I believe), and sells it to very elegant shops everywhere. She does not conduct a retail business, strictly speaking; but she will sell to you here, and at prices very much lower than you would pay for her lovely articles in the rue de la Paix. Besides her lingerie and lingerie dresses, see her embroidered bedspreads and other household embroideries. She has some rare old laces, too. It is one of the places to which I like best to come of all Paris shops, not only for the joy of seeing such handiwork, but for the atmosphere of the establishment. I have gone there for many years, and it does not change. Madame Marguerite, who has been with Mademoiselle Féhner for twenty years or thereabouts, speaks English perfectly, and will make you very glad you came.

Almost opposite the Cité Trévise is rue du Conservatoire, where the Conservatory of Music used to be; it was founded in 1784 to furnish singers and actors for the Court Theatre. Talma was trained there, and among the conservators were Cherubini, Auber, and Ambroise Thomas.

A little farther on you come to rue du Faubourg-Poissonnière; turn north on this street, and then to your right, into rue de Paradis, which is the centre for dealers in porcelains, potteries, crystals — "a veritable museum of ceramics," but much more trying to the lover of such things, because these are purchasable, and those in museums are not.

At number 58 in this street, Corot had a studio while he was living around the corner at 56 rue du Faubourg-Poissonnière, where he died, in 1875. At number 51, the capitulation of Paris was signed in the night of March 30–31, 1814.

The first street you cross, as you go eastward on rue de Paradis, is rue d'Hauteville, which need not concern you unless you are a Napoleon enthusiast — in which case, you will be very interested to know that Bourienne, his school-mate, companion-in-poverty, secretary and biographer, lived for twenty-three years (1801–24) at number 58 where you may see some of the apartments which were decorated for Bourrienne in the florid style of the Consulate. The Marquis de Rochegude (who certainly ought to know) says that this is the only example remaining in Paris of this "pompous style."

Rue de Paradis ends at rue du Faubourg-Saint-Denis, one of the most ancient streets in Paris and one that has seen memorable sights a-plenty. The kings of France made their "joyous entries" into Paris down this street; and up it they came, solemnly, on their way to burial. There are many venerable houses remaining, and the saunterer along its pavements has much to recall.

You will, I think, want to turn north a little way for a glimpse of Saint-Lazare Prison for women (which you cannot visit without an order from the Préfecture), the successor of an ancient leper-house founded during the Crusades, by the Hospitaliers de Saint-Lazare. The domain was a vast one — even as late as 1808, it was much greater in extent than the Gardens of the Tuileries — and the kings, entering Paris, always alighted there; their coffins always lay here the last night before the tombs of Saint-Denis closed over them. Saint-Lazare was a Revolutionary prison, and it was from here that André Chénier went to his death — we shall recall him more particularly, in a few minutes. Here he wrote, during his one hundred and forty days of imprisonment, that poem of poignant pathos, "The Young Captive," and those stinging "Iambics" wherein he tried, condemned, and consigned to everlasting obloquy

ANDRÉ CHÉNIER AT SAINT-LAZARE
Painting by Charles-Louis Muller

the Convention which had travestied the Rights of Man.
No painting of the Revolutionary period is more familiar
than Muller's "Calling the Last Victims of the Terror,
July 25, 1794," with Chénier in the foreground. Ten days
before, Suvée, the painter, had made, here, the portrait of
his fellow-prisoner, the exquisite young poet. The existing
buildings at Saint-Lazare date back more than a hundred
years before Chénier's death; and for his sake, if for no
other, the place is of supreme interest to many.

If you were to follow rue du Faubourg-Saint-Denis some
distance farther, you would come to the Maison Dubois,
the municipal hospital for the insane, where poor Henri
Murger died in 1861, at the age of thirty-four. But there
are not many reasons why the average visitor to Paris
should come so far. For those few who might care to see
the chapel where Jeanne d'Arc received communion in
November, 1429, the hospital where Murger died is on the
way; for the chapel is at the end of rue du Faubourg-Saint-
Denis, where it is crossed by boulevard de la Chapelle — a
short distance beyond the Maison Dubois. Any one who
cared to see that would probably like also to follow rue
Louis-Blanc, in a southeasterly direction, to the Place du
Combat where the gibbet of Montfaucon stood for centuries. Hard by here (in rue des Écluses Saint-Martin) is the
cemetery for Protestant strangers, where John Paul Jones
was buried in 1792, and whence his remains were removed
to Annapolis in 1905. From this place to the beautiful
park of the Buttes Chaumont is but a short distance, and I
heartily commend it to all who can take time for a visit to it.

But, on the presumption that you have completed your
détour, or that you are not going to make it, let me go back
to Saint-Lazare Prison and direct you thence down to the
porte Saint-Denis which is at the east end of boulevard de
Bonne-Nouvelle. This section of the boulevard is interest-

ing for many reasons. It gets its name from the Church of Notre-Dame-de-Bonne-Nouvelle (or Our Lady of Good Tidings) which was frequented by Anne of Austria during those long years when she was so wistful to hear that *she* was to have a son. The church is in rue de la Lune, at the beginning of which (where it leaves boulevard de Bonne-Nouvelle) is the ancient stall where Brioches de la Lune are sold, in close proximity to Brioches du Soleil (of the Sun). At number 38 boulevard de Bonne-Nouvelle is Marguery's, and at number 39 is Café Prévost, frequented by journalists and celebrated for its chocolate.

Rue de Cléry runs southeast from the porte Saint-Denis. It was at this corner (of the boulevard and rue de Cléry) that the Baron de Batz made his d'Artagnanesque attempt to wrest Louis XVI from his executioners.

The boulevard was narrower then, and had not been levelled; and along the north side of it (where Marguery's is now) was the cemetery de Bonne-Nouvelle. The slow pace necessary in traversing this bit of the way to the scaffold and the composition of this curious "pocket" full of tiny streets caused de Batz to fix upon this as the best possible place to effect the rescue.

The early morning of January 21, 1793, was raw and damp — a thick fog enshrouded Paris. It was about eight o'clock when Louis — under the escort of Santerre, the brewer — left the Temple. He rode in a green carriage and read the psalms for the dying. His face was calm. Beside him sat the Abbé Edgeworth, and, on the seat opposite, two gendarmes.

The people of Paris had been given the most severe orders; and a terrifying display of military force was made, so that the futility of resistance might be apparent to all. Four deep, the troops lined the route of the cortège, standing stiff like lead soldiers. At every street corner along the line of march was a detachment of artillery, with guns ready to bark; and behind them masses of infantry reserves from the camps around Paris.

Shop-shutters were not taken down, and there were (by command) no loiterers on doorsteps, no faces peering from windows. Many silent spectators were there, however — terror and sympathy on the faces of most of them.

"As the carriages drew near," writes Georges Cain, "an irrepressible murmur ran through the crowd; in the distance could be heard the mournful beating of drums muffled by the humidity; then the escort, formidable and sinister, appeared in the fog. First, the Marseillais; then the national gendarmerie, mounted and on foot; finally, two batteries preceding the carriage which, its windows clouded with moisture, was framed in a forest of pikes and bayonets.

"The cortège advanced slowly. Suddenly, at the porte Saint-Denis, at the top of rue de Cléry, before starting up the slopes of Bonne-Nouvelle, it came to a sort of halt or hesitation — . . . cries, jostling, some shadows soon swallowed up in the mist; then some men knocked down, thrust through — some pools of blood on the pavements."

What happened? This: the evening before, the Committee of Public Safety had been advised that an attempt would be made to assassinate Louis, to spare him the shame of the scaffold. They were told the place where this would occur, and the names of five hundred men who were to rally around de Batz when he gave the cry. Before dawn they had posted an armed guard at the home of every conspirator, and egress was forbidden to all.

The Baron, however, was at his post when his house was surrounded; and about twenty-five of his supporters who had not slept at their homes were mingled in the silent, mist-enshrouded throng, awaiting his signal.

It was nine o'clock when the King's carriage halted here. So far as "D'Artagnan" de Batz could see, everything favored his bold enterprise.

"Follow me and save the King!" he cried, waving his hat in one hand and a sabre in the other.

Of those who attempted to follow him, only six were able to break through the rim of steel surrounding Louis. All were killed except "D'Artagnan" — who disappeared "as by enchantment."

Some of the conspirators, whose movements betrayed them, but did not get them past the cordon of soldiery, were chased as they fled into this network of tortuous little old streets behind the boulevard; and those who attempted to seek refuge in the Church of Notre-Dame de Bonne-Nouvelle were nailed to its doors with bayonets.

It all lasted but a minute or two, and delayed the cortège scarcely that long. Before it was over, the last ranks of the death procession were lost to view in the thick fog hanging low under the great trees of boulevard Poissonnière, and Louis — still calm — continued to read the psalms for the dying. He must have heard de Batz's cry. He may have had a moment of expectancy. There was little or nothing in the attitude of the populace — so far as he could gauge it — to indicate that they desired his death. Perhaps he was still hopeful when he tried, on the scaffold, to make that speech which Santerre silenced by ordering the drums to beat.

Where — on that sombre morning — was the exquisite young poet, André Chénier, beneath the windows of whose home this attempt at rescue took place? He had risked his life to help Malesherbes prepare the King's defence. Was he ready to risk it also to snatch Louis from the executioner's hands?

Born at Constantinople, of a beautiful and highly cultivated Greek mother and a French father who was consul and cloth-merchant, André lived in France from the time he was three years old (part of the time in that poet's town, Carcassonne), except for visits to Italy and to England. His mother's salon, although a modest one, was frequented by some of the most thoughtful men in Paris, and André was nurtured on idealistic talk of the glorious days that were dawning. "He foresaw the peaceful triumph of philosophy, and conceived a regenerated human race, worthy of the blessings of liberty and obedient to the dictates of reason." He was an ardent Constitutionalist, but he was not a Republican. As the tempest about him increased in violence, he wrote, in prose and verse, and orated at the Feuillants, pleading with his countrymen that freedom and happiness were to be won through devotion to duty; would be lost through frenzied repudiation of all old allegiances, old obedience. "But there were too many who hoped to profit by a hurricane. And of his dreams, André Chénier soon had nothing left but inconsolable regret for having too easily believed 'not in those ideas, which had not deceived him, but in the men who exploited and corrupted the ideas.'" He was bitterly chagrined at the action of his younger brother, Marie-Joseph (the brilliant dramatist, whose "Charles IX" was played by Talma at the Comédie-Française and had an immense success, when the youthful author was only twenty-five, and was followed in quick succession by other pieces immensely influential against hereditary privilege), in entering the Convention as a deputy — and voting for the King's death. André excoriated violence, whilst Marie-Joseph did much to incite it. André congratulated France on the courage of Charlotte Corday, thanks to which "one fanatic the less wallows in this mire." Marie-Joseph was of those who ordered her death.

Finally, sick at heart, André sought solitude at Versailles, "not because he was afraid; he was fleeing from the spectacle of men's baseness. His weary soul fraternized voluptuously with the marble gods, the devastated porticoes, the vast basins where the clear sky was reflected." There he communed with nature and with those works of art which the Sun-King had commanded for his pleasances. There he wrote his exquisite "Ode to Versailles." Thence he often made his way through the woods to Louveciennes, where he had a lady-love, and to Marly, where he visited his friends the Trudaines at the villa which was to be for many years the home of Victorian Sardou (and where the author of "Thermidor" piously preserved everything associated with the young poet).

At the beginning of March, 1794, André heard from some one in Paris that his friend Pastoret was to be arrested. Immediately, he set out to find Pastoret at Passy, where he had taken refuge in the home of his wife's parents. André's hope was that he might induce Pastoret to return with him to the cottage at Versailles; but Pastoret had already been warned, and had fled. His wife and her mother, in tears, received André, who comforted and reassured them as best he could, and persuaded them to hide themselves for a while in his retreat.

They agreed, and he was about to go for a carriage to take them when the house was surrounded by armed men seeking a suspect who was not there. What did it matter? There was an aristocratic-looking young gentleman who must be a villain because he was intelligent and mannerly. So they took him. And that night he was lodged in Saint-Lazare Prison. The King's neglected gardens knew him no more.

Marie-Joseph has been painted a veritable Cain compassing his brother's murder either through active denunciation or through inactivity to help him. There is no evidence in support of either charge. Marie-Joseph and his mother seem to have agreed that André's best hope lay in being forgotten. They were, however, unable to convert the distracted old father to their way of thinking. He wore out, with his agonized importunities, everybody whose influence he sought to sway for André.

One day when the aged man arrived at Saint-Lazare to visit his son, he was told that an order of the dread Committee of Public Safety forbade Chénier to receive him. In tears, the terrified father came home (that house at the convergence of rue de Cléry and rue Beauregard was their home; it is numbered 97 rue de Cléry) and besought Marie-Joseph to act. But Marie-Joseph had reason to believe that the end of the Terror was near — that Robespierre was doomed. He counselled patience. The frantic father, however, could not keep quiet. He hovered about the prison, and saw the daily "batch" sent off to feed the guillotine. One day, a prison-guard told the wretched old man that thirty victims a day were being haled hence to the Tribunal and the scaffold. Frenzied with fear, the father ran to Barère (whose word was then next to Robespierre's if, indeed, it was not already better, and who was supposed to be a stanch friend of Marie-Joseph's) and pleaded as he could not have done for his own life, that care be taken lest André perish.

"Your son shall come out in three days," promised Barère — grimly. But the old man did not grasp the sinister meaning; he was radiant, believing that his entreaties had saved his idolized son.

Three days later he sat at home, listening for the footfalls of André returning home.

Toward evening, some one knocked. He ran to the door and opened it. Not André, but Marie-Joseph, stood on the threshold. One look at his son's face, frozen with horror, and the father fell, with a heartrending cry, on the dining-room floor.

Standing here in the shadow of this old house, we may easily picture the scene of that hot July evening. "On the doorsteps," says Lenôtre (in his "Last Days of André Chénier," to be found in his first series on "Vieilles Maisons, Vieux Papiers"), "people of the neighborhood laugh and talk, trying to get a breath of air; little girls in the street play noisily; the stifling air is full of the joyous sounds of a Paris summer evening . . . and up there, near the open window, the father of André Chénier sobs, blames himself for his son's death and prays that he, too, may die.

"At this same hour a cart loaded with twenty-five headless bodies left the Place de la Barrière-de-Vincennes (the Place du Trône) where the execution had taken place, and went along the outer boulevards to an abandoned quarry where, for six weeks past, carts had gone every evening with similar loads for dumping." . . . It was thus that André Chénier was buried, in the big ditch wherein 1307 victims were thrown between June 14th and July 27th. In Chapter X you have further details of that ditch, and urgings to visit it.

Rue Chénier, which runs south from André's home, was call d rue Saint-Claude from 1660; during the Revolution the "Saint" was eliminated (at number 10 you may see the old designation, with the prefix effaced), and in 1804, ten ye rs after the poet's death, his name was given to this little street.

Some among you may be interested to walk the length of rue de Cléry. A few steps beyond Chénier's house is the shortest "street" in Paris, consisting of a flight of fourteen steps. It is called rue des Degrés, and dates back to the seventeenth century.

The brothers Corneille (Pierre and Thomas) lived in rue

de Cléry at one time. Madame de Pompadour was born in this street near its junction with rue du Sentier. Numbers 19 and 21 rue de Cléry once belonged to Molière's brother, who was a priest. In 1778 Pierre Lebrun, art dealer, bought this property. Here his beautiful, talented and immensely popular wife, Madame Vigée-Lebrun, lived until 1793, when she fled as an émigré, to save her life; here she gave "fêtes à la grecque" (Greek) or exhibitions of classic beauty in dancing, tableaux vivants, etc.; and here, in a house he had built at the back of his property, opening on rue du Sentier at number 8, Lebrun's wife found him when she returned from her nine years' stay abroad.

Number 33 rue du Sentier (which will take you back to the boulevard) is where Madame de Pompadour lived at the time of her marriage with Le Normand d'Étioles; and numbers 22–24 is where the latter lived after his separation from the King's mistress. When she died, he married a dancer at the Opéra. Across the street from him, at number 23, lived the President Hénault, the close friend of Louis XV's neglected Queen, Marie Leszczynka. And, some-where in the street, Nattier died, in 1766.

Now, supposing you to be back at the porte Saint-Denis, and proceeding eastward on the boulevard, I do not know that there is anything to which I should call your special attention until you reach the porte Saint-Martin (erected, like its neighbor, to glorify Louis XIV) beneath which the Allies entered Paris in 1814.

Where the Théâtre de la Renaissance stands there used to be a famous restaurant, Deffieux, which did business on that site for one hundred and thirty-three years, until it was burned by the Communards in 1871. The theatre has many interesting associations with Bernhardt, Guitry, and other famous artists. The Théâtre-de-la-Porte-Saint-Martin, next door, was first built in 1781, when the Opéra auditorium at the Palais-Royal was destroyed by fire. This theatre was completed in seventy-five days; and the populace was so suspicious of the solidity of a building thus rapidly run up that the first performance in it was given free. If lives were lost, at least no one would have paid for risking his! But it was found to be very substantial, and was the home of opera for twelve years.

In February, 1787, Marie Antoinette, attending the opera here, was applauded as usual; but as the applause subsided, some one was heard to hiss. The Queen was much disturbed by this, and declared that in future when she came to the opera the public must be excluded.

The hiss emanated from a young nobleman, the Marquis de Saint-P——, who belonged to the class corresponding to our "drawing-room *pinks*" of to-day, priding themselves on their sympathy with the oppressed who want the world *red*.

For his show of irreverence, he was hustled out of the theatre and into the Châtelet Prison. A little more than fifty years later, he was brought to trial for that hiss!

His family had hastened to secure his release from the dungeons of the Châtelet; and, either because they disliked his "pinkness" or because they were fearful for him, they got him committed, on a plea that he was "weak-minded," to a luxurious sanitarium where he employed his abundant leisure in the study of the Greek and Latin historians. Years passed by; the Marquis seemed to have no interest in getting out, and no one evinced any concern to have him liberated. When the storm broke, his relatives emigrated. His board was no longer paid, but he was supported by the state which accepted him, without inquiry, as an "incapable." He refused to see a visitor, and he did nothing but read. What further proof of insanity could any government ask?

In 1837 the "mad" Marquis completed a comparative study of the historians of the Greek decadence, and determined to have it printed and to dedicate it to King Louis XVI. He sent for a printer, who suggested that the dedication read "to the *Memory* of Louis XVI."

"He is dead, then?" said the Marquis. "Recently?"

He began to question. But the printer fled before the task of trying to recapitulate the history of those fifty years.

This served to call attention to the case of the Marquis, and he was brought to trial in that very room where, four-and-forty years before, Marie Antoinette was condemned to death by accusers who would have regarded a mere hiss against her as almost a betrayal of Royalist sympathy.

In those days the Théâtre-de-la-Porte-Saint-Martin, had long since ceased to house the opera, and was the scene of Frédéric Lemaître's triumphs as an actor in melodrama. The old theatre was burned by the Communards, and rebuilt in 1873. It was there that in 1897 Coquelin produced "Cyrano de Bergerac," with overwhelming success for himself and the author, Rostand; it was there, while rehearsing "Chantecler" that the superb actor was stricken with his mortal illness, in 1909.

If you were to walk up rue du Faubourg-Saint-Martin, you would find that the first street which crosses it is rue du Château-d'Eau, the part of which to your left used to be called rue Neuve-Saint-Jean when Charles-Henri Sanson lived on it. He was the executioner from 1778 to 1795, and officiated either actively or nominally (his son Henri acting for him) at all the guillotinings of the Terror. His family had been executioners at Paris for more than a hundred years. Charles-Henri, born in 1739, was one of seven brothers, all of whom earned their livelihood on the scaffolds of France; and it is said that not infrequently they all sat together at the table in Charles-Henri's well-appointed and spacious residence.

The headsman's house was painted red, and it was practically impossible for any man of that calling to get a wife except from among the daughters of headsmen elsewhere. Yet the Sansons do not seem to have been held in any special abhorrence, and they were quite like gentry in their parish of Saint-Laurent (near the Gare de l'Est) where they had their family burial vault. In the last days of 1767, Henri Sanson was christened at the font of Saint-Laurent; and on September 1, 1768, at five o'clock in the morning, Jeanne Bécu, or Vaubernier, was married to Guillaume du Barry, and immediately thereafter returned to Versailles there to be domiciled — almost enthroned — as a countess. It was almost certainly Henri Sanson who officiated at her execution twenty-five years later.

Boulevard Saint-Martin ends at Place de la République, and there the line of interior boulevards (following the old walls of Charles V) turns south, toward the river; becoming, first, boulevard du Temple, where, before and during the Revolution, was the home of the Swiss doctor, Kurtz (Latinized to Curtius), uncle and teacher of Madame Tussaud. Curtius had an exhibition room in the Galerie Montpensier of the Palais-Royal, where he showed his life-size portrait models (in wax) of celebrities. In the house on the boulevard du Temple was his workshop, his dwelling, and an exhibition of a different character, the forerunner of "The Chamber of Horrors," in which he showed portrait figures of noted criminals.

Some years ago, in London, when I was haunting Madame Tussaud's exhibition (which has, all my life, been one of the most fascinating places in the world to me), Mr. John Tussaud, Madame's great-grandson, the present head of the enterprise, loaned me a copy of Madame's memoirs, published in 1838 or thereabouts and relating graphically her extraordinarily eventful life. She was brought in contact with practically every notable of her time, and made portraits of most of them. For nine years she lived at Versailles as the intimate companion of young Madame Elizabeth, Louis XVI's sister; and there she became ardently attached to the members of the royal family and to many of their close friends. From there her uncle recalled her just before the storm of the Revolution broke. Thence she came here to boulevard du Temple. Here she saw the mob sweep by on its way to take the Bastille; thence she went, with her uncle, to visit the famous dungeons when their captives (seven criminals) had been set free — and there she was kept from falling on the slippery winding stairs by a young man whose touch, she said, made her shudder; whereat her uncle said she was a goose, for the young man was a very clever and promising young lawyer from Arras, named Maximilien Robespierre. There she lived while the royal family was in captivity. There she was forced, by the butchers of the Princesse de Lamballe, to model the beautiful head they were bearing aloft on a pike. There she was visited by persons ordering her to be present, on the morning of January 21, 1793, in the graveyard of the Madeleine, to model the severed head of "the tyrant," Louis XVI, fresh from the knife. They made her do it. When Marat was murdered, one of the first commands was to fetch Marie Grosholtz (that was her name) and have him modelled as he lay in his bath. There she saw Charlotte Corday before the latter was haled to prison; and within the next day or two she modelled Charlotte. In October, the command came to her, early in the morning of the 16th, to proceed to the cemetery of the Madeleine prepared to make a copy of Marie Antoinette's head. The following May she had the same unspeakably terrible task with the head of her beloved Madame Elizabeth. And so on, until she did Robespierre's own. She was in prison with Joséphine de Beauharnais and through her was brought, later, into contact with Napoleon.

Long before that day boulevard du Temple had been "the great white way" of Paris — only, its distinguishing color was green when its arching trees were in foliage. The gay world flocked there in such throngs that, toward four o'clock in the afternoons, it was impossible to move faster than a snail's pace. Where the crowds are, the entertainers soon come. First it was a famous monkey which imitated the mannerisms of a popular actor; then it was a man who made a fortune with grimaces which amused the idlers; then a tight-rope walker; all these in open air or in temporary booths. Then theatres, and more theatres of every sort. At the time of the Revolution there were ten theatres on this street. And soon thereafter the Parisians began to call this "the boulevard of crime," because every evening between six and eleven there were perpetrated here (on the stages) so many crimes; and virtue never triumphed before eleven-fifteen or even later.

"Each evening," says Georges Cain, "this gay boulevard was invaded long before the box-offices opened; and patiently the public stood in line between the long wooden rails, devouring garlic sausage and fried potatoes, drinking glasses of cocoa or peeling oranges — the peels of which were carefully saved by the boisterous young gallery-gods to hurl at the bald heads in the orchestra seats."

In February, 1847, when Dumas's "La Reine Margot" was given its first performance, at his own theatre, the Théâtre-Historique, the public was standing in line full twenty-four hours before the sale of tickets commenced. And the play, which began at 6 P.M., was not over until three in the morning!

The boulevard loved historical drama; and at one time (October 20, 1830) the "Courrier des Théâtres" advertised the following:

Vaudeville: Bonaparte, lieutenant of artillery.

Variétés: Napoléon at Berlin, or the Gray Redingote.

Nouveautés : The Schoolboy of Brienne, or The Little Corporal, with Mademoiselle Déjazet.

Ambigu: Napoléon.

Cirque-Olympique: The Crossing of Mont Saint-Bernard, military glory in seven tableaus.

I probably shall not surprise you if I say that I should like to have been there then.

There is another memory of this boulevard that I am sure you will be glad to have in mind as you traverse it; and that is Massenet's, as he communicated it to Georges Cain for the latter's "Promenades dans Paris." I am sure that the genial conservator of the Carnavalet, whose passion was Paris, would have been far from minding my drafts upon his vast funds of Paris lore, since it is in the interest of helping many Americans to know and love Paris that I make them. He is gone now, and I cannot ask him; but I am confident what his answer would have been.

M. Cain had asked his distinguished friend for reminiscences of those days when the future composer of "Manon," "Thaïs," etc., at the age of fifteen, studied by day at the Conservatoire, and in the evenings was a drummer at the Théâtre-Lyrique earning forty-five francs (nine dollars) a month.

"I lived at number 5 rue Menilmontant," he told M. Cain, "occupying a little room high up in a strange house whose other lodgers were almost all acrobats, bare-back riders, aërialists, pretty 'clownesses' who did their little housekeeping tasks and watched the soup-kettle while they practised their 'stunts.' . . . Sunday mornings, this gorgeous company used to set out for the country to picnic on the grass . . . and when one of us had spent thirty cents he was accused of prodigality. . . .

"After I had spent the day at the Conservatoire, I betook myself at half-past five o'clock to rue Basse-du-Temple, a sort of alley parallel to the boulevard, where the stage-doors opened. The 'shows' then began at six o'clock. [This was from 1856 to 1861.] What a crowd! What a court of miracles! Imagine all the 'supers,' all the mechanics, all the wardrobe women and dressers, all the choruses of ten theatres packed into this narrow, muddy alley, full of venders of sausage, of wine, of tarts . . . it was dirty, it was verminous, and it reeked of garlic. . . . But how amusing, how picturesque, how living!

"In my orchestra pit I worked during the dialogues — of which there were many in the opéra-comiques. I had drawn some staves on the heads of my drums, and there I worked out my lessons in fugue and saved myself the price of some sheets of music-paper which cost three sous for five sheets. . . . During the intermissions, we gathered in the former stable of the Théâtre-Historique that the good Dumas had built for the horses of D'Artagnan and of Bussy d'Amboise. . . .

"What fine artistic battles were fought in the theatre, then! . . . The first performance of 'Faust' was in our theatre on the 19th of March, 1859. Gounod had won us all to faith in his ability, and Madame Carvalho was sublime; but this new music was so different to that which was then popular. Léon Carvalho had given the opera an adorable setting; Léo Delibes was the conductor; all the principal parts were superbly sung. But the audience was restless. They hissed the soldiers' chorus and the final trio. . . . Gounod wept.

"It was not until two years later that a second attempt to popularize the opera met with triumphant success."

The Théâtre-Lyrique (formerly Dumas's Théâtre-Historique) was where one now descends to the Métro at Place de la République. For nothing now remains of the old "boulevard of crime" except its name and its happy memories. We must see it all with our mind's eye; what's stamped on our retina is a modern street due to Baron Haussmann. All that is left of yester-years are the houses numbered 42, 44, 46, 48, at the first of which Gustave Flaubert lived during six months annually for fifteen years, and where he wrote "Madame Bovary," "Salammbo," etc. Here he was visited on Sunday afternoons by the brothers Goncourt, Théophile Gautier, Taine, and others of lesser note.

Beyond here there is nothing of special interest on the boulevards until you come to the Bastille, which is described in our Chapter Five.

XVI

A THIRD SUNDAY IN PARIS

You may be so fortunate as to have a third Sunday in Paris; and if you do, you may like this outline, in whole or in part. Most of it may be followed on any day of the week; but I put it in a Sunday class because of the Beaux-Arts, whose visiting-hours are from twelve to four on Sundays. It seems to me that every intelligent visitor to Paris should come away with some impression of the Beaux-Arts. If your Sundays are fewer than three, you could easily make the Beaux-Arts and Saint-Germain-des-Prés part of your first Sunday, going to them after your luncheon and on your way to the Luxembourg Gardens.

There are a few more things I'd like to have you see in the Marais quarter; and if that phase of Paris interests you, I suggest that you spend part of the morning there. You may prefer, however, to have this morning for the Louvre — Sunday morning is one of my favorite times for going there — or for some of the other museums; in the latter event, you have only to omit the Old Paris stroll, or transfer it to another day, and "pick up the trail" at the Bœuf-à-la-Mode, for luncheon.

Now, then, for the Marais!

Take the Métro, or tram 3 or 4 to the Saint-Paul station (whence you have twice before set out), and turn west into rue François-Miron which used to be part of rue Saint-Antoine, the main highway from the east gate into the city. This easternmost end of it ran through the great tournament field where Henry II was mortally wounded by Montgoméry; and the western end, in Roman and much later times, bordered a vast cemetery, or "field of rest."

The street has many old houses; but the one to which I specially direct you is the Hôtel Beauvais, at number 68 — built in 1655, on ground where once stood a house in which Tasso wrote part of "Jerusalem Delivered." The present mansion was erected for Catherine Bellier, wife of Pierre de Beauvais, who had been a peddler of ribbons, then a store-keeper, and had grown rich enough to buy a title and a place at Court — which latter he got by marrying Catherine, a one-eyed wanton who as first lady of the bed-chamber to Anne of Austria came to know so many things that she had to be treated deferentially. It was this woman who instructed Louis XIV in many things which were to his discredit and — therefore — to her profit.

Anne used to come here frequently to visit her confidante; and she accepted Catherine's hospitality on August 28, 1660, to see the gorgeous entry of her son, Louis XIV, into Paris with his Spanish bride, Marie-Thérèse. Beside Anne that day sat her unfortunate sister-in-law, Henrietta Maria of England, and the latter's youngest daughter who was soon to be Anne's other daughter-in-law. Turenne, the great marshal, was there also; and Mazarin — too ill to ride in the procession, in his gorgeous coach painted by Lebrun, escorted by his Musketeers, and *drawn by mules* because He whom Mazarin was supposed to serve had entered Jerusalem on an ass. Nothing could more perfectly illustrate how little, after all his bitter experience, Mazarin had learned of the Parisian populace, than his ordering that coach, thus drawn, to be a part of that parade; a better butt for ridicule could scarcely have been devised.

The procession was the most magnificent that Paris had ever seen, requiring nearly twelve hours to pass. There were balconies on Hôtel Beauvais then (you may see a somewhat similar one now on number 82), and thereon sat the notables who were not in the passing pageant. The throng in this street was dense; and it may have been here that young Madame Scarron stood, and had her first glimpse of the resplendent sovereign who was one day to be her husband.

You may like to fancy what were Anne of Austria's thoughts as she looked down on the young Spanish bride (her niece) and recalled her own bridal procession into Paris from Spain, five-and-forty years before. Beside her, hastening toward his grave, sat that prelate-minister whose relations with her had scandalized the world and brought on a civil war. Was there, in Anne's mind, doubt or certainty as to the paternity of that young King who was riding by?

Christina of Sweden was a later tenant of this mansion. And in 1763, when the Bavarian ambassador owned and occupied it, Mozart was his guest. The next proprietor perished on the guillotine, in 1794. (See the beautiful oval court.)

Turn down (on your left) rue Geoffroy-l'Asnier, a delightful old thirteenth-century street, at number 26 in which is what remains of the Hôtel Châlons-Luxembourg, with a doorway worth travelling miles to see. D'Annunzio once lived here. At number 19 there are the remains of a house which dates back at least to 1350 (according to the Marquis de Rochegude) and was confiscated by the English in 1422.

The sinister rue Grenier-sur-l'Eau which faces you, with the belfry of Saint-Gervais dominating its west end, is worth walking through, to give you impressions which may help to vivify for you, some day, stories of "the mysteries of Paris"; and also because of another reason:

At the end of this short street is rue des Barres; and thereby hangs a tale — one of the best tales that any man

ever wrote: "Marguerite de Valois." (One cannot re-read,
in Paris, all the books one would like to. But I will guarantee that every one who has his copy of "Marguerite"
with him, and its topography fresh in his mind as he goes
about Paris, will be richly rewarded therefor.)

Do you remember the mysterious rendezvous of La Môle
and Coconnas after they and Marguerite and the Duchesse
de Nevers had left the abode of the Florentine sorcerer on
the pont Saint-Michel? La Môle and Coconnas were sitting
in the inn, the Belle Étoile, in rue de l'Arbre-Sec, when a
man entered and gave them each a letter saying: "You are
waited for in rue Saint-Antoine, opposite rue de Jouy."
(That is, rue François-Miron; and rue de Jouy runs southeast from it, near Hôtel Beauvais.) And there two duennas
met the ardent lovers, and told them that they must be
blindfolded and led the rest of the way. So they came to
the house in rue Cloche-Perce, where their ladies awaited
them. (Rue Cloche-Perce runs north from rue François-
Miron, almost opposite rue Geoffroy-l'Asnier.)

This house had two entrances exactly alike, you will recall; and on a later night when Henry of Navarre, his
brothers-in-law, Charles IX and Anjou (later Henry III),
with the Duc de Guise, had tracked Marguerite thither,
the ladies and the lovers fled out the other street (rue
Tiron), leaving the four men wondering. In rue François-
Miron (then called rue Saint-Antoine) the men separated
into two pairs. And Charles IX with Henry of Navarre
went down rue Geoffroy-l'Asnier to rue Grenier-sur-l'Eau,
and through the latter to rue des Barres. There they
stopped before a small lone house in the middle of a garden,
enclosed by high walls. Charles took a key from his pocket
and opened the door.

"'Henriot,' said the King, 'I told you that when I go out
from the Louvre I go out from hell. When I enter here I
enter Paradise.'"

The scene that follows, in the house of Marie Touchet ("the only being," Charles told Henry, "who loves me for myself"), has for me an extraordinary pathos and vividness, so that it seems impossible for me to walk hereabouts except in company with those two young men on that midnight visit to Marie and the sleeping baby boy who, but for the bar-sinister on his birth, would have made so different the history of France.

Long before Charles's day there was another royal romance associated with rue des Barres. In the fourteenth century a lover of Isabeau of Bavaria was proprietor of Hôtel des Barres; his name was Boiserédon, and Charles VI had him thrown into the river in a sack, with these words: "Let the King's justice be executed."

There was a church here dedicated to Saint-Gervais as early as the sixth century. It was rebuilt in the thirteenth century, again in the fifteenth, and lastly in the sixteenth.

Madame de Sévigné was married here. And here Paul Scarron was buried. It is, of all the interesting events associated with Saint-Gervais, the latter that I always seem to "see" there; it must have been a goodly company that paid its last respects to the little man with the pain-twisted, impotent body and the agile tongue. And there was the penniless young widow, whose existence had been hand-to-mouth enough as wife, but was to be even more precarious for some years hence.

There is a chapel here called Chapelle de Scarron, which Madame de Maintenon is supposed to have erected to the memory of her first husband. But the truth (as established by MM. de Boilisle and Hallays) is that a hundred and ten years after Scarron's burial its expenses were still unpaid and the parish had not ceased complaining of the fact. And, furthermore, his widow was very far from wishing to do anything to conserve his memory. His works were not permitted to be reprinted in France. Racine was disgraced for mentioning them at Court. By Madame's express commands, no mention of her first marriage was made in her epitaph.

The interior of Saint-Gervais is little changed since the end of the fifteenth century, and has always been impressive, but is more so than ever now, because one must be far from sentient who does not feel the atmosphere of that Good Friday, 1918, when a great congregation had gathered here to pray and to listen to the Ténébræ chanted by the famous choir of Saint-Gervais. Every heart there must have been heavy-laden that day, and lifted up in agonized supplication to the Crucified, when the shell from "Big Bertha" struck the north side, and seventy-five of the kneeling suppliants were killed, ninety others injured.

Note, in the left aisle, the tablet bearing the names of men of this parish who died in the late war. Note these commemorative tablets in every church, school, and public building you enter. A moment of reverence and of emotion before each and every one of them is, it seems to me, the least we can do, "lest we forget." Such a toll as was taken! And in the night that still covers us, it is hard for some to see for what they died.

Go into Saint-Gervais by all means. It is full of artistic treasures; it is in itself greatly impressive; and you may be fortunate enough to hear the Chanteurs.

The Place Baudoyer, north of the church, occupies part of the site of the old cemetery of Saint-Jean-en-Grève which was not removed until 1830. Where the former Caserne Napoléon is (now an annex of the Hôtel-de-Ville), on the opposite side of the square from the Mairie, there was once (in 1379 and thereabouts) the Paris mansion of the sires of Coucy, those great feudal lords who dared to defy the kings of France. And it is a curious coincidence that "Big Bertha" was located near Coucy, their famous castle, nearly ninety miles northeast.

On the south side of Saint-Gervais is the rue de l'Hôtel-de-Ville, one of the most ancient-appearing in Paris, with many very old houses. If you don't care about that walk with Charles IX and Henry of Navarre to Marie Touchet's house, take the rue de l'Hôtel-de-Ville all the way from rue Geoffroy-l'Asnier to the Place de l'Hôtel-de-Ville.

When you came here, early in your Paris stay, to visit the great City Hall of Paris and the little Ward Hall of the Fourth Arrondissement, close by, I did not urge upon your attention anything of the history of this famous square of which the Marquis de Rochegude says that "its history would be the history of Paris, and even the history of France."

I doubt if you want to linger, now, long enough to recall much of it. The outstanding feature of it in most people's minds, I find, is the fact that here for more than five hundred years executions took place.

The first Town Hall here was a mansion called "The House of Pillars," in which, Victor Hugo says, Charles V lived when dauphin. Étienne Marcel, whose bold equestrian statue stands here overlooking the Seine (which is his grave), bought that house for headquarters for the people's interests, in 1357. Nearly two hundred years later, Francis I laid the cornerstone of a new Hôtel-de-Ville which was not finished until 1628 — nothing at all was done on it from 1548 to 1600. This building, which was the theatre of much drama in the unfolding of history, was burned by the Communards in 1871; and the one we see was built between 1874 and 1882.

The square was, however, an important gathering point for the Paris populace long before Marcel gave it official headquarters there. Away back even in Roman times this bit of ground (whose other name is the Grève, or Strand) was the scene of so many disputes between masters (usually boat-owners, who docked here) and men, that the French word for a labor strike is "une grève." And all through the centuries this has been a favorite place for the people of Paris to vaunt their grievances.

You will recall Hugo's descriptions of the square in "Notre Dame de Paris." Many other romances also present pictures of it — notably your "Marguerite," with the unforgettable scene of the execution of La Môle and Coconnas.

It was here that Henry II saw Anne Dubourg strangled and then burned as a heretic; and here that Montgoméry, whose lance caused Henry's death, was beheaded. (For the romance of Montgoméry, read Dumas's "The Two Dianes.") Here Ravaillac suffered those varied tortures which may have been devised in punishment and may have had something to do with the effort to make him name accomplices. Here died one who, if she had nothing to do with causing Henry IV's death, certainly was in no wise cast down by it: that Eléonore Galigai (or Concini), Marie de Médicis's half-sister, who came from Florence with Marie and kept Marie well supplied with mischievous advice whenever Marie had overdrawn her own funds of intrigue, rapacity, etc. The Marquise de Brinvilliers was executed here in 1676, in the presence of a vast and fashionable throng; and four years later this was the setting for another poisoner's death: Catherine Monvoisin, known as "La Voisin," through whom Olympe Mancini had sought to poison Louise de la Vallière, and Madame de Montespan tried to do away with Louis XIV. So many personages in very high places were implicated with La Voisin that the dignity of the throne was conserved only by great secrecy in dealing with the affair. Sardou used this for the plot of his play, "Affaire des Poisons," and Funck-Brentano quotes freely from the long-suppressed documents concerning it, in the Bastille archives, in his fascinating book "La Drame de Poisons."

Damiens, who tried to kill Louis XV, was done to death here with a variety of tortures which might have indicated exasperation at his non-success. And here the guillotine functioned for the first time, on April 25, 1792, to behead an assassin, Pelletier. Carrier, the arch-terrorist of Nantes, and Fouquier-Tinville, the prosecutor who had sent so many hundreds to the guillotine, both perished here. The last execution here was in 1832.

The square is more than twice as spacious now as it used to be; and whole streets have been swept away in its aggrandizement. One of these was the rue du Mouton on the corner of which stood the "house with the lantern" (or lamp-pole) where Foulon and others were hanged early in the Revolution, giving rise to the cry: "Aristocrats to the Lantern!" Gone, too, is the charming turret which Hugo loved; and all trace of that Tour-Roland, or "Rat-Hole," he describes so vividly, wherein misguided women walled themselves up and existed in squalor on the alms of passers-by.

If you started this walk fairly early (say ten-thirty), it should not be now more than verging toward noon. Perhaps you would like to take the Métro again, at the Hôtel-de-Ville station, and find yourself in a very few minutes (five, maybe) at the Tuileries station, close to the entrance of the Musée du Louvre. If, on the other hand, you spent a couple of hours at the Louvre before taking this walk, you may leave the Métro at the Palais-Royal station, which is close to the rue de Valois and the Bœuf-à-la-Mode. (I seldom find myself in the Métro, because I am so loath to whizz along underground, beneath places which infinitely

invite sauntering; but I suggest it to more hurried travellers, as a time-saver.)

If you do not feel like lunching at the Bœuf-à-la-Mode,
try the Café de Rohan in the Place du Palais-Royal, or the
Régence in the Place du Théâtre-Français.

One reason why I suggest the Bœuf-à-la-Mode is that I
never tire of it; and another is that there is a "bit" near by,
in rue des Bons-Enfants, which I think you will like to see
and to associate with Dumas.

He was one-and-twenty when he came to Paris to seek
his fortune, in 1823 — that dusky lad from Villers-
Cotterets; slim, then, and most romantic-looking, unless
Deveria greatly idealized him in the portrait that gives us
our impression — and was set down from his diligence in
rue du Bouloi, and betook himself and his few belongings to
a hotel at number 9 in that street, whence he immediately
set out for the home of his father's old comrade-in-arms,
General Foy, who lived at the corner of rue de la Chaussée-
d'Antin and rue de la Victoire. Alexandre wanted a job —
or, more strictly speaking, he needed one; but his qualifica-
tions for any sort of job were exceedingly meagre, and
seemed to begin and end in good penmanship. On the
strength of that, and General Foy's influence, he was given
a petty clerkship in the chancellery of Orléans — which is
to say, in the offices where accounts were kept for that
gentleman who was shortly to become King Louis-Philippe.

This office was at number 19 rue des Bons-Enfants, and
hither came Alexandre, at a salary of twelve hundred
francs a year (about five dollars a week), and was so dashing
in his manner of opening envelopes and sealing them that
he attracted the attention of his department chief who reported to the Duc d'Orléans that the young man not only
wrote a very good hand, but "even is not lacking in intelligence."

But Alexandre had scarcely set foot to those magic pavements of Paris when he was spoiled for clerkship. He began hearing voices, encountering gallant phantoms, living in those yesterdays which are never dead in Paris.

I would that I dared to take space here for an extract from his "Memoirs," wherein he tells of his first theatre-going in Paris, and how he found himself seated beside Charles Nodier, and how he got into conversation with that remarkable man who had so much to do with the Romantic movement in French literature. But you will go on a regular "Dumas spree" after you have been in Paris; and you will want to read the "Memoirs," too. So I shall do no more here than commend to you the whole "orgy."

Dumas's first efforts in writing were dramas: "Christine [of Sweden] at Fontainebleau," then "Henry III and his Court," which was produced at the Comédie-Française on February 11, 1829, and was an immediate triumph. It had need to be! For the young author, when his scribbling proclivities had been discovered in the office, was ordered to choose between his job and his folly — and he stuck to the latter.

His pay had risen, then, to twenty-five dollars a month; so it was a bold, if not a foolhardy, young man who came out of number 19 rue des Bons-Enfants, his back turned upon his means of support and his face grave with worry; for he had his mother to care for, and there was little Alexandre, then four years old, whom the young father regarded with full as much paternal responsibility as if a bishop had blessed the union of which he was the fruit.

The Duc d'Orléans was in the audience at the Théâtre-Français for that first performance of "Henry III"; and so was his office-manager who had made Dumas choose between sealing letters and scribbling plays. And when Dumas reached his humble home that night, after the wild acclaim of the theatre, he found an effusive note of congratulation from the man who had, in effect, "fired" him.

It has had much other history — that building at number 19 — but none that you will, I think, care about except that of the clerk who, although he was not lacking in intelligence, was not permitted to draw twenty-five dollars a month and have his head full of plays.

This is an ancient street. When Philippe-Auguste was King, they called it "the Clichy road"; then, in 1202, a hospital of Bons-Enfants, or Good Children, was built here, and the street took its name.

You will be interested in the vaulted passage (at number 8) that was once the entrance to the cloisters of Saint-Honoré, the old convent, founded in 1204 and destroyed in 1793; and in the many other "passages" in which this corner of Paris abounds.

In rue Montesquieu (on the site of the old hospital and college of Bons-Enfants) is the "mother-house" of the Duval restaurants, and quite the best of them all. It is lodged in a building (number 6) wherein there was once a shop in which M. Chauchard worked as clerk — he who founded the Magasins du Louvre, owned the beautiful white house in the Bois de Boulogne, and left the superb Chauchard collection of paintings to the Louvre.

The Bank of France is at the other (north) end of rue des Bons-Enfants, housed, partly, in a mansion which once belonged to the Comte de Toulouse, one of de Montespan's sons, by Louis XIV. His son, the Duc de Penthrièvre, was father-in-law of the Princesse de Lamballe, and her home was there. The corner of rue Radziwill and rue La Vrillière contains what is left of the famous mansion.

Now to the Bœuf-à-la-Mode, at number 8 rue de Valois, in the old Hôtel Mélusine that Richelieu built and Boisrobert occupied, as I reminded you in our first chapter; and

which later belonged to the founder of the Arsenal library
— as I did not then remind you because you would probably have cared less about this fact than (I hope) you
care now. (At number 10 is the façade of the Orléans
Chancellery, which runs through to 19 rue des Bons-
Enfants.)

After a luncheon there, which should be deeply restful,
satisfying to the mind as the delicious food is to the body,
fare forth again across Place du Palais-Royal, beneath the
Pavillon Richelieu, and (unless you are an indifferent
walker) stroll across Place du Carrousel and over pont du
Carrousel to quai Malaquais. If you must save steps, take
a bus (A V, A G, A M, A N) across the bridge, and get off
on the quai. The entrance to the Beaux-Arts is on rue
Bonaparte, a few doors south of the quai.

If you are a lover of Anatole France, you will love quai
Malaquais for his sake; his "Little Pierre" has given this
vicinity an exquisite interest which will, doubtless, remain
freshly charming as long as that which La Fontaine left in
the same places.

You will recall that when Marguerite of Valois had cried
for vengeance upon one of her young lovers for slaying another of them, and had seen that vengeance done, outside
her Hôtel de Sens, she was smitten with horror of that place
and asked her obliging ex-husband to give her another.
He complied gallantly and understandingly with her request,
and gave her an extensive property on this side of the river.
Her new residence was on rue de Seine, the next street running south from the river, east of rue Bonaparte. She had
not many neighbors, for this part of Paris was still little
more than fields rolling riverwards from the hoary old abbey of Saint-Germain-des-Prés; and with that good nature
which characterized her, she was far from selfish with her
new domain, but allowed her meadows and gardens and

shaded paths to go on giving pleasure (as they had done before her coming) to the simple folk of the crowded quarters east of her. Which so popularized Marguerite that Marie de Médicis, her successor, had to think of something similar to bring herself forward as a "friend of the people" — and caused the Cours la Reine to be laid out, on the other bank of the river, west of what is now Place de la Concorde.

Another thing that Marguerite did when she got her new property was to recall that once upon a time in the days of her captivity in Auvergne she had vowed to Jacob that if he, who knew how to wrestle with the angel of the Lord, would intervene on her behalf, she would erect an altar to him as soon as she was free. In obedience to this vow, she now built a chapel — here where you are about to enter the Beaux-Arts — and put it under the care of the barefoot friars who were called Petits-Augustins. To do this, she had to dislodge some other monks who had been camped on this site. They moved to what is now rue Jacob (in memory of Marguerite's deliverer) around the corner; and there Marie de Médicis founded for them the Charity Hospital which is still there. A noble rivalry of royal dames was that.

The convent of the Petits-Augustins was suppressed in 1790, and this place then entered upon an extraordinary new phase of its sufficiently varied history.

Although the Revolution was scarcely launched, it had already become evident that some of its partisans were going to be very destructive of everything which seemed to them associated with the old privileges — ecclesiastical or seignorial.

There was then in Paris a young man of thirty, known to few, who was a student of painting and a critic of it in a small way. His name was Alexandre Lenoir, and so great was his love of France's heritage in art, so desperate his anguish at the thought of mobs destroying it, that he was

finally instrumental in getting authority to save what he
could, *as* he could, and to store the books and manuscripts
in the convents of the Cordeliers and of the Capucines, and
the paintings and sculpture in the convent of the Petits-
Augustins.

What a task for one man to undertake in behalf of posterity! He had, says Edouard Drumont in his admirable chapter on Lenoir, in "Mon Vieux Paris," to be forewarned of
everything, to be everywhere at the same time — or almost
that; now to demand some statues of precious metals which
had been carried to the Mint for coinage, again to save
some of bronze which were being hauled to a cannon-foun-
dry; now at Saint-Denis when the kings were being
snatched from their sepulchres, and now in cemeteries where
the ashes of Molière and La Fontaine were in danger of being scattered. While he was striving to preserve the abbey
of Cluny, the refectory and library of Saint-Germain-des-
Prés went up in flames. A bayonet pierced him when he
threw himself upon Richelieu's tomb, in the church of the
Sorbonne, to save it from a mob.

One day he hurried out to the Faubourg-Saint-Honoré
and arrived just in time to rescue from some quarrelling
second-hand dealers Michelangelo's "Captives," the only
work of the great master now owned by the Louvre. (The
figures are in the Salle de Michel-Ange, of the Renaissance
Sculptures.) These figures, designed for the tomb of Pope
Julius II, were given by Michelangelo to one of the Strozzi
who in turn presented them to the Constable de Montmorency, from whose château at Écouen they were taken by
Richelieu and carried to his own place in Poitou. The last
Marshal Richelieu brought them to Paris, and it was from
among his widow's goods that Lenoir rescued them. On
that same expedition of salvage, he found a Raphael in a
loft near by.

Sometimes he bought what he could not otherwise preserve. Witness these extracts from his accounts:

"Four bas-reliefs in white marble, one by Jean Goujon, 500 francs."

"Six stained-glass windows painted by Pinaigrier in 1600, 400 francs."

And so on!

He got them as he could, and he gathered them in, until this old convent of Marguerite's was such a storehouse as had never been seen before and will never be seen again: "eighteen centuries represented by their most eloquent creations. Fragments of altars to Jupiter and of Christian churches, Gallo-Roman sarcophagi and tombs of great knights and nobles, Gothic statues expressing the tender, touching faith of the Middle Age, the masterpieces of the Renaissance full of pagan beauty; architectural fragments from Clairvaux where Saint Bernard prayed, from Anet where Diane de Poitiers reigned supreme, from Versailles where Du Barry was thrust into prominence; salvage of palaces, of oratories, of boudoirs; all that was eloquent of the former world whose most illustrious representatives were daily mounting the scaffold."

When the Terror was over, Lenoir had more time to contemplate his great salvage piles, and to realize what an opportunity was there for a museum of French monuments; he brought this idea before the committee on public instruction, where it was well received. He was authorized to constitute and to direct such a museum, and it was opened to the public on September 1, 1795. The entrance was here where you are now going in from rue Bonaparte — which was then called rue des Petits-Augustins. And the loveliness with which the treasures were displayed has probably never been equalled in any museum. I would like to quote at great length from M. Drumont's book, but am fearful of making this chapter too long. Those among you who read French would do very well to get the book for yourselves. Ernest Flammarion is the publisher — buy the book at his stalls beneath the Odéon arcade.

For those who do not read French, let me summarize a bit, and quote Drumont's closing paragraph.

The Museum of French Monuments lasted throughout the rest of the Directory, through the Consulate and the Empire. Napoleon, with his zeal for the glory of France in the arts, was a good friend to it. But it was closed under Louis XVIII, and the incomparable collection dispersed. Louis, when reproached for this, disavowed responsibility for the order. It was just one of the many stupidities of his régime. Lenoir was heartbroken. Four years later he was one of those charged with the restoration of the Cluny; and when M. du Sommerar rented it to house his collection, Lenoir — who was still living— had every right to believe that but for his efforts a man like du Sommerard would have had neither the taste nor the desire to amass such a treasure, nor would the cultured people of Paris have been so appreciative of it.

"And with regard to the literary movement which was taking place around him," M. Drumont continues, "he also had his indisputable reason to know tha' he was a part of it. Many of the historians who preceded the poets and the artists in the return to the study of the past — Guizot, Augustin Thierry, and others — had been able in their youth to visit the Museum of French Monuments, to stand in awe before its marvels, and to resolve that they would know more about that ancient civilization which expressed itself in such beauty. It seems to me that Michelet speaks somewhere [he does, indeed!] of his first sensations on visiting this museum, and one loves to think of him in his ardent youth evoking before those assembled masterpieces, those

Middle Ages which his prodigious imagination has recalled to life in pages luminous and living."

The School of Fine Arts (École des Beaux-Arts — called "Bōze R") was founded in the year that the museum was suppressed. Your guidebook will tell you what there is to see at the famous school, and I hope I have helped you to feel that you must salute the bust of Lenoir as you go by it. How much we owe to his vision and his courage, no one will ever be able to compute.

It is a charm-full place. And after you have seen it you will comprehend why most of the men who create distinguished beauty all over the modern world are Beaux-Arts men.

Rue Bonaparte is one of my favorite Paris streets, and one which I most delight to introduce to my friends.

You may not feel its charm in a single and hasty visit, although even then you can scarcely fail to be attracted by its little shops selling copies of art masterpieces. Over here, better than elsewhere in Paris, one finds those post-cards (so precious after one's return home) reproducing choice etchings of Old Paris, engraved portraits of historic personages, facsimiles of famous documents in the National Archives, and the like. Prodigality in the purchase of these will, I assure you, never be regretted.

The Academy of Medicine next door to the Beaux-Arts is little likely to interest you. Across the street is the short rue des Beaux-Arts, which was cut through in 1825, destroying a mansion which belonged to Turenne and then to the Duc de La Rochefoucauld-Liancourt, and which had as tenants, after the Revolution, David, the painter; David d'Angers, the sculptor; and Talma, the tragedian. Among those who have lived in the little street are Prosper Mérimée, the friend of Empress Eugénie and author of "Carmen"; Pradier, the sculptor; Corot; Ampère; and Fantin-

Latour whose studio was there for thirty-six years. About 1835, Thackeray lived in rue des Beaux-Arts, while he was bent upon making a painter of himself; and it is doubtful if any other period of his life was so happy. "What a Paradise this gallery [of the Louvre] is for French students, or foreigners who sojourn in the capital!" he wrote, describing his life in those days. "They sleep, perhaps, in a garret, and dine in a cellar; but no grandee in Europe has such a drawing-room. King's houses have at best but damask hangings and gilt cornices. What are these to a wall covered with canvas by Paul Veronese, or a hundred yards of Rubens?"

"La Revue des Deux-Mondes" was for many years published at number 17 rue Bonaparte. Among its contributors were Balzac, Dumas, Hugo, George Sand, Alfred de Vigny, Musset, and Eugène Sue.

Number 19 was the home of the Princess Charlotte-Dorothée de Rohan-Rochefort, niece of the Cardinal de Rohan of "necklace" fame, and wife of the young Duc d'Enghien shot at Vincennes by Bonaparte's orders.

Friends of mine who live at number 18 and who are ardent antiquarians maintain that it is this house which belonged to César, Duc de Vendôme, son of Henry IV and Gabrielle d'Estrées, and in which he died. The Marquis de Rochegude believes that César's house was the one now numbered 20. I don't know anybody in number 20, so I like to believe that this may be the one time when the Marquis nods. Benjamin Ellis Martin, in "The Stones of Paris" (a delightful book, albeit the authors — Mr. and Mrs. Martin — "nod" frequently, and sometimes startlingly), says that the house, numbered 18, in this street to which Madame Hugo brought her boys in 1818, stood on ground now covered by the entrance court of the Beaux-Arts. The building in which they lived was part of the old convent, and is now demolished and cannot be identified with the present number 18. André Hallays, who has made a very serious study of Victor Hugo's Paris dwellings, says that the room of Victor and his brother overlooked the court of the convent wherein still stood many of the sculptured treasures saved by Lenoir, and that these wrought a profound impression upon the imagination of the young poet.

Hugo himself tells us with what distress he saw from his window Lenoir's collection being dispersed.

Up this street toward the Church of Saint-Germain-des-Prés, there used to go, in those evenings when Madame Hugo and her boys lived here, a little group which you may still see — if you care to, and know how. The brothers walked arm-in-arm ahead. Their mother, wearing a gown of coxcomb-colored merino and a yellowish cashmere shawl, followed, carrying her little work-bag. You shall go with them, presently, to the Hôtel de Toulouse, where Adèle Foucher, Victor's childhood sweetheart and future wife, lived with her parents. Just now, I must ask you to let them disappear beyond rue Jacob, while you stroll down this delicious old rue Visconti, opposite number 20.

The Hugos are very modern folk, now, and you have come here to call on — whom? I shall let you choose.

If you are a Calvinist, you may be in search of some of your co-religionists who, about the time of the Saint Bartholomew massacre, lived here in such numbers that the street was called "Little Geneva." In the year of Henry II's death, a householder in this street was prosecuted for meat-eating on Friday. Perhaps you belong to the period a hundred years and more later, and have come to call on Racine who spent the last seven years of his life in number 21 (not 13 as many of the guidebooks say) and died there in 1699. A few years later this was Adrienne Lecouvreur's home; here that fine creature died, in the arms of her lover, the Marshal de Saxe, and hence she was carried in the dead of a moonless night, March 2, 1730, to be buried like a pet dog, in a vacant lot of rue de Grenelle. You may be going with Voltaire to visit her. Or you may be accompanying David Garrick, thirty-five years later, on a visit to Mademoiselle Clairon, also of the Comédie-Française, who lived here in this same house for eighteen years during all her great triumphs in the House of Molière where the audience, cheering, used to cry: "Vive le roi et Mademoiselle Clairon!"

The tablet on the house says that La Champmeslé, once Racine's mistress, lived in this house, too. But M. Hallays says that it is highly improbable, and tells why.

Perhaps it is to number 17 that your footsteps are directed, to call on the young printer, Honoré de Balzac, who is faring so badly with his business venture that for many years after his failure here he will not be able to pass the street without a groan in memory of all that failure made him suffer. He lived here, as well as worked here, having a "bachelor apartment" above his print-shop.

Later, both Delaroche and Delacroix were tenants — successively — of a vast studio atop this same house. It was there that Delacroix painted "The Shipwreck of Don Juan" and "Constantinople taken by the Crusaders," which you may see in the collection of French works of the nineteenth century at the Louvre.

If you have left rue Visconti at its east end and do not want to retrace your steps, you may follow rue de Seine to rue Jacob (remembering Marguerite and her prayer to Jacob and his angel) along which, on the south side, used to run the walls of the abbey garden of Saint-Germain-des-Prés. At the corner of rue Jacob and rue de Furstemberg you may see a pillar of one of the old abbey gates. Go up rue de Furstemberg where the abbey stables used to be, and at number 6 in which Delacroix died (glancing into the twisting little rue Cardinale), to rue de l'Abbaye which was cut through the grand cloister of the abbey after the Revolution; and take a good look at the abbot's palace (number 3) which was built by the Cardinal Charles de Bourbon in 1586 — four years before the Duc de Mayenne, leader of the Ligue, proclaimed the Cardinal King of France, in opposition to the claims of that other Bourbon, Henry of Navarre. The beautiful refectory and the Lady-Chapel built by Pierre de Montereau, architect of Sainte-Chapelle, were where this street now runs.

My recommendation to you is to see this corner in daylight, and then to come back to it well after dark and stroll through it again — for reasons which I shall presently tell you.

Now for some details of the abbey of Saint-Germain-des-Prés, or Saint Germain of the Fields, which, like very many old churches, was built to house a "relic" believed to be miracle-working. This particular relic was the tunic of Saint Vincent (I have to confess the deepest ignorance of this saint and why his tunic was venerable) which Childebert, son of Clovis, brought back with him from Saragossa in Spain. When Childebert was besieging Saragossa, in 542, he saw that the inhabitants were defending their city, not with arms, but with chanting and carrying a reliquary — which so awed Childebert that he raised the siege. How he persuaded the Bishop of Saragossa to part with such a valuable relic I do not dare to guess; but he got it (that tunic of Saint Vincent's) and brought it to Paris, and built this church to house it. It was called "the golden basilica" of Saint Vincent, so splendid did it become with gifts from kings and queens and other magnates of those days. And when Saint Germain, Bishop of Paris, was buried in it, in 576, his name began to be attached to it, along with Saint Vincent's, and finally to the exclusion of the latter.

Nearly all the kings and queens of France's first regnant race were buried here; but nothing is left of that first church, which the Normans destroyed, except some fragments of columns in the apse. Of this "comparatively modern" structure, nothing is more than some nine centuries old, except the base of the belfry, which is of the ninth century.

The abbey domain of Saint-Germain-des-Prés was a vast one, stretching from the river literally miles away to the southward; but the actual, walled, fortified abbey precincts lay between the present boulevard and rue Jacob, and rue Saint-Benoît and rue de l'Échaudé. So great was the prestige of it, and so enormous the revenues, that kings coveted the abbotcy and frequently got it for themselves or for their children.

It is, however, not the early nor the ecclesiastical history of Saint-Germain, I find, that chiefly interests most Paris visitors; it is the Revolutionary scenes in and about the old prison of the Abbaye; the September massacres; Charlotte Corday; Madame Roland. The prison-site is now covered by the boulevard Saint-Germain (cut through in the middle of the nineteenth century) a little west of the passage de la Petite-Boucherie. The massacres took place (on that Sunday we have recalled in our second chapter) in a court or garden which used to cover ground that now is the junction of rue Bonaparte with the Place Saint-Germain-des-Prés. We read so much about the Abbaye Prison in the Revolution that I am sure many of you will appreciate this bit of topography.

Do not miss the little garden, close to the scene of the massacre, wherein are preserved, in a charming setting of green, some of the fragments of Montereau's exquisite

Lady-Chapel, demolished in 1802. This corner, in the shade of the venerable gray tower, is one of the spots in Paris you will, I think, most delight to recall when you have left this enchanting city behind you in point of physical fact — to leave her otherwise seems to me an impossibility. Young Republicans of these years of grace sleep refreshingly in this bit of the old royal abbey; young lovers seek its friendly shadows in the evenings, nor care that here were cloisters once. Gone are the entrenched privileges of church and class, in assaults upon which so much blood flowed, hereabouts and elsewhere. The world about us seems very noisy yet, very unsettled; but if this little corner speaks to us as it should, I opine that we shall take heart a bit. Substantial, peaceful blessings *do* come out of "ructions" — sometimes!

Across from the portal of the church is the Café des Deux-Magots which is an excellent place to sit and watch the world go by, especially "of an evening."

Now, cross the boulevard, saluting the statue of Diderot — to whose memory you have already paid tribute in rue de Richelieu — placed here because this is almost the exact site of his dwelling, in the thirteenth century rue Turanne; and a step or two down rue de Rennes, enter the Cour du Dragon, walking through it to rue du Dragon on its other side.

This court looks as if it must have been the scene of countless episodes historic, romantic, picturesque; as a matter of fact it is not very old, as antiquity goes in Paris, having seen less than two centuries, and I don't know of a single celebrated happening that had its background there. Nevertheless, it is exceedingly interesting. In many places in Paris you may step with a single stride out of bustling modernity into the past; but unless you can stand there quite alone, some insistent reminder of the twentieth cen-

tury is almost sure to mar the illusion for you. Not so in the
Cour du Dragon; not even the people in it seem to have any
relation with a world later than that which knew Marat,
and mourned him.

A woman named Champagne who lived in the Cour du
Dragon in 1792, bought the clothes, "in very bad condition
and much-mutilated," of the victims massacred at the Abbaye Prison that September Sunday, paying "375 livres 10
sols" for the lot, and for their boots and shoes "76 livres 5
sols." (I quote the figures, for to me they are eloquent of
the bargaining which must have gone on over these slashed
and blood-drenched garments.) She was probably just such
a one as Anatole France's "Widow Bargouiller" whom he
found here when he was twelve and bent on largesse to the
"deserving poor." That was about the beginning of the Second Empire. If you were bent on finding the Citizeness
Champagne now, or the Widow Bargouiller (gin-faced and
viper-haired), you would probably have little difficulty —
they might have changed their names, but they would not
have changed their clothes (much) nor their outlook upon
life.

The court has always been inhabited by many metal-
workers. My only point of personal contact with it is
through an exceedingly affable, kindly little old woman who
sells copper basins and pans in a dark little shop on the
court's south side. Perhaps she would trade in the gashed
and gory garments of privileged persons to-day, if the
chance came to her. I don't know. She certainly betrays
no blood-thirstiness, nor greed, when she sells her beautiful
coppers.

Rue du Dragon has a house, numbered 24, where Bernard Palissy, the great potter, is supposed to have lived in
1585 what time he thrust his last sticks of furniture into his
furnace to get the heat requisite for his glaze. But the

house's claim to veneration on that account is disputed by authorities I dare not gainsay. I'm sorry. I've stood in front of the house, before I knew what those authorities say, and had emotions which were very good for me. Now I don't know where to have them. I can't do it in the Louvre, where so many of his priceless productions are — nor at the Cluny, where there are others. When persons have become immortals and taken up their position forever-more in niches in the Hall of Fame, they have become re-mote from me. I always seek them out before they've got so far; feel most at home with them when they are strug-gling.

Very well! I can take all the emotion I used to expend on two houses in this street, and address it, entire, to number 30, where Victor Hugo very certainly lived in an attic, in 1821, after his mother's death. M. Foucher had said that Victor might have Adèle when he could take care of her. And Victor, with his four shirts and his seven hundred francs, took up his mansard abode here with his cousin come from Nantes to study law. Those who would know how he lived have only to read the budget of Marius in "Les Misérables." Without borrowing a sou, and even with loans of five francs to a friend now and then, he man-aged to buy a gorgeous suit of blue with gilt buttons and to carry himself very well indeed in excellent society, although his sufferings and privations were terribly acute.

"Sometimes," he wrote, describing himself in Marius, " an embarassed young man, carrying books under his arm, might be seen entering the butcher shop on the corner, crowded with jeering cooks whom he jostled, awkwardly; his manner was timid, yet wrathful, but he doffed his hat to the astonished butcher, with a profound bow, and did the same for the butcher's boy as he asked for a mutton chop. Sweat stood in beads on the brow of this extraordinary

young man as he waited for his chop, paid six or seven sous
for it, put it (wrapped in paper) between two books, and
then went home. . . . On that chop, cooked by himself, he
lived three days. The first day he ate the meat, the second
day he ate the fat, and the third day he gnawed the bone!"

Thus the "Sublime Child" of nineteen who was to as-
tound the world a year later with his Odes and Ballads;
and, fortified by the pension of a thousand francs accorded
him by the King, to leave his garret and take unto himself
a wife. I have almost as great awe of Hugo in later years as
Théophile Gautier had when he climbed the stairs of Hugo's
house (in rue Jean Goujon) three times before he could
muster courage to ring the bell; but here in rue du Dragon I
feel on very easy terms with him, and share his indignation
at the way poets are treated by this contumelious world.

Those little streets, rue Bernard-Palissy and rue de
Sabot, which branch to right and left from rue du Dragon,
are very quaint and picturesque.

At the end of rue du Dragon is the Carrefour de la
Croix-Rouge, which dates from the fifteenth century and
was named for a red cross which once stood there.

If you are interested to see the military prison of the
Cherche-Midi, and the neighborhood where Victor Hugo
courted Adèle, take rue du Cherche-Midi from the Carrefour de la Croix-Rouge for a short distance — a little more
than a block. (Otherwise take rue de Sèvres.) The prison
is at number 38 rue du Cherche-Midi; the Hôtel de Toulouse, where Adèle Foucher lived, was across the street,
until boulevard Raspail cut through here.

If you have come to look at the prison, follow the boulevard northward for a short block, past the big modern
Hotel Lutétia. The pretty little Square Boucicault is on
your left, named in memory of the admirable woman who
founded the Bon-Marché and instituted so many favorable

VICTOR HUGO
By Devéria

conditions for her employés, and containing also a statue to another woman of great benevolence, the Baroness Hirsch.

The site of the Abbaye aux Bois (to your right on rue de Sèvres) where Madame Récamier lived for thirty-odd years, much of the time in blindness, is covered in part now by a little street which, though it bears her name, was not named for her. The demolition of that convent (in 1907 and 1908) has been greatly deplored by lovers of Old Paris. In the new building at number 16 rue de Sèvres, Boutet de Monvel lived.

If it is a week-day on which you are making this saunter, you will, of course, make some acquaintance with the Bon-Marché. And if you are feminine, you will not get quickly past the shops on the south side of rue de Sèvres, opposite the Bon-Marché, which flaunt such quantities of laces in the fluttering breezes. (Some of it is cheap in quality as in price; but there are fine laces to be had there, too, and not too dear — if you know how to bar ain.)

I am not greatly addicted to the Bon-Marché, except for ribbons and some kinds of gloves; but some of my friends swear by it, and issue from its portals with surprisingly good-looking frocks. Its January white sales were the first of their kind, I believe, and are eagerly awaited by house-wives all over France — for the great shops do an immense mail-order business.

Quite apart from interest in what the big magasins of Paris purvey, I find them interesting for the way they do it. It is very different from our way of doing the same thing. Some of my compatriots seem to like the magasins less than our department stores, in the degree that they differ from ours. I do not urge their methods on our merchants; but when I travel four thousand miles from home, it is not in search of just such perfections as I leave behind me.

Rue du Bac runs behind the main building of the Bon-Marché, and on the other side of that street the big store has an annex. Beyond that annex, all the way to rue Vaneau, is the Hôpital Laënnec, or Home for Incurables.

On the 12th of April, 1796, there came here, to spend the rest of her days, Marie-Jeanne Simon, widow of the shoemaker, and co-guardian with him of the Dauphin in the Temple. She was destitute, ailing, unable to work, though only just past fifty years of age. Of course the other women (the institution was for women only then; now it cares for both sexes) were curious about the newcomer; and of course they asked questions about her. When they heard who she was, they made remarks about her and her treatment of the Dauphin which stung her, finally, into self-defence. "He isn't dead," she declared furiously; "I took him away." She called him "my Charles," and spoke of him with the greatest tenderness. To one of the young sisters, Sister Lucie, she said: "You will see him on the throne, but I shall not live to see it." Complaining to one of the internes about something in the hospital she said: "If my children knew of this, they would not suffer it — my little Bourbons that I love with all my heart."

Under the Directory, the Consulate, and the Empire it was not politic to speak of loving the Bourbons; but Marie-Jeanne continued to do so. One day in July, 1805 (ten years after the death of the child in the Temple), a young man accompanied by a negro entered the dormitory where Marie-Jeanne was, passed before her without stopping, but with his hand on his heart and a gesture of silence, saluted her, and then, when he saw that she had recognized him, drew nearer to her and murmured, "I see that they did not deceive me." He came again, many times. Marie-Jeanne said he was her Charles. The incurables, the doctors, the nurses, talked about it; but nobody seemed to feel that it was of any great importance where the Dauphin was. When the Restoration came, many people showed sudden interest in her story. She had many visitors, and convinced them all of her sagacity and sincerity. Even the Duchesse d'Angoulême came, in disguise, but was promptly recognized by Marie-Jeanne.

Louis XVIII sent some officers to question her. They knew their business, those officers! They reported that her "faculties were enfeebled." They ordered her to say no more of the matter. The Duchesse d'Angoulême was not satisfied. She went again to the Incurables, this time without disguise; but the moment her carriage appeared in the court, some strong hand seized Marie-Jeanne and hustled her into a hiding-place. She talked no more about the Dauphin; but when she was dying, on June 19, 1819, and the priest who gave her extreme unction asked her if there was anything on her soul that she wished to confess, she answered: "I shall always say just what I have said."

She had a pauper's funeral.

A later inmate here was Rosalie Lamorlière, the jailer's servant at the Conciergerie, who rendered so many loving services to Marie Antoinette in prison. The Duchesse d'Angoulême gave Rosalie a tiny pension (two hundred francs) and secured for her this asylum, but never came to see her, although Rosalie said she would gladly give up all her comforts for the joy of looking once upon "the daughter of *Madame*."

Turn up rue Vaneau, now, at number 40 in which (close to rue Babylone) is the home of M. Gosselin who adds Lenôtre to his name for a nom-de-plume.

A few steps farther up rue Vaneau you will come to the Hôtel de Chanaleilles (number 24) which was the home of Thérézia Tallien while she was living with the banker Ouvrard.

You may not care to take even a few steps to see that; in which case turn back (to your right) on rue de Babylone to rue du Bac, and follow the latter to number 118–120, where Chateaubriand died, on July 4, 1848, with Madame Récamier sitting, blind and helpless, beside him. His funeral was from the Church of the Foreign Missions, next door, and his body was carried to his native Saint-Malo to be buried on a rock in the harbor. Madame Récamier went back, desolate, to her rooms in the Abbaye-aux-Bois which once had been thronged by nearly all who were most illustrious in France. The following May, there was cholera in the Abbaye, and she left it, to take refuge with her niece, Madame Lenormant, at the Bibliothèque Nationale, where M. Lenormant was librarian; and on the night of her arrival, she died — of the plague she had fled.

A few doors up the street (at number 110) is the home of M. André Hallays, of "Le Journal des Débats," whom we have so often quoted in these pages.

If you want to go home and rest now, you will find a Métro station at the junction of rue du Bac and the boulevards Saint-Germain and Raspail. (See the bewitching faience shop there!) Also many bus and tram lines, concerning which I cannot be more definite because I don't know where you wish to go.

You now know so many of the best places to dine that I hesitate to suggest any others. But if you haven't been to Ciro's, you ought not to miss it. And Griffon, 6 rue d'Antin, is super-excellent.

If you feel like dining out-of-doors, try Laurent in the Champs-Élysées, or drive out to Château de Madrid at the edge of the Bois.

Larue, at the corner of rue Royale and Place de la Madeleine, is also celebrated; but all these, I must warn you, are dear.

Have I told you of the Brasserie des Pyramides, at

number 3 rue des Pyramides, close by the Jeanne d'Arc statue on rue de Rivoli? It is a great favorite with some of my friends when they feel a bit frugally inclined.

What I would like to beg of you to-night, if the night be favorable, is a rendezvous on one of the bridges — probably the pont des Arts. And you may remember that I expressed the hope that you would care to wander about the vicinity of Saint-Germain-des-Prés, after dark.

Let ardent souls, whose delight in Old Paris transcends fatigue, get on bus U, coming down from the Chambre des Députés, and ride the short distance to the junction of rue d'Assas, boulevard Montparnasse and avenue de l'Observatoire; descend there, enjoy the superb vista north through the Luxembourg Gardens, and then — when hungry — walk along boulevard Montparnasse and dine either at Sainte-Cécile (140) or at Jouvin (124) on the south side of the boulevard; both inexpensive and both good. At the latter you will dine in company with many artists of the Quarter, some of them very well known to you by name if not by countenance.

After dinner, you may take bus O, near the Gare Montparnasse, and go to Saint-Germain-des-Prés.

Walk now past the site of the September massacres, and along rue de l'Abbaye, where the cloisters used to be, and down rue Furstemberg. I don't know how worth while this will seem to you. I only know that friends who have taken this stroll with me have said that it left ineffaceable pictures in their minds, and they recall it with delight as a memorable experience. This, and a long lingering on the pont des Arts, preferably quite late at night, especially if the moon be riding toward her last quarter.

This bridge is for foot-travellers only, and you may sit there in delicious reverie, close to the "prow" of the boat-shaped Île de la Cité, reviewing Paris as you have come to know her.

XVII

HERE AND THERE

SAINT-DENIS AND CHANTILLY

SAINT-DENIS seems difficult for the Paris visitor with limited time to "fit in" on his schedule. It is only four miles
from the Gare du Nord; but there is little or nothing to be
seen there except the basilica and the royal tombs; the
latter cannot be visited, unless one has a student's permit,
before noon; there is no good place to lunch out there; and
so —! Unwilling to take a whole afternoon for one "sight,"
however notable, a great many visitors forego Saint-Denis.
This is a pity — almost as great a pity as missing Westminster Abbey on a visit to London.

For those who would like to see Saint-Denis, let me make
a few suggestions.

First of all, get a students' ticket. Ask for it at the Administration des Beaux-Arts, at 3 rue de Valois, opposite
the Bœuf-à-la-Mode. Your hotel concierge will write you
an application for the ticket, if you wish; and of course he
will send a chasseur to get it for you — but I urge that you
give yourself a glimpse of that important department of
the Ministry of Education. Some day *we* shall have a
Ministry of Education with an Administration of Fine Arts;
it is well that Americans of our sort should be thinking
about it.

This ticket will permit you to see the royal tombs in the
morning and at your leisure, and to make sketches or
photographs of them.

Then —! If you go to Chantilly (as you certainly
should!) you can make your plans so as to leave the Gare du

Nord by nine o'clock (go in the Métro) and be in Saint-
Denis in ten or fifteen minutes. (I hesitate to mention
train times, lest you be led to depend upon them; and
schedules *do* change! Get all this information from your
hotel concierge or from a tourist agency.) Those who are
staying in the vicinity of the Madeleine or the Opéra may
find it just as time-saving to take tram number 42 or 48;
for thus they can be set down considerably nearer the
basilica. If you must take a conveyance to reach either of
these trams, you would do better to use the Métro and the
railway; take rue Ernest Renan and rue de la République
to the basilica. Those who go by tram debark at rue de
Paris and rue de la République. I am explicit about all of
this, because I know the need to be. Saint-Denis is an industrial town which apparently gives little thought to the
tombs of kings; tourists are not an important part of its
life, and it is quite possible for a bewildered pilgrim to
wander about there for some time (if he doesn't speak
French) without meeting any one who suspects what he
has come to see, and directs him to it.

Your guidebook (if you have a Blue Guide) gives you a
very complete enumeration of the monuments, and reminds you of Alexandre Lenoir's part in saving church and
tombs; of Jeanne d'Arc's presence here; of Henry IV's ab-
juration. Those readers who would like a vivid picture of
the profanation of the royal tombs will find it in Lamartine's "History of the Girondists."

If you have planned a full day and must not linger here
for more than an hour or so, you may — unless you are a
special student of Gothic sculpture — pass rather quickly
along the north (left) aisle (remembering only that many of
those tombs were originally in the Church of the Jacobins,
near the Panthéon in Paris) to the magnificent tomb of
Louis XII and Anne of Brittany, in which French sculpture

of the Renaissance attains one of its most perfect expressions. The superb tomb of Henry II and Catherine de Médicis is just beyond; it was designed soon after Henry's death, by Primaticcio, who did so much at Fontainebleau, and some of the sculpture is by Germain Pilon, one of those to whom the Louvre of Francis I and Henry II owes much of its sculptural glory. After you have ascended the stairs into the ambulatory, you will see two other statues of Henry and Catherine, by Pilon. Catherine died at Blois, on the eve of Twelfth Night, 1588; "and she had no sooner given up the ghost than she was made no more account of than a dead goat would have been. Never were fewer tears shed for any long-lived woman who had been wife and mother, than fell for Catherine de Médicis." Burial in this tomb that she had caused to be made was refused her — not evasively, either! If her body were brought thither, said the Council of the Sixteen who were bent upon making a Guise (Mayenne) King, they would "drag it to the banks of the Seine and throw it in." It was only after many years that hatred of her subsided sufficiently to permit her burial here. Near these statues, where now you see the kneeling statue of Marie de Bourbon (aunt of Henry IV, and betrothed of James V of Scotland — Mary Stuart's father, — though she died before her marriage could take place) is where Turenne was buried. His body, venerated by the Revolutionists, was preserved for nine years in the garrets of the Museum of Natural History at the Jardin des Plantes, among the stuffed animals, and was interred at the Invalides by Napoleon's orders.

See the apse chapels, and be sure to note the altar, the Oriflamme, and the choir-stalls. The Sacristy paintings of historic episodes in the abbey help one to re-people the basilica.

In the crypt are the tombs of all royalties from Henry IV

to Louis XVIII. Most of the tombs are empty, but it is an impressive place, nevertheless, if only for the gloom and dust and air of a neglected cellar, in which lay the bones of Louis XIV and Louis XV until they were flung out by the Revolutionists. Henry IV's body was so skilfully embalmed that his chest still displayed the two wounds Ravaillac had dealt him; and for two days the crowd that had come to dishonor kings filed in silence before the corpse of one they found it hard to hate; then a demagogue persuaded them that their veneration was venial. "Louis XIII was only a mummy, and Louis XIV a black, amorphous mass of spices. [I quote Lamartine.] Louis XV came last from the tomb. The infection of his reign seemed to rise from his sepulchre. A mass of powder had to be burned to dissipate the mephitic odor of the corpse." (Louis XV, it will be remembered, died of a most virulent small-pox.) In spite of the quicklime said to have been used in the cemetery of the Madeleine, there are probably more remains of Louis XVI and Marie Antoinette here than of any who preceded them. Note the monumental statue of Diane de France, natural daughter of Henry II and (perhaps) of Diane de Poitiers.

When you return to the upper church, you enter the Chapelle des Connétables, beside the Sacristy, in which is the very interesting tomb of Duguesclin, brother-in-arms of Olivier de Clisson whose Paris home is now the Archives. Charles V (for whom Duguesclin and Clisson fought to dislodge the English from France) lies close by (or did — until dislodged) with his queen beside him. Her statue came from the Church of the Célestins at Paris (near the Arsenal) where her entrails were buried — the bag in her hands indicates her offering them, as 'twere. This is one of the antiquities that Lenoir saved. Many, many others from his Museum of French Monuments are also here.

Beside Charles V and Jeanne de Bourbon lie their son, Charles VI, the mad king, and his wicked wife, Isabeau of Bavaria, who died at Vincennes and was brought here "like a mere demoiselle unattended, by boat and under cover of darkness."

After leaving the Chapel of the Constables, be sure to see the beautiful door of this (the south) transept. Close to it, on the south wall, is the canopied tomb of a seven-year-old girl who died in 1515 and was buried in the Church of the Célestins. Also near this door is the tomb of the abbot, Suger, who built the greater part of Saint-Denis and was the power behind the throne of Louis VII. This good and able man, who with all his might opposed the divorce of Louis and Eleanore of Acquitaine, died just before that divorce was pronounced which permitted Eleanore to marry young Henry Plantagenet and annex vast, rich domains of southern France to the English Crown.

Here you turn to your right and enter the Ritual Choir where are many monuments of very early royalties, erected by Saint Louis's order. The temptation to linger and remind you of stories is very strong, but must be resisted except for one little instance. Look, on your diagram in the Blue Guide (page 392) for the tomb numbered 50. In it lay Louis X, who died when he was twenty-seven, and his little posthumous son who was King John I for the seven days of his existence. Some said the baby life was snuffed out by orders of Uncle Philippe, the regent, who then became King Philippe V; some said the living child was stolen and a dead child substituted for him — which either caused a "lost Dauphin" to appear, later, and claim the throne, or was so substantiated. At any rate, if that baby boy had lived and continued to wear the crown, there would have been no cause for the Hundred Years' War, no House of Valois on the French throne. It was the death, without male issue, of both his uncles who succeeded him, that gave his aunt's son, Edward III of England, his claim to the crown of France. It was this baby's grandfather who caused Jacques de Molay, Grand Master of the Templars, to be burnt (at what is now the west end of the Île de la Cité) in 1314; and Molay's prophecy, "God will avenge our death," may have had its fulfilment in the extinction of the direct line of Capet. "Grandpa" (Philippe IV) lies in the tomb numbered 54 on your diagram. Number 55 is the tomb of Saint Louis's father.

After leaving the Choir, you have a notable group of tombs in the right aisle, including the superb monument of Francis I and his first wife, Claude, daughter of Louis XII and Anne of Brittany; and that of Louis of Orléans (killed by his cousin of Burgundy's minions, in the rue Vieille-du-Temple) and his wife, Valentine, and their son, the poet-duke, Charles of Orléans, father of Louis XII. This latter monument was brought from the Church of the Célestins.

If it should happen that the day you visit Saint-Denis is a racing day or other day when the Château of Chantilly is closed, you might enjoy going on to Montmorency, seven miles farther, and seeing Rousseau's Ermitage, where Robespierre spent his last free night on earth (girding himself, perhaps, for what he knew was coming), and wandering in the forest. This latter is supremely worth while in early May, when the chestnut trees are in bloom. The Musée Jean-Jacques-Rousseau is in the Hôtel-de-Ville.

Chantilly is twenty miles from Saint-Denis. If you leave the basilica at eleven, you should be in Chantilly before noon, and through with your luncheon almost as soon as the château is open, at one. The Hôtel du Grand-Condé is excellent, but expensive. We are very fond of taking luncheon with us when we go to Chantilly, and eating it in the forest into which you may plunge directly you get off the train.

There is so much to see in the château and in the park that you will do well to study the catalogue (in your Blue Guide) quite carefully before you go, so that you may not miss the things you would most like to see.

You will feed the famous carp, of course. Within the château, the first apartment entered from the Grand Vestibule is the Galerie des Cerfs, so called from the stags' heads and antlers which are a feature of its decoration. Beyond this is the Picture Gallery which you may walk through rather briskly if you do not find your interest readily challenged; there are things more choice in rooms beyond, and, if you must economize time, this is not the worst place to do it. In the Rotonde at the end of this gallery, to which you pass through a doorway I find out-of-place, is the Chapu Jeanne d'Arc which, through copies of it in many museums, is familiar to millions.

Those who are interested in portraits or in drawings will find much to admire, lingeringly, in the Galerie du Logis, Vestibule du Logis, and Petite Galerie du Logis; others may be satisfied to walk through these apartments and the Salle de la Smalah without lingering. The Greek sculptures in the Rotonde de la Minerve are worthy of much study; but if your time is limited (if, for instance, you are hoping to go on to Senlis) you may continue to economize it until you come to the Galerie de Psyche, with its wealth of sixteenth-century stained glass, its Clouet portait drawings, and other treasures. The Sanctuaire, opening off the Galerie de Psyche, contains the exquisite little Raphael, "The Madonna of the House of Orléans," "The Three Graces," also by Raphael, and the Fouquet miniatures to which I hope you will feel like devoting a great deal of the time you have saved elsewhere.

The Cabinet des Gemmes will interest some, and the large octagonal room called the Tribune has many things in it which nearly all visitors will want to see: Delaroche's famous and familiar picture of the murder of the Duc de Guise; a Perugino Madonna; three Luinis; a portrait of Simonetta Vespucci, by either Pollaiuolo or Piero Cosimo; Mignard's portrait of Molière; some more of the wealth of Clouet portraits which are such a notable feature of the Chantilly Collection.

Now, back through the Galerie des Cerfs, to the Grand Vestibule and into the apartments of the Grand Condé which will be to many visitors the most interesting part of the château.

In the library (or Cabinet des Livres) be sure to see the Duc de Berri's Book of Hours, with its superb illuminations.

You may look at the Grand Staircase, and then pass on to the chapel.

If the day is fine, spend as much time as you can in the Park. But sacrifice something of your delight in lingering there, to press on to Senlis, which you reach from Chantilly in twenty-five minutes. You can see a good deal of Senlis in an hour or so, and if you are under no special urge about returning to Paris for dinner, I suggest that you dine — simply, but memorably — at the little Hôtel du Grand-Cerf.

FONTAINEBLEAU

(This is one trip that may be made on Monday.)

Another of the days you spend out of Paris will undoubtedly be that devoted to your trip to Fontainebleau.

If you can afford a car for one day, you might take it for this journey; although there are at least two others which will, I think, yield you a larger return on the investment, inasmuch as they make practicable for one day's sight-seeing what you could scarcely accomplish in two if you went by train.

Going by train to Fontainebleau is not at all difficult; and the drive through the forest to Barbizon is really more fittingly made in a little carriage than in a motor. So, with all possible appreciation of the delightful ride it is by car, I say that you need not feel too sorry for yourself if you must go by rail. (Those who can motor, and who are interested in the great body of literature centring about Fouquet, Louis XIV's minister of finance, should secure a permit to visit his famous estate of Vaux. Apply, for this permit, to M. Sommier, 37 avenue George-V, Paris.)

Take the Métro to the Gare de Lyon, and try to "make" a train not later than nine-thirty. A second-class ticket will give you more company in your compartment than a first-class, but for an hour or so this ought to be diverting. Do not buy a return-trip, as you will come back from Melun. It is a long walk from the railway station to the château; take the tram, or a bus, and save your steps for the palace, the park and gardens, the forest and Barbizon. If, however, you have reached Fontainebleau as early as ten-thirty, and the morning is fine, and your energy is abundant, you may like to walk through the park to the château; in this case, follow avenue du Chemin-de-Fer for a short distance to avenue des Carrosses and turn here, to your left, toward the porte Blanche. Keep on, past the Labyrinth, to the porte de Changis, and take the allée d'Avon, across the canal from which is the famous Artillery School of the École Militaire where both Joffre and Foch were students, in the early seventies, and where many of our American officers had special training in the late war.

The château, or palace, is open every day from eleven to four or five; but you are not permitted to roam about, as at Versailles; you must go through in a herd, led by an attendant with the usual sing-song about clocks, carpets, chairs, and candelabra. His one object is (not unnaturally) to get through as fast as he can; the collection he takes up, at the end of the tour, seems to be the only thing about it that interests him. But some, at least, of these men have "two soul-sides," as I have often found; "one to face the world with" (the tourist world, that arrives in wagon-loads and seems only half-certain whether it is seeing Versailles or Fontainebleau) and "one to show a woman" when she loves France and knows her history. The latter soul-side is not wholly dissociated from lucre; but I don't mind! This is not Arcadia; and things worth having are worth paying for.

Buy a history of the palace, on sale in the vestibule where you wait for a party to form; and read as much as you can in it and in your guidebook before you start through — leaving the purchase of post-cards until you have come out. Stick close to your guide as he leads his flock from room to room; even if you can't understand what he says, *look* as if you have heard, before, of Diane de Poitiers, Madame de Maintenon, and Pope Pius VII.

Then, when the tour is over, hang back as the others go out, and (if you can't say it) show a card on which is written: "Les Appartements Privées de Bonaparte — rez-de-chaussée." Murmur *"S'il vous plaît,"* and indicate as best you can that you expect to pay for this privilege. If this seems to you like a subversion of the law, you can, I believe, go to the Conservator's office and ask for a permit. However you do it, it is well worth doing; for in those ground-floor apartments the Bonapartes lived their family life and left an impress on it more indelible than any they left upstairs except in the Cour des Adieux and the Cabinet d'Abdication. In those lower rooms, Joséphine heard the decree of Napoleon to divorce her. That episode effaces all others which shared with it these backgrounds.

If I embark on "reminders" of the events in the upper rooms, I shall never know where to leave off; but let me at least say that no ghost glides hereabouts more pervasively, to me, than little Louise de la Vallière's.

Be sure to visit the carp pond and the English Garden.

When you are ready for luncheon, I hope you can go to the Hôtel de France, across the way from the Cour des Adieux. I must warn you that it is expensive. But it is "an experience." I say, go to it even if you can afford only a plain omelet and one of the humblest bottles of wine from its famous cellars. See the proprietor's great collection of old colored prints; his other collection of "fire-backs." The place has distinction, personality — and many memories; it is pervaded by the genial hospitality of the host. You will find that, in discussing Fontainebleau with "seasoned" travellers, they will nearly always say, "And I hope you went to the Hôtel de France." I dare say there are other good places to lunch and dine at Fontainebleau — but I never shall be able to pass an opinion on them.

After luncheon, arrange with one of the drivers in front of the hotel (or have a chasseur do it for you; I think there is always some one about who speaks English) for your drive through the forest and to Barbizon. If you are fairly expert in asking your way, I say go to Barbizon by carriage; finish your visit there, then take the steam-tram for Chailly, and ask directions to the cemetery; afterwards proceeding to Melun by the tram, and there taking train for Paris. If you are not successful in comprehending directions given (and after all, there's the rub; *any* one can say, "*Où est la cimetière?*" but only the expert can profit by the reply), I advise your spending a few francs more to be driven first to Chailly, and then to Barbizon where you can dismiss your "equipage." I urge that you do not yield to a temptation to "pass up" Chailly. Nowhere else in France, perhaps, will

JOSEPHINE INFORMED BY NAPOLEON OF HIS WISH TO DIVORCE HER

THE EMPEROR BIDS BAUSSET, PREFECT OF THE PALACE, CARRY THE

EMPRESS TO HER APARTMENTS

your way take you to a village churchyard; and this one is likely to linger in your memory as a spot you would not, for a great deal, have missed.

If, before making this trip to Barbizon, you have gone into the American Reading Rooms on the rue d'Élysée and refreshed your memory of certain books, your pilgrimage will be ten times better for your soul. The books I specially suggest are Julia Cartwright's "Jean François Millet: His Life and Letters"; "The Barbizon Painters," by Arthur Hoeber; Will H. Low's "A Chronicle of Friendships"; and "The Life of Robert Louis Stevenson," by Graham Balfour; also Stevenson's essay on Fontainebleau.

For those among you who won't do this, I'll offer a few reminders:

Jean François Millet, the Norman peasant-painter, was living, early in 1849, at number 8 rue du Delta in Montmartre (off rue du Faubourg-Poissonnière, near boulevard de Rochechouart), with his wife and three children, and having a bitter struggle to support them.

In April he finished his first important canvas of rural life ("Haymakers Resting in the Shadow of a Haystack") and was paid eleven hundred francs; the commission for it was from the new Republican Government, and the price was eighteen hundred francs, of which seven hundred had been advanced when the order was given.

The final payment came most opportunely. Cholera had broken out in Paris, and was very violent in the quarter where Millet lived. He had determined, even before this hastening factor, to leave Paris and devote himself to painting peasant life; the cholera and the eleven hundred francs accelerated his departure. He went to his friend, Charles Jacque, who lived near by, and said: "Here is a thousand francs; I will lend you half. Let us go together into the country."

Jacque said that "he knew of a little place on the edge of
the Forest of Fontainebleau . . . he could not remember the
name of the place, but he knew that it ended in *zon*. . . .
And so, one fine summer's day in early June, 1849, the two
families set off in the diligence for Fontainebleau." They
were in such high spirits that they forgot to ask which edge
of the forest the village ending in *zon* might be, and passed
within sight of it as they drove through to Fontainebleau
and to the Cadran Bleu on rue Grande, where they stayed
several days — until Madame Millet became frightened by
the expense. Urged by her, the two artists set out in search
of the village, and after a long walk they found a wood-cut-
ter who showed them the path to a village ending in *zon*.
They were charmed with it, and the next day moved
thither with their families. Rousseau, Diaz, and some
other artists were already there — for about twenty-five
years painters had been going to Barbizon — and Corot,
Barye, came soon after. Long before Stevenson went there,
in 1875 (the year in which both Millet and Corot died),
Barbizon had become a shrine for pilgrims as well as a
haunt for artists from many lands.

Your driver will take you to the Rousseau-Millet memorial by Chapu at the forest's edge, and after that to the Hôtel de la Forêt, rich in artistic associations. You should dismiss him here, and wander about Barbizon on foot.

Chailly is about a mile and a half north of Barbizon, and
its church is the one you see in so many pictures of the Barbizon painters — most notably, perhaps, in Millet's "Angelus." The ancient churchyard that surrounded the church
was dug up, in 1863, and some (only some!) of the bones of
the "forefathers of the hamlet" were transferred to the new
cemetery outside, where Rousseau was laid to rest in the
Christmas holidays of 1867. It was Millet who had the
rocks from the forest brought there, with a fine young oak,

and holly planted; it was his hand that kept Rousseau's grave bright with flowers while they were in bloom; it was on his invitation that many a visitor to Barbizon came to the Chailly cemetery with him, to stand by Rousseau's resting-place. "Let us talk of our dear dead together," he said.

It was a cold, gloomy day in January, 1875, when Millet was brought here to rest beside his friend, in "this quiet spot, near the old church which he had so often painted, on the edge of that plain where the sound of the Angelus still seems to float in every wind that blows."

You may not, if you are not steeped in the art and literature of Barbizon, share my feeling for this spot. I hesitate to urge it upon any one whose tastes I do not know. But I can only hope you will thrill to find yourself there; and, early next morning, will be at the Louvre, in the Chauchard Collection and in the Salle des États (see page 215 of your Blue Guide) revelling in the Barbizon School as you could not have done before.

The steam-tram which passes through Chailly (Shy-ye) goes on to Melun, five miles beyond. There you take train back to Paris.

NOTE

Detailed descriptions for other day trips out of Paris are in "Your Trip to France" of the Clara Laughlin Travel Study Courses; also itineraries, prices, suggestions for the Châteaux, for Normandy, for the Battlefields, for Provence and the Riviera, etc.

APPENDIX

I

RESTAURANTS, TEA-ROOMS, CAFÉS, CABARETS BARS, ETC.

(In the district bounded by the rue de Rivoli and the Grand Boulevards, and the rue Royale and rue Vivienne — the centre of Paris for most visitors.)

Alice, 21 rue Saint-Roch. Alsatian cooking. Pâté de foie gras, sauerkraut, creamed chicken or chicken with tarragon. Alsatian wines and fruit brandies. Prices modest.

Bœuf à la Mode, 8 rue de Valois. In my very frequent experience, unfailingly excellent. Fine courtesy. Prices moderate, but not cheap.

Beaugé, 10 rue Saint-Marc (off rue de Richelieu, near boulevard) delicious food, excellent cellar, genial service. Ask for the proprietor, M. Jules. Moderate prices.

Bonne Auberge, 7 rue Sainte-Anne. Excellent. Prices very moderate.

Brasserie Universelle, 31 avenue de l'Opéra. Specially celebrated for its hors-d'œuvre. Prices moderate.

Coupe d'Or, corner rue Saint-Honoré and rue Saint-Roch. American food — inexpensive.

Café de Paris, avenue de l'Opéra. Very famous; very expensive; very gay. Patronized by the lavish spenders.

Café de la Paix, place de l'Opéra. Everybody goes there to sit on the sidewalk and watch the world go by. But it is also a restaurant. Prices fairly moderate.

Café de Rohan. 1 place du Palais-Royal.

Café de la Régence, 161 rue Saint-Honoré. Historic house,

identified with chess-players. (See 'So You're Going to Paris!' pp. 157–58.)

Café de l'Univers, 1 rue de Rohan. 'Regional' specialties. Good cellar — prices moderate.

Au Caneton, rue de la Bourse. Specializes in Russian cooking. Very good, but not cheap.

Crillon Hotel, place de la Concorde. Dine on the roof terrace some warm evening. Expensive.

Cigogne (La), 17 rue Duphot (near the Madeleine). Alsatian — prices moderate.

Continental Hotel, rue de Rivoli and rue de Castiglione. Very good food. Fine table d'hôte. Prices moderate.

Ciro's, 6 rue Daunou. Very gay. Expensive. You can eat better for less money in dozens of places. But most people go to 'look,' and to be seen.

Columbin, corner rue Cambon and rue du Mont-Thabor. Tea-room. Nice for light luncheons. Prices moderate.

Drouant, place Gaillon. Fine cooking, celebrated clientèle. There the Council of Ten meets, in November, to award the Prix Goncourt. Prices moderate.

Delmonico, 39 avenue de l'Opéra. Good, but not cheap.

Duval, rue de Rivoli — avenue de l'Opéra — rue Montesquieu, and other places. The 'Childs' restaurants of Paris.

Gauclair, 86 rue de Richelieu. Fine old house. Cellar notable for its wines of Touraine and Anjou. Moderate prices.

Griffon, 6 rue d'Antin. Good. Prices not too high.

Henry, 30 rue Saint-Augustin (near avenue de l'Opéra); delightful place — elegant clientèle — finest food and wines — especially Burgundies. Prices rather high.

Ixe, 24 rue Royale. Luncheon, tea, candies, soda water, sandwiches; good foods; rather indifferent attitude; prices fairly 'stiff.'

Larue, 27 rue Royale. High-class — delicious food — attentive service — expensive, but well worth it.

Lucas, 9 place de la Madeleine. No better food, anywhere. Pleasant atmosphere. Quite expensive, but you don't grudge the price!

Maxim's, 3 rue Royale. 'Sporty' clientèle. Expensive. Popular at apéritif hour, just before dinner.

Maisonette Russe, 36 rue du Mont-Thabor. Delicious Russian food. Inexpensive at luncheon, but very dear at dinner when you have also the Russian musicians. After the theatre, go to the annex, at no. 38, called the Lido.

Maisonette des Comédiens Russes, 36 rue Vivienne. Tiny place — inexpensive at luncheon; very dear at dinner and after the theatre. Exquisite music.

Maza, 50 rue Richelieu. Basque restaurant. Very good. Not expensive.

Maillabuau, 68 rue Sainte-Anne. Plain surroundings, brief menu, superlative foods and Burgundy wines unsurpassed in Paris. Prices fairly high, but what you pay for is what you consume — not the surroundings, nor the music (there is none).

Meurice Hotel, 228 rue de Rivoli; has a very high-class restaurant. Expensive.

Montagné, 5 rue de l'Echelle, corner rue Saint-Honoré. One of the choicest spots in Paris for the gourmet. Delightful, intimate 'background.' M. Montagné is a distinguished writer on the fine art of cooking. His bill of fare is never lengthy; but oh! what food. Yes, the prices are high. But eating here is 'an experience.'

Philippe, 10 rue Daunou. Alsatian cooking. Very 'smart' and interesting clientèle. High prices.

Poumot, 33 rue Saint-Roch. The landlord here (Georges Poumot) used to be proprietor of the famous Cochon d'Or at Villette. He is a supremely good chef, and gives of his best to each patron. His place is small and simple; prices modest.

Prunier, 9 rue Duphot (near the Madeleine). Most celebrated (and justly so!) restaurant in the world for seafood. Always crowded. Everything delicious. Prices moderate. Don't miss it!

Peny, place de la Madeleine. Luncheon and tea. American foods.

Ritz Hotel, place Vendôme. Packed at luncheon and at tea-time. Sunday dinner-dances very smart and popular. Food no better than many other de luxe places, but nowhere else is there a more varied throng to look at. The Ritz Bar on rue Cambon is a favorite rendezvous.

Rumpelmayer, 226 rue de Rivoli — luncheon and tea; always crowded. Very dainty 'fixed price' luncheon at about one dollar. Famous pastries. Very good ice cream sodas. Delicious candies. Rather expensive.

Sherry, Louis, 6 rue de Castiglione. Breakfast (American coffee!), luncheon, tea. Candies; sodas. Tiny tables and much crowding. Expensive.

Savoy Hotel, 194 bis rue de Rivoli. Food so good that the restaurant is frequented by Parisians I know who spend a good part of their lives in discovering 'what's what.' Prices moderate.

Smith, W. H. and Son — 248 rue de Rivoli. Tea-room. English teas.

Shevlin's, 79 rue des Petits-Champs. Breakfast, luncheon, tea, dinner. American food. Friendly atmosphere. Prices very moderate.

Volney-Chatham, rue Daunou and rue Volney. Restaurant of this hotel much patronized by connoisseurs. Pleasant garden for outdoor lunching or dining. Prices rather moderate. English grill.

Voisin, corner rue Saint-Honoré and rue Cambon. Very
famous, very expensive. Quiet place, rather 'devoutly'
attended by worshippers of culinary art and rare vintages.

Weber, 21 rue Royale. Originally Alsatian, and still excels
in Alsatian food and beer, but now has varied menu.
Very popular with Parisians. Good place to go after
theatre if you want supper rather than 'distractions.'

At the East End of Paris

Au Cochon d'Or, 192 avenue Jean Jaurès. (This avenue is
the continuation of rue de Lafayette, northeast to the
Porte Jean Jaurès where one leaves the city on the great
national route for Metz.) The 'stockyards' are out here,
and the slaughter houses — and several of the best
restaurants in Paris! The gourmets rave about the
Cochon d'Or.

Dagorno, at 190 (next door), is specially celebrated for his
thick, tender, juicy steaks, broiled over grape-vine
shoots. Marvellous!

Café-Restaurant du Lac, Parc des Buttes-Chaumont. I
love to drive out here about 6.30 or 7.00, when this great
industrial quarter is full of the home-going throngs.
Dine at this restaurant if it's a fine evening; and perhaps
'take in' the Gaumont Palace (cinema and vaudeville)
at boulevard de Clichy, on your way home. Or go to the
place du Tertre for coffee and liqueurs.

In and Near the Champs-Élysées

Ambassadeurs, Champs-Élysées Gardens. One does not
know whether to list this among restaurants with entertainment or among theatres where one may eat and drink.
Whichever way you reckon it, it is an expensive business — but gorgeous, as to setting, entertainment, and
patrons.

Chez Francis, 7 place de l'Alma, at the angle of avenue George V, and avenue Montaigne, with a 'terrace' overlooking the river and the Eiffel Tower. Much frequented by Americans from the near-by hotels and apartments, and by persons who are going to attend one of the theatres on avenue Montaigne. Good food, moderate prices.

Claridge's Hotel, 74 avenue des Champs-Élysées — gay, expensive.

Au Cabaret, 4 avenue Victor-Emmanuel III. Grill-room. Prices moderate, food and cellar good.

Le Coup de Fusil, 28 avenue Victor-Emmanuel III; in the style of a hunter's inn. Prices moderate.

Le Cheval Pie, 8 avenue Victor-Emmanuel III. Normandy setting. Always crowded. Prices moderate.

Douchka, 8 rue Brey (avenue Wagram). Russian. First-class. Fashionable.

L'Ermitage, 72 avenue des Champs-Élysées. Cabaret at night.

Fouquet, 99 avenue des Champs-Élysées. Everybody knows the 'terrace,' but not everybody knows that the food served in the restaurant is superlatively good.

Florian, 78 avenue des Champs-Élysées, is part of the 'Venetian' scheme at Claridge's Arcade des Champs-Élysées, which also includes the Lido, a swimming-pool place where the pool is used principally as an excuse for dining and dancing in bathing costumes. Florian's is not part of the Lido, but another 'bit of Venice,' close by. Prices high.

Le Fin Gourmet, 15 avenue Victor-Hugo. 'Regional' dishes, moderate prices.

Franco-Italien, 5 avenue Matignon (north of the Rond Point) excellent Italian food and wines. Very popular. Prices reasonable.

George V. Hotel, 31 avenue George V. Magnificent. Food and cellar unsurpassed in Paris.

Restaurant Jean Goujon, 8 rue Jean-Goujon, near the Grand Palais. In a famous mansion of the First Empire. The manager, M. La Broue, is a well-known writer on food as a fine art. Expensive, but choice.

Joseph, 56 rue Pierre Charron (between avenue des Champs-Élysées and avenue George V), a small, quiet, elegant, expensive place. Delicious food, notable cellar. Joseph used to be at Martin's and at Sherry's, in New York, and has a devoted clientèle.

Langer, Champs-Élysées. Good food; expensive; dancing.

Laurent, 41 avenue Gabriel. Distinguished, delightful — don't miss it! Prices moderate, considering the quality, the setting, and the hospitality. M. Henri Secheresse, the manager, was liaison officer for General Bullard's army; and this place is a great rendezvous for the devotees of Franco-American friendship.

Ledoyen, Champs-Élysées. Famous place. Particularly good when out-door lunching or dining is possible. Excellent food. Prices high but not exorbitant. If there is any 'personality' about it, any interest shown in clients, I have never encountered it, though I have eaten there frequently, for many years.

Plaza-Athénée, 25 avenue Montaigne, is much frequented by quiet, elegant folk for entertaining. Many notable luncheons and dinners are given there, many fashionable wedding-breakfasts. The garden court is lovely. No better food in Paris; no more restful, charming place; no more delightful attention paid to guests anywhere in Paris.

Petit Durand, 27 avenue Victor-Hugo. Successor to the very celebrated Durand which used to be at place de la Madeleine where Cook's is now. First-class.

Traktir, 16 avenue Victor-Hugo — 'West-End' branch of
Prunier's. Excellent, of course! Prices not too high.
Specially attractive Sunday evenings.

The Grand Boulevards
(From the Madeleine to the Bastille)

Hôtel de Paris, boulevard de la Madeleine. Viel's restaurant is here, in the new hotel which is on Viel's old
site. No better food in Paris. Not cheap.

Marguery's, 38 boulevard Bonne-Nouvelle. The famous
Sole Marguery is still a marvel. Other foods good, but
not superlative. Prices moderate. No feeling of hospitality or welcome.

Nöel-Peters, boulevard des Italiens, in the Passage des
Princes (at rue de Richelieu). Delicious food, Italian
and French-Moorish setting. Good music at dinner.
Prices very moderate for the quality. Service inclined to
be indifferent. No welcome — no attention.

Café Prévost, 39 boulevard Bonne-Nouvelle; frequented
by journalists; celebrated for its chocolate and brioche.

Quick, corner rue des Italiens and rue Taitbout. 'Quick'
lunch or dinner.

Quatre Sergents de la Rochelle, 3 boulevard Beaumarchais;
a famous old house near the site of the Bastille. I love to
go there. The cooking is excellent, the wines superior,
the management is attentive, the prices are extremely
reasonable, and one sees interesting types of French
people there; many of them might (one thinks) have been
known to Balzac when he lived in this quarter.

Samaritaine, 27 boulevard des Capucines. The restaurant
on the top floor has a terrace whereon it is very pleasant
to lunch or 'tea' or dine. Good food at reasonable prices.

Sam's, 26 boulevard des Italiens — American food and
drinks, including coffee, cocktails, and ice cream sodas.

Breakfast and every other meal and 'between-meal.'
Reasonable.

LEFT BANK
(South of the Seine)

Auberge de la Cloche, 30 rue Saint-André-des-Arts, near
place Saint-Michel. Dates back to the days of the
Three Musketeers. Good food, modest prices, interesting
background.

Aux deux Tours, 204 boulevard Saint-Germain, near the
Ministry of War. If you know Bologna and its famous
old 'two Towers,' you will understand why Signor Sarti
chose this name for his reproduction of an old inn in
Bologna, his home city. Here he serves excellent Italian
food and wine, and also maintains a permanent exhibition of Italian art.

Auberge du Vieux-Colombier, 21 rue du Vieux-Colombier
(west from place Saint-Sulpice). Patronized by authors
and artists of the 'new schools.' Modest prices.

Caveau des Oubliettes Rouges, 11 rue Saint-Julien-le-
Pauvre. (Off rue Saint-Jacques — near the quai Saint-
Michel.) This is a cabaret, reached from the courtyard
of the ancient church of Saint-Julien-le-Pauvre. The
cellar is said to be part of the old prison of the Petit
Châtelet, and boasts its association with Dante. There,
surrounded by reminders of eight or nine centuries that
are gone, one may hear the songs of old France sung,
evenings from about nine o'clock, on. Upstairs, in the
Auberge des Oubliettes, you may see a little museum of
Old Paris.

Café des Deux Magots, place Saint-Germain-des-Prés
(corner rue Bonaparte and boulevard Saint-Germain), a
favorite evening resort of students; in the Beaux-Arts
neighborhood.

Café Harcourt, Café Soufflot, Café, or Taverne, du Panthéon, are three places on boulevard Saint-Michel, near the Panthéon, where you may lunch or sup or dine, as well as sit, between meals, and watch the 'Boul' Mich'' world go by. Panthéon best for food.

Café du Dôme and Café de la Rotonde, are the best-known and most-frequented cafés of boulevard Montparnasse. They are at the intersection of that boulevard with boulevard Raspail, not far from the Gare Montparnasse. Good food at the Rotonde, music and dancing. But the chief attraction is the artists and authors of the 'Quarter' who frequent the place.

Jouvin's restaurant, 124 boulevard Montparnasse; and Restaurant Sainte-Cécile at 140, same boulevard, are inexpensive places, much frequented by residents of the 'Quarter.'

Lavenue, opposite the Gare Montparnasse, is a trifle more expensive, and larger. There is a pleasant garden for outdoor dining on summer evenings. Sometimes the music is exceptionally good.

Restaurant des Trianons, 5 place de Rennes (at Gare Montparnasse), is excellent. And Café-Restaurant de Versailles, next door, has been highly commended to me by friends; I have not tried it.

Restaurant Strix, 4 rue Huyghens, back of Café du Dôme, is a good Swedish restaurant.

The Viking, 29 rue Vavin (other side of boulevard Montparnasse) is a Norwegian restaurant.

Café Voltaire, place de l'Odéon, beneath Camille Desmoulins' home, was interesting chiefly for association's sake the last time I visited it, on my way to Foire Saint-Germain. The service was very poor. But I have eaten well there on more than one occasion.

Little Brown Jug, at 15 carrefour de l'Odéon (up near

boulevard Saint-Germain). American food. Reasonable prices. Friendly atmosphere.

Elza Lee, 130 boulevard Saint-Germain (in the historic Cour du Commerce). American food. Reasonable prices.

Grill Room de Médicis, 17 rue de Médicis (opposite Luxembourg Gardens), near 'Boul' Mich'' and Panthéon. Moderate prices, good food. Pleasant place to dine on 'terrace' (or sidewalk) some warm evening. Very popular.

Foyot's, corner of rue de Tournon and rue de Vaugirard (opposite the Palais du Luxembourg, now the French Senate), one of the most celebrated of all the shrines of French cuisine and French vintages. Very quiet and reposeful. Everybody seems in a reverent mood, in the presence of such food, such drink, such service. Many distinguished French gourmets to be seen. Expensive — but 'an experience' you'll never regret, and will repeat as often as you can.

Le Pain et le Sel, 42 rue de la Montagne-Sainte-Geneviève (a fascinating street running down toward boulevard Saint-Germain from place Sainte-Geneviève behind the Panthéon and in front of Saint-Étienne-du-Mont). This is a tiny place, where delicious Russian food is served — no better Russian food in Paris. Not cheap — but less expensive than some of the others, across the river.

Grill Room Saint-Michel, 2 place Saint-Michel, was created to take care of the lawyers from the Palais de Justice. The clientèle now is varied and very numerous. Space at a premium. Good food — regional menus.

Michaud, corner rue Jacob and rue des Saints-Pères, near the Beaux-Arts, is an unpretentious place with a very considerable reputation. Some like it very much, and

some like it not at all. I have sometimes agreed with
each camp of opinion. In any event, it won't cost you a
great deal to find out what you think of it.

Lapérouse, 51 quai des Grands-Augustins (near the southern end of le pont Neuf) is one of the houses of the great
old tradition. Superlative food, marvellous cellar, perfect service — quiet, reposeful. No one's knowledge of
Paris restaurants of the first order is complete unless he
knows Lapérouse. Yes — it is expensive; but not exorbitant.

La Tour d'Argent, 15 quai de la Tournelle (opposite Île
Saint-Louis). Founded in 1562, this is not only the oldest restaurant in Paris but the most celebrated in France
and throughout the world. Every lover of good living
who goes to Paris, goes there inevitably — as he goes to
Foyot and to Lapérouse, and l'Escargat, and Montagné,
and certain others I might mention. Years ago, he was
certain to go to the Café Anglais, equally celebrated for
its cuisine and for its cellar. The cellar is at la Tour
d'Argent, now; the daughter of M. Burdel, under whom
Café Anglais enjoyed its palmiest days, is now Madame
Terrail, whose husband is proprietor of la Tour d'Argent
and of so many other distinguished places in Paris. The
best-known specialty of la Tour d'Argent is its duck in a
sauce of pressed blood; but there is a multitude of marvels to choose from. On no account miss going there, if
you can possibly afford it.

Rendez-vous des Mariniers, 33 quai d'Anjou, on the north
side of Île Saint-Louis, has become popular with many
kinds of clients other than the old barge-men who were its
principal patrons until a few years ago. Specially celebrated for Madame Lecomte's roast chicken. Best to
order before you go a-sightseeing in that story-book
vicinity.

Restaurant du Lac, Parc de Montsouris. (Parc de Montsouris is at the southern edge of Paris. Follow boulevard Raspail to place Denfert Rocherau — where the Lion de Belfort is — and continue down avenue Parc de Montsouris to the park; the restaurant is on the west border of the lake, near avenue Reille where you enter the park. You will go out there to see the new Cité Universitaire. Choose a late afternoon for that; and, if it be warm, dine at this restaurant.)

Chicago Inn, 31 avenue de la Bourdonnais (near the Eiffel Tower). Fried chicken, waffles, and other American foods, prepared by a colored cook from Texas.

In the Bois de Boulogne

Armenonville (near the Porte Maillot, entered from avenue de la Grande Armée). Exquisite, as to surroundings and food, at any time while the weather is good (closed except in summer). But specially perfect, I think, for luncheon, beside the tiny lake, on a summer day. Oh, yes! it *is* expensive. And after races at Longchamps it is thronged for tea.

Pré-Catélan, under the same management as Armenonville, Café de Paris, and Fouquet's (M. Louis Barraya), is reached by taking the route de Suresnes which runs between the Lac Inférieur and the Allée de Longchamp. Idyllic surroundings, here; and, of course, the perfection of food, drink, and music. Lovely at any time, but particularly on the gala dinner nights.

Château de Madrid, at Porte de Madrid, near Bagatelle, and reached from the bottom of the Lac Inférieur by the route de Madrid aux Lacs, or by direct route from the Porte Maillot. Has less natural beauty than either Armenonville or Pré-Catélan; but presents, on gala dinner nights, with the lighting effects and the Renais-

sance Château background, one of the most ravishing
settings in which any one ever dined and danced. Fear-
fully expensive — but well worth it, if you have the
money!

Pavillon Dauphine, at the Porte Dauphine, entrance from
avenue du Bois de Boulogne, is attractive for luncheon or
tea; and I find it delightful for dinner on warm evenings.
A bit less expensive than the three before-mentioned —
but still not cheap.

La Cascade, near the cascade at the end of the Allée de
Longchamp. Very gay at tea-time on days when there is
racing at Longchamps.

Pavillon Royal, at the bottom of Lac Inférieur, is less expensive than the three first named. Popular with wedding
parties.

L'Ermitage, on the river, near the pont de Suresnes, is the
only place in the Bois of which I cannot speak from much
personal knowledge. Every time I have tried to go there,
it has been just opening or just closing, or something.
But I'm sure it's excellent.

The Jardin d'Acclimatation in the Bois has a Café-Restaurant which is popular-priced.

The island in the Lac Inférieur has a café, reached by
boats.

Near the Élysée Palace

La Crémaillère, place Beauveau (facing the palace). Here
one finds, now, M. Marius and his staff, erstwhile of the
once-very-famous Paillard's. Everything very choice.
Not cheap, of course.

Comm' Chez-Soi, 17 rue Roquepine, is around the corner.
Here you may lunch or dine very well at a very moderate
price — although the proprietor, M. Blondet, spent
many years in New York, at the Ritz and the Plaza,

catering to lavish spenders. He has, also, La Bonne
Auberge, rue Sainte-Anne.

Near Gare Saint-Lazare

La Reine Pédauque, 6 rue de la Pépinière (westward continuation of rue Saint-Lazare, running from rue de
Rome to where boulevard Haussmann crosses boulevard
Malesherbes). Many unusual and intriguing ways of
serving food. Good food — but little elbow-room. Not
expensive.

Chateaubriand, 98 rue Saint-Lazare. Famous for its
steaks.

North of the Grand Boulevards

Au Caneton, 3 rue de la Bourse, good French cooking, but
largely patronized for its Russian specialties. Rather
expensive.

Restaurant de la Dame Blanche, 6 rue Chauveau-Lagarde
(back of place de la Madeleine, between rue Tronchet
and boulevard Malesherbes). Delicious food and fine
wines, in quiet, tasteful surroundings. Same management as la Tour d'Argent and l'Escargot.

Escargot, 38 rue Montorgueil. (This street runs north
from the place de la Pointe Saint-Eustache, north of the
great central markets. If you follow rue du pont Neuf
from the pont Neuf straight north, through the centre of
the markets, you will find yourself continuing in rue
Montorgueil.) Little needs to be said of this very famous
place, to which lovers of good eating unfailingly find their
way. Not cheap. Ask for M. Lespinesse.

Pharamond, 23 rue de la Grande-Truanderie (east from the
beginning of rue Montorgueil). Frequented by revellers,
after a night on Montmartre, for onion soup and tripe à
la mode de Caën, in the dawn when the markets are live-
liest.

Grill Room du Helder, 6 rue du Helder (north from the beginning of boulevard des Italiens). Especially for luncheon, if you happen to be in that vicinity. Modest prices.

Restaurant Hubin, 22 rue Drouot (the continuation of rue de Richelieu, north of boulevard Montmartre). Good food, good wines, reasonable prices. Ask for the proprietor, M. Pichenot.

Lapré, across rue de Provence from Hubin's. Quiet, restful place. Delicious food. Excellent wines. I never fail to go there several times on each visit to Paris. Managed by the genial M. Jules, owner of Beaugé, and brother-in-law of the celebrated André Terrail. Moderately expensive.

À la Biche, 19 rue Grange-Batelière, a block nearer the boulevards than the two foregoing, is run by M. Laurin who was formerly with The Savoy Hotel, and also The Carlton, in London, and has a host of friends who frequent his place.

Montmartre

(For lunch or dinner, as distinguished from the places frequented for dancing or as cabarets.)

L'Âne Rouge, 28 avenue Trudaine. Cooking of high excellence. First-class cellar. Moderately expensive.

Écrivisse, 32 avenue Trudaine. Very attractive. Good orchestra, excellent cellar, delightful cooking. Rather expensive.

Auberge du Clou, 30 avenue Trudaine. Picturesque interior, and some picturesque customers. Supposed to be very Bohemian, but a little 'on parade,' now. Some of my Paris friends like it very much. Not expensive.

Au Bouquet de Montmartre, 28 rues des Abbesses (runs east from rue des Martyrs, north of boulevard de Clichy). Worth investigating, if you don't know it.

Au Bon Vigneron, 67 rue Blanche (runs north from rue Saint-Lazare to boulevard de Clichy). First-class food, excellent wines, fine clientèle. Ask for M. Jules Breton, the director.

À la bonne Franquette, 18 rue Saint-Rustique (up near the old church of Saint-Pierre). A garden, a charming view, an outdoor rotisserie, reasonable prices.

Lizeux, 24 rue Fontaine (southeast from place Blanche). Very fine cooking, rare old wines.

L'Auberge du Coucou, place du Calvaire, off the place du Tertre. Every one whose time in Paris permits and whose stay there is in weather favorable for outdoor dining, should give one evening to dinner in the vicinity of place du Tertre (la bonne Franquette is near there). Wandering 'artists' of many sorts offer varied entertainment; the view is lovely; 'one could,' one writer on Paris has said, 'imagine one's self eating with Charpentier's *Louise*.' The Coucou was specially commended to me by a distinguished New York lawyer resident in Paris, who felt that readers of 'So You're Going to Paris!' would be glad to know about it. I'm sure they will!

Restaurant de la Savoyarde, 2 rue Lamarck (alongside Sacré-Cœur) on one of the highest spots of Paris, is famed as that place from which was painted the setting for the fifth act of 'Louise.' View forever memorable. Good food. Interesting in every way. Consecrate to it some evening when the sunset's fine.

Out of Town

Bois-Joli, also known as 'Cent-Quatre' because it is one hundred and four kilometres from Paris, is on National Route 12 to Mont Saint-Michel, reached through Versailles, Houdan, and Dreux. It is at Tillières-sur-Avre, a little beyond Nonancourt, and stands close to the road,

on your left-hand side going west. Most 'story-book'
kind of place. Eat under the apple trees, or in any one of
a wide variety of indoor settings. Very good food —
Normandy! Wonderful antique furnishings. One hundred and four kilometres is sixty-five miles. If you stop
at Dreux (as you should) you will 'make it' in about
three hours. After a leisurely lunch you could, if so-
minded, return to Dreux and take the road to Chartres
(twenty miles), see the town and cathedral, and return
to Paris via Maintenon and Rambouillet, stopping for
dinner at any of the delightful places I shall mention in
the Valley of the Chevreuse.

Chantilly, whither some go to visit the superb château and
some to attend the races, is twenty-five miles from Paris
on the route to Amiens and Calais. The Grand-Condé is
the principal hotel — handsome and beautifully situated.
Food pretty good, and (especially on race-days) expensive. At Lys-Chantilly, a new 'subdivision' just south of
the town, there is an Alsatian restaurant, 'La Clairière
aux Chênes,' which serves excellent food. Every place
frightfully crowded on race-days.

Chevreuse, Valley of. This lovely district south of Paris is
full of delightful eating places to which 'all Paris' resorts
a-pleasuring. The nearest-to-Paris, on this route, is
Robinson (twelve and a half miles) where you may
lunch or tea or dine on a platform high up among the
branches of a huge chestnut-tree — and descend to dance
or to watch others dancing. *Paliseau*, which is about an
equal distance from Paris, has the very attractive 'Moulin
de la Planche' where (weather permitting) you may eat
outdoors in a big garden and then wander beside a tiny,
meandering stream — the Yvette. Terribly crowded on
Sundays and holidays; but I lunched there without difficulty on a recent Sunday in June. At *Saint-Remy-les-*

Chevreuses there is the Hôtel de l'Yvette, with a fine
garden and some noted recipes. At *Dampierre* there is the
Auberge Saint-Pierre, an old inn with fine old furniture,
excellent food, a notable cellar. At *Rambouillet*, the
Hôtellerie de la Garenne is famous for its fare, and for its
twenty-two-acre 'park' on the edge of the forest. The
Presidents of France are frequently in residence at the
Château of Rambouillet; and the 'Garenne' entertains
many of the best epicures of France. Most celebrated of
all in the Valley is probably La Rôtisserie du Moulin de
Bicherel, which you reach by leaving the Grande Route
from Paris to Rambouillet at Verrières and taking the
road to Montfort-l'Amaury. One is offered opportunity
for bathing and boating in the mill-pond around the
edges of which the most desirable tables are set. Unless
it is a very varied crowd that you want to see, and an
enormous collection of expensive automobiles, don't go
on a Sunday or a holiday.

Château-Thierry, fifty-one miles from Paris, is much visited
by Americans. (See 'So You're Going to France!' pages
510–20.) A most interesting day may be spent going to
Château-Thierry for luncheon at Hôtel Bonhomme (see
Madame Pullin), visiting Belleau Wood, and returning
to Paris by way of Mildred Aldrich's 'Hilltop on the
Marne,' near Huiry.

Chennevières-sur-Marne, l'Hostellerie de l'Écu de France.
Here is a delicious spot, near Paris, for luncheon or dinner
on a summer day! And one of the many lovely things
about it is that the best route to it is through the heavenly
Bois de Vincennes — which far too few visitors to Paris
see. I drive in this Bois by the hour, whenever I can
make time for it — up one road and down another;
never, never getting enough of its beauty and restfulness.
Drive out avenue Daumesnil from place de la Bastille;

or follow the quais straight out to the confluence of the
Seine and Marne, then turn up into the Bois and drive in
it as long as you can. When you leave the Bois, do it by
way of the pont de Joinville (at the southeast corner) and
follow the left bank of the Marne a short distance to
l'Écu de France, in one of the most idyllic settings im-
aginable. Eat beside the Marne. Excellent food. This
is an old posting-inn; and beside one of the doors there
hangs a pair of very high boots said to have belonged to
d'Artagnan.

La Closerie des Saules, at Tessancourt, twenty-five miles
from Paris, is a hotel-restaurant set in very large and
charmingly picturesque grounds. Very crowded on Sundays and holidays. Other times extremely restful. Has a
fine clientèle. Very good food. Go to Saint-Germain-en-
Laye, and from there take the route to Poissy and Meulan.
Tessancourt is near Meulan.

Compiègne. The famous Rond-Royal hotel is closed, as I
write. I am told that Hôtel de Flandre has exceptionally
good food, but I haven't tried it — being addicted to pic-
nics in Compiègne forest. You must go there, of course!
See Compiègne, the forest, and Pierrefonds. (See 'So
You're Going to France!' page 548.)

Fontainebleau. There's the very famous (and expensive!)
Hôtel de France, opposite the gates of the palace. There's
the palatial Savoy, on the avenue du Chemin-de-Fer,
near the railway station. There's the Grand Hôtel
François I, at 23 rue Royale, near the palace gates, and
not expensive. In the forest depths, there's the Restaurant de l'Ermitage, at the Gorges of Franchard. At Barbizon, there's the Hôtel de la Forêt, at the edge of the
forest close to the Millet-Rousseau memorial; and the
Hôtellerie du Bas-Bréau, made famous by Robert Louis
Stevenson's sojourn there: and the Hôtel des Charmettes,

also well liked. At Arbonne, not far from Barbizon, nor from the Gorges of Franchard, is the Hôtel Cornebiche, on the west edge of the forest, with bungalows in its park, a swimming-pool, and tennis. At Grez-sur-Loing, about seven and a half miles from Fontainebleau on the road to Nemours is La Poule d'Eau, a thoroughly up-to-date, delightful hotel in large grounds, with a terrace on the river, and many attractions — including good food, best vintages, an American bar, boating, fishing. And of *course* Grez is a place of pilgrimage to all lovers of Robert Louis Stevenson. It was there that he met and loved 'the woman whom Fate had brought halfway across the world to meet him.'

Forest of Senart, about fifteen miles from Paris on the route to Melun, is celebrated for its lilies-of-the-valley, in May; and has some attractive resort places. Try the Moulin de Jarcy, near Brunoy, for luncheon some day in May.

Mon Village is an interesting place for lovers of antiques, which are displayed and sold there in a Normandy cottage setting. Go to Enghien-les-Bains, at the foot of the Montmorency hills, seven and a half miles from Paris. Then four and a half miles to Saint-Leu, and ask for 'Mon Village.' A little farther on is L'Isle-Adam where there is a fine sandy beach on the Oise, and a gay little summer-resort, close to the fine forest of L'Isle-Adam. The Royal Conti is a hotel and restaurant in the historic castle of the princes of Conti; and the Metairie Cottage-Hotel is comfortable, attractive, and sets a good 'home-like' table. Inexpensive.

Saint-Germain-en-Laye is ten miles from Paris; on the route, by road, is Malmaison, and Marly. There is a boat 'La Madelon,' which goes to Saint-Germain each day from the quai d'Orsay, at 10.35, serves luncheon on board, allows time for a visit to the town (see 'So You're Going

TO PARIS!' pages 87–92) and gets back to Paris at 5 P.M.
If you lunch at Saint-Germain (or 'tea' or dine there)
you will doubtless choose Pavillon Henri IV — see the
room in which Louis XIV was born, enjoy the glorious
view from the glass-enclosed terrace, and eat notable
food. Not cheap — but worth all it costs. Should you
stop before reaching Saint-Germain, at Louveciennes
(where Du Barry had her fine estate), you will find La
Pomme d'Api, by the roadside, overlooking the Seine, a
delectable place to lunch or dine, in the terraced gardens.
Yes, it's expensive. At Villennes-sur-Seine, fifteen and a
half miles from Paris, in a fine private park, with a superb
view over the Seine Valley, is 'La Nourrée,' managed (I
believe) by M. Jules, the genial proprietor of Restaurant
Beaugé, in Paris.

At Mantes-la-Jolie, thirty-one miles from Paris on the road
to Deauville, I have eaten many a fine meal in charming
setting in the garden of Hôtel du Grand Cerf. At the
Grand-Cerf in Senlis, thirty-three miles from Paris on
the edge of the forest of Chantilly, you may have fine
hospitality in a sixteenth-century mansion which has been
a hostelry for some three hundred years. And at the
Grand-Cerf in Grand-Andely (see 'So You're Going to
France!' pages 84–90) you may — en route to Rouen,
perhaps — enjoy good fare and good cheer in a mansion
of Francis I's time which has been catering to wayfarers
through Normandy since 1749.

Versailles offers you a considerable range of choice. There's
the Trianon Palace Hotel, with its terraces and gardens.
There's the Hôtel des Reservoirs in Madame de Pompadour's old mansion. There's the Vatel, on rue des Reservoirs, which is said to be good; but I can't report from
personal knowledge. And only on hearsay can I speak of
Pilloud's, 12 rue André-Chenier — said to be excellent.

BARS

Henry's, 11 rue Volney (near Chatham Hotel). Much frequented by Americans.

Harry's New York Bar, 5 rue Daunou (around the corner from the above). Sort of an American Club without initiation fee other than 'setting 'em up.' Cabaret from 10.30 P.M. to 2 A.M., in basement.

The Chatham Bar, 17 rue Daunou.

The Cintra, rue Edouard VII. Like an old tavern. Barrels of port; barrels for tables; barrels everywhere. Port and sandwiches and oyster cocktails — and conviviality.

The Bodega, at the corner of rue de Rivoli and rue de Castiglione, also specializes in ports and sherries.

The Cecil, 16 rue de Caumartin (the continuation of rue Cambon north of the boulevards). Usually known as 'Jack Bushby's.'

Fouquet's, 99 avenue des Champs-Élysées.

Select, 100 avenue des Champs-Élysées.

Maxim's, 3 rue Royale.

The Ritz Bar, entered from rue Cambon side of hotel.

The Scribe Bar, 1 rue Scribe.

Fred Payne's, 14 rue Pigalle. Cliff Thompson, one-time actor in America, owns an interest here and makes it a rendezvous for Thespians from the U.S.A., and those who like theatrical society.

Napoleon Bar, 30 Arcades Champs-Élysées (next to Claridge's). Excellent champagne cocktails.

MONTMARTRE NIGHT PLACES

(For cabaret entertainment and dancing. Remember that a city tax of twenty-five per cent is charged on everything served after 10 P.M. in restaurants where there is dancing and music.)

Le Bal Tabarin, 34 rue Victor-Massé. Best on Saturday

nights. Girls of the streets, tourists, and a few low-class French.

Le Bal du Moulin Rouge, place Blanche. Clientèle of street girls, pretty shop-attendants, chambermaids, tourists. Big floor, usually crowded. You can sit in a *loge* (box) and watch, if you buy champagne.

Bruant (Cabaret), 84 boulevard Rochechouart. Fewer tourists, more French; more of the atmosphere of the old-time cabaret before it became a stop on the 'rubber-neck' routes.

Caveau Caucasien, 54 rue Pigalle. High-grade cabaret, fine foods, and wines, good dance-floor. Quite expensive, but really worth-while performance.

Cabaret du Néant, 34 boulevard de Clichy. Coffins, human bones, skulls, undertakers, dancing skeletons. Somebody enters a coffin, and, through 'trick' lighting and mirrors, seems to decompose. A woman visitor sits on a chair on the little stage of a cavern, and by more illusion seems to be divested of her clothes. One of the old, old 'attractions' of Montmartre, always new for 'rustics' from somewhere.

Ciel et l'Enfer (Heaven and Hell), 53 boulevard de Clichy. Much on the order of side-shows at a fair.

Le Chat Noir (Black Cat), 68 boulevard de Clichy. A good deal of what entertains many of the guests is lost on those who do not understand colloquial French — and 'argot.' But the place is so widely known that it's worth a look-in if you're 'doing' Montmartre.

Le Rat Mort (the Dead Rat), place Pigalle. Dancing—thick crowd, small space, lots of noise, crowds of street girls.

Le Lapin Agile, 2 rue des Saules. Used to be 'genuine,' but has become rather a show for tourists. Setting is picturesque, and the old songs are still sung. Worth a visit. Not dear.

La Florida, 20 rue de Clichy. Very dressy — pecks of
diamonds — can't get in unless you're in evening dress.
Glass dance-floor which gradually disappears from sight
as night wears on and tables thicken. Top-notch exhibition dancers. But as for the dancing that the guests do,
it might better be done in a subway express at the rush
hour. Everybody *must* buy champagne, which is likely to
be inferior, at a high price. Expensive dolls and other
favors for the ladies. Marvellous clothes.

Le Perroquet, 16 rue de Clichy. Much like La Florida.

Pigalle's, 77 rue Pigalle, is on the order of the above, but
less fashionable and perhaps a shade less expensive.

L'Abbaye de Thélème, place Pigalle. One of the most interesting places in the Montmartre district. Expensive.

Palermo, 6 rue Fontaine. Smart, expensive, gay. Said to
have enjoyed much favor of the Prince of Wales.

Casanova, 12 avenue Rachel. Handsome place — Russian
— good entertainment. Not cheap.

Chez Fysher, rue d'Antin (not Montmartre, but avenue de
l'Opéra). Very *chic* from midnight till 2 A.M.

Zelli's, 16 rue Fontaine. Probably the best-known of the
Montmartre night resorts. On the order of Pigalle's.

Bi-Ba-Bo, 12 rue Frochot (place Pigalle). Gypsy cave.
Argentine and Spanish dancing; celebrated violinist.
Charming favors.

Imperial Soupers, 59 rue Pigalle. Very good.

Kounak, 29 rue Henri-Monnier. Good entertainment of
Caucasian and Russian music.

Russian Artistic Club, 4 rue des Batignolles. First-class
entertainment. Fashionable.

Troïka, 26 rue Fontaine. Russian and gypsy dancers and
singers. Ukrainian chorus. Good entertainment.

Caveau de Montmartre, 30 boulevard de Clichy. Like a
vagabonds' retreat. More amusing if you know French.

II

SOME ADDRESSES

(For many other shopping addresses, see *Clara Laughlin's Paris Address Book*, in handy pocket-book size)

WHEN I put a few of my Paris addresses into the first edition of 'SO YOU'RE GOING TO PARIS!' because I knew that they were among the things my friends always wanted when Paris-bound, it was an innovation; and I was told that it might cause my book to be looked upon as an advertising proposition. Naturally, I did some serious thinking before going on with a policy which might reflect upon my attitude toward my readers, toward myself, and toward my subject. But, the more I thought about it, the more it seemed to me that what the stranger in Paris wants as much as any other one thing is not just sight-seeing directions, but hints as to which of Paris's myriad doors he may open with best expectation of feeling welcome and finding what he wants.

So I scattered restaurants through the text, and a few shop addresses, and trusted that I might serve my readers without bringing my motives under their suspicion. There are, of course, some persons who always suspect. One may as well make up one's mind to that. But there are a great many others. And now that this book has been five years in circulation, I know that there are many, many thousands of visitors to Paris who, using it constantly, have found out that if an address is in these pages, it is because I believed it would be serviceable to my readers — and not for *any* other reason.

As a matter of fact, aside from the small number of places

to which I went for years before this book was thought of, there are exceedingly few of those mentioned in it who know me, or — so far as I am aware — anything about me; I still come and go, in their restaurants or shops, without making myself known to them; and only once or twice have I had even a card of thanks, by mail, acknowledging any benefit the book may have been to them. (This refers to a majority of those mentioned — not to the small group of those I have known and dealt with for many years.)

So appreciative has your attitude been toward addresses, that I have now complied with your repeated requests for more of them, issued in small pocket-book size, to be always in hand even when your 'SO YOU'RE GOING TO PARIS!' is in your hotel-room. I would have put many more of these into this volume, but for consideration of space.

In trying to make this Fourth Edition more serviceable to you than any of the predecessors, I have enlarged the restaurant list and made a separate feature of it, by locations.

Here, I have collected the various addresses of other sorts that are scattered through the earlier editions, making them easier for you to consult.

They were not many, I find.

There was, in the domain of clothes:

Blanche Lebouvier (Marie Louise, directrice), at 3 rue Boudreau, corner of rue Auber, near the American Express Office. For dresses, coats, evening gowns, sports wear. The longer I know this place, the more reasons I have for commending it to those who want beautiful clothes, beautifully made; and treatment of the greatest courtesy and integrity. Ask for Madame Marguerite. She speaks perfect English.

Fehnér, 2 cité Trévise (near rue Richer, north of boulevards), for lingerie, table and bed embroideries, handkerchiefs, hand-made frocks, infants' wear, etc. A place I have gone to for nearly twenty years. Ask for Mme. Marguerite Menneret. She speaks beautiful English.

Réjane, 10 rue Daunou (near rue de la Paix), for hats. Ask for Mlle. Jenny who had five years selling experience in America. Large assortment of hats to try on.

Guy, 26 rue Bayard (near Rond Point des Champs-Élysées), 'the architect of feminine headgear.' Immensely clever designer. Brings out 'personality' of customer, quite wonderfully. Ask for Mr. Stanley Forster, Guy's partner.

Antoinette Germaine, 8 rue de Louvois (off rue de Richelieu, beside Bibliothèque Nationale) loveliest artificial flowers in the world. Ask for Mlle. Marie Louise.

Aux Tapisseries de France, 1bis rue Montaigne (near Rond Point des Champs-Élysées), for lovely tapestries copied from the finest old ones; needlepoint. Bags, purses, furniture coverings, decorative pieces. Ask for Mme. Gasnot, who speaks excellent English.

Sandalari, 364 rue Saint-Honoré. Beautiful French, bench-made shoes on American lasts. Designed by Mary Bendelari, the American girl you've read so many magazine articles about; and made in her own factory. This is her retail salesroom. Stock in hand, and orders taken. American silk stockings for sale, too.

Cadolle, 14 rue Cambou (near rue Saint-Honoré), for corsets and lingerie and négligées, and silk hose.

Zavrel, 18 rue Daunou (between boulevard des Capucines and rue de la Paix), for furs. Absolutely reliable, and remarkable values. M. Zavrel is a highly expert furrier whose knowledge of pelts and workmanship cannot be excelled. Whatever you want, from fur-trimming to a superb fox or sable, or from remodelling an old fur coat to ordering a fine new one, I'd at least consult Zavrel about it. Mlle. Zavrel speaks English; and both M. and Mme. speak some, and understand a good deal.

The Grande Maison de Blanc, boulevard des Capucines, for table and bed linens, lingerie, handkerchiefs, sports wear, evening wraps, dresses, fine furnishings for the home, etc. Every sales person speaks English. Beautiful goods in every line they carry, and prices not too high.

Bon Marché, rue de Bac (near boulevard Raspail). Department store. Excellent for many things.

Grand Magazin du Louvre, place du Palais-Royal. Department store. Excellent for silks, gloves, and many other things.

Then there were some that had to do with 'personal' wants. Like:

Elizabeth Arden, 2 rue de la Paix, for facial and body massage, beauty exercise, electric light cabinet, etc. Also for buying lingerie, and many choice small novelties.

Frances Fox Institute, for the scientific care of the hair, 5 rue Cambon.

Harper Method — 3 rue Tronchet, for shampoos.

Ogilvie Sisters — shampooing — 23 rue de la Paix.

American Institute for hair treatment, 35 rue Godet de Mauroy.

Waegili, chiropodist, 31 rue Boissy-d'Anglas.

Lelong, laundry, 12 rue de la Sourdière.

Rosa Brun, dry-cleaning; magic cleansing fluid — 54 rue François Premier.

Guy Créquigné, 37 rue Lauriston, veterinary.

There was Prouté, for etchings and engravings, at 12 rue de Seine. And Leroy, for Brittany china, at 19 rue de Miromesnil.

There was Marguerite Shelley, 21 rue du Mont-Thabor, for antiques.

And there were four schools:

L'Institut du Panthéon, for French, at 38 rue de Écoles, with a delightful summer school in Brittany. I know that this address has been much appreciated.

The School of Fine and Applied Art, under the Regents of the State of New York, at 9 place des Vosges. Directed by Frank Alvah Parsons.

The School of Fine Arts and The Music School at Fontainebleau.

The Cordon Bleu, for cooking lessons, at 129 rue du Faubourg Saint-Honoré.

(For all these and others, see the new Appendix on 'Study in Paris.')

A very few of the others in the Address Book, that I want to incorporate here, for those readers who may not happen to have the Address Book, are:

Bags

Bossac, 5 rue Boudreau. Finest leather and antique fabrics.

Painted Velvets and Silks

Gallenga, 17 rue de Miromesnil. Also, most beautiful Italian Art Crafts products of many sorts, in La Boutique Italienne, managed by Madame Gallenga. One of the most fascinating places in Paris. Don't miss it if you are in search of lovely things.

Felt and Fancies

Lenci, 402 rue Saint-Honoré; for the adorable Lenci dolls; also for frocks for wee folk and hats for women, and a variety of entrancing things. Take home to somebody very nice, a few of Lenci's pussycats!

Toiles de Jouy

Au Vieux Jouy, 108 rue du Bac.
Delepoulle, 25 rue Saint-Augustin.

Old Maps

Mercator, 50 rue du Colisée.

Old Pewter

T. Lematte, 14 rue Saint-Sulpice.

Danish Silver

Georg Jensen, 239 rue Saint-Honoré.

Casts of Antique Sculpture

Heckman and Ossant, 57 rue Bonaparte.

III

PARIS IN FIVE DAYS

MANY persons have asked me to suggest what an average traveller may see of Paris in an average stay — which seems to be about five days.

It's hard to say, because so much depends on the individual and on the weather and on the season of year.

But suppose we say something like *this:*

First day: I'd begin with the place de la Concorde (page 2), finding a safe spot near the Obelisk from which to look about me, map in hand, and get the lay of the land.

After that, I'd walk east, in the Tuileries Gardens toward where the Tuileries Palace used to be, or in the rue de Rivoli which fringes them on the north, till I came to rue de Castiglione, where I'd turn north, toward the place Vendôme and the rue de la Paix, loitering along the latter till I reached the Opéra and the boulevards (Chapter I to page 10).

Next I'd turn east in the boulevards (which change their name every few streets) and find a place to lunch (see the restaurant list).

After luncheon, I'd probably shop a while. I might spend an hour at the Musée Grevin, 10 boulevard Montmartre — the waxworks show which does so much to vivify what we see in Paris (page 72). Or, I might go to the races (page 483). In any case, if the weather were at all propitious, I'd go out to the Bois de Boulogne (page 13). I might have tea there at one of the famous restaurants (see list). I might even stay out there to dine under the trees, were the evening a fine and warm one. Were it not, I'd dine in town, and probably I'd find myself (after a very early dinner) at the Opéra Comique.

Second day, or *another* day, I'd go to the Louvre in the morning (pages 74–84) while I was feeling fresh and fit, and see the things I cared most about, and I'd make acquaintance with that superb vista from in front of the Gambetta Monument, looking westward for miles. Then, if I didn't have to go home to lunch (that is, to my hotel), I might cross the pont du Carrousel to the left Bank, and turn to my left, browsing at some of the bookstalls along the embankment on Quai Malaquais, or in some of the book and picture shops (pages 313–15, 388). I'd stroll down rue Bonaparte, past the Beaux-Arts, looking up and down the quaint old streets, till I came to boulevard Saint-Germain (page 393). I'd get some luncheon — lots of places not too far from there — and in the afternoon I'd see the Panthéon (page 179), glimpse the Sorbonne (pages 182–83), in passing, and I might visit the Cluny Museum (pages 281–85), or I might go to Napoleon's Tomb and the Church of Saint Louis (behind it) and the military museum of Des Invalides (pages 167–70).

A third day, if I could afford an automobile, I'd start out soon after nine in the morning, and get to Malmaison (page 85), as near ten as possible. Then to Versailles (Chapter XI) to visit the palace before luncheon, and after luncheon the Trianons and the gardens. After seeing these, drive to Saint-Germain (page 86) for dinner on the terrace, and a walk in the town or in the park. This is a perfectly feasible and thoroughly delightful day for travellers with few days for Paris. But no excursion does it. And you couldn't compass it except by motor. I like going to Versailles by the electric road, and advise spending money on a first-rate guide rather than on a motor if one is going only there. But if you want to include Saint-Germain (and I think even the five-day sojourners should try to dine out there and glimpse the château from without if not from within), you must have a car. This will enable you to see something also of the forests of Marly and Saint-Germain.

I don't think that Versailles *and* Fontainebleau are advisable on so short a stay. Each requires a whole day; and that would leave but three days for Paris itself. Some travellers may prefer to take their one full day excursion to Fontainebleau (page 417) because it is so much more furnished, has a much longer history, and because of the magnificent forest of Fontainebleau, and the delightful village of Barbizon, home of Millet and Corot and other noted painters. But Fontainebleau is thirty-six miles from Paris, and Versailles is eleven.

A fourth day might begin with a drive over the pont Neuf (page 125) to the Île de la Cité, where Paris was cradled, and a visit to the Conciergerie, the Palais de Justice, the Sainte-Chapelle, and Notre-Dame (pages 129–42). After luncheon, visit the Hôtel de Ville, or City Hall of Paris, to see the magnificent state apartments where Paris offers her municipal hospitality to so many distinguished visitors (page 71). Then I'd shop a while, for whatever interested me most. I'd see at least one of the Parisian *magasins*, or department stores. Our own at home are more elegant; but the Paris stores are interesting, and have lots of attractive goods at reasonable prices. And I'd make acquaintance with a number of the small specialty shops which are so many and so beguiling in Paris.

When I got tired shopping, I'd have tea in a 'smart' place where Parisians as well as visitors go. And if I felt like a drive before dinner, I'd say *this*, or *show* this, to a taxi-driver, or (preferably) to the *cocher* of a little old fiacre with a sleepy nag:

Pont de la Concorde (page 109); Quai d'Orsay (pages

318–20); Tour Eiffel; Parc du Champ de Mars (pages 323–26); Pont d'Iéna; Trocadéro; avenue Kléber; Étoile (where the Arc de Triomphe is); avenue Hoche; Parc Monceau (pages 20–21); boulevard Malesherbes. This is a drive that will give you lovely glimpses of several beautiful residential sections of newer Paris.

A *fifth day* might start with the Musée Carnavalet (pages 93–95), the Museum of the City of Paris, housed in a beautiful old mansion where Madame de Sévigné held her salons, and filled with things interesting, historic, and beautiful, *some* of which must surely appeal to every visitor.

Thence it is but a few steps to the place des Vosges (page 112), with its variety of interests, including that most storied house in which Victor Hugo lived, and which you may visit. Go thence to the site of the Bastille (page 104) and lunch near there. Then take a cab and say: Cimetière de Picpus — (Sim-tee-air de Pick-poos), where, in the yard of a convent of the Perpetual Adoration, you may visit Lafayette's grave (pages 238–40), see the last resting-place of André Chenier (pages 362–66) and many other victims of the last days of the Terror, and visualize some of the most thrilling scenes of 'Les Misérables' — for this yard is where Jean Valjean and Cosette escaped from Javert and were hidden by old Fauchlevent.

It might be that thence you would like to go to the cemetery of Père Lachaise (pages 231–33), where so many eminent persons lie buried; and to drive thence along avenue de la République to place de la République and follow the line of boulevards to the Opéra or the Madeleine. Or, you might like to cross by the pont d'Austerlitz (which Valjean crossed, carrying Cosette and closely followed by Javert) to the Jardin des Plantes, or Botanical Garden (Zoölogical, also!), lovely in itself and dear to many for its association with eminent naturalists (page 195). And continue, past the great wine markets, to pont Sully, and drive around quiet Île Saint-Louis (pages 310–12), which is still so much a seventeenth-century place. Or, go along boulevard Saint-Germain to its intersection with the 'Boul' Mich'' (boulevard Saint-Michel), and turn down the latter toward the Luxembourg Gardens (pages 31–33, 45–46).

A section that may be substituted for the Picpus is the ancient part of Paris around the Central Markets (Les Halles Centrales) (pages 201 *et seq*.) and from there west to the Palais-Royal (page 51).

Whatever you do, be sure you go along rue du Faubourg Saint-Honoré from rue Royale west at least to avenue Marigny, past the British Embassy and the President's palace (page 333).

If you love very ancient and picturesque old narrow streets, go exploring on the Left Bank between quai Montebello (page 274), and boulevard Saint-Germain, and then up rue de la Montagne Sainte-Geneviève toward the Panthéon — a quarter Villon knew well.

Not many persons know much better than I do how tragic are the omissions from this list. But this may serve some as a suggestion, and I'd try to get *these* things into a five-day visit to Paris:

At least five of her famous restaurants, besides several cafés. Among the latter, I'd try some on the grand boulevards and one or two of those on boulevard Montparnasse, in the evening. And I'd dine once in the *Bois* or Champs-Élysées, weather permitting.

At least one opera at the Comique and one at the Grand Opéra. I'd probably see a French 'revue,' and might go thence to one or two typical night-restaurants in Montmartre — though the next day I might wish I had saved my money and energy for something less like what I could

have at home. One night I'd dine out at Saint-Germain.
So there'd be but one more evening — perhaps for Montparnasse and its cafés; perhaps for a fairyland, dinner-dance
in the Bois on a gala night; perhaps for the Comédie Française or Odéon; perhaps (who knows?) for the Fratellini at
the Cirque d'Hiver.

I'd try to see Le Bourget.

I'd shop, and not be apologetic about it, to myself or to
others. It's a very important part of a Parisian experience.

I'd loaf around some place like the Luxembourg Gardens,
or the Palais-Royal Gardens, or the Parc Monceau, when
I was tired, and watch French parents and their adorable
babies.

I'd consider a ride on a river steamer, sometime, so I
could watch 'folks.' If there were a fair on — and there
usually is, somewhere — I'd go to it by all means.

IV

PARIS FOR CHILDREN

LITTLEST ONES

Parc Monceau, in fashionable 'West End' quarter of Paris. Charming small park, where many of the picture-book-y French babies play, attended by their nurses in peasant costumes. Sand-pits — duck-ponds — many flowers (page 20).

Champs-Élysées. A Paradise of toy-booths, merry-go-rounds, puppet-shows, goat carriages, donkeys for riding, swings, sand-pits, and every delight, under the splendid trees.

Tuileries Gardens. Especially the 'yachting' on the big basin of the fountain.

Luxembourg Gardens. Swings, games, toy-booths; always full of French children and their mamas and (Sundays) their papas; *much* 'yacht-sailing' here! Yachts may be rented beside the fountain.

Jardin des Plantes, East end of Paris. Fine 'Zoo' (page 195).

Bois de Vincennes, East end of Paris. Beautiful big park. Famous castle. May be reached by river steamer to Charenton (page 242).

Bois de Boulogne. Boating — tea on the island — play under the trees (page 14).

Jardin d'Acclimatation (porte de Neuilly entrance of Bois de Boulogne). *Every*thing blissful for babes! Ride on camel, elephant, zebra, or what-you-will, or in carriage drawn by ostrich. Aviary — monkey-house — pheasant-ries — sheep-fold — kangaroo house (babies in mamas' pockets!) reindeer paddock — rabbit house — kennels with puppies for sale — bunnies for sale — warm milk from the dairy — waffles — a riding school — a gymnasium — band concerts.

Palais-Royal Gardens. Children like playing there, close to the arcades and their shops (page 51).

Versailles. The Trianon Gardens are especially dear to children, with the Queen's 'playhouses,' etc. (page 247).

Not very far from Versailles is Sceaux, with the park called Robinson, where one eats high up in the great old chestnut trees, which have platforms built among their branches. One can go from Versailles to Robinson if motoring, and return to Paris by way of Bourg la Reine.

Toy-shops on rue de Rivoli; and especially Le Nain Bleu, 410 rue Saint-Honoré.

The Bird Market on Sundays, on the Île de la Cité — quai aux Fleurs. Rabbits and kittens and little monkeys for sale, too!

Be *sure* not to miss the puppet-shows (guignols) in Champs-Élysées, AND the circus, especially the one at which the famous Fratellini clowns are performing (Cirque d'Hiver).

Musée Grévin (10 boulevard Montmartre) has some features the littlest ones will enjoy — the distorting mirrors near the entrance; the wax policemen who look alive, the 'people' who seem to be looking at the figures, and are figures themselves. The images of Charlie Chaplin, Lindbergh, etc.

The Fairs!! There is always one in or on the near outskirts of Paris. No child should leave Paris without having visited one of these street fairs and carnivals — The Foire Saint-Germain reproduces a mediæval city.

River steamers to Charenton or Auteuil; or the all-day ride to Saint-Germain.

Ride on the tiny railway in the Bois de Boulogne, from the Porte Maillot to the Jardin d'Acclimatation.

Eat outdoors whenever possible — restaurants in the Bois or Champs-Élysées.

Picnic when possible — especially in the grand old forests near Paris.

Go *behind* the Cascade at the Trocadéro Park — visit the Aquarium.

Visit the Dogs' Cemetery (tramway 39, from the Madeleine).

For the Older Children

All the foregoing, and much more. Especially —
Napoleon's tomb and the Musée de l'Armée.
  Things which belonged to Napoleon.
  Relics of the late War — such as Guynemer's plane.
  Museum of armour (page 168).

Carnavalet Museum — fascinating to children. Old shop-signs, models of old Paris streets, Roman remains recovered from river bed, old costumes, playthings of the little Dauphin in prison, rope-ladder by which Latude escaped from Bastille; and *hundreds* of things of interest (page 94).

Conservatoire des Arts et Métiers has many things the boys will be especially interested in. The plane, for instance, in which Blériot made the first flight across the Channel; the original model for Bartholdi's Statue of Liberty in New York Harbor, etc. (page 220).

Musée de Cluny. The Roman baths interest children; also the collection of shoes, and the state carriages. Also, many of the old furnishings; and the musical instruments, although a much better collection of the latter is at the Conservatoire National de Musique, rue de Madrid (page 281).

The Musée Ethnographique du Trocadéro has many things
that children like — girls must see the collection of five
hundred dolls. Boys will be delighted with the Dahomey
exhibits, etc. (page 323).

The Arc de Triomphe and the Unknown Soldier's Grave,
one passes en route to the Bois de Boulogne.

Picpus Cemetery and the Grave of Lafayette should be
visited, for many reasons. This convent garden plays a
great part in 'Les Misérables.' And the reason why Lafayette lies there is one of the most interesting stories in
all French history (page 238).

Chapelle Expiatoire, where many victims of the guillotine
were buried. Also, the Swiss Guard in whose honor the
Lion of Lucerne was carved (page 21).

The Conciergerie and Palais de Justice and Sainte-Chapelle
are full of interest for young folks of school age (page
128).

The Panthéon, with its mural paintings telling many of the
great stories of France, should by all means be seen
(page 179).

A visit to the state apartments of the Hôtel de Ville (City
Hall) is most impressive. Many of the paintings there
illustrate episodes in French history (page 71).

See, if possible, the historical paintings of the Sorbonne
(page 285).

The Natural History collections at the Jardin des Plantes
are intensely interesting to those who are fond of those
sciences (page 195).

Get a glimpse of the École des Beaux-Arts on rue Bonaparte (page 383).

Visit the Mint (Hôtel des Monnaies, quai Conti) on Tuesday or Thursday, 1 to 3, by special permission, for which
written application must be made. Your hotel concierge
will get it.

Eiffel Tower — and, near by, École Militaire, where Napoleon went to school (page 176).

Le Bourget Flying Field, and marked spot where 'Lindy' landed.

The House of Victor Hugo, place des Vosges, near the site of the Bastille (pages 115 and 104).

See more of Musée Grévin than the very young ones should see — the historical tableaux are fine (page 71).

The stamp market on Sunday afternoons near the puppet-shows of the Champs Élysées. Other times, see the shops for stamps in the Palais-Royal.

Le Semaine de Suzette, quai des Grands Augustins, is a dolls' outfitting shop. Everything for the dolly's needs.

Children are interested to see the front of the War Office, pocked with shell scars; the Church of Saint-Gervais, back of the Hôtel de Ville, where the first shell from Big Bertha killed nearly one hundred persons, on Good Friday, 1918.

They should have a definite impression, a mental picture of the Chamber of Deputies, quai d'Orsay, the Senate (Luxembourg), and the Élysée Palace, the President's home.

The Louvre and the Luxembourg Galleries; but not too much!

The markets of Paris are interesting — the great Halles Centrales and the street markets all over the city. And they love the Flea Market at porte de Clignancourt, up at the north edge of the city.

The Salon in the Grand Palais, particularly the sculpture exhibit on the ground floor, impresses young visitors very happily.

And the streets of Paris are a never-ending story-book.

Fontainebleau and Barbizon (with Millet's house) should be seen, if possible. And by all means see Malmaison, on the way to Versailles. To these, I would add Compiègne if it can possibly be done — including a picnic in the forest where Charlemagne used to hunt. There they see where the Armistice was signed, where Guynemer lived, where Jeanne d'Arc was taken prisoner, where Louis XVI and Marie Antoinette first saw each other. And from there they can (if motoring) go on to Pierrefonds, a perfect story-book castle.

These suggestions are but a *beginning*. Paris for the young visitor is inexhaustible. See 'Where It All Comes True in France!' by Clara E. Laughlin, with the aid of her nieces, Betty and Mary Clara.

V

RAINY DAYS

THEY happen in Paris as elsewhere. And I have thought that perhaps a few suggestions about how to use them might be helpful.

There's always shopping, of course. And with a bit of 'organization' before you start out — grouping places that you're interested in — it need not entail too much paddling around in the wet. Moreover, cabs are plentiful and very cheap.

On some rainy afternoons there are circus performances. On others there are matinées at Opéra Comique and theatres. Frequently, there is a salon of some sort at the Grand Palais, which is well lighted. The lovely collections of the City of Paris, housed in the Petit Palais across the street, can be seen to fair advantage on a rainy day. The Musée Grévin is just as well seen in a pouring rain as in sunshine — in fact, better; because you're not missing the sunshine that's outdoors.

The treasures of the National Archives may be seen on a rainy Sunday afternoon; and those of the Bibliothèque Nationale on Monday or Thursday from 9 A.M. on.

I wouldn't go to the Conciergerie on a rainy day; because, when you are there, you'll want to see, also, Sainte-Chapelle (for which you should have sunshine) and to wander about in the Cour du Mai. I wouldn't choose a rainy day for Napoleon's tomb; because when you are there, you should see the Musée de l'Armée, and on rainy days it's as black as a pocket. So is the Cluny. The Carnavalet is better. And as I write, electric lighting has just been introduced into the Louvre.

You could see the Hôtel de Ville satisfactorily on a rainy afternoon. You could visit Victor Hugo's house. You can enjoy the Trocadéro.

There are movies. There are entertaining tea-places with good music. One need not be disconsolate in Paris if it rains.

VI

HOLIDAYS AND FAIRS AND FÊTES

EUROPE has many holidays; and it is quite necessary for the traveller to be aware of them, because they may affect his program either to his inconvenience or his greater pleasure. The closing of banks and business houses and travel agencies may be a serious annoyance, if you haven't reckoned on it in advance. And the crowding of museums and amusement places on holidays makes it advisable for the traveller to avoid them at such times, although observation of people (particularly French people), when on pleasure bent, is one of the things which should be an important part of a visitor's business abroad.

The principal holidays which may affect your Paris stay are:

January 1 — A general holiday, as everywhere. But more generally celebrated in France even than Christmas which is primarily a religious festival.

Mardi Gras — Much merriment on the boulevards and in the cafés and cabarets.

Mi-Carême, or Mid-Lent (fourth Thursday) — Even more observed, and gayer, than Mardi Gras. Fancy-dress ball at the Opera; confetti-throwing on boulevards; etc.

Holy Week — The picturesque Foire aux Jambons (Ham Fair) is held in Holy Week on boulevard Richard-Lenoir east of place de la République. Notable music at Church of Saint-Gervais; and in other churches impressive services.

Easter — Magnificent music in many churches. Much

gaiety everywhere. Foire aux Pains d'Épices (Ginger-bread Fair) begins in place de la Nation and cours de Vincennes (see page 238).

May 1 — Labor Day in Europe. Everybody who can, stops work. It is particularly noticeable in transportation — cabs almost impossible to get. On this day (and a few days succeeding) the streets are filled with vendors of *muguet* (lily-of-the-valley) which everybody buys and gives to some one 'for luck'; the French say it is a *porte-bonheur*, or happiness-bringer.

May 5 — Anniversary of Napoleon's death; there are picturesque and impressive ceremonies under the Arc de Triomphe and at Les Invalides.

May 8 — Jeanne d'Arc Day, anniversary of her raising the siege of Orléans. Celebrations at her various statues, services in churches; some of the churches have a military mass — very impressive. Great to go to Orléans for this day, if you can.

The Foire de Paris is held in May, and extends from the porte de Versailles (at the southwest edge of the city) along the outer boulevards; and in town has an extension around the Champ de Mars. This is a 'buyers' fair,' exhibiting many kinds of French products. The porte de Versailles is at the far end of rue de Vaugirard. It is reached by Métro to the porte de Versailles station. Tram 89 goes there, following a very interesting route from the Hôtel de Ville. Bus AG goes there from the Bourse.

The Foire Saint-Germain, place Saint-Sulpice, is held in May, beginning about the middle. It re-creates an old-time city, each year of a different epoch.

Ascension Day is very generally observed as a holiday — also the day before it and the day after.

Whitsun is as general a holiday time as any in the year

— a three-day holiday. Everybody who can goes to the country. Those who can't, go to the parks. Everything shut *tight*, at least from Saturday noon till Tuesday morning.

Corpus Christi (in France, *la Fête Dieu*) is about mid-June. Very picturesque ceremonies in the Catholic churches. I specially love the procession at the Madeleine.

The Foire de Neuilly begins about Corpus Christi and lasts for three weeks; it stretches for an interminable length along avenue de Neuilly from the porte Maillot to the Seine. This is the National Route to Cherbourg, out which one goes to Saint-Germain, Mantes, etc. If you do not find yourself driving along it, make an errand of the Fair. Take tram 41 from the Madeleine.

The Foire des Antiquaires at Versailles, in late June, should attract lovers of antiques. Versailles, being full of dealers in antiques, is probably not a place where one may hope to pick up an unsuspected treasure. But a fair out there is good fun.

July 4 — Many pleasant events in honor of American visitors.

July 14 — Bastille Day — the equivalent of our Fourth of July. The grand exodus from Paris begins just before July 14th; everybody who can go away, goes. But there are always a lot left! Celebrating begins on the 12th (see page 55) and is even livelier on the 13th than on the 14th. On the 14th the parks and suburban resorts are thronged. If you stay in the city, and want to see the fun, go up to Montmartre and along the boulevards to the place de la Bastille.

August 15 — Assumption. General holiday, like Easter.

November — During the first week there are picturesque festivities at Chantilly in connection with the fête of Saint Hubert.

November 11 — Armistice Day. Very generally and
solemnly observed.

November 25 — Sainte Catherine's Day — the day of the
midinettes or sewing-girls in the dressmaking establish-
ments. Much merriment, not only among the girls but
for the public.

Christmas —

VII

STUDY IN PARIS

The Sorbonne is the University of Paris (see page 285). Many of the lectures are open to any one who cares to attend and has sufficient knowledge of French to 'follow' what's said. I very heartily advise those who can to attend the courses of lectures on French Civilization. One course begins early in November and finishes at the end of February; and the other begins early in March and finishes at the end of June. The lectures occur twice a week, in the morning; and there are classes which may be taken in conjunction with the lectures. The terms are 100 francs per month, or 300 francs for four months if all paid in advance. A certificate of attendance is given, if desired. There is a vacation lecture course from July 1 to November 1.

Free lectures on the History of Art are given in the Louvre on Sunday mornings at 10 and Thursday evenings at 8.45, under the direction of professors headed by L. Hourticq, whose manual on 'Art in France' should be part of every art-loving traveller's 'suitcase library.' It is published, in English, by Scribner's. Cards for these lectures (thirty in the course) may be had by writing to 'Direction des Musées Nationaux' au Louvre, giving your name and profession.

The Paris College of New York University has many exceedingly interesting and valuable things to offer Americans resident in Paris for sufficient time to do some studying. Inquire at 4 quai des Tuileries.

The New York School of Fine and Applied Art at 9 place

des Vosges, under the direction of Frank Alvah Parsons. This school is incorporated under the Regents of the State of New York, and is not a private enterprise. It has a faculty of forty-five members. The courses include interior architecture and design, stage design, costume design, decorative design, and commercial art. There are branches in London and Florence. Apply to the New York School, 2239 Broadway, New York; or to the secretary of the school in Paris.

The Fontainebleau School of Fine Arts, in the Palace of Fontainebleau, under the patronage of the French Government, is a summer school for advanced American students in architecture, painting and sculpture. New York address (for applications): Fontainebleau School of Fine Arts, 119 East 19th Street. Paris address: American University Union, 173 boulevard Saint-Germain, where a representative of the Fontainebleau School can be found Mondays and Fridays from 4 to 6 P.M., January to June. Board, lodging, and tuition about $100 per month.

The Fontainebleau School of Music, Walter Damrosch, President, New York address: 119 East 19th Street. In Paris, as above. Rates similar. Knowledge of French essential.

The Institut du Panthéon, 38 rue des Écoles (near the Cluny Museum and the Sorbonne), is excellent for the study of French. In addition to the Paris school, specializing in private lessons, there is a delightful summer school in Brittany where adult pupils are accepted for one month or more, boarding in the institution, receiving private instruction according to their needs, joining in the classes on French literature and art, making excursions to places of historic and artistic interest, and listening to plays and lectures in French. They are required to give their promise that they will not speak a word of English while they are pupils of this school; and friends of mine who have patronized it report with the highest praise of the pleasantness and profitableness of the experience.

L'École Moderne de Coupe de Paris, 43 rue de Rivoli, is subsidized by the City of Paris, and gives courses of instruction in cutting and making dresses, lingerie, corsets, hats, artificial flowers. Instruction given in all languages.

Le Cordon Bleu, 129 rue du Faubourg Saint-Honoré, gives lessons in cooking. Learn how to make anything you specially like as the best French cooks make it.

Schools and Camps for Young Americans in and out of Paris

MacJannet Schools and Camps are as follows:

The Elms — day and boarding school for boys at Saint-Cloud — auto service from and to Paris.

The Junior School for girls and boys — Trocadéro Gardens.

Summer Camps on the shore of Lake Annecy in the French Alps.

The Vacation House at Houlgate (Normandy shore) open from June to September for children whose parents are travelling abroad. Address Miss Charlotte Wiggin, Juanita, rue des Dunes, Houlgate, Calvados.

Mlle. Marguerite Clément, 4 Impasse Jouvencel, Versailles. Takes young ladies for "a year in France" with travel and instruction.

Paris American Day School, for boys and girls, 37 rue Boileau.

American High School of Paris, 5bis rue d'Auteuil.

The American Normandy Camps — under the direction of Paul G. De Rosay (Harvard), associate director Paris American Day School — La Clos, for boys — La Falaise, for girls. Inquire at 37 rue Boileau.

VIII

CHURCHES

American Cathedral-Church (or Pro-Cathedral) of the Holy Trinity, 23 avenue George V. This much-beloved church seems always full to overflowing, what with American residents in Paris and American visitors. There is a notably fine spirit toward strangers; and attending a service there is one of the real 'experiences' of Paris, almost sure to leave an unforgettable and stirring memory. The Memorial Battle Cloister is a very sacred and lovely place. And the Memorial Pews, with the State flags hanging above them, are one of Dean Beekman's many ideas for making the traveller feel truly at home in this house of God. The Cathedral-Church maintains a Chapel (Saint Luke's) in the Students' Quarter, at 5 rue de la Grande-Chaumière, off boulevard Montparnasse; and a U.S. Students' and Artists' Club at 107 boulevard Raspail.

British Embassy Church, 5 rue d'Aguesseau (near British Embassy, which is at 39 rue du Faubourg-Saint-Honoré).

The American Church, uniting all Protestant denominations, which has for many years worshipped at 21 rue de Berri (north from avenue des Champs-Élysées), is building a splendid new house of worship on quai d'Orsay.

Presbyterian Church (Church of Scotland), 17 rue Bayard, near Rond-Point des Champs-Élysées.

Methodist Church, 4 rue Roquépine (near Élysée Palace).

Methodist Episcopal Church, 89 boulevard Haussmann.

Saint Joseph's Church, for English-speaking Catholics, 50 avenue Hoche, near Arc de Triomphe.

First Church of Christ, Scientist, 184 boulevard Saint-Germain.

Second Church of Christ, Scientist, 58 boulevard Flandrin, near the Porte Dauphine.

Jewish Reformed Congregation, 24 rue Copernic (from place Victor-Hugo to avenue Kléber), three blocks south of Arc de Triomphe.

Church Music

Notre-Dame. Louis Vierne, organist. Lovers of organ music should hear his offertory solo at about 10.45 on Sunday mornings.

The Madeleine has very fine music, not confined to organ and choir, but frequently augmented by harp, violin, and trumpet.

Saint-Eustache, beside the Central Markets, is where Joseph Bonnet plays. He sometimes has week-day recitals there. Watch out for them.

Saint-Sulpice, near the Luxembourg, is noted for its congregational singing. Go at 9 some Sunday morning (see page 290) and hear the little organ in the Students' Chapel, on which Mozart played.

Saint-Gervais, back of the Hôtel de Ville, has a superb choir, specially celebrated for its 'plain-song.' The Passion Week music, 'the Tenebrae,' is very famous.

Saint-Severin (near rue Saint-Jacques — not far from Notre-Dame), where Saint Saëns was so long the organist, still has very fine music. Don't miss visiting this church! (See page 275.)

Saint-Roch, rue Saint-Honoré, has fine music.

The Russian Church, rue Daru (from rue du Faubourg-Saint-Honoré to boulevard de Courcelles, west of Parc Monceau). Marvellous choir.

IX

CONCERTS — THEATRES — MUSIC HALLS

(See daily papers, or La Semaine à Paris, for programs
of current concerts)

Concerts Calonne, at the Théâtre du Châtelet. Saturday
and Sunday afternoons. Gabriel Pierne, conductor. One
of the best places in Paris to hear new compositions,
especially of the 'new school.'

Concerts du Conservatoire, 14 rue de Madrid. Orchestra
composed of remarkable musicians, under the direction
of M. Philippe Gaubert. Sunday afternoons. Classical
compositions and the best of the generally accepted
newer music.

Concerts Lamoureux, Sunday afternoons at Salle Gaveau,
45 rue de la Boëtie. Orchestral. Classical compositions.

Concerts Pasdeloup. Fortnightly, from October to Easter,
in Théâtre Mogador. Classical and modern music.

Concerts Touche, 25 boulevard de Strasbourg. Every
evening at 8.30, and Sunday matinée. Classical concerts.
Thursday afternoons, chamber music.

Trocadéro — The Salle des Fêtes, seating 6000, has frequent concerts.

Sacred Music at the Church of the Sorbonne, under the
direction of the university and the Ministry of Education
and the Fine Arts.

Les Chanteurs de Saint-Gervais give concerts of secular
music, also. Inquire at 36 boulevard Saint-Germain.

Lecture-concerts, in English, on the History of French
Music, are being given (as I write) in Sainte-Chapelle, by
the Paris College of New York University, under the

patronage of the Sorbonne and the École du Louvre.
The illustrative singing is by the Schola Cantorum. Ask
at the Paris College of New York University. Palace of
the Louvre, 4 quai des Tuileries (porte des Lions).

Opéra. Some of the greatest individual artists (like Krise-
ler, Casals, Cortot, etc.) give their concerts at the Grand
Opéra. Others appear at Théâtre des Champs-Élysées,
avenue Montaigne. Still others are heard in recital halls,
like Salle des Agriculteurs, Salle Gaveau, Salle Érard,
Salle Touche.

OPEN-AIR CONCERTS

At the Tuileries Gardens, the Luxembourg, the Palais-
Royal, and the Jardin des Plantes; and the Jardin d'Ac-
climatation in the Bois de Boulogne. Also in the park at
Saint-Cloud, and at Versailles (Quinconce du Midi)
Tuesday, Thursday, and Sunday afternoons in summer,
from 3 to 4.30.

THEATRES

Of these, not many can interest the visitor who has not a
very good understanding of rapidly spoken (fluent) French.
Classic plays, which one may buy and study before attend-
ing, are given at the Comédie Française and the Odéon.
There is frequently an English company at the Albert
Premier, 64 rue du Rocher (near Gare Saint-Lazare). And
sometimes there are performances in French of familiar
plays by English and American authors, at the Théâtre des
Arts, 78 *bis* boulevard des Batignolles (north of the Gare
Saint-Lazare). This is where one sees the Pitoëff players.
Their presentation of Bernard Shaw's 'Saint Joan' was a
revelation. At the Mogador, one is quite likely to find a
French version of a great American or English success in
musical comedy.

Most visitors to Paris want to go to the Grand Guignol, 20 *bis* rue Chaptal (Montmartre, east of rue Blanche) to see the 'horrors' — which are so realistically presented that one may have cold chills or hysterics without understanding a word that's spoken. And I believe that a good many go to Théâtre Édouard VII, place Édouard-VII, to see Sacha Guitry and Yvonne Printemps — even if unable to understand what they say.

Visitors who are interested in modern theatre movements and new dramatists, should make acquaintance with what is going on at L'Atelier, place Dancourt (north of boulevard de Rochechouart, in Montmartre), where Charles Dullin's pupils, schooled in every need of the theatre, develop unusual and most interesting performances of plays by authors who are still scorned (or at least rejected) by the more commercial theatres. The Studio des Champs-Élysées, 15 avenue Montaigne (above Théâtre des Champs-Élysées), is a tiny 'laboratory' theatre for ultra-modern and 'precious' presentations. La Maison de l'Œuvre, 55 rue de Clichy, has been in existence since 1893, and here were produced early works of Maeterlinck, Bataille, Bordeaux, Claudel, and many more. La Petite Scène, 27 rue Saint-Sulpice (near the Luxembourg), is a society of amateurs devoted to productions of old French plays, in an atmosphere as much as possible like that in which plays were produced at the court of France two centuries and more ago.

MUSIC-HALLS

Les Ambassadeurs, in the Champs-Élysées, ranks as a Music-Hall by the quality of its entertainment, rather than as a restaurant with diversions, though the restaurant, also, is of the highest class. Very expensive.

Restaurant de la Michodière, 4 rue de la Michodière (south
from boulevard des Italiens, two blocks east of place de
l'Opéra) is under the same management, and of much the
same sort.

Apollo Music-Hall, 20 rue de Clichy (Montmartre).

Empire, 41 avenue de Wagram (near Arc de Triomphe).

Spectacles — Follies — Revues

Casino de Paris, 16 rue de Clichy. Gorgeous shows —
world-renowned 'stars'; much nudity.

Folies Bergères, 32 rue Richer. The spectacles here are
sumptuous beyond description. The nudity is less
obtrusive than it used to be — one can almost forget
about it in the sheer beauty of the tableaux. Last year
(1928) prudent parents were even taking their young
folks. The *promenoir* was still very much as of old; but
one may pass through it as if it were part of a seething
street.

The Moulin-Rouge, place Blanche (Montmartre), rebuilt,
after the fire of 1915, on a handsomer scale than the
famous old music-hall, is now perhaps the finest of its
sort in Paris. There is a movable ceiling, so that in
summer the spectacles may be given in open air.
Gorgeous shows. Growing more decorous.

The Palace, 8 rue du Faubourg Montmartre. Celebrated
music-hall stars, like Raquel Meller, Maurice Chevalier.
Splendid tableaux. Nudity emphasized.

The Théâtre Marigny, avenue Marigny, between avenue
Gabriel and Champs-Élysées. The revues at this theatre
are a feature of Paris that should not be missed. There
is no nudity, and much cleverness. Some of the most unforgettable 'bits' I have ever seen in a theatre, were in
revues at the Marigny.

Cinemas (Moving-Picture Theatres)
(*English titles*)

The Colisée, 28 avenue des Champs-Élysées; near the Rond-Point. Evenings at 9. Good films, excellent orchestra, smart audience.

The Cameo, 32 boulevard des Italiens. English and American.

The Madeleine, 14 boulevard de la Madeleine. Usually occupied by great successes enjoying long runs — like 'Ben Hur.'

The Paramount, boulevard des Italiens. Handsome new theatre of the sort Americans and Londoners are accustomed to at home.

The Gaumont, boulevard de Clichy (Montmartre). Very large (5000 seats). Variety program between films.

Circuses

The Cirque d'Hiver is where the famous Fratellini are. Everybody who can should see them. Though you may not understand a word they say, you'll laugh till you cry. I recommend a matinée, when many children are present. To hear their glee is delicious. The Cirque d'Hiver is at place Pasdeloup, which is the end of boulevard du Temple (see page 372).

Cirque de Paris, 18 avenue de la Motte — Piquet (between Les Invalides and l'École Militaire), is another circus of which I am specially fond.

Cirque de Medrano, 63 boulevard Rochechouart (continuation eastward of boulevard de Clichy, Montmartre), is where the Fratellini used to be. Still good.

X

SPORTS

1 — Sports for the Onlooker
2 — Sports in which You may Participate

I

Racing — Polo — Tennis Matches — Stadium
Exhibitions — Golf Tournaments — Motor and
Cycle Races — Pelôte Basque — Baseball —
Football — Fencing Exhibitions

Horse-Racing

February to December on the principal courses around
Paris. These courses are:

Auteuil, where much of the hurdle-racing and steeple-chasing is done. Very beautiful course and superb grounds,
on edge of the Bois de Boulogne. Métro, line 8 or 16;
no. 12, 15, 19, 23, or 25 tram from the Madeleine. Bus
AB, AS, or AX. Three great days in June here are the
Grand Steeple-chase, the Hurdles, and the Drags. Also,
Easter Sunday, and the Fall.

Chantilly. Flat racing. Thirty-five minutes by train from
the Gare du Nord. In June, the Prix du Jockey Club is a
big day, and the Prix de Diane. Nothing in May; not a
great deal in July; little in August. September has
several days. Then, nothing more till the following June.
Chantilly was the birthplace of French racing.

Compiègne. Flat racing. Sixty minutes by train from the
Gare de Nord. Principal races in July.

Enghien. Hurdle and steeple-chase. Ten minutes from the

Gare du Nord or forty-five minutes by tram 54 from the Opéra.

Longchamps, Bois de Boulogne. Flat racing. The Grand Prix and other important events here. Transportation terribly inadequate for 'big' days, except by taxi (which you should keep waiting) or private car.

Maisons-Laffitte. Flat racing. Thirty-five minutes from the Gare Saint-Lazare. Tram 62 from Porte Maillot. Many English and American horses trained here.

Le Tremblay. Flat racing. Fifteen minutes by tram from the Gare de l'Est. On the Marne, near the old inn, l'Écu d'Or.

Saint-Cloud. Flat racing and trotting. Tram 44 or 75 from Porte Maillot.

Vincennes. Trotting, steeple-chase, and hurdle. Twenty-five minutes from the Bastille Station of the Ceinture (Belt) Railway, to Joinville-le-Pont. A winter track.

Tickets of admission are, generally: To the Pelouse, 5 to 10 francs. This is what we might call 'general admission' to the centre of the oval. To the Pavillons, where there are stands, usually 15 francs. To the Pesage, where the grandstands are and the fashionable promenades, men 40 francs, ladies 20.

Going to the races is one of the easiest things in the world to do if you hire a car with an experienced chauffeur; buy a ticket to the pelouse for the car and chauffeur, then cross the track to the pesage. When the races are over, you get to your car in five minutes, or less, and drive away without the slightest difficulty. If you are a party of four, an afternoon at Longchamps or Auteuil or Saint-Cloud will probably cost you, with private car, about twenty dollars, exclusive of your bets and of your tea at a smart place afterwards. Don't 'pick up' a car at a public stand like the Opéra. (I never did that but once, and the driver was highly recommended to me by friends. But he abandoned us halfway, and returned to Paris.) Go to a thoroughly reputable, reliable travel agency and have them arrange everything for you. Another excellent 'Don't,' in general, is 'Don't' hire from your hotel concierge. He usually has 'fish to fry,' and they may not be the kind you prefer. When you have 'learned the ropes' about going to the races, you may feel equal to trying a less expensive way.

POLO

At the Polo Club of Bagatelle, and at the Saint-Cloud Country Club. April to July and in September and October. Very smart.

ROWING

Contests for championship of the Marne and of France, in the Bassin de Neuilly-sur-Marne-Bry — near Joinville-le-Pont where the charming Écu d'Or inn is — loveliest place to do your rowing — much like Thames at Henley.

STADIUM EXHIBITIONS

The Stade Français (or French Stadium) is at the Faisanderie in the park of Saint-Cloud.

The Stade Olympic is at Colombes. It seats 60,000 spectators. Reached in about eighteen minutes from the Gare Saint-Lazare, and also by tram from the Porte Maillot.

The Stade Pershing, presented to Paris by the American Army and the Y.M.C.A., is in the Bois de Vincennes over near the Marne side.

GOLF TOURNAMENTS

These are played at the Saint-Cloud Country Club, at La Boulie (near Versailles), at Fontainebleau, and on other courses near Paris. Watch the Paris papers or inquire at the Golf School on the avenue Gabriel, just beyond the place de la Concorde.

Motor and Cycle Races

The Motor Drome, or Autodrome, the fastest track in the world, is at Montlhéry, sixteen miles south of Paris near the lovely Valley of the Chevreuse. If you don't motor down, you can go by the steam-tramway from the porte d'Orléans to which the Métro will take you; or buses AE and AR will take you within a short walk of the porte d'Orléans — which is near parc de Montsouris on the southern edge of the city.

For information about races at the Autodrome — if you don't find what you want in the papers — inquire of the Autodrome's information office, 23 avenue de Messine (near parc Monceau). Telephone Élysées 16–70.

There are three Velodromes, or bicycle-racing tracks, in Paris. The best known is the Velodrome d'Hiver, rue Nélaton, near the Seine on the Left (or south) bank a short distance beyond the end of quai d'Orsay — near the Eiffel Tower. Métro to Grenelle station. The other tracks are at Bois de Vincennes (where the Grand Prix de Paris is run in July) and at parc des Princes, between the portes d'Auteuil and Saint-Cloud. Information about races may be had from the Société des Courses Cyclistes de France, 37 rue Saint-Georges (north from boulevard Haussmann, near the Ambassadors Hotel).

Pelôte Basque

At Montrouge, just beyond the porte d'Orléans.

Baseball

At the Stade Burgatti, Reuil. Take the Saint-Germain or Malmaison tram at porte Maillot and get off at the Parc station, Malmaison.

Women play baseball at the Stade Elizabeth, near the porte d'Orléans.

FOOTBALL

Matches are played at the Parc des Princes in the Bois de Boulogne; at the Stade Français, Saint-Cloud; and in the Bois de Vincennes. Information on this, or any other phase of sport, from the Sports Information Office, 14 Rond Point des Champs-Élysées.

FENCING EXHIBITIONS

Inquire at the Federation des Sociétés d'Escrime, 10 rue Blanche.

BOXING

Public matches are held at Wonderland, 74 avenue de Suffren, near the Eiffel Tower.

II
SPORTS IN WHICH YOU MAY PARTICIPATE
TENNIS

Where you may play, on the many superb courts in and near Paris, depends so much on your introductions and affiliations (just as it does everywhere!) that it is hard to say, in a general way, what you may do. Ask at the Sports Office, 14 Rond-Point des Champs-Élysées — or have your hotel concierge do it for you. Or, if you are a student, go to the American Methodist Centre, 79 rue Denfert-Rochereau. Or ask at the American University Union, 173 boulevard Saint-Germain. Or see what you can do at the Cité Universitaire on the boulevard Jourdan, south of parc de Montsouris.

Golf

Inquire at the Golf School, avenue Gabriel near place de la Concorde, or at the Golf Training Club, 147 avenue des Versailles. (This is not out at Versailles, but in Paris, close to the Seine. Tram 1 or 2, from the Louvre, will take you past the door — and a beautiful ride it is! Or you can take the Métro — though it doesn't go very near.)

There are many fine golf courses near Paris.

Chess

Headquarters are at the Café de la Régence, 161 rue Saint-Honoré.

Cycling

Cyclists should join the Touring Club de France, 65 avenue de la Grande-Armée, for a few francs a year. Its privileges are worth a hundred times what they cost.

Riding

Saddle horses may be hired of: Manège de la Faisanderie, 26 rue de la Faisanderie — which runs from avenue du Bois de Boulogne, just before it reaches the Porte Dauphine, to avenue Victor-Hugo. From Marion Walcot, 8 rue Benouville — which runs into rue de la Faisanderie near the porte Dauphine end. From Blum, 50 rue Saint-Didier, near place Victor-Hugo — back of the Trocadéro.

Swimming

Palais de la Natation, 26 rue de Chazelles, north of parc de Monceau, from boulevard de Courcelles. Physical training here, too. Fencing and boxing. Turkish baths.

Claridge's Pool, 74 avenue des Champs-Élysées.

Outdoor swimming at L'Isle Adam on the Oise, forty-five

minutes from Paris by train — Gare du Nord. Rowing and tennis here, too. Good hotels.

WHERE TO DANCE

Ciro's, 6 rue Daunou (at dinner or supper).

Claridge's, 74 avenue des Champs-Élysées (tea, dinner, or supper).

Embassy, 136 avenue des Champs-Élysées (tea, dinner, or supper).

Ermitage Muscovite, 24 rue Caumartin (tea, dinner, or supper).

Florida, 20 rue de Clichy (after 11 P.M.).

Langer, Champs-Élysées (tea and after dinner).

Lido, Arcades Champs-Élysées (tea, dinner, or supper).

Laurent, Champs-Élysées (tea).

Noël-Peter's, Passage des Princes, boulevard des Italiens — (dinner).

Ritz, Place Vendôme.

(See also, under Montmartre, in Restaurant lists.)

XI

DOCTORS — AND OTHERS TO AID US

I HAVEN'T a long list to offer, though there are, I'm sure, many in Paris whom I'd be proud to include did I but know about them. The only doctor in Paris with whom I've ever had any personal experience (or *nearly* personal! the patient was one of my small nieces, with a carbuncle on her arm) is Dr. George Imbert, 50 rue Pierre-Charron (telephone, Élysée 12–74), who impressed me as one I'd turn to with confidence in a much more serious need.

An osteopath who is in great favor with my friends is Katherine Gray Lynch, at 20 rue de la Paix.

Of Dr. Waegili, chiropodist, 31 rue Boissy d'Anglas, I can speak from many personal experiences. He is very popular and almost continuously busy. Telephone for an appointment, Élysée 26–65. He speaks perfect English, and so does his assistant.

I am told that Guy Créquinge, 37 rue Lauriston, is an excellent veterinary. His consultation hours are from 3 to 5 P.M. His telephone is Passy 54–70. He has a hospital for pets, and 'boards' them; also gives them baths.

XII

CLUBS

The Union Interalliée, 33 rue du Faubourg Saint-Honoré,
next door to the British Embassy, in the former mansion
of Baron and Baronne Henri de Rothschild, is probably
the 'smartest' club in Paris as well as the most interesting. Its membership includes residents of Paris whose
places of origin were in the many countries which fought
together as Allies in the Great War; and non-residents
who are the outstanding notables of those countries.
Marshal Foch was, up to the time of his death in 1929,
chairman of the executive committee. The mansion is a
superb background for the brilliant international affairs
which occur there. And the deep, shady garden, reaching to avenue Gabriel, is one of the loveliest in Paris.
Admission by invitation only — of course.

The American Club, 3 rue Taitbout (off boulevard des
Italiens), is a vigorous organization which seems to overlook no opportunity for furthering Franco-American
friendship and fostering fine American feeling in the
American colony of Paris. The Thursday luncheons of
the Club are among the most delightful affairs in Paris.
Men only.

The American Women's Club of Paris, Inc., 61 rue Bois-
sière, near place Victor-Hugo. This club, organized in
1921, has now its own home in a fine mansion, with garden, in the fashionable residence district of Passy.
American women travelling abroad who can present
references to two Paris residents, may have a three-
months' membership for two hundred francs. There are
a few attractive bedrooms which may be occupied by

members for a period not longer than two weeks. The meals are excellent and there are many entertainments.

The Lyceum Club (of Women) now occupies a fine mansion at 17 rue de Bellechasse (back of the Palais de la Légion d'Honneur on quai d'Orsay), which formerly belonged to the Rochefoucauld family and dates back to 1730. The members belong to many different nations.

The Travellers' Club, 25 avenue des Champs-Élysées (for men), with an important membership and many interesting guests always 'dropping in.'

Rotary Club, 36 rue de l'Echiquier (back of Marguery's on boulevard Bonne Bouvelle). Luncheons on Wednesdays.

The Club Soroptimist, 47 avenue de l'Opéra. For business and professional women; hoping to be a link between the active women of France and America.

Special Sports Clubs

Aero-Club de France, 35 rue François-Premier.
Automobile Club de France, 6 place de la Concorde.
Touring Club de France, 65 avenue de la Grande-Armée.
Yacht Club de France, 82 boulevard Haussmann.

Students' Clubs

American University Union, 173 boulevard Saint-Germain. All men and women from American colleges invited to register.

American Students' Club, 107 boulevard Raspail.

American Methodist Memorial Centre, 79 rue Denfert-Rochereau (south end of boulevard Raspail).

American Women's University Club, 4 rue de Chevreuse (off boulevard Montparnasse near its intersection with boulevard Raspail). Attractive living quarters for graduates of American colleges for women. Inexpensive. Pleasant.

XIII

WHEN YOU PREPARE TO LEAVE PARIS

Travel Agencies

THERE is a considerable, but rapidly diminishing, number of persons who go abroad with no plans made; and who, in consequence, spend no small part of their precious time in Europe doing what they could have done much more satisfactorily before they left home.

The smart, sophisticated traveller now has his travel agent just as inevitably as he has his bank and his lawyer and his broker and his doctor, and even his accustomed salespersons in the shops he frequents; they know his needs, they don't waste his time, and if he has chosen them well they are a part of his prestige.

When he is in Paris, the Paris office of his agent serves him. When he is in Rome, or in Berlin, or in Budapest, or elsewhere, there is always at his service some one affiliated with his agency and notified to look after him.

There is another type of traveller, who is haunted by the fear that he may contribute something to the upkeep or profits of a travel agency. He uses its service to handle his mail, and answer his questions; he hails and endlessly interrogates its interpreters and station-men; he does everything he can to make the travel agency serve him, but is constantly careful to keep from supporting it in any way. You have met this type only too often. He will borrow your itinerary, to copy in the train; he will quiz you for information about hotels; he will even 'tag onto' you if you have some one looking after you. He fancies that he is saving money. He is probably spending more than you are, and getting less for it.

European travel with the travel agencies taken out of it would be a chaos for about ninety-five per cent of the English-speaking travellers.

Of course they have to earn their 'overhead' and a little more — or they couldn't exist. So does every business. But if you contribute anything to their maintenance, you need not feel that you have *robbed your heirs!* Not if you have chosen your agent wisely! Your bank makes money out of your account. But how much better off would you be if you tried to do your own banking?

Have a good, reliable agent looking out for your travel affairs and serving you in a multitude of ways. If you haven't chosen your agent at home, when you began to plan your trip, choose one in Paris. There are many good ones — and some who do *not* know the business; some whose credit is not sound; some whose comprehension of American travellers is almost totally lacking; some who are good for one special phase, but not for others.

Here is a list of agencies I know and have done business with. I list them alphabetically:

American Express Co., 11 rue Scribe.

Amerop, rue Edouard VII (especially for Germany, but good everywhere).

Benedict Bureau, 6 rue Mont-Thabor.

Bennett, 4 rue Scribe (especially for Scandinavian travel).

Cook (Thos. and Sons), 2 Pláce de la Madeleine.

Dean and Dawson, 2 rue Edouard VII, and 212 rue de Rivoli.

Franco-Belgique, 19 avenue de l'Opéra.

Frank Tourist Company, 11 rue Edouard VII.

Fraser McLean, 56 rue du Faubourg Saint-Honoré (especially for motor touring).

Knickerbocker Tours, 12 boulevard Malesherbes (espe-

cially fine for Holland and Belgium, but good all over
Continent).

Lewis Travel Service, 12 rue d'Aguesseau. Good general
service; specially fine Pullman coach tours in France and
to Spain; excellent for motor hire and motor touring.

Pisa Brothers, 56 rue du Faubourg Saint-Honoré (de luxe
motor touring — superb service).

Raymond and Whitcomb, 20 Place Vendôme.

Yana Travel Service, 56 rue du Faubourg Saint-Honoré
(especially for motoring; North Africa, Italy, France,
Spain in particular).

If you like a big company, you have American Express,
Cook, Dean and Dawson, and Raymond Whitcomb, to
choose from. If you like an old-established firm, over fifty
years in the business, with a very strong support, but not so
multitudinous, you have the Frank Tourist Company.
Franco-Belgique is fast coming into the category of the
'big ones.' Knickerbocker Tours is a younger concern, still
under the close, constant, personal direction of its owners,
who have impressed many persons in the travel world as
being among 'the livest' in the business, as well as among
the most reliable. And so on; the others I have already
designated for their specialties.

INDEX

CLARA LAUGHLIN TRAVEL SERVICES

410 South Michigan Ave., Chicago
18 East 53rd St., New York

Authorized Agents for ALL Foreign Steamship Lines. Representing Everything WORTH WHILE in Foreign Travel

The same thorough planning that has made the "So You're Going" books such widely sold and helpful guides to many thousands of enthusiastic travellers is available to our CLIENTS

Without Extra Charge

Many of the most discriminating American travellers entrust all their travel arrangements to us, and send their friends to us to

TRAVEL THE CLARA LAUGHLIN WAY

Steamship Accommodations — Motor and Rail Trips
Hotel Reservations — (personally tried LIST)
Independent TRAVEL — with or without escort
Conducted Tours — CRUISES — Planned Itineraries
TRAVEL Counsel — that saves your TIME and MONEY

A COMPLETE FOREIGN TRAVEL SERVICE